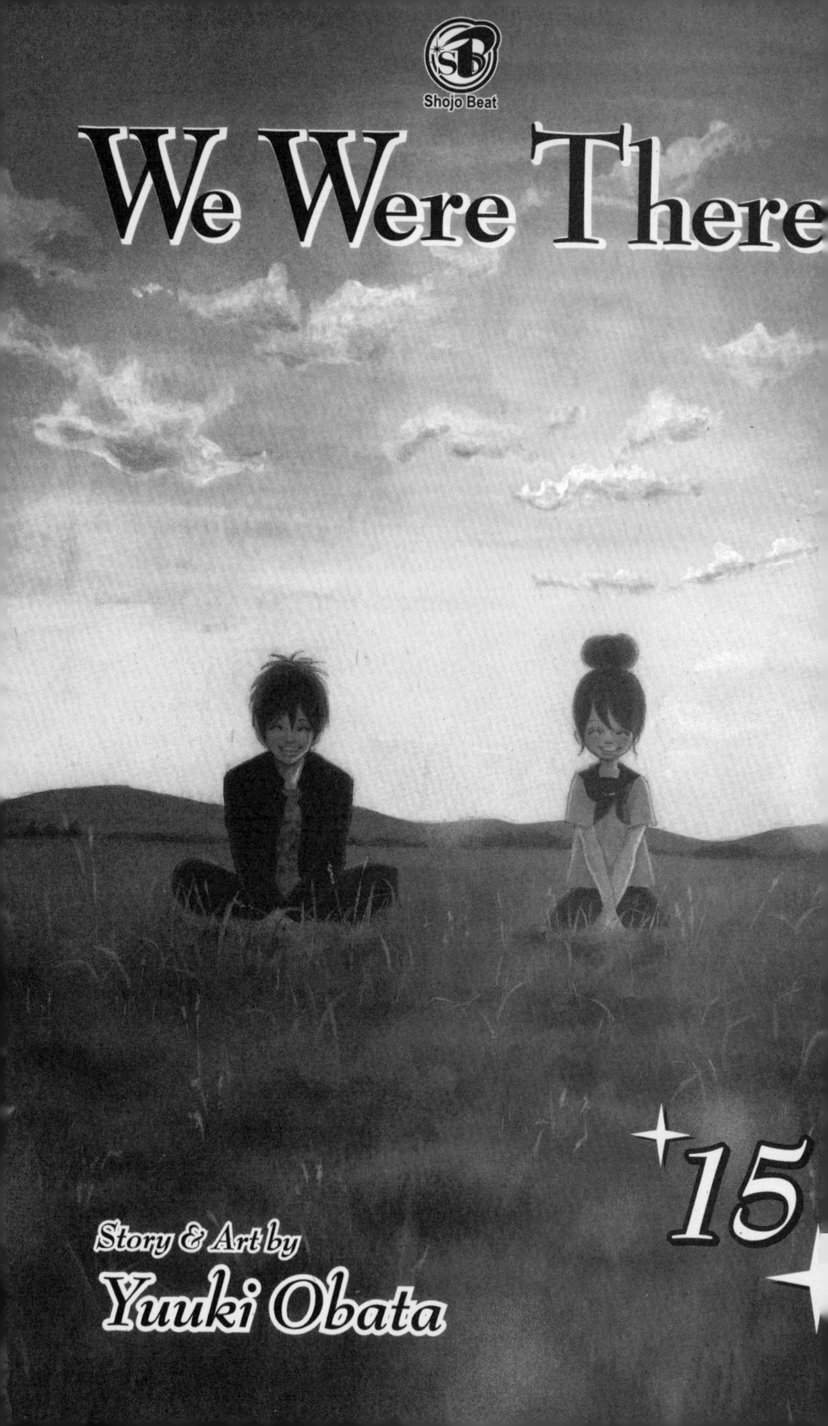
Shojo Beat
We Were There
15
Story & Art by
Yuuki Obata

Contents

Characters

Masafumi Takeuchi
Yano's best friend. He works for a foreign finance company. He used to date Nanami, but...

Nanami Takahashi
Nanami works at a publishing company in Tokyo. She is unable to forget her feelings for Yano.

Motoharu Yano
Nanami's ex-boyfriend. He works for an architecture and design firm. He is currently living with Yuri.

Story

Yano tells Nanami about his past after she confronts him about living with Yuri. Nanami accepts Yano's strong wish for her to "go on without me." Takeuchi decides to cut all ties with Nanami. He tosses the engagement ring he bought her into the sea, but then tells Yano that Nanami is the one drowning...?!

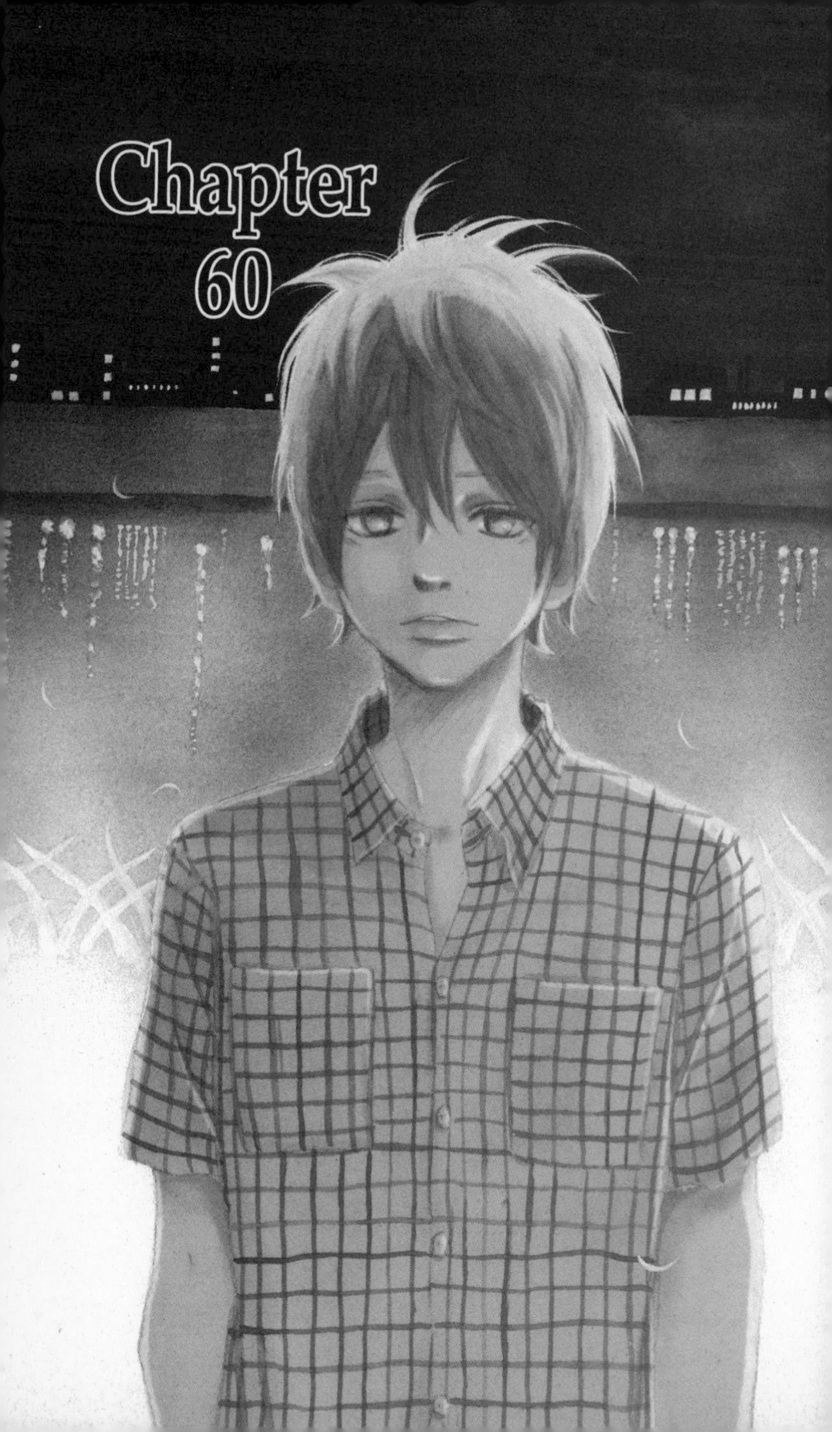
Chapter
60

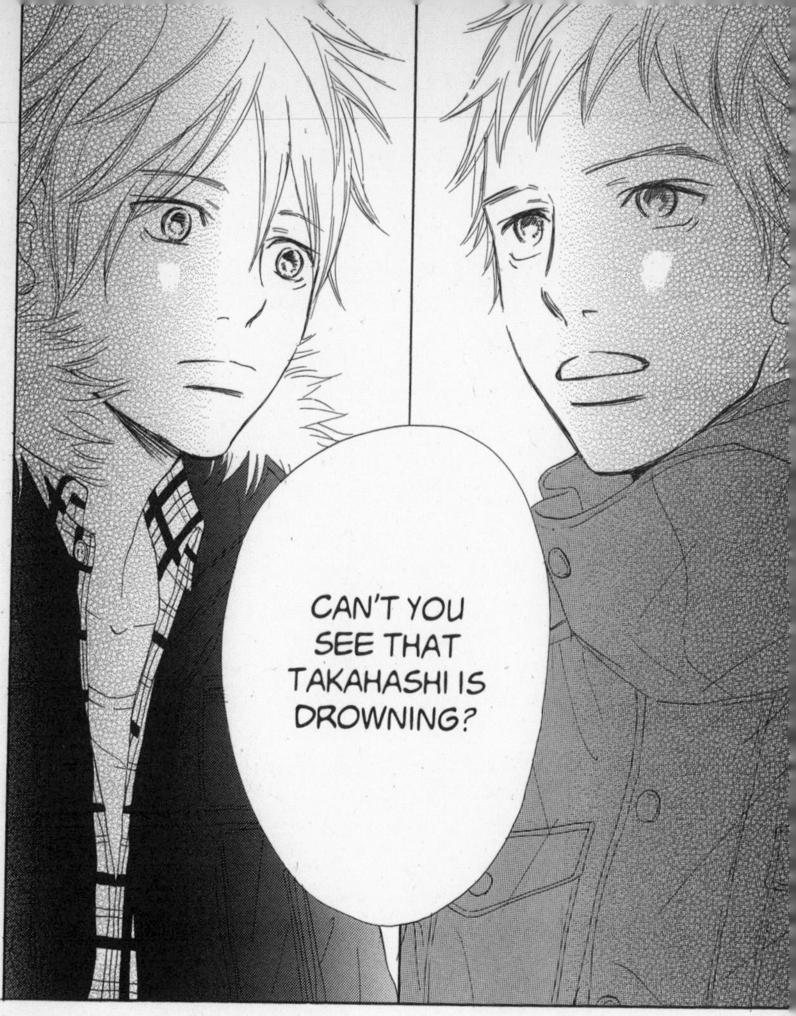
CAN'T YOU SEE THAT TAKAHASHI IS DROWNING?

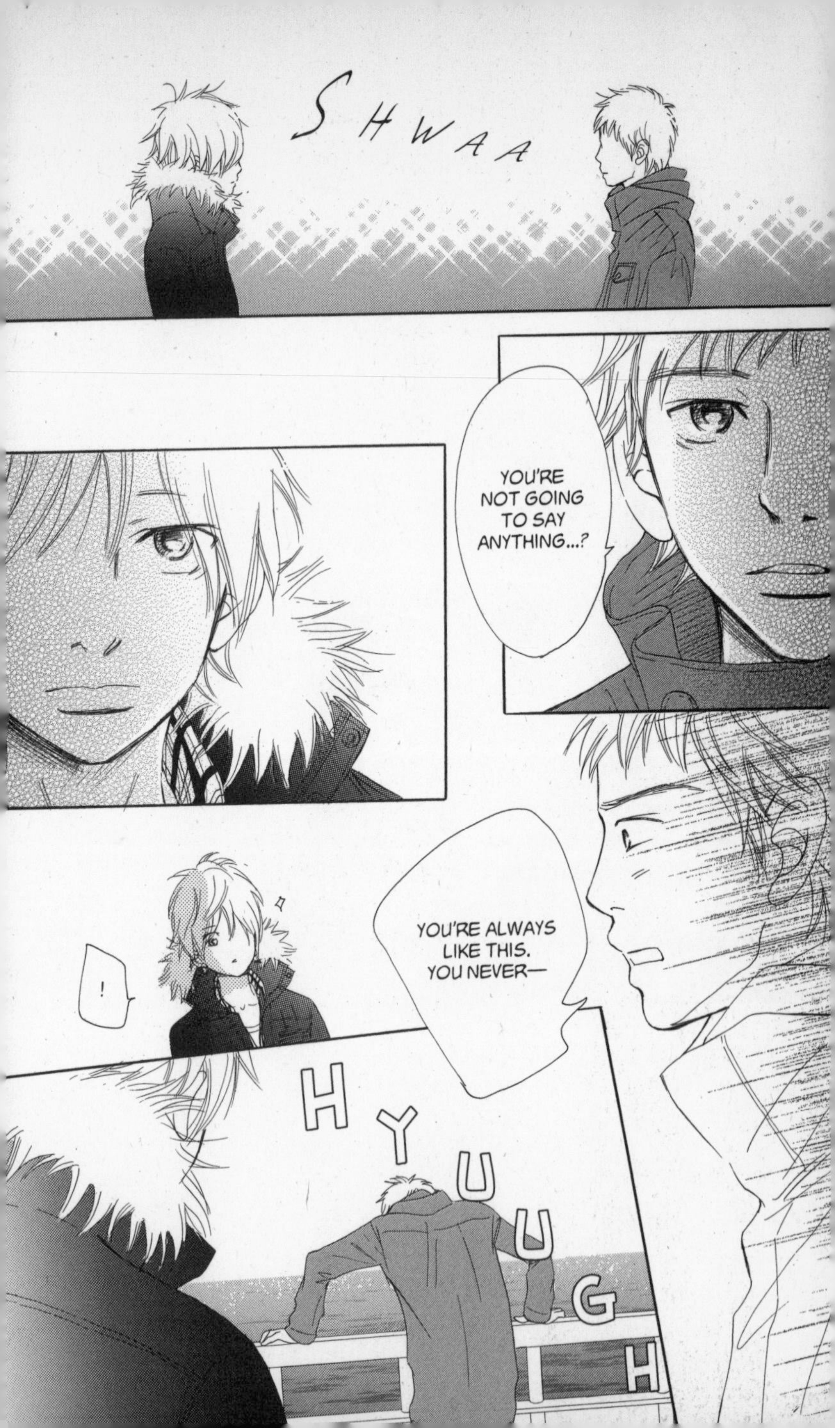
SHWAA
YOU'RE NOT GOING TO SAY ANYTHING...?
YOU'RE ALWAYS LIKE THIS. YOU NEVER—
!
HYUUGH

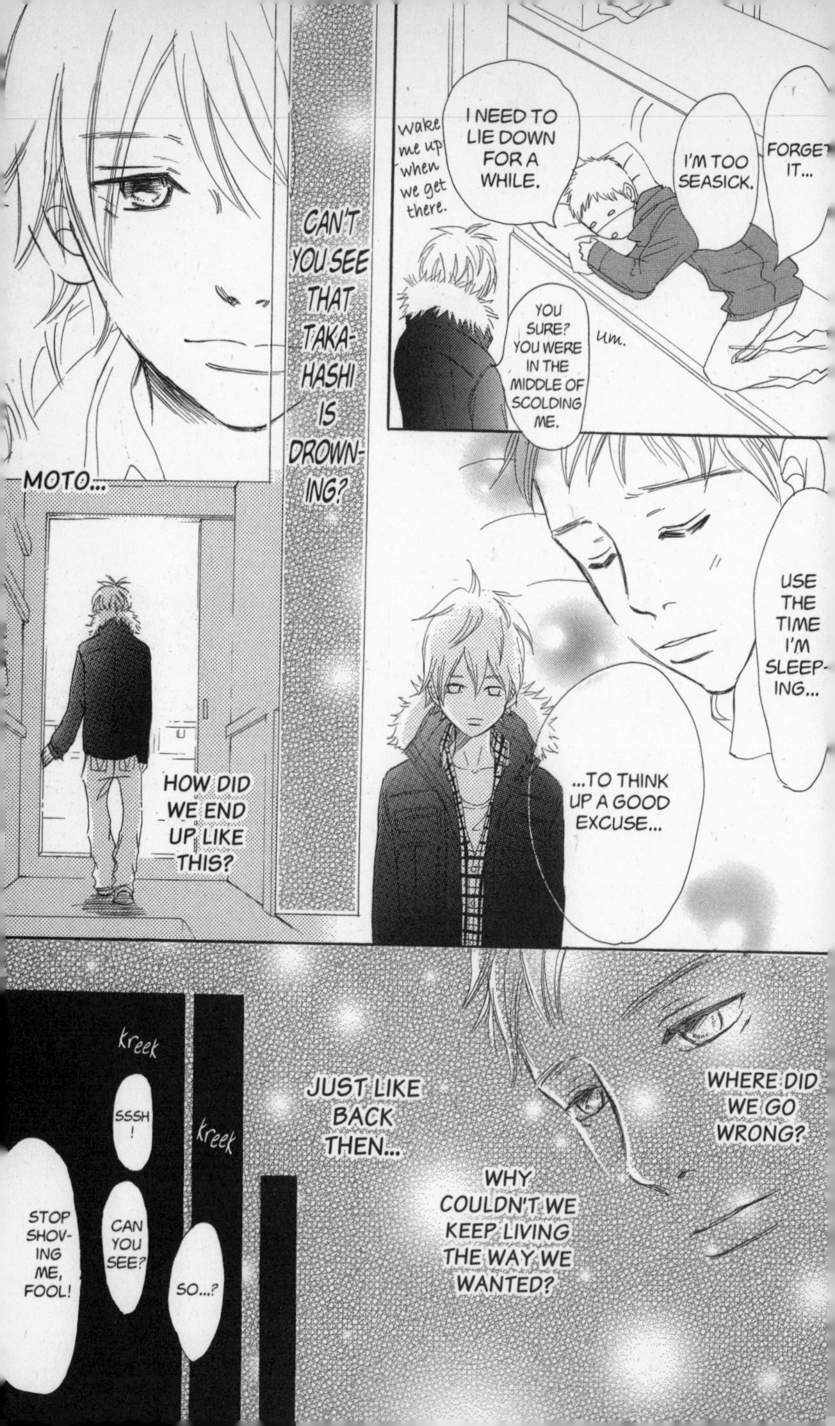

FORGET IT...
I'M TOO SEASICK.
I NEED TO LIE DOWN FOR A WHILE.
Wake me up when we get there.
um.
YOU SURE? YOU WERE IN THE MIDDLE OF SCOLDING ME.
USE THE TIME I'M SLEEPING...
...TO THINK UP A GOOD EXCUSE...
CAN'T YOU SEE THAT TAKA-HASHI IS DROWN-ING?
MOTO...
HOW DID WE END UP LIKE THIS?
WHERE DID WE GO WRONG?
WHY COULDN'T WE KEEP LIVING THE WAY WE WANTED?
JUST LIKE BACK THEN...
kreek
kreek
SSSH!
SO...?
CAN YOU SEE?
STOP SHOV-ING ME, FOOL!

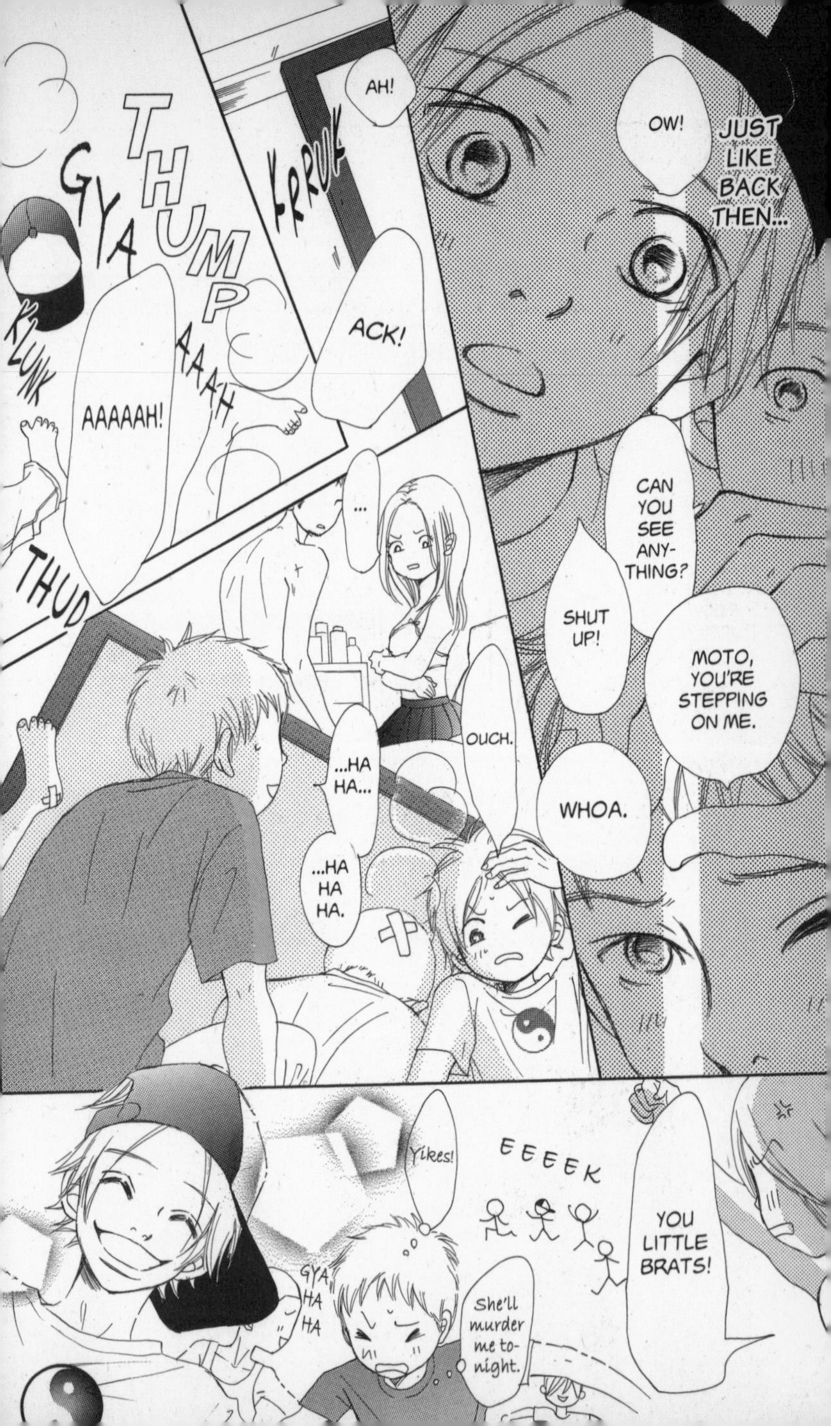

JUST LIKE BACK THEN...
OW!
CAN YOU SEE ANY-THING?
SHUT UP!
MOTO, YOU'RE STEPPING ON ME.
WHOA.
AH!
KRRUK
ACK!
THUMP
GYA
AAAH
KLUNK
AAAAAH!
THUD
...
OUCH.
...HA HA...
...HA HA HA.
YOU LITTLE BRATS!
EEEEK
Yikes!
She'll murder me to-night.
GYA HA HA

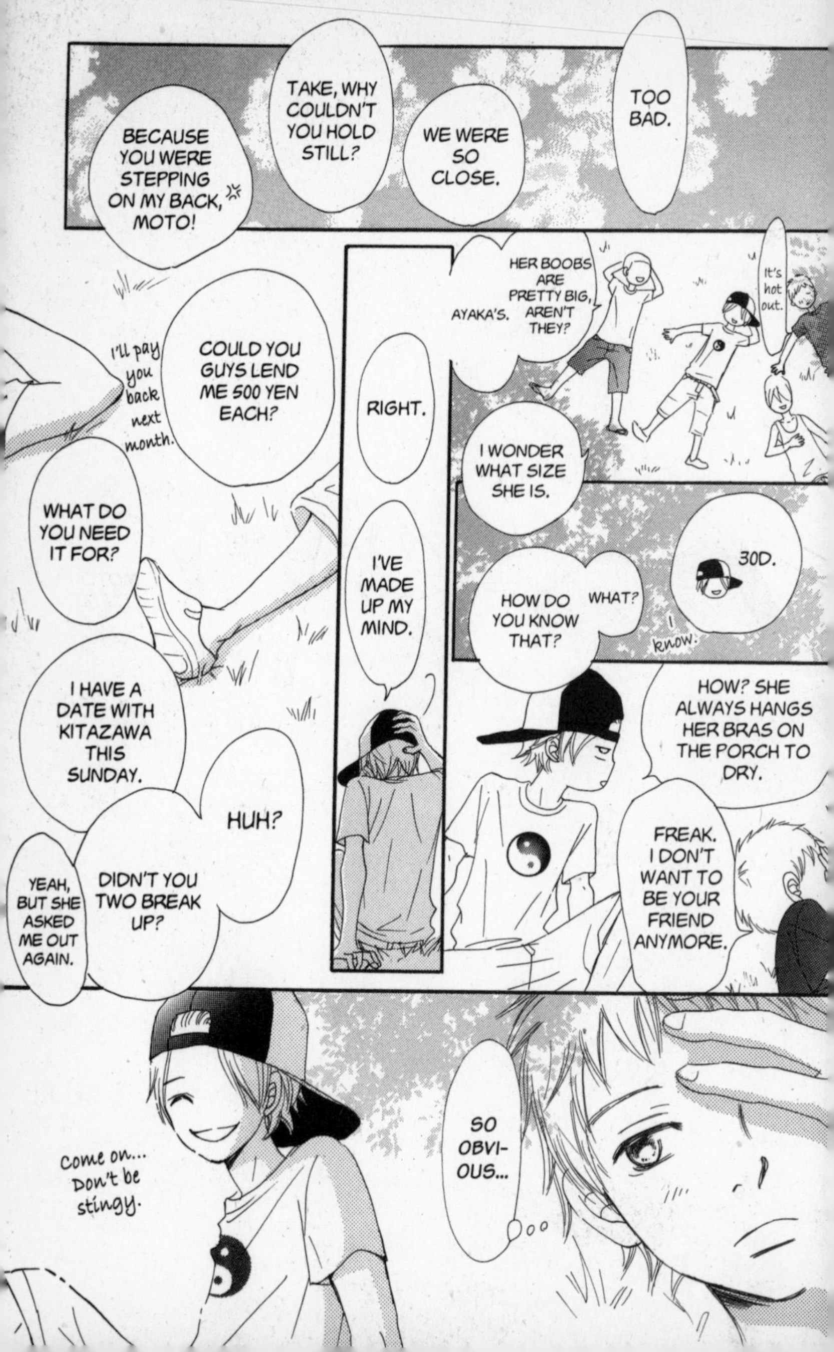
TOO BAD.
WE WERE SO CLOSE.
TAKE, WHY COULDN'T YOU HOLD STILL?
BECAUSE YOU WERE STEPPING ON MY BACK, MOTO!
It's hot out.
HER BOOBS ARE PRETTY BIG, AREN'T THEY?
AYAKA'S.
I WONDER WHAT SIZE SHE IS.
30D.
I know.
WHAT?
HOW DO YOU KNOW THAT?
HOW? SHE ALWAYS HANGS HER BRAS ON THE PORCH TO DRY.
FREAK. I DON'T WANT TO BE YOUR FRIEND ANYMORE.
RIGHT.
I'VE MADE UP MY MIND.
COULD YOU GUYS LEND ME 500 YEN EACH?
I'll pay you back next month.
WHAT DO YOU NEED IT FOR?
I HAVE A DATE WITH KITAZAWA THIS SUNDAY.
HUH?
DIDN'T YOU TWO BREAK UP?
YEAH, BUT SHE ASKED ME OUT AGAIN.
SO OBVI-OUS...
Come on... Don't be stingy.

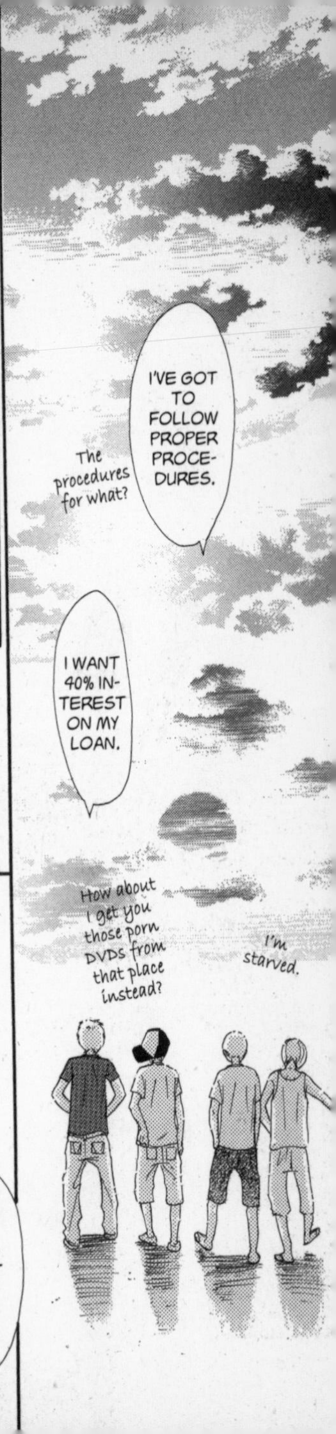
I'VE GOT TO FOLLOW PROPER PROCEDURES.
The procedures for what?
I WANT 40% INTEREST ON MY LOAN.
I'm starved.
How about I get you those porn DVDs from that place instead?

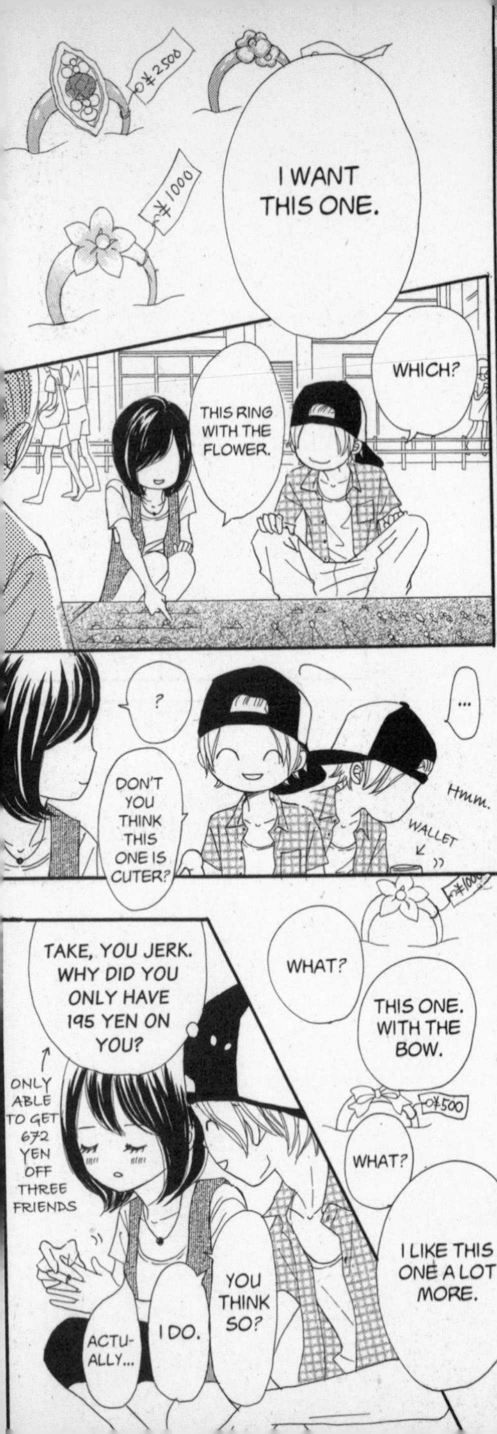
¥2500
¥1000
I WANT THIS ONE.
WHICH?
THIS RING WITH THE FLOWER.
...
?
Hmm.
WALLET
DON'T YOU THINK THIS ONE IS CUTER?
¥1000
WHAT?
THIS ONE. WITH THE BOW.
¥500
WHAT?
I LIKE THIS ONE A LOT MORE.
YOU THINK SO?
I DO.
ACTUALLY...
TAKE, YOU JERK. WHY DID YOU ONLY HAVE 195 YEN ON YOU?
ONLY ABLE TO GET 672 YEN OFF THREE FRIENDS

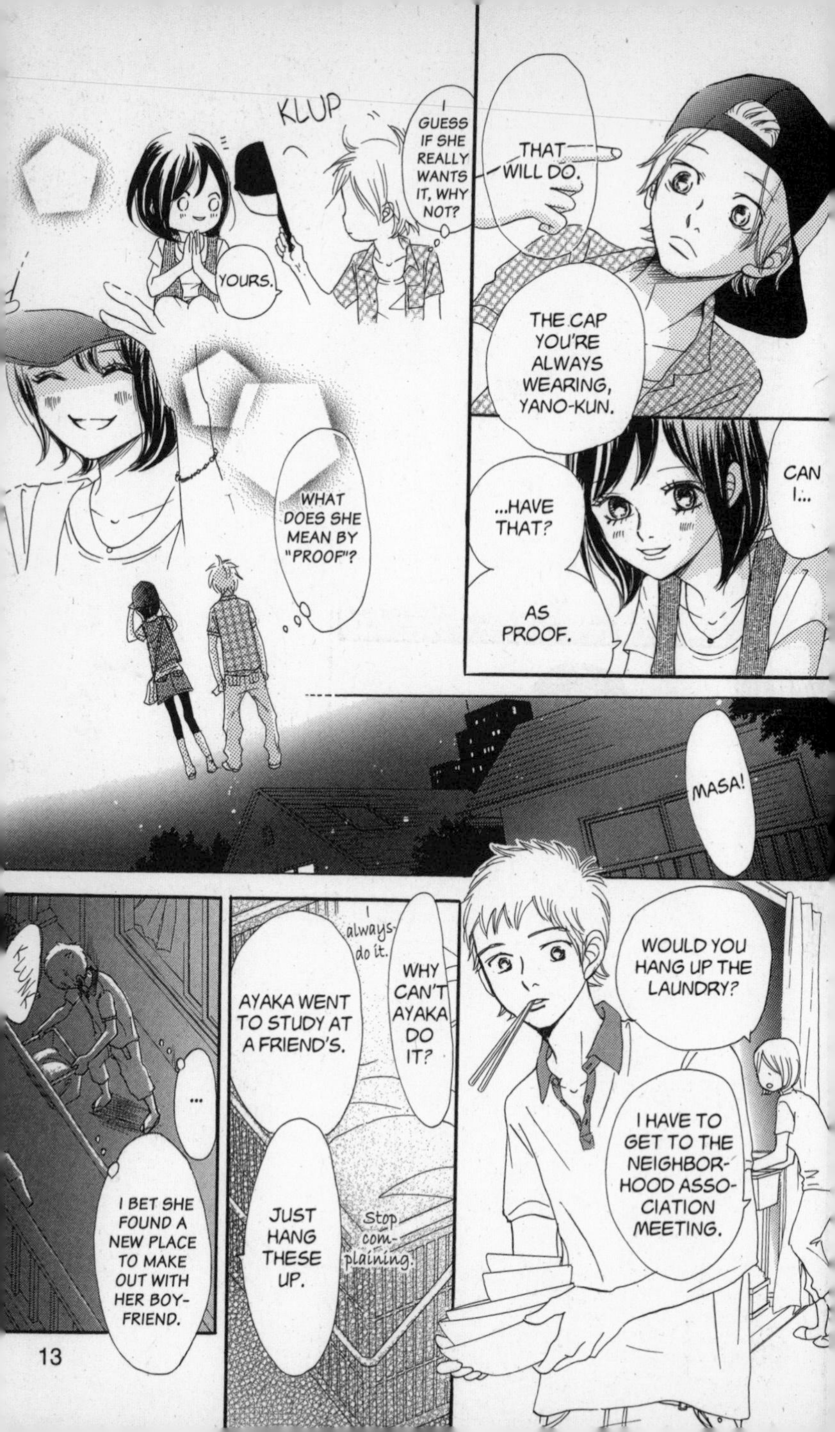
THAT WILL DO.
THE CAP YOU'RE ALWAYS WEARING, YANO-KUN.
CAN I...
...HAVE THAT?
AS PROOF.
I GUESS IF SHE REALLY WANTS IT, WHY NOT?
KLUP
YOURS.
WHAT DOES SHE MEAN BY "PROOF"?
MASA!
WOULD YOU HANG UP THE LAUNDRY?
I HAVE TO GET TO THE NEIGHBOR-HOOD ASSO-CIATION MEETING.
WHY CAN'T AYAKA DO IT?
I always do it.
AYAKA WENT TO STUDY AT A FRIEND'S.
Stop com-plaining.
JUST HANG THESE UP.
KLUNK
...
I BET SHE FOUND A NEW PLACE TO MAKE OUT WITH HER BOY-FRIEND.

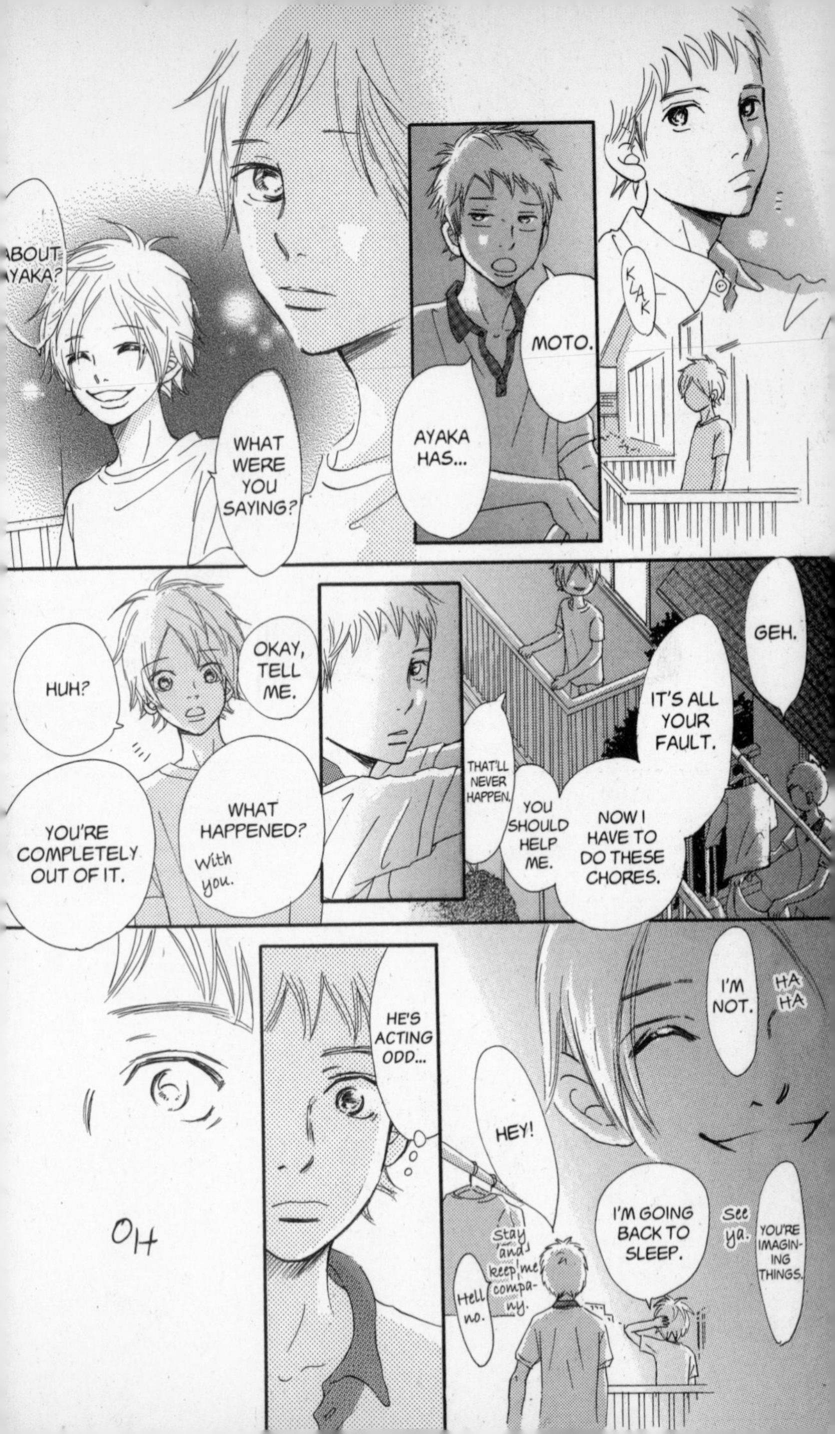
KLAK
MOTO.
AYAKA HAS...
WHAT WERE YOU SAYING?
ABOUT AYAKA?
GEH.
IT'S ALL YOUR FAULT.
NOW I HAVE TO DO THESE CHORES.
YOU SHOULD HELP ME.
THAT'LL NEVER HAPPEN.
OKAY, TELL ME.
HUH?
WHAT HAPPENED? With you.
YOU'RE COMPLETELY OUT OF IT.
I'M NOT.
HA HA
YOU'RE IMAGINING THINGS.
See ya.
I'M GOING BACK TO SLEEP.
HEY!
Stay and keep me company.
Hell no.
HE'S ACTING ODD...
OH

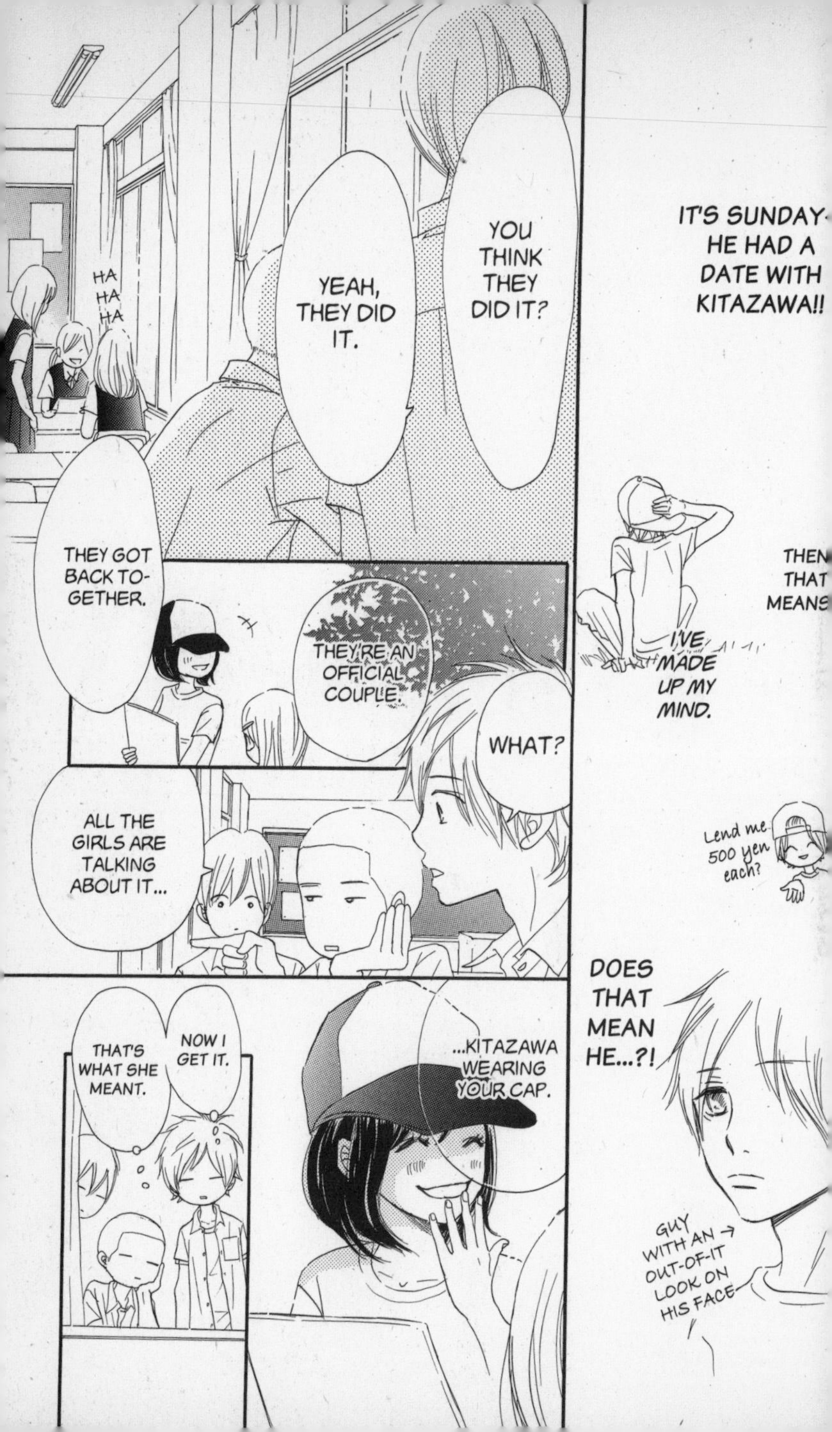
IT'S SUNDAY. HE HAD A DATE WITH KITAZAWA!!
THEN THAT MEANS
I'VE MADE UP MY MIND.
Lend me 500 yen each?
DOES THAT MEAN HE...?!
GUY WITH AN OUT-OF-IT LOOK ON HIS FACE
YOU THINK THEY DID IT?
YEAH, THEY DID IT.
HA HA HA
THEY GOT BACK TO-GETHER.
THEY'RE AN OFFICIAL COUPLE.
WHAT?
ALL THE GIRLS ARE TALKING ABOUT IT...
...KITAZAWA WEARING YOUR CAP.
NOW I GET IT.
THAT'S WHAT SHE MEANT.

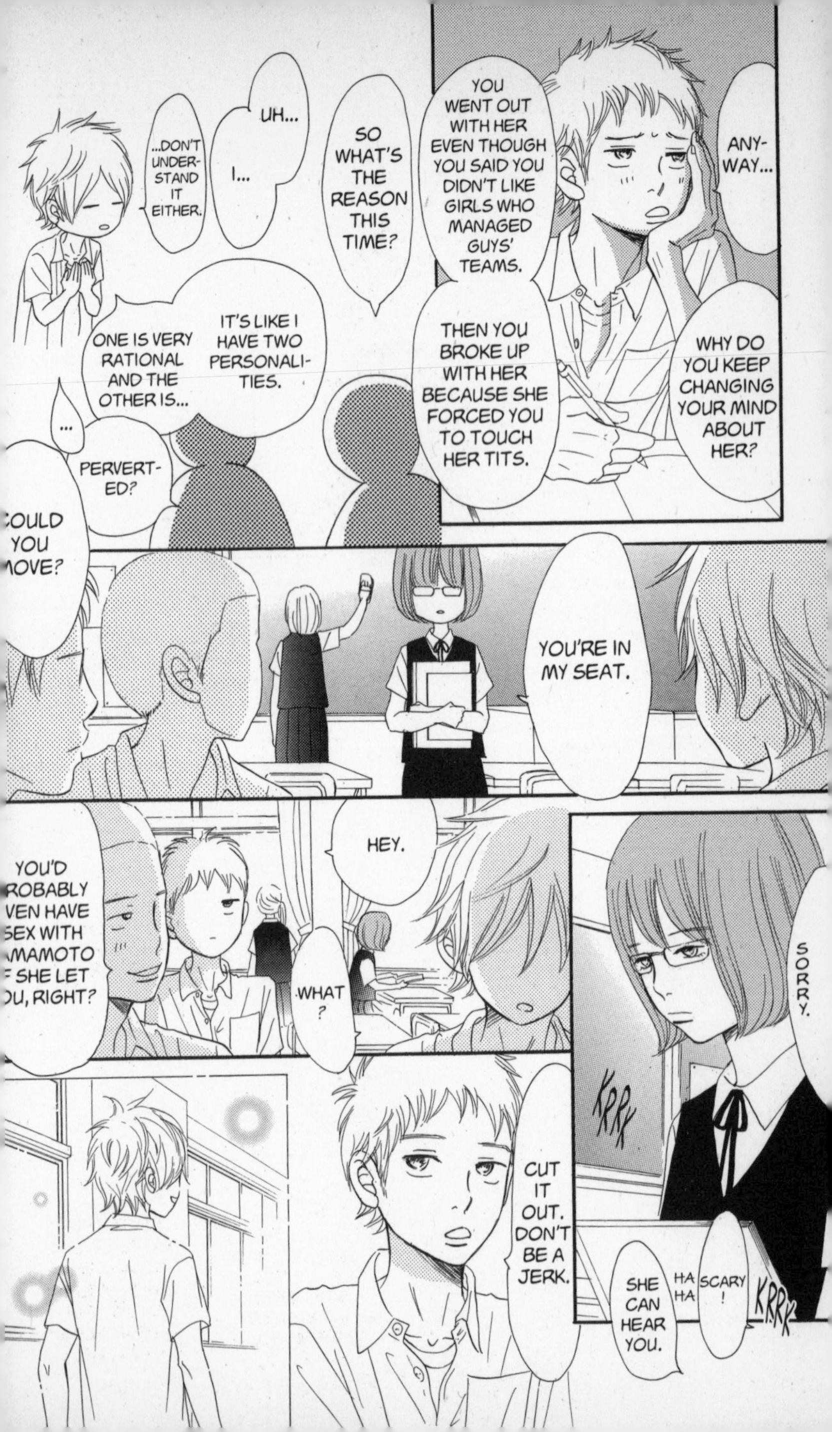
ANYWAY...
YOU WENT OUT WITH HER EVEN THOUGH YOU SAID YOU DIDN'T LIKE GIRLS WHO MANAGED GUYS' TEAMS.
WHY DO YOU KEEP CHANGING YOUR MIND ABOUT HER?
THEN YOU BROKE UP WITH HER BECAUSE SHE FORCED YOU TO TOUCH HER TITS.
SO WHAT'S THE REASON THIS TIME?
UH...
I...
...DON'T UNDERSTAND IT EITHER.
IT'S LIKE I HAVE TWO PERSONALITIES.
ONE IS VERY RATIONAL AND THE OTHER IS...
...
PERVERTED?
COULD YOU MOVE?
YOU'RE IN MY SEAT.
SORRY.
KRRK
HEY.
WHAT?
YOU'D PROBABLY EVEN HAVE SEX WITH YAMAMOTO IF SHE LET YOU, RIGHT?
KRRK
SCARY!
HA HA
SHE CAN HEAR YOU.
CUT IT OUT. DON'T BE A JERK.

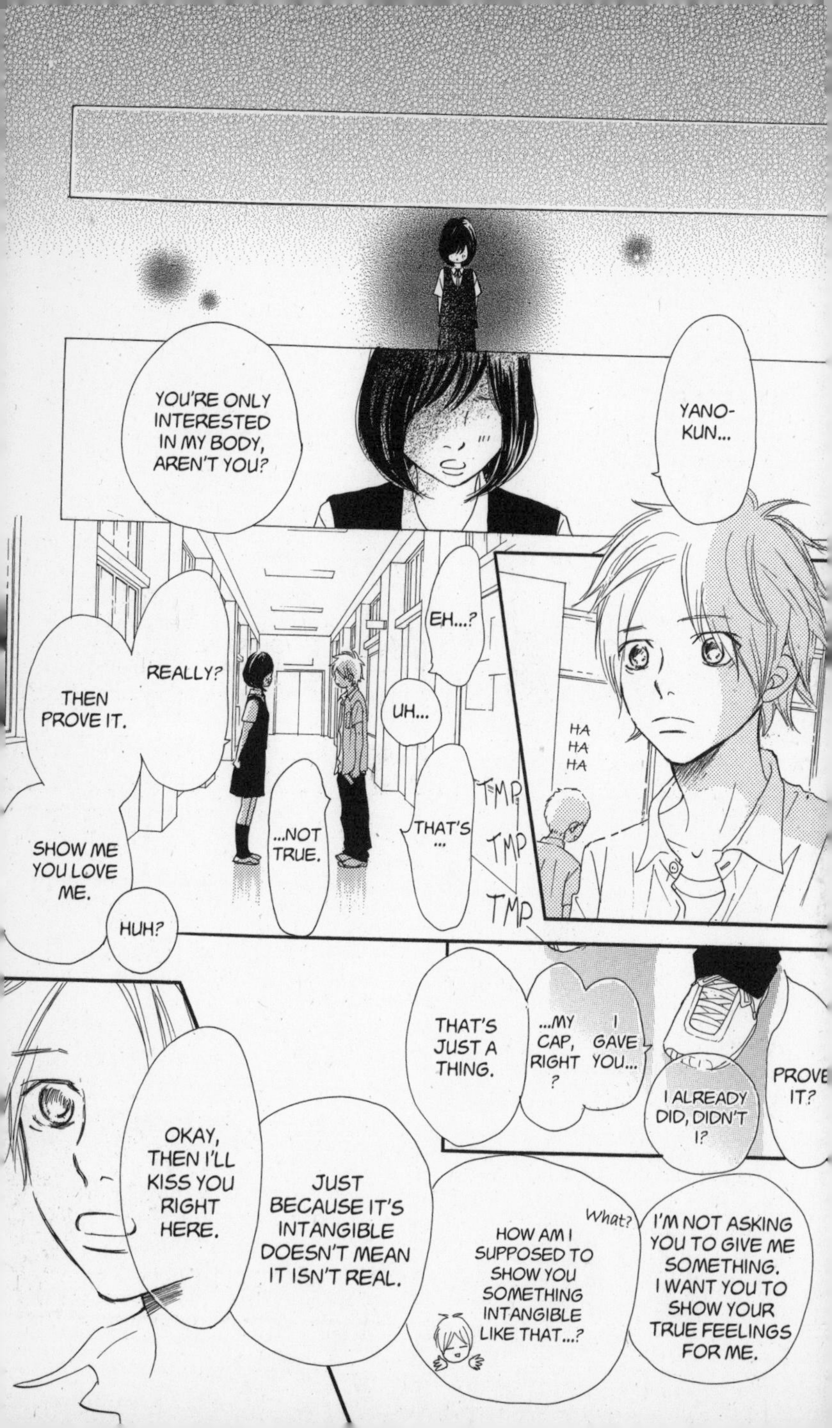
YANO-KUN...
YOU'RE ONLY INTERESTED IN MY BODY, AREN'T YOU?
HA HA HA
TMP TMP TMP
EH...?
UH...
THAT'S...
...NOT TRUE.
REALLY?
THEN PROVE IT.
SHOW ME YOU LOVE ME.
HUH?
PROVE IT?
I ALREADY DID, DIDN'T I?
I GAVE YOU...
...MY CAP, RIGHT?
THAT'S JUST A THING.
I'M NOT ASKING YOU TO GIVE ME SOMETHING. I WANT YOU TO SHOW YOUR TRUE FEELINGS FOR ME.
What?
HOW AM I SUPPOSED TO SHOW YOU SOMETHING INTANGIBLE LIKE THAT...?
JUST BECAUSE IT'S INTANGIBLE DOESN'T MEAN IT ISN'T REAL.
OKAY, THEN I'LL KISS YOU RIGHT HERE.

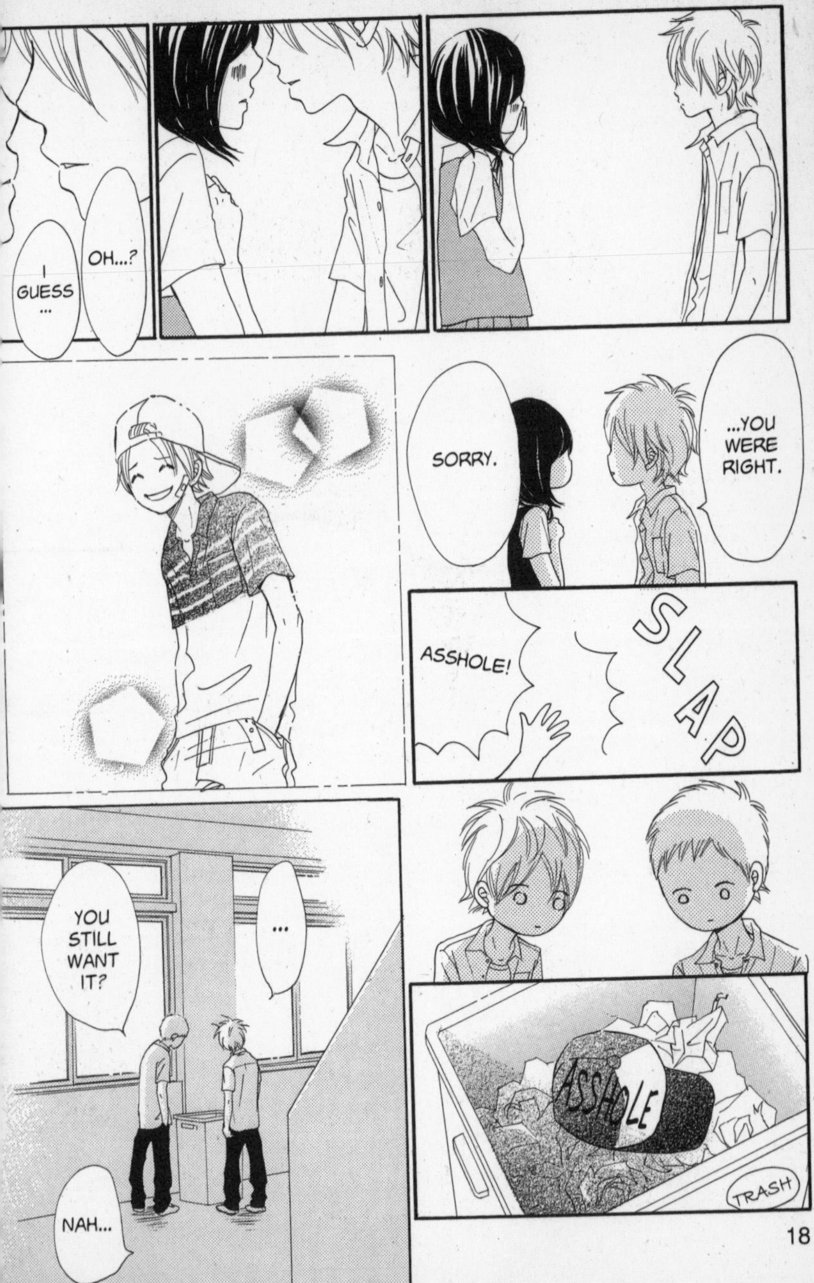
OH...?
I GUESS ...
...YOU WERE RIGHT.
SORRY.
SLAP
ASSHOLE!
ASSHOLE
TRASH
...
YOU STILL WANT IT?
NAH...

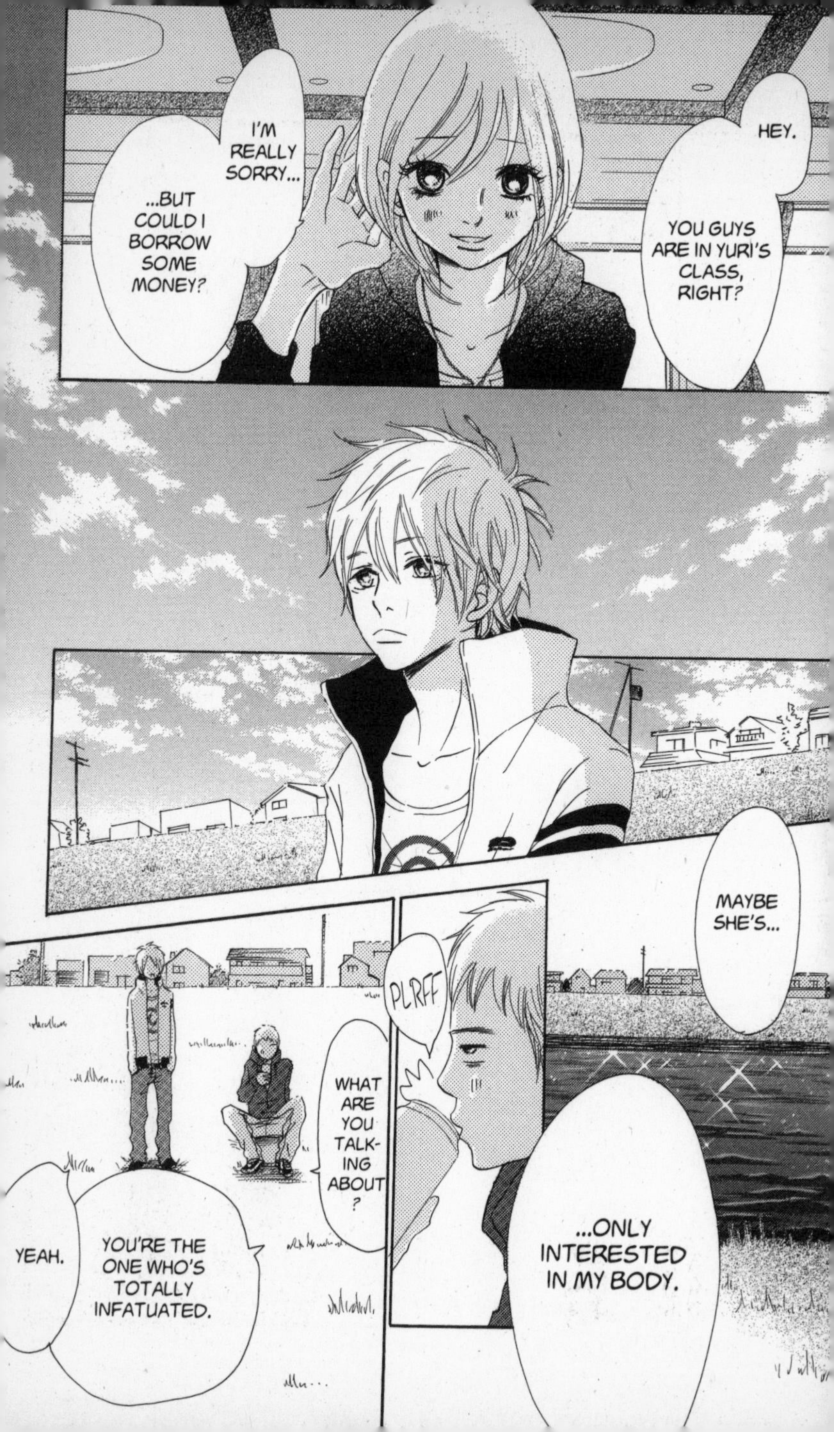
HEY.
YOU GUYS ARE IN YURI'S CLASS, RIGHT?
I'M REALLY SORRY...
...BUT COULD I BORROW SOME MONEY?
MAYBE SHE'S...
...ONLY INTERESTED IN MY BODY.
PLRFF
WHAT ARE YOU TALK-ING ABOUT?
YOU'RE THE ONE WHO'S TOTALLY INFATUATED.
YEAH.

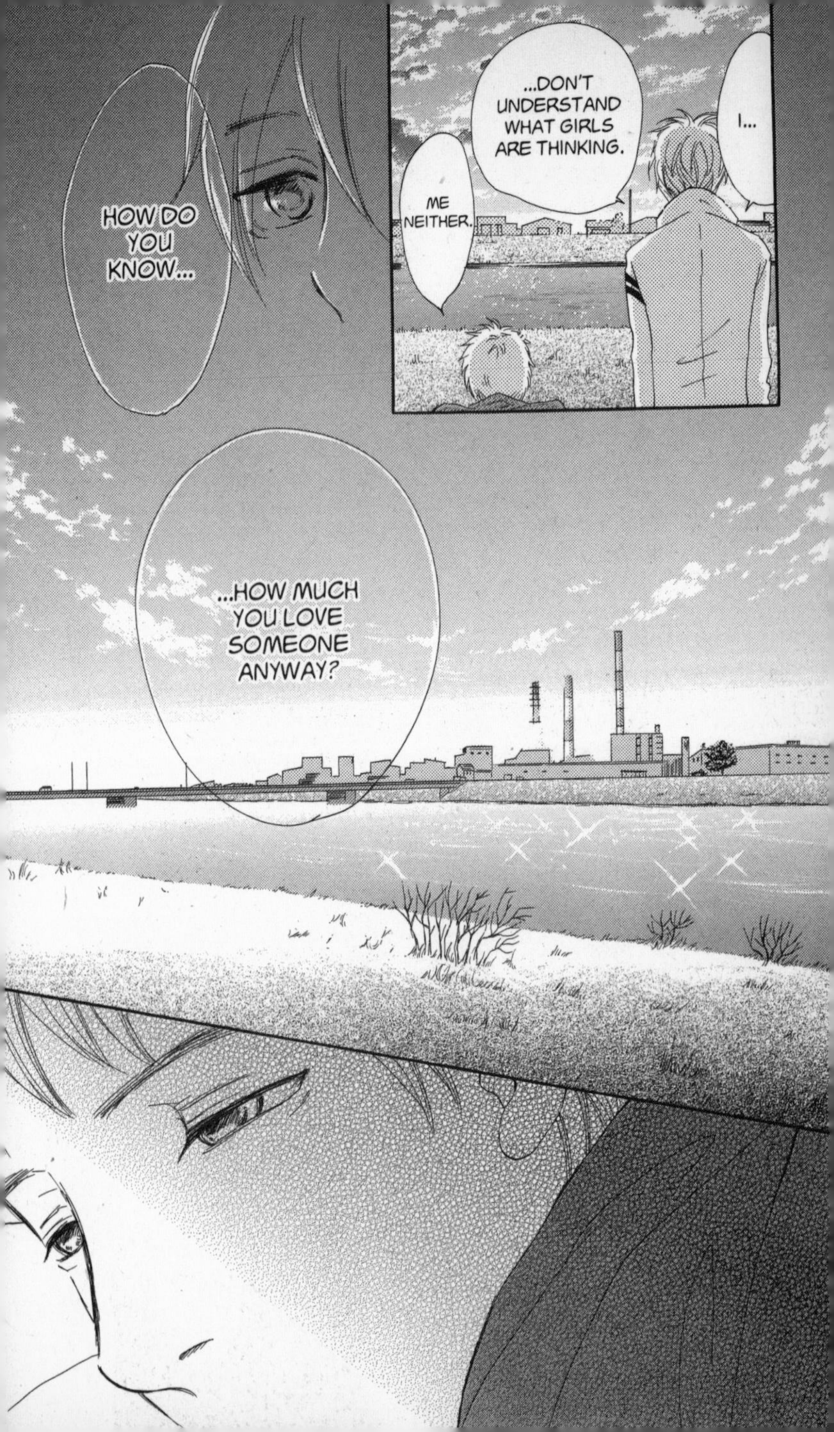
I...
...DON'T UNDERSTAND WHAT GIRLS ARE THINKING.
ME NEITHER.
HOW DO YOU KNOW...
...HOW MUCH YOU LOVE SOMEONE ANYWAY?

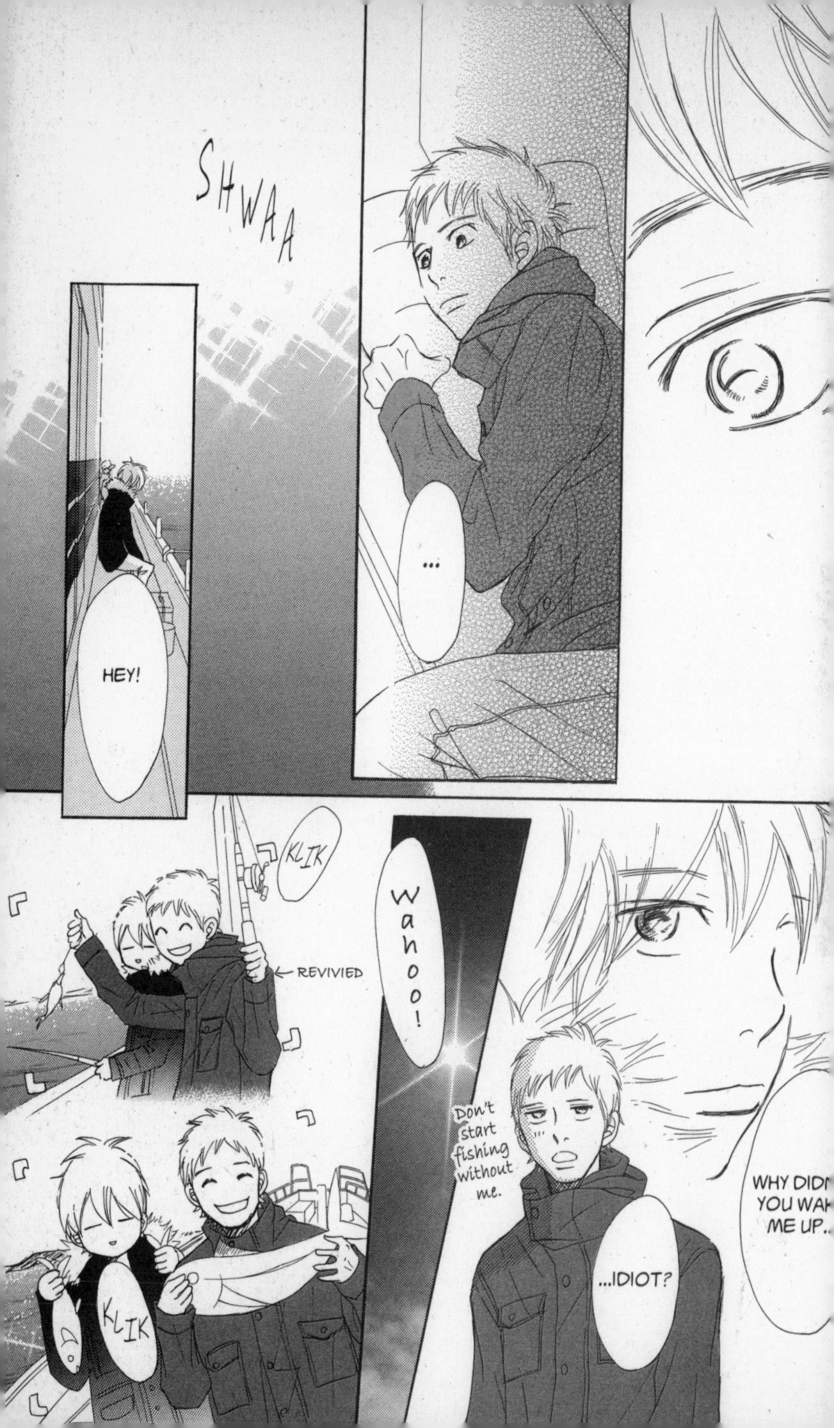
...
SHWAA
HEY!
WHY DID YOU WAK ME UP...
...IDIOT?
Don't start fishing without me.
Wahoo!
KLIK
REVIVIED
KLIK

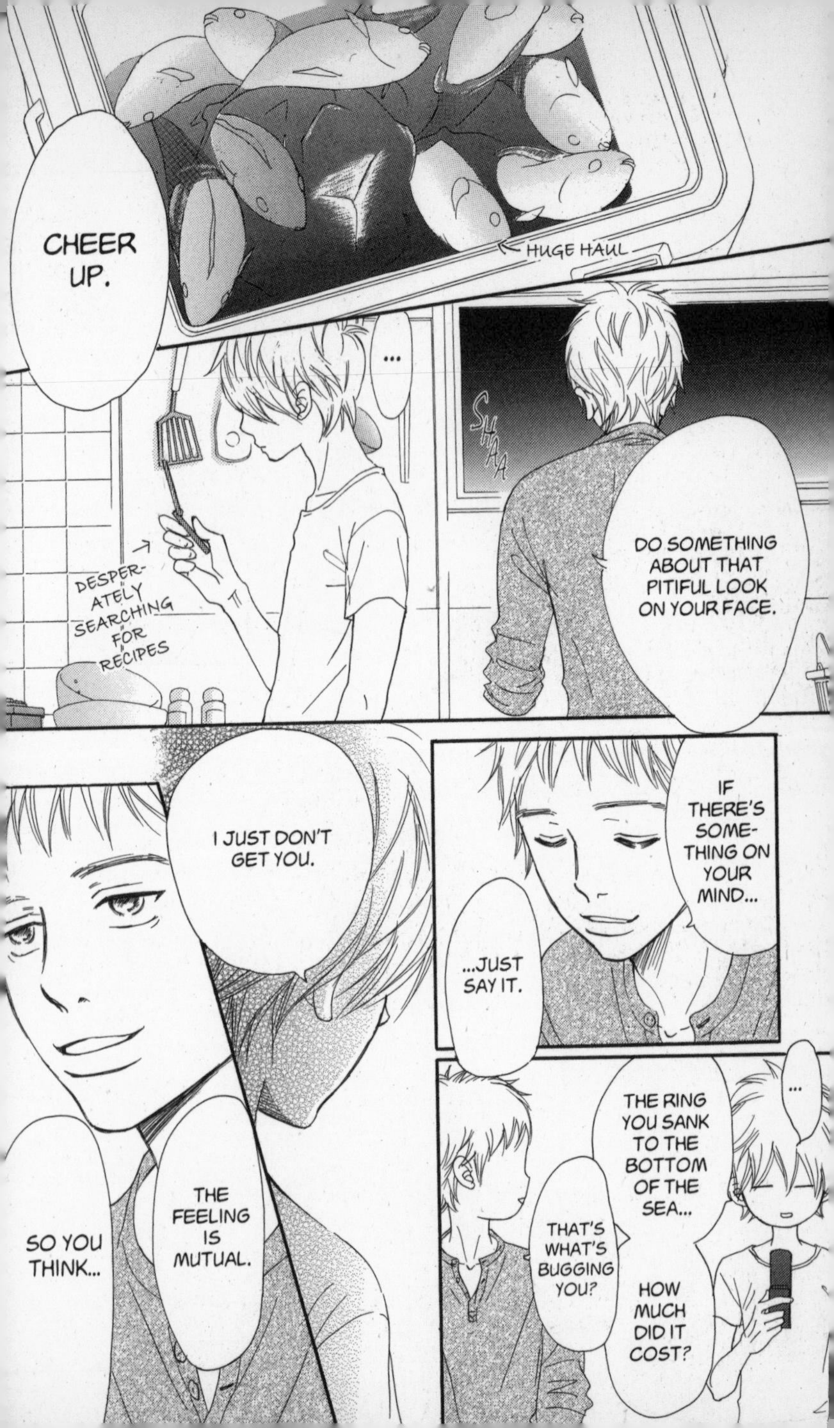
HUGE HAUL
CHEER UP.
DO SOMETHING ABOUT THAT PITIFUL LOOK ON YOUR FACE.
...
SHAA
DESPERATELY SEARCHING FOR RECIPES
IF THERE'S SOMETHING ON YOUR MIND...
...JUST SAY IT.
...
THE RING YOU SANK TO THE BOTTOM OF THE SEA...
THAT'S WHAT'S BUGGING YOU?
HOW MUCH DID IT COST?
I JUST DON'T GET YOU.
THE FEELING IS MUTUAL.
SO YOU THINK...

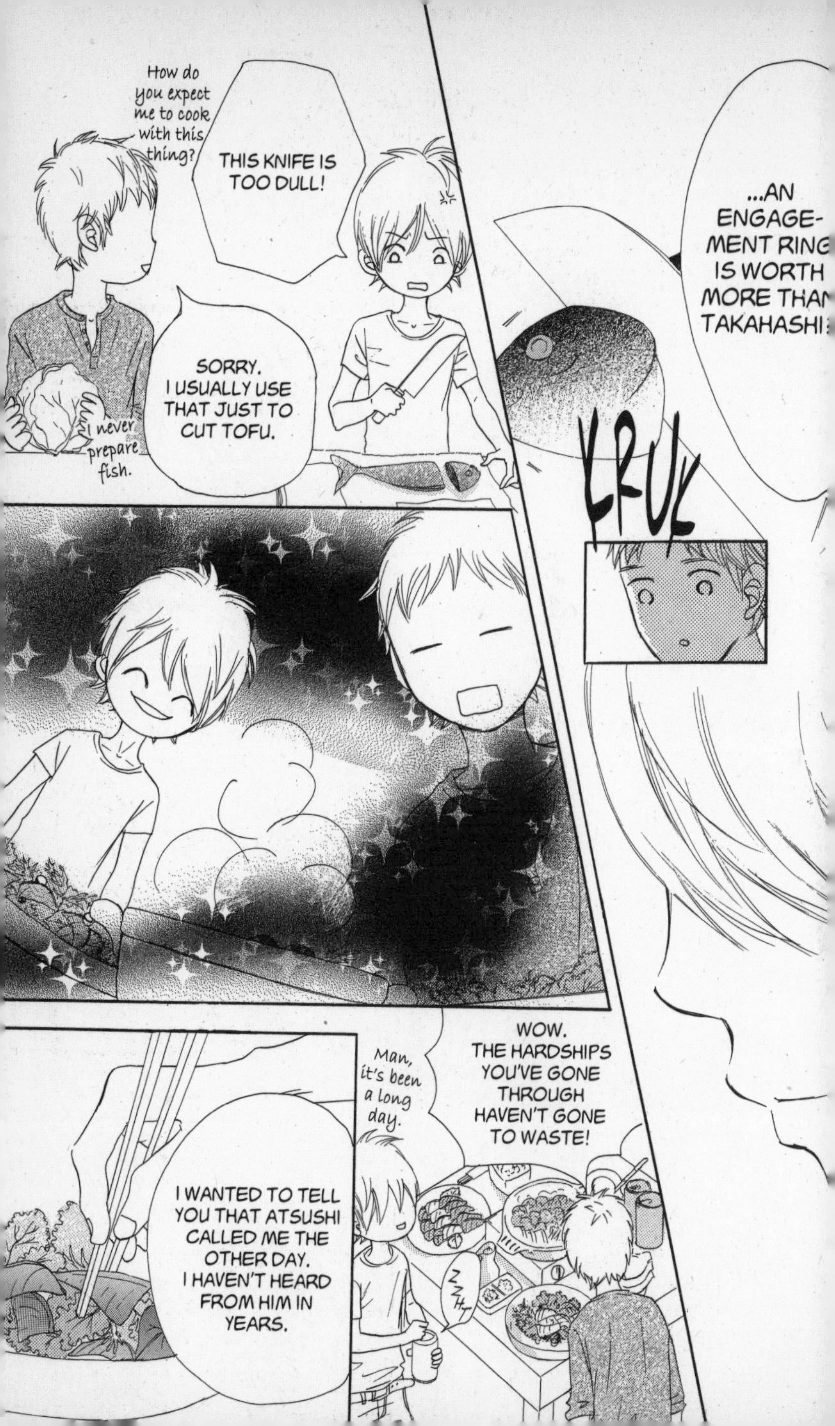
...AN ENGAGEMENT RING IS WORTH MORE THAN TAKAHASHI
KRUK
THIS KNIFE IS TOO DULL!
How do you expect me to cook with this thing?
SORRY. I USUALLY USE THAT JUST TO CUT TOFU.
I never prepare fish.
WOW. THE HARDSHIPS YOU'VE GONE THROUGH HAVEN'T GONE TO WASTE!
Man, it's been a long day.
I WANTED TO TELL YOU THAT ATSUSHI CALLED ME THE OTHER DAY. I HAVEN'T HEARD FROM HIM IN YEARS.

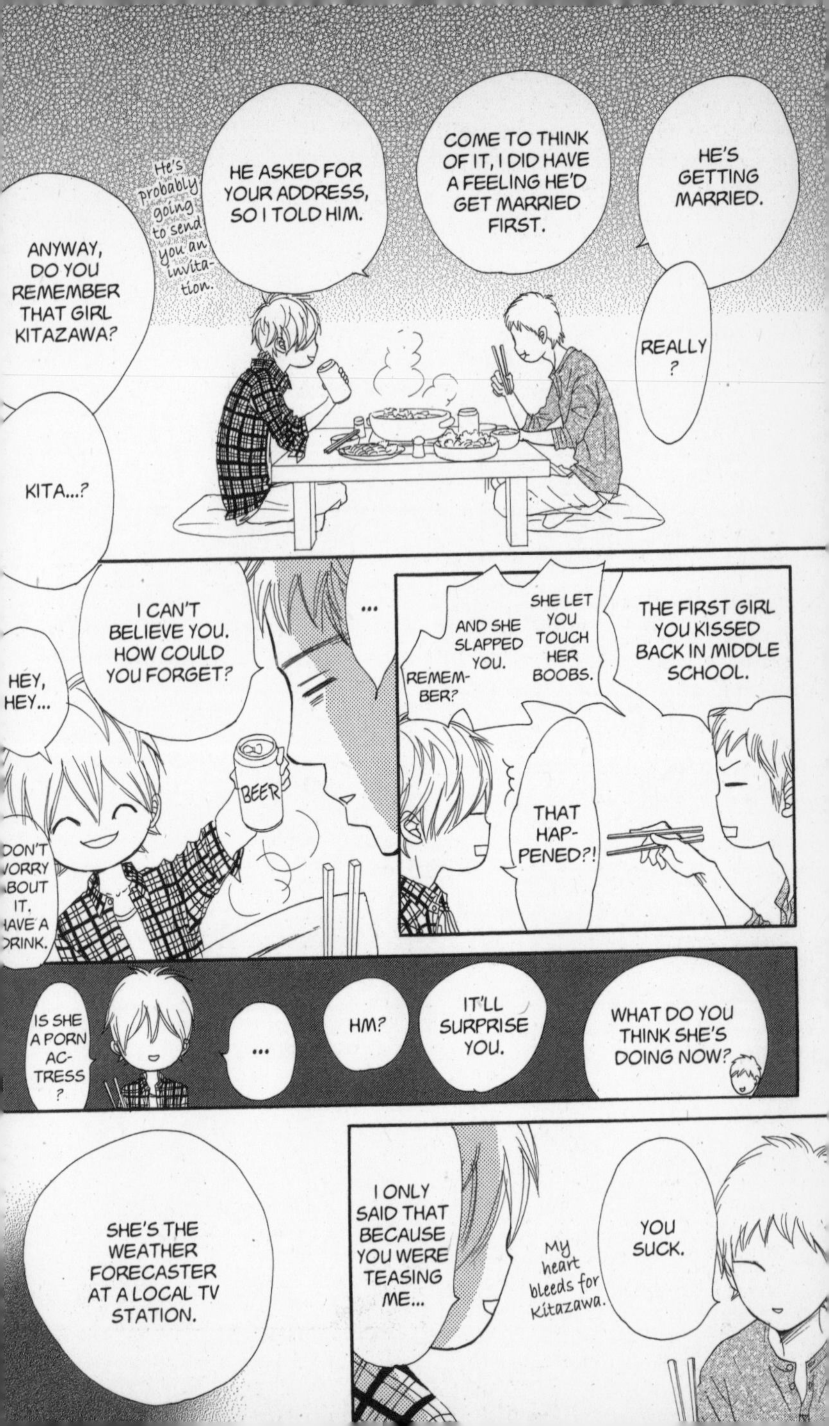
HE'S GETTING MARRIED.
REALLY?
COME TO THINK OF IT, I DID HAVE A FEELING HE'D GET MARRIED FIRST.
HE ASKED FOR YOUR ADDRESS, SO I TOLD HIM.
He's probably going to send you an invitation.
ANYWAY, DO YOU REMEMBER THAT GIRL KITAZAWA?
KITA...?
THE FIRST GIRL YOU KISSED BACK IN MIDDLE SCHOOL.
SHE LET YOU TOUCH HER BOOBS.
AND SHE SLAPPED YOU.
REMEMBER?
THAT HAPPENED?!
...
I CAN'T BELIEVE YOU. HOW COULD YOU FORGET?
HEY, HEY...
BEER
DON'T WORRY ABOUT IT. HAVE A DRINK.
WHAT DO YOU THINK SHE'S DOING NOW?
IT'LL SURPRISE YOU.
HM?
...
IS SHE A PORN ACTRESS?
YOU SUCK.
My heart bleeds for Kitazawa.
I ONLY SAID THAT BECAUSE YOU WERE TEASING ME...
SHE'S THE WEATHER FORECASTER AT A LOCAL TV STATION.

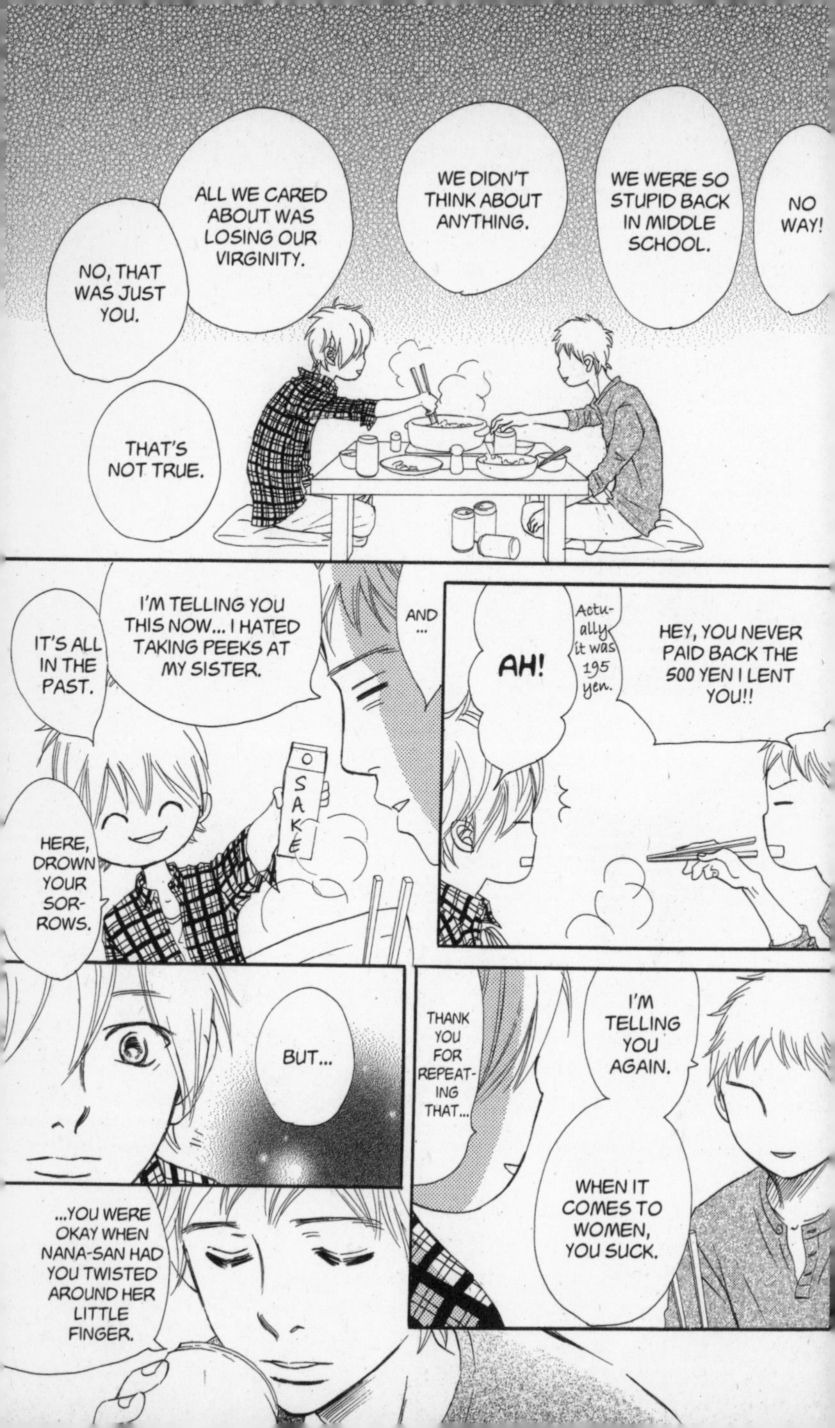
NO WAY!
WE WERE SO STUPID BACK IN MIDDLE SCHOOL.
WE DIDN'T THINK ABOUT ANYTHING.
ALL WE CARED ABOUT WAS LOSING OUR VIRGINITY.
NO, THAT WAS JUST YOU.
THAT'S NOT TRUE.
HEY, YOU NEVER PAID BACK THE 500 YEN I LENT YOU!!
Actually it was 195 yen.
AH!
AND ...
I'M TELLING YOU THIS NOW... I HATED TAKING PEEKS AT MY SISTER.
IT'S ALL IN THE PAST.
SAKE
HERE, DROWN YOUR SORROWS.
I'M TELLING YOU AGAIN.
WHEN IT COMES TO WOMEN, YOU SUCK.
THANK YOU FOR REPEATING THAT...
BUT...
...YOU WERE OKAY WHEN NANA-SAN HAD YOU TWISTED AROUND HER LITTLE FINGER.

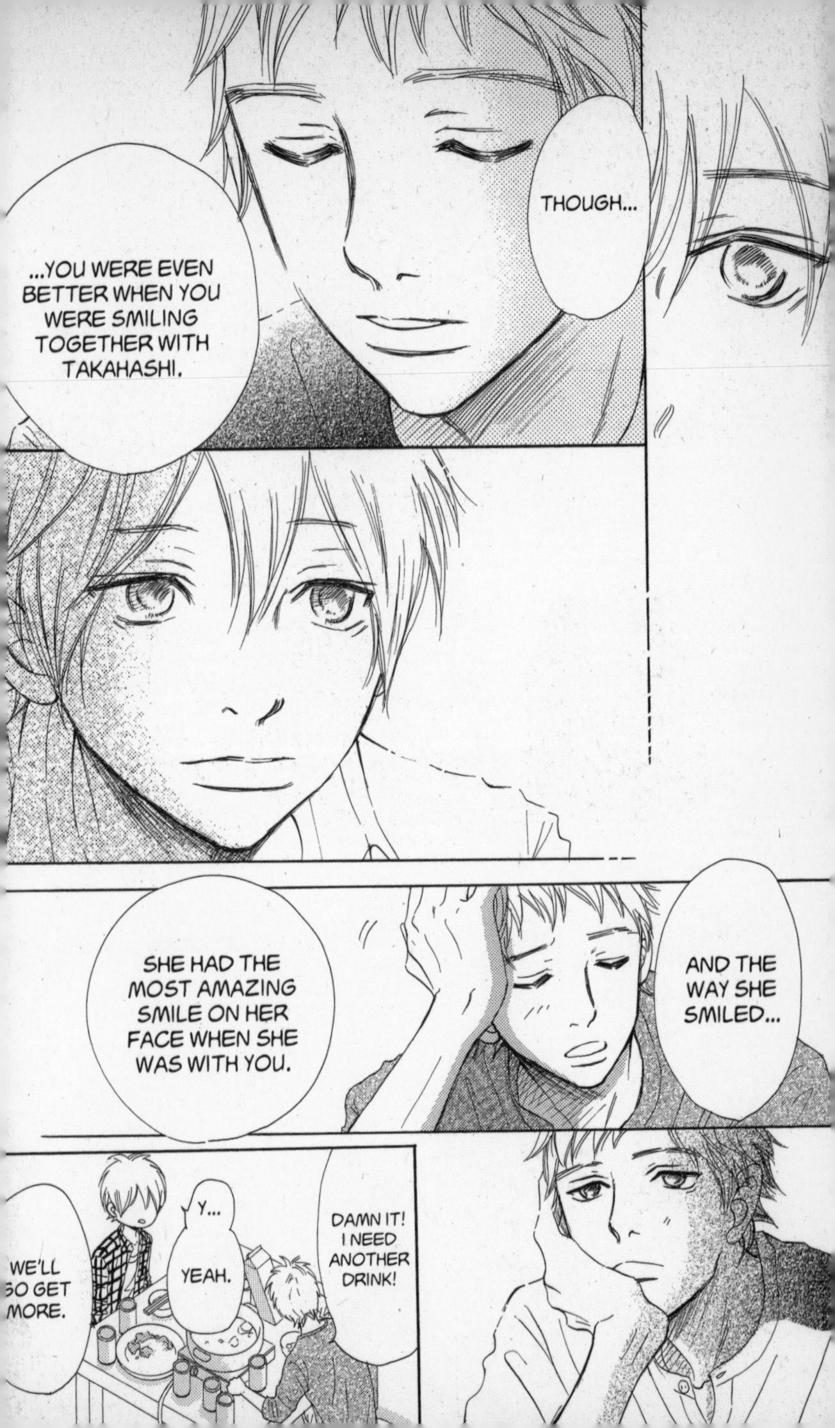
THOUGH...
...YOU WERE EVEN BETTER WHEN YOU WERE SMILING TOGETHER WITH TAKAHASHI.
AND THE WAY SHE SMILED...
SHE HAD THE MOST AMAZING SMILE ON HER FACE WHEN SHE WAS WITH YOU.
DAMN IT! I NEED ANOTHER DRINK!
Y...
YEAH.
WE'LL GO GET MORE.

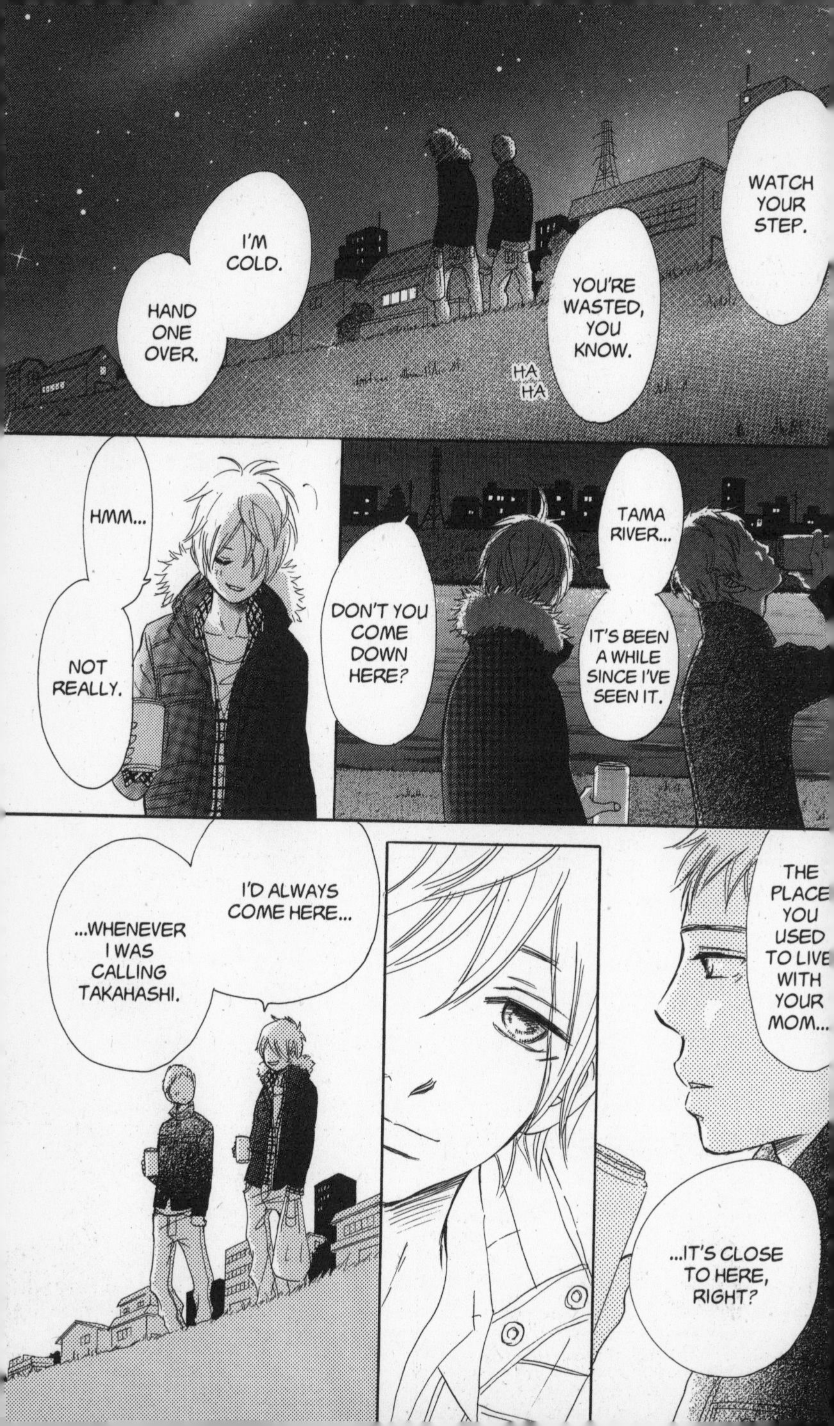
WATCH YOUR STEP.
YOU'RE WASTED, YOU KNOW.
HA HA
I'M COLD.
HAND ONE OVER.
TAMA RIVER...
IT'S BEEN A WHILE SINCE I'VE SEEN IT.
DON'T YOU COME DOWN HERE?
HMM...
NOT REALLY.
THE PLACE YOU USED TO LIVE WITH YOUR MOM...
...IT'S CLOSE TO HERE, RIGHT?
I'D ALWAYS COME HERE...
...WHENEVER I WAS CALLING TAKAHASHI.

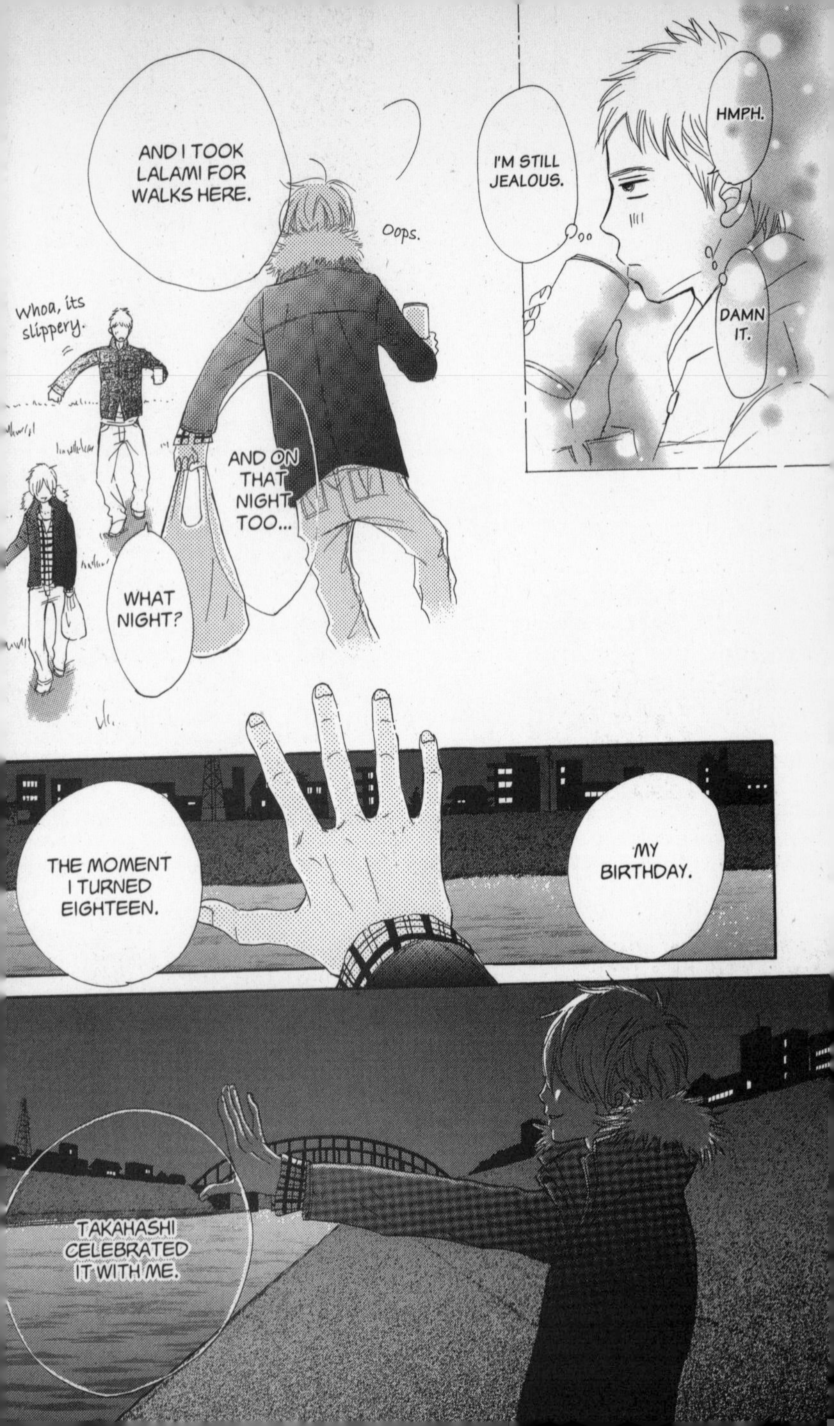
HMPH.
I'M STILL JEALOUS.
DAMN IT.
AND I TOOK LALAMI FOR WALKS HERE.
Oops.
Whoa, its slippery.
AND ON THAT NIGHT TOO...
WHAT NIGHT?
MY BIRTHDAY.
THE MOMENT I TURNED EIGHTEEN.
TAKAHASHI CELEBRATED IT WITH ME.

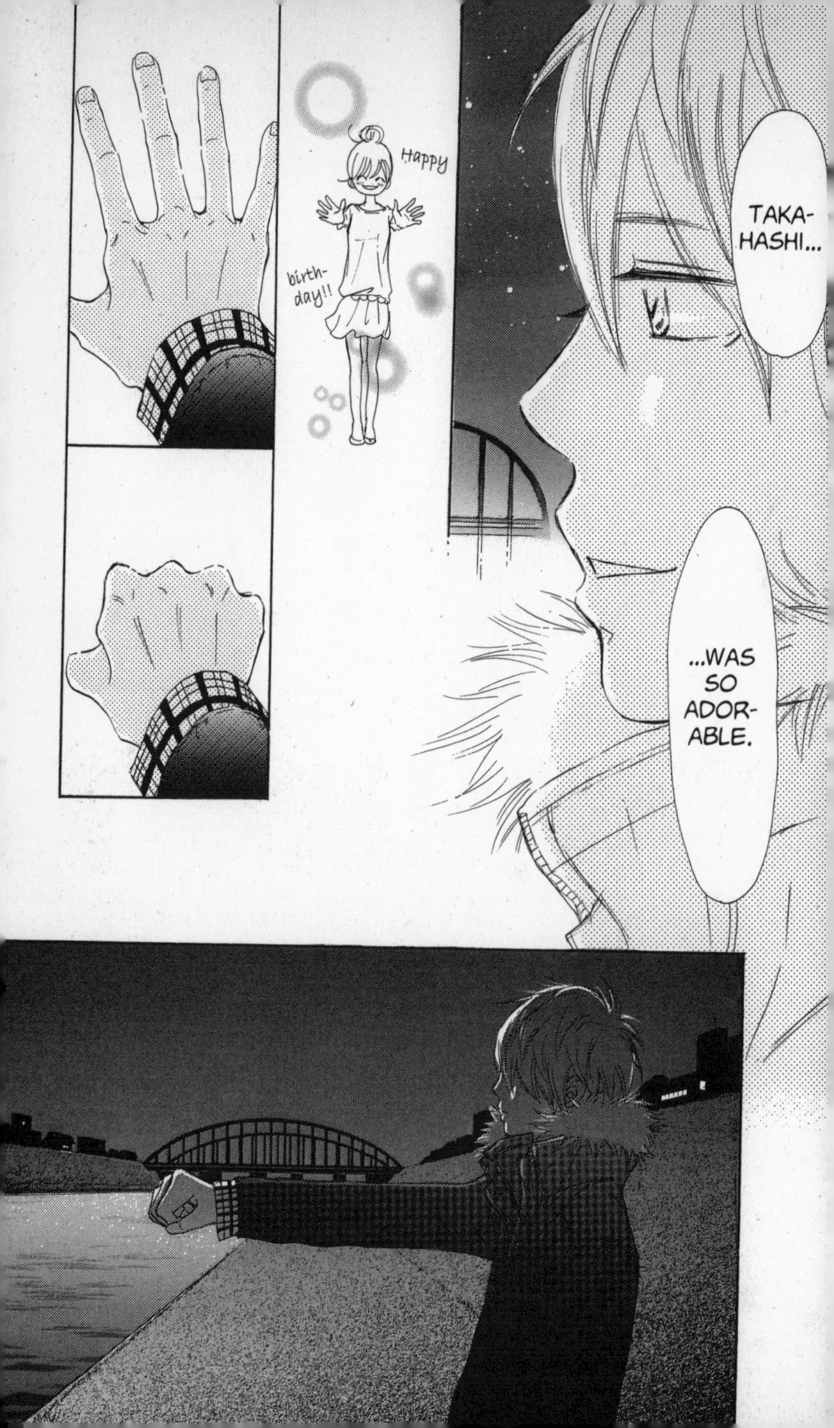
TAKA-HASHI...
...WAS SO ADOR-ABLE.
Happy
birth-day!!

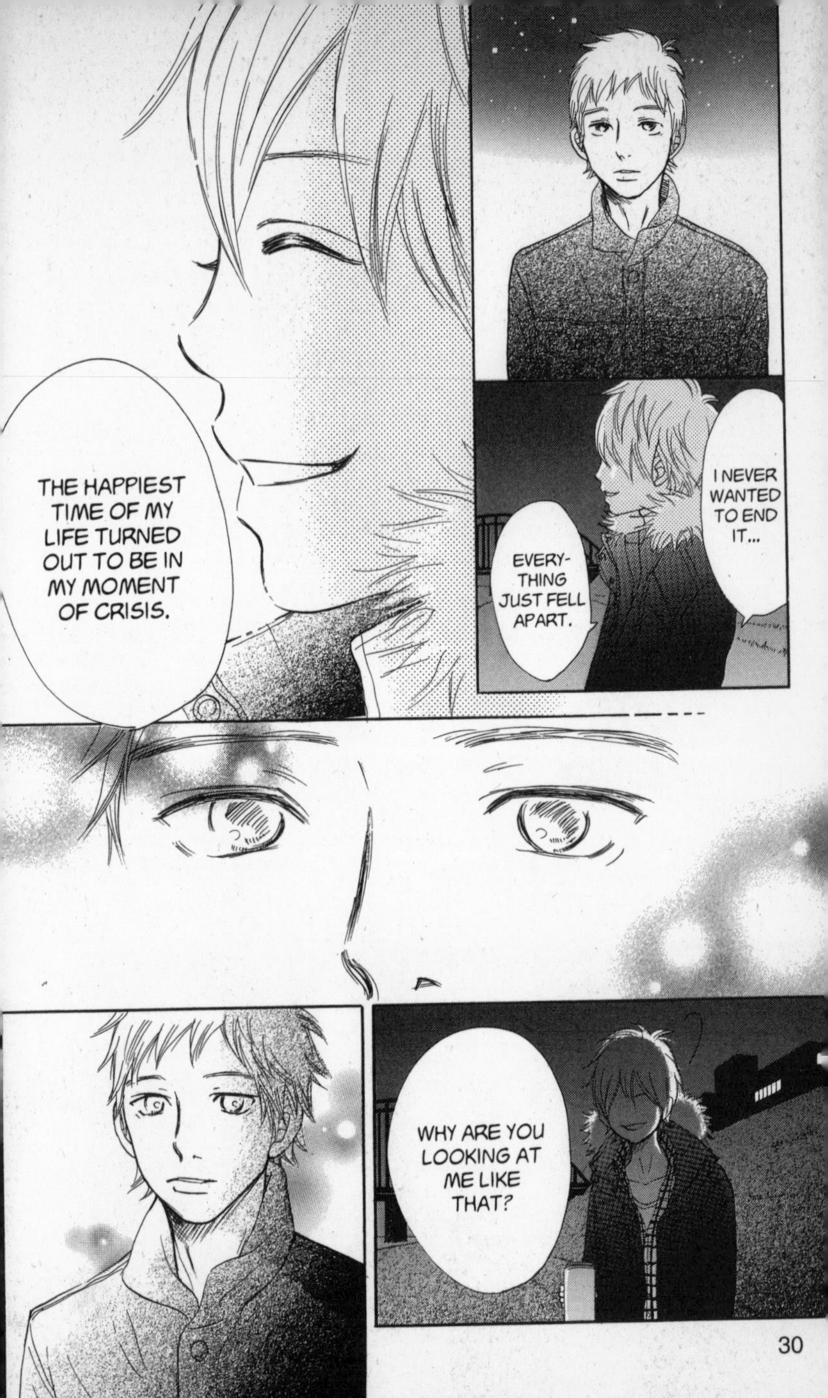
I NEVER WANTED TO END IT...
EVERY-THING JUST FELL APART.
THE HAPPIEST TIME OF MY LIFE TURNED OUT TO BE IN MY MOMENT OF CRISIS.
WHY ARE YOU LOOKING AT ME LIKE THAT?

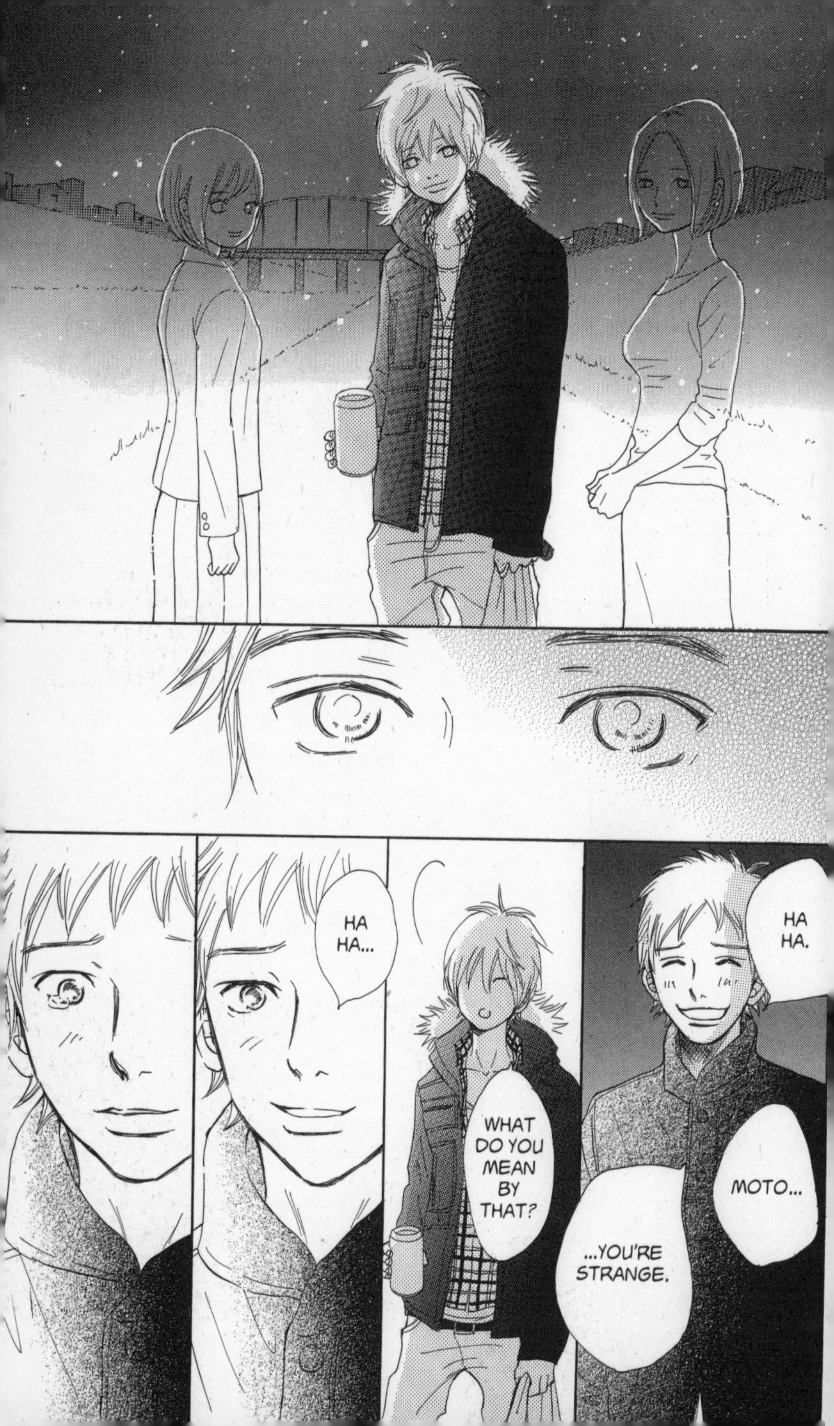
HA HA.
MOTO...
...YOU'RE STRANGE.
WHAT DO YOU MEAN BY THAT?
HA HA...

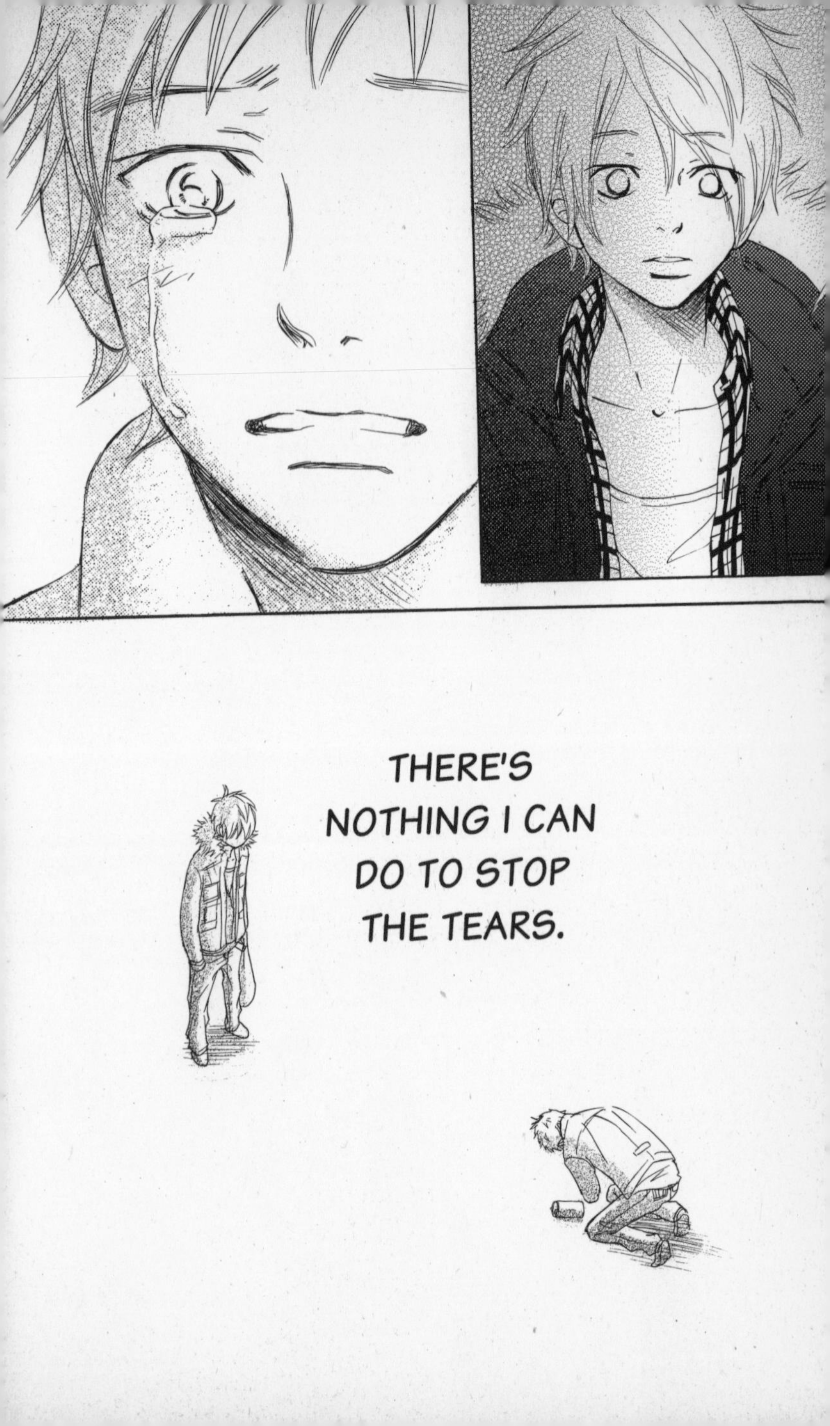
THERE'S NOTHING I CAN DO TO STOP THE TEARS.

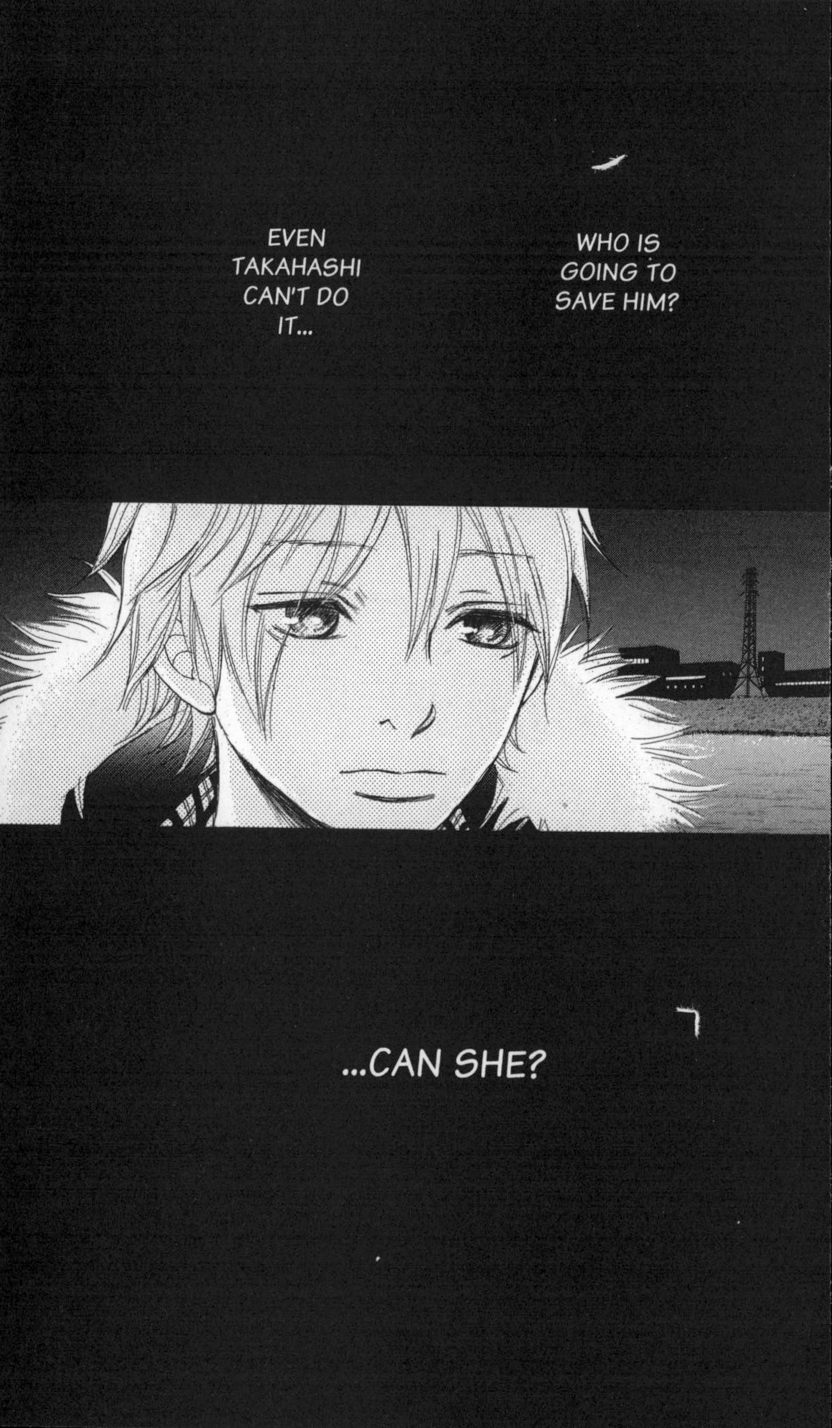
WHO IS GOING TO SAVE HIM?
EVEN TAKAHASHI CAN'T DO IT...
...CAN SHE?

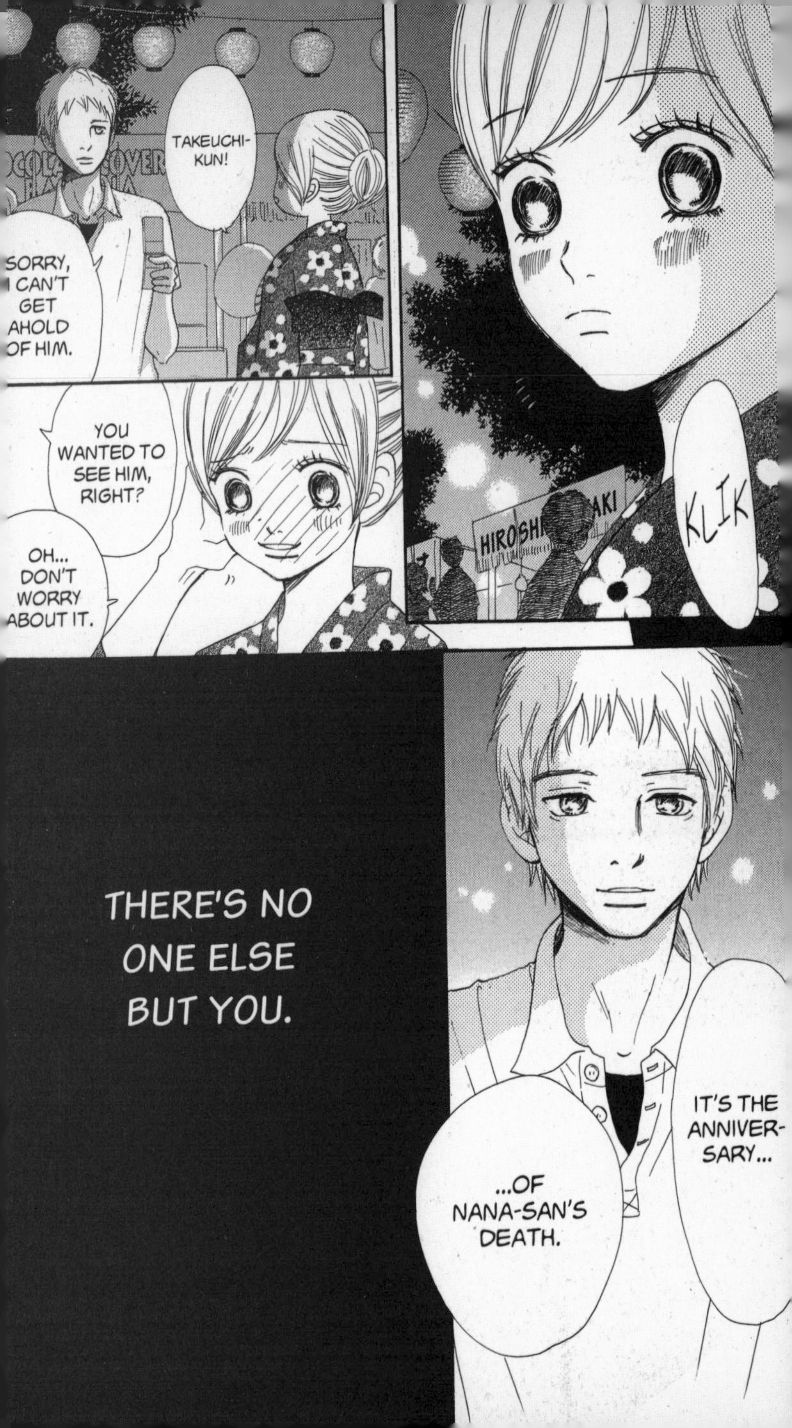
KLIK
TAKEUCHI-KUN!
SORRY, I CAN'T GET AHOLD OF HIM.
YOU WANTED TO SEE HIM, RIGHT?
OH... DON'T WORRY ABOUT IT.
IT'S THE ANNIVERSARY...
...OF NANA-SAN'S DEATH.
THERE'S NO ONE ELSE BUT YOU.

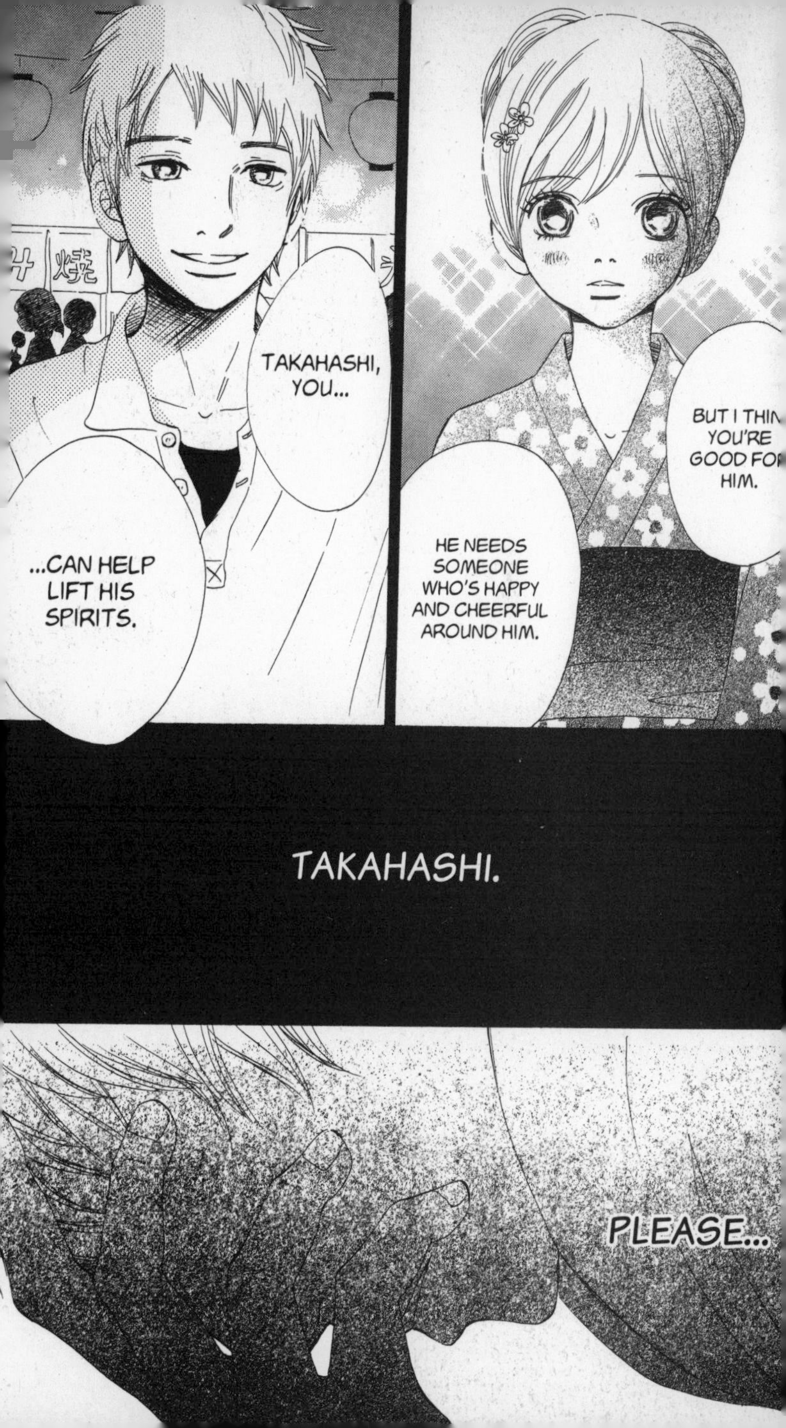
BUT I THIN
YOU'RE
GOOD FO
HIM.
HE NEEDS SOMEONE WHO'S HAPPY AND CHEERFUL AROUND HIM.
焼
TAKAHASHI, YOU...
...CAN HELP LIFT HIS SPIRITS.
TAKAHASHI.
PLEASE...

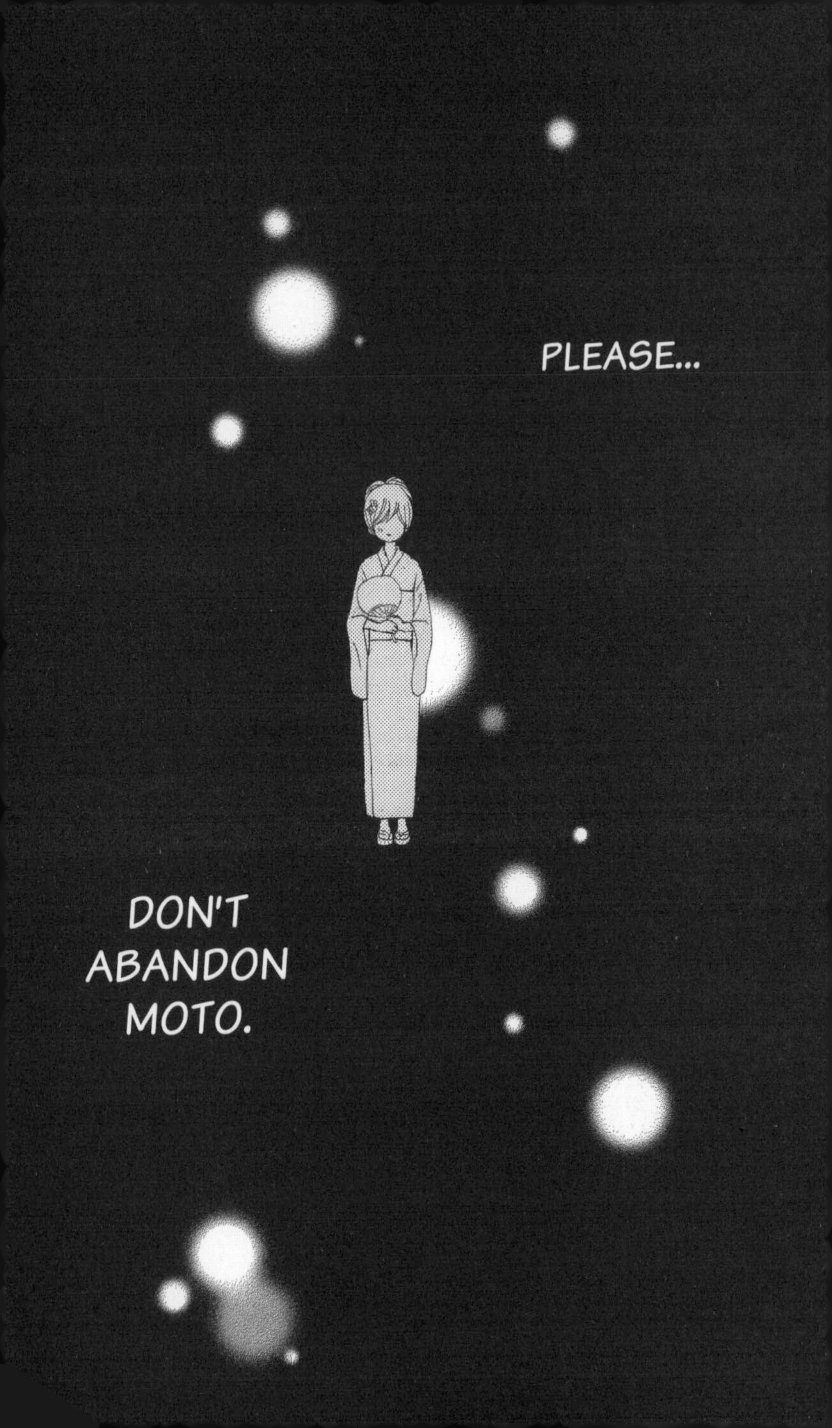
PLEASE...
DON'T ABANDON MOTO.

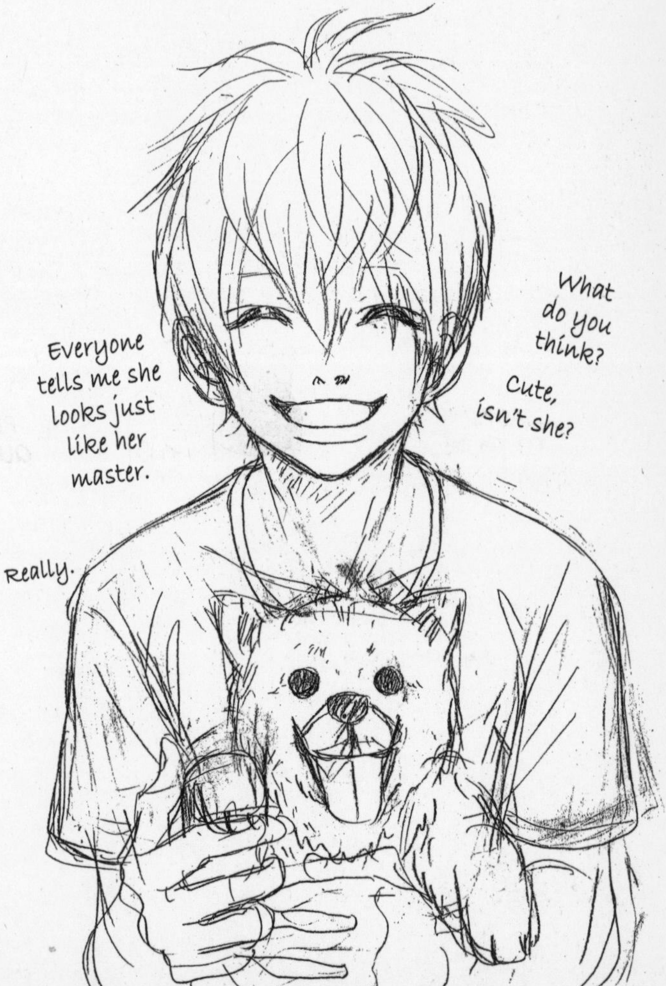

What do you think?
Cute, isn't she?
Everyone tells me she looks just like her master.
Really.

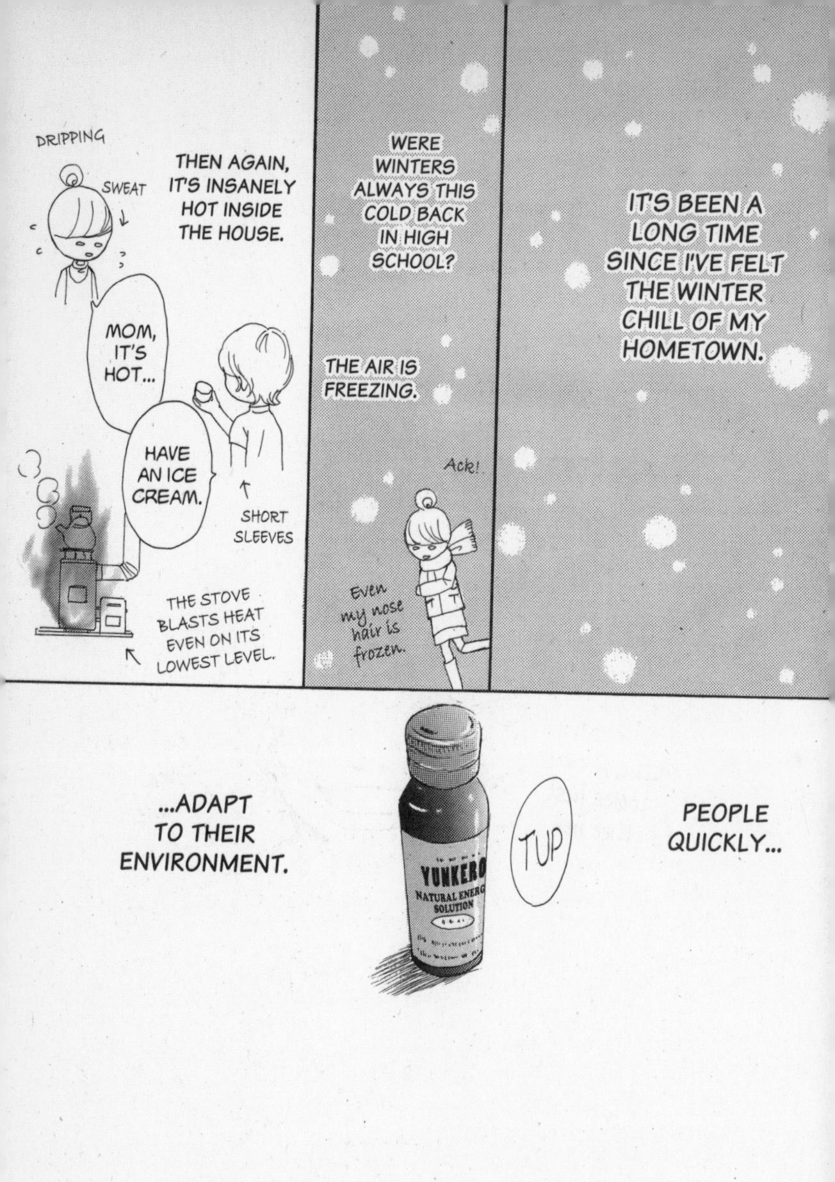
IT'S BEEN A LONG TIME SINCE I'VE FELT THE WINTER CHILL OF MY HOMETOWN.
WERE WINTERS ALWAYS THIS COLD BACK IN HIGH SCHOOL?
THE AIR IS FREEZING.
Ack!
Even my nose hair is frozen.
THEN AGAIN, IT'S INSANELY HOT INSIDE THE HOUSE.
DRIPPING
SWEAT
MOM, IT'S HOT...
HAVE AN ICE CREAM.
SHORT SLEEVES
THE STOVE BLASTS HEAT EVEN ON ITS LOWEST LEVEL.
PEOPLE QUICKLY...
TUP
YUNKERO
NATURAL ENERG
SOLUTION
...ADAPT TO THEIR ENVIRONMENT.

Chapter 61

Chapter 61

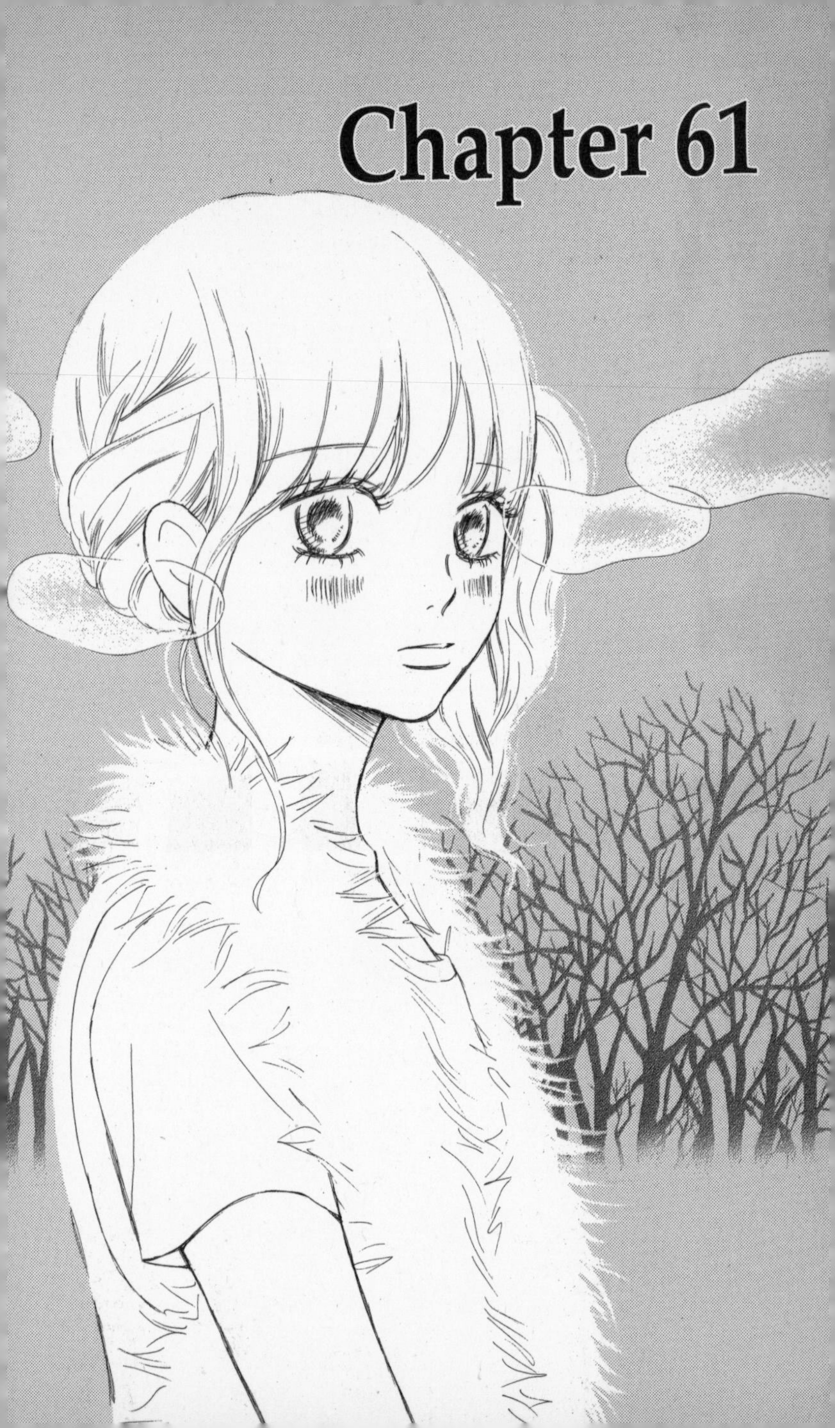

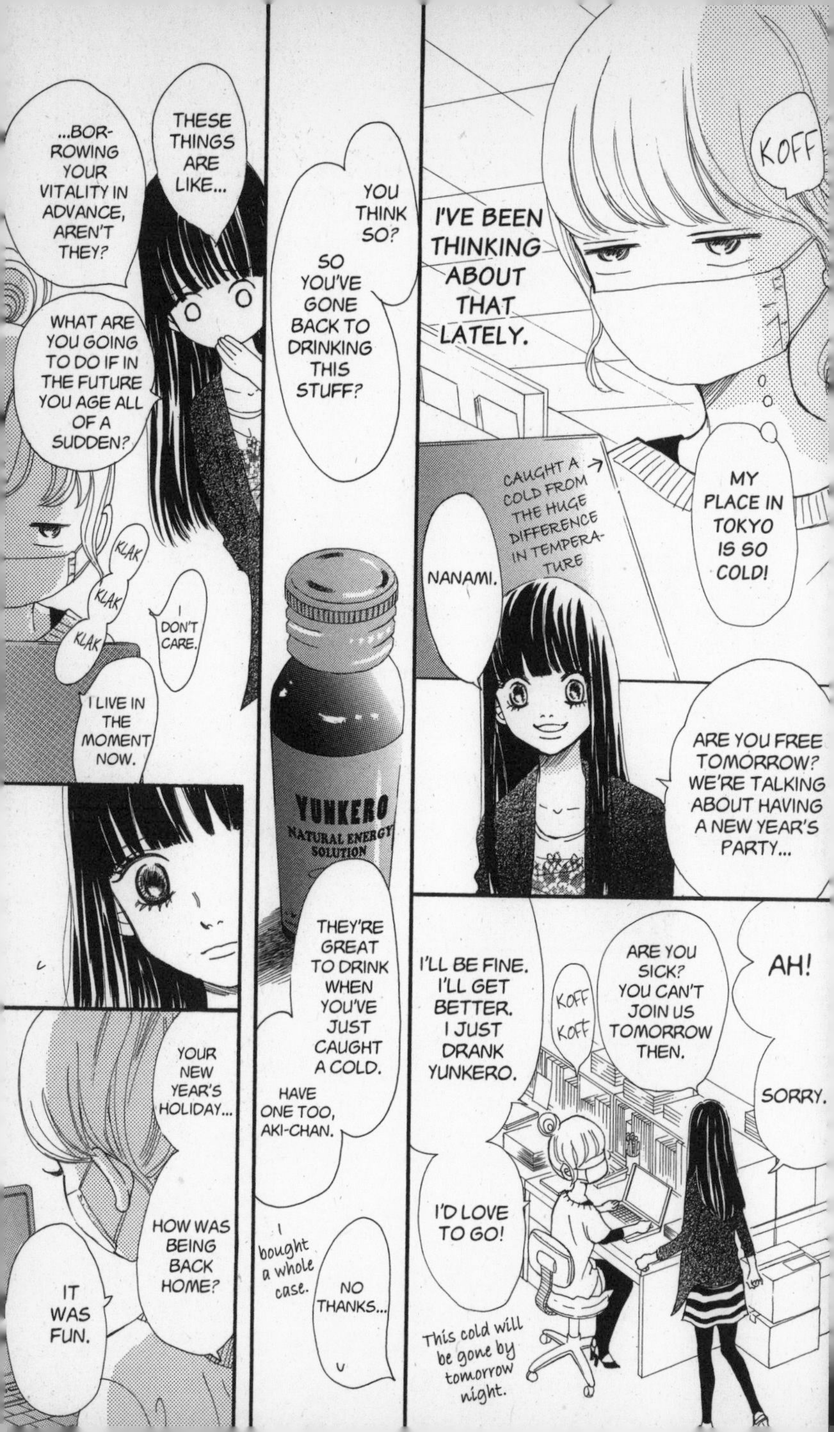
KOFF
I'VE BEEN THINKING ABOUT THAT LATELY.
MY PLACE IN TOKYO IS SO COLD!
NANAMI.
ARE YOU FREE TOMORROW? WE'RE TALKING ABOUT HAVING A NEW YEAR'S PARTY...
CAUGHT A COLD FROM THE HUGE DIFFERENCE IN TEMPERATURE
AH!
ARE YOU SICK? YOU CAN'T JOIN US TOMORROW THEN.
KOFF KOFF
I'LL BE FINE. I'LL GET BETTER. I JUST DRANK YUNKERO.
SORRY.
I'D LOVE TO GO!
This cold will be gone by tomorrow night.
YOU THINK SO?
SO YOU'VE GONE BACK TO DRINKING THIS STUFF?
YUNKERO
NATURAL ENERGY SOLUTION
THEY'RE GREAT TO DRINK WHEN YOU'VE JUST CAUGHT A COLD.
HAVE ONE TOO, AKI-CHAN.
NO THANKS...
I bought a whole case.
THESE THINGS ARE LIKE...
...BOR-ROWING YOUR VITALITY IN ADVANCE, AREN'T THEY?
WHAT ARE YOU GOING TO DO IF IN THE FUTURE YOU AGE ALL OF A SUDDEN?
KLAK
KLAK
KLAK
I DON'T CARE.
I LIVE IN THE MOMENT NOW.
YOUR NEW YEAR'S HOLIDAY...
HOW WAS BEING BACK HOME?
IT WAS FUN.

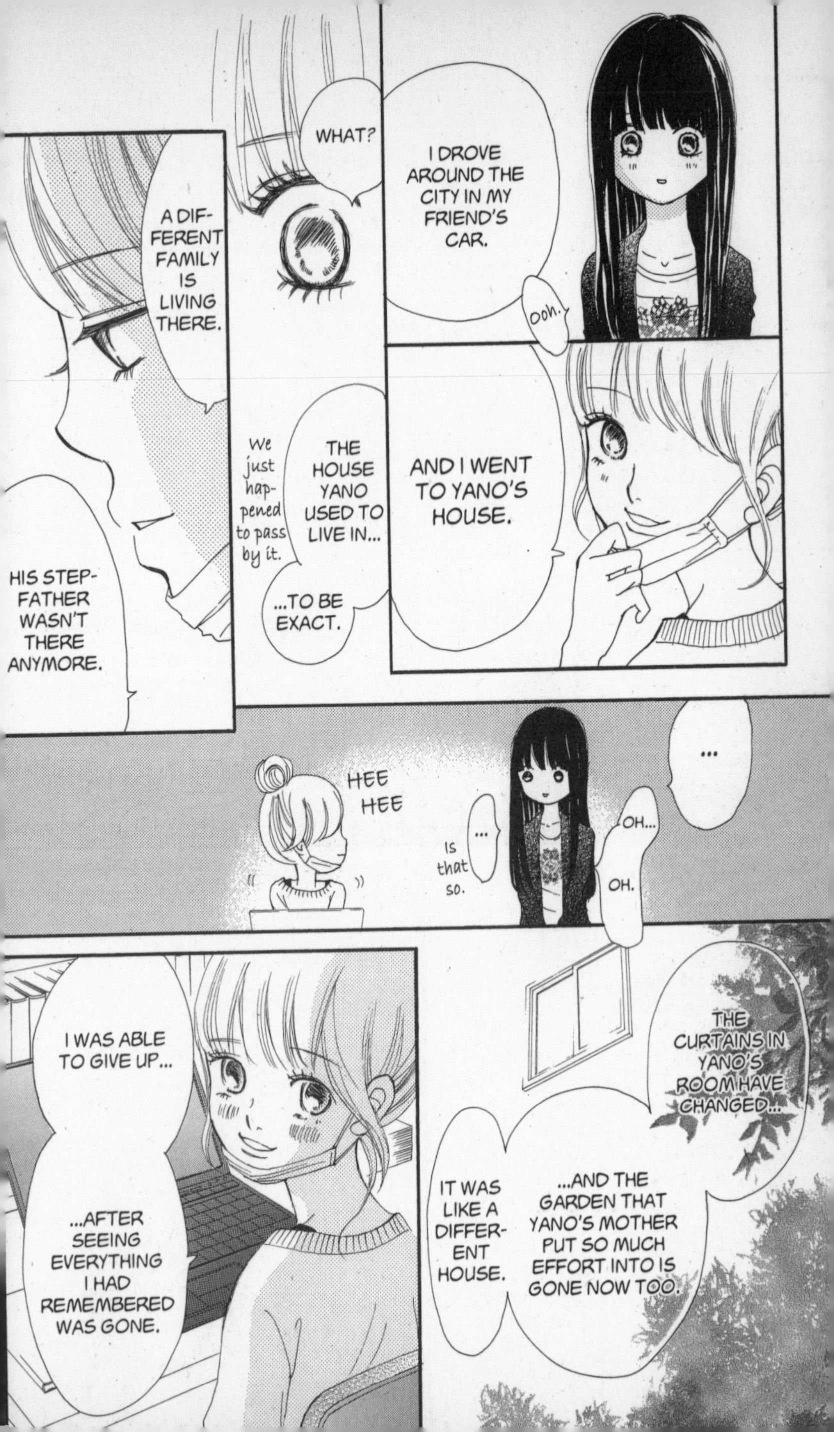

I DROVE AROUND THE CITY IN MY FRIEND'S CAR.
Ooh.
AND I WENT TO YANO'S HOUSE.
WHAT?
THE HOUSE YANO USED TO LIVE IN...
We just happened to pass by it.
...TO BE EXACT.
A DIFFERENT FAMILY IS LIVING THERE.
HIS STEPFATHER WASN'T THERE ANYMORE.
...
OH...
OH.
...
Is that so.
HEE HEE
THE CURTAINS IN YANO'S ROOM HAVE CHANGED...
...AND THE GARDEN THAT YANO'S MOTHER PUT SO MUCH EFFORT INTO IS GONE NOW TOO.
IT WAS LIKE A DIFFERENT HOUSE.
I WAS ABLE TO GIVE UP...
...AFTER SEEING EVERYTHING I HAD REMEMBERED WAS GONE.

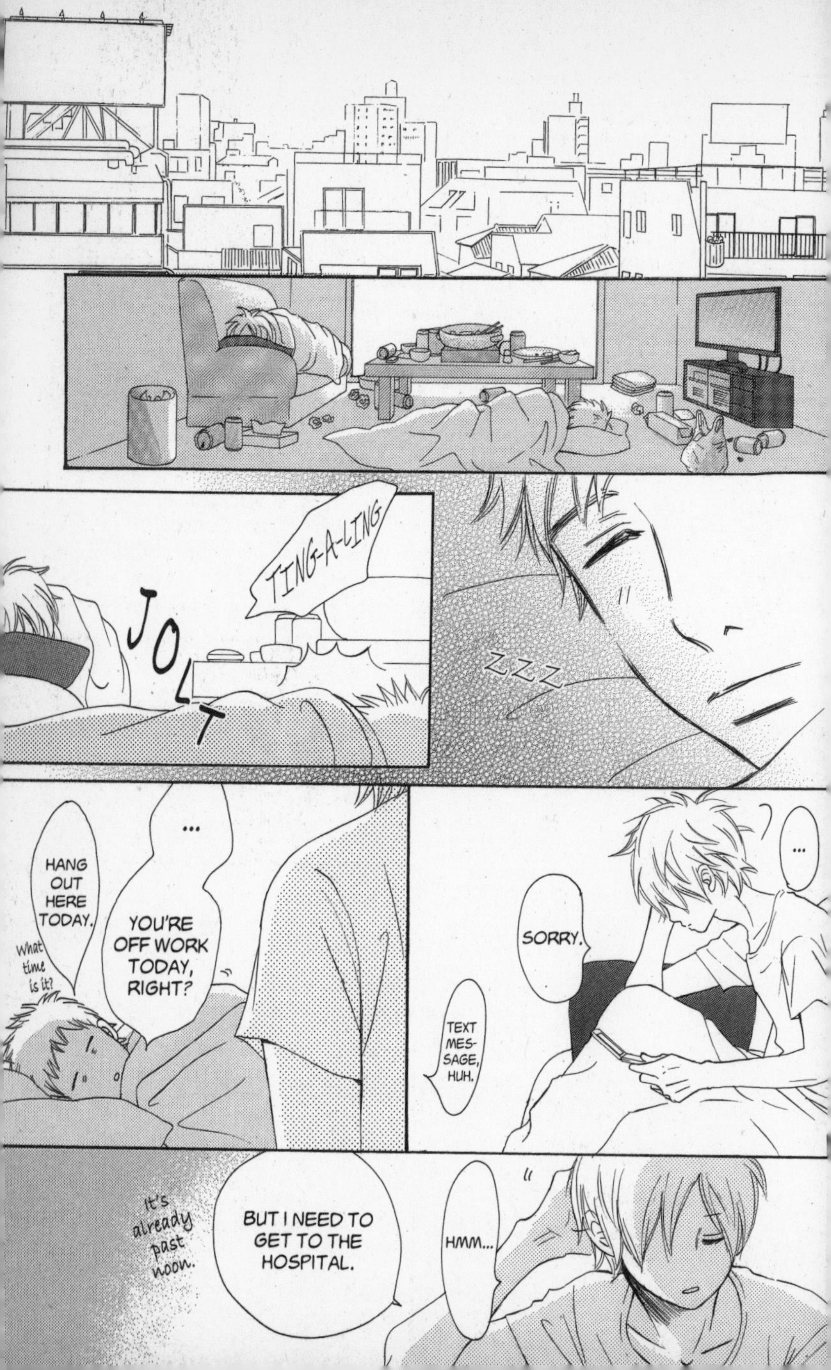
ZZZ
TING-A-LING
JOLT
...
SORRY.
TEXT MES-SAGE, HUH.
...
YOU'RE OFF WORK TODAY, RIGHT?
HANG OUT HERE TODAY.
What time is it?
HMM...
BUT I NEED TO GET TO THE HOSPITAL.
It's already past noon.

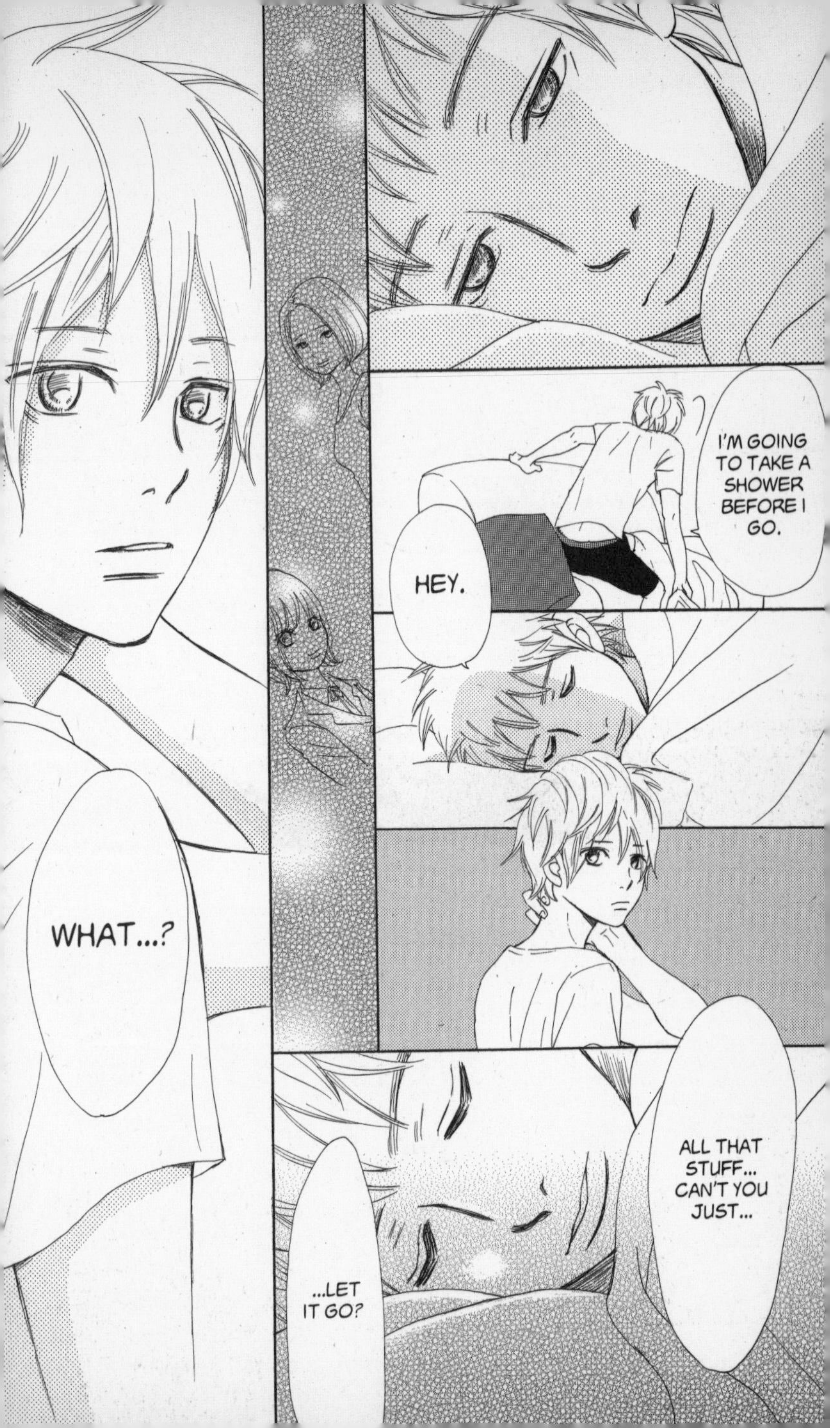
I'M GOING TO TAKE A SHOWER BEFORE I GO.
HEY.
ALL THAT STUFF... CAN'T YOU JUST...
...LET IT GO?
WHAT...?

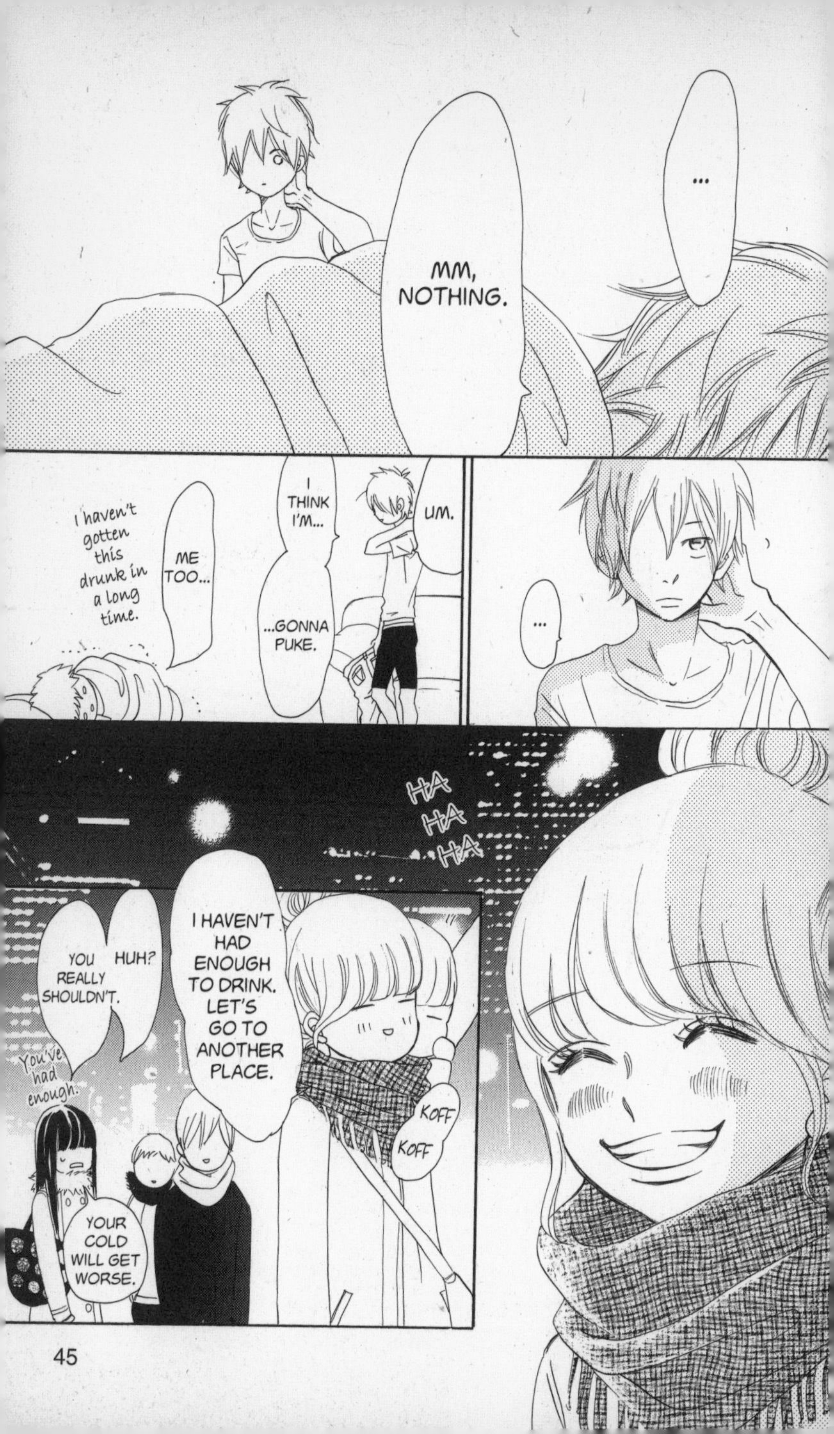
...
MM, NOTHING.
...
UM.
I THINK I'M...
...GONNA PUKE.
ME TOO...
I haven't gotten this drunk in a long time.
HA HA HA
I HAVEN'T HAD ENOUGH TO DRINK. LET'S GO TO ANOTHER PLACE.
KOFF KOFF
HUH?
YOU REALLY SHOULDN'T.
You've had enough.
YOUR COLD WILL GET WORSE.

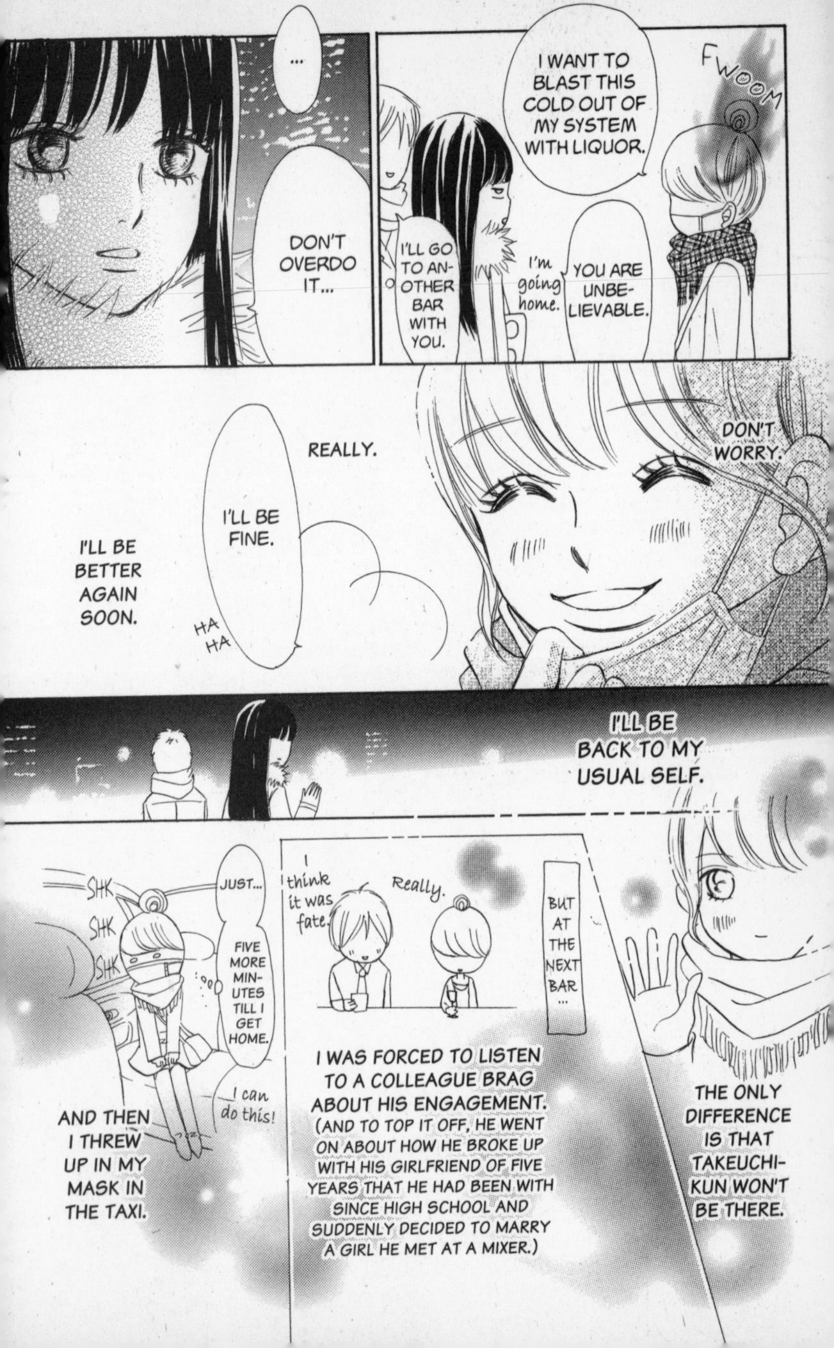
FWOOM
I WANT TO BLAST THIS COLD OUT OF MY SYSTEM WITH LIQUOR.
YOU ARE UNBELIEVABLE.
I'm going home.
I'LL GO TO ANOTHER BAR WITH YOU.
...
DON'T OVERDO IT...
DON'T WORRY.
REALLY.
I'LL BE FINE.
HA HA
I'LL BE BETTER AGAIN SOON.
I'LL BE BACK TO MY USUAL SELF.
THE ONLY DIFFERENCE IS THAT TAKEUCHI-KUN WON'T BE THERE.
BUT AT THE NEXT BAR...
Really.
I think it was fate.
I WAS FORCED TO LISTEN TO A COLLEAGUE BRAG ABOUT HIS ENGAGEMENT. (AND TO TOP IT OFF, HE WENT ON ABOUT HOW HE BROKE UP WITH HIS GIRLFRIEND OF FIVE YEARS THAT HE HAD BEEN WITH SINCE HIGH SCHOOL AND SUDDENLY DECIDED TO MARRY A GIRL HE MET AT A MIXER.)
JUST...
FIVE MORE MINUTES TILL I GET HOME.
SHK SHK SHK
I can do this!
AND THEN I THREW UP IN MY MASK IN THE TAXI.

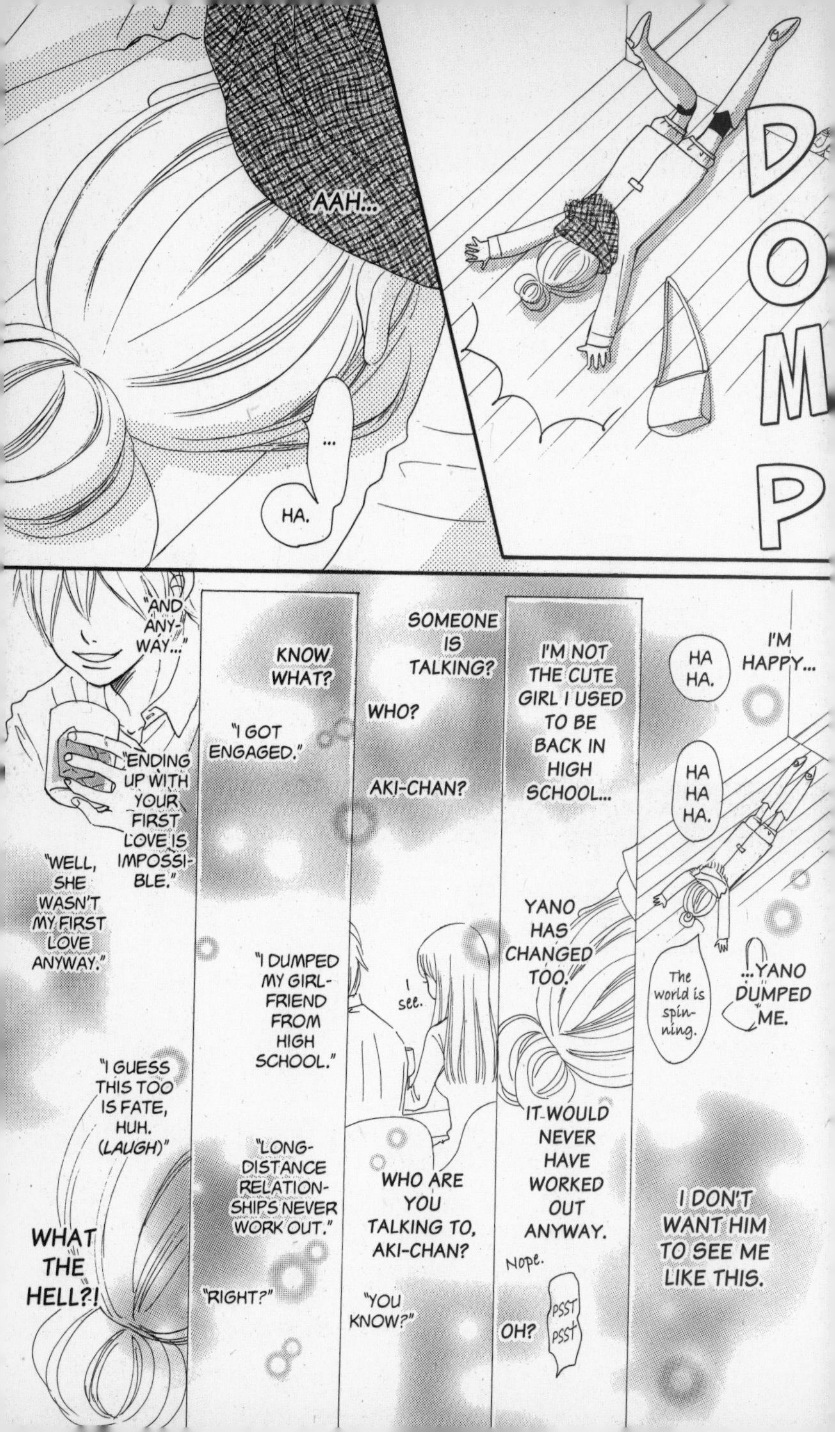
DOMP
AAH...
...
HA.
I'M HAPPY...
HA HA.
HA HA HA.
The world is spinning.
...YANO DUMPED ME.
I DON'T WANT HIM TO SEE ME LIKE THIS.
I'M NOT THE CUTE GIRL I USED TO BE BACK IN HIGH SCHOOL...
YANO HAS CHANGED TOO.
IT WOULD NEVER HAVE WORKED OUT ANYWAY.
Nope.
PSST PSST
OH?
SOMEONE IS TALKING?
WHO?
AKI-CHAN?
I see.
WHO ARE YOU TALKING TO, AKI-CHAN?
"YOU KNOW?"
KNOW WHAT?
"I GOT ENGAGED."
"I DUMPED MY GIRLFRIEND FROM HIGH SCHOOL."
"LONG-DISTANCE RELATIONSHIPS NEVER WORK OUT."
"RIGHT?"
"AND ANYWAY..."
"ENDING UP WITH YOUR FIRST LOVE IS IMPOSSIBLE."
"WELL, SHE WASN'T MY FIRST LOVE ANYWAY."
"I GUESS THIS TOO IS FATE, HUH. (LAUGH)"
WHAT THE HELL?!

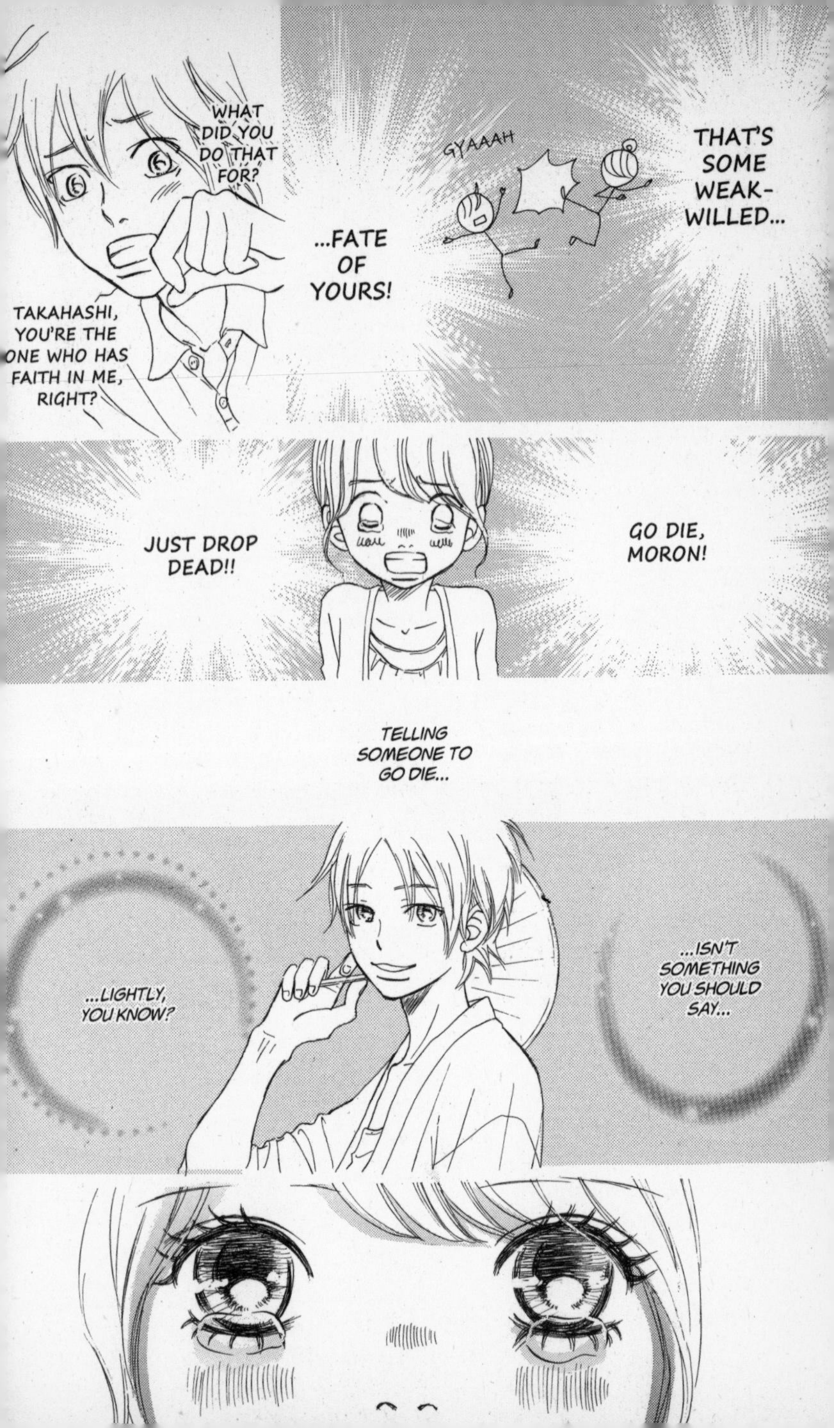
THAT'S SOME WEAK-WILLED...
GYAAAH
...FATE OF YOURS!
WHAT DID YOU DO THAT FOR?
TAKAHASHI, YOU'RE THE ONE WHO HAS FAITH IN ME, RIGHT?
GO DIE, MORON!
JUST DROP DEAD!!
TELLING SOMEONE TO GO DIE...
...ISN'T SOMETHING YOU SHOULD SAY...
...LIGHTLY, YOU KNOW?

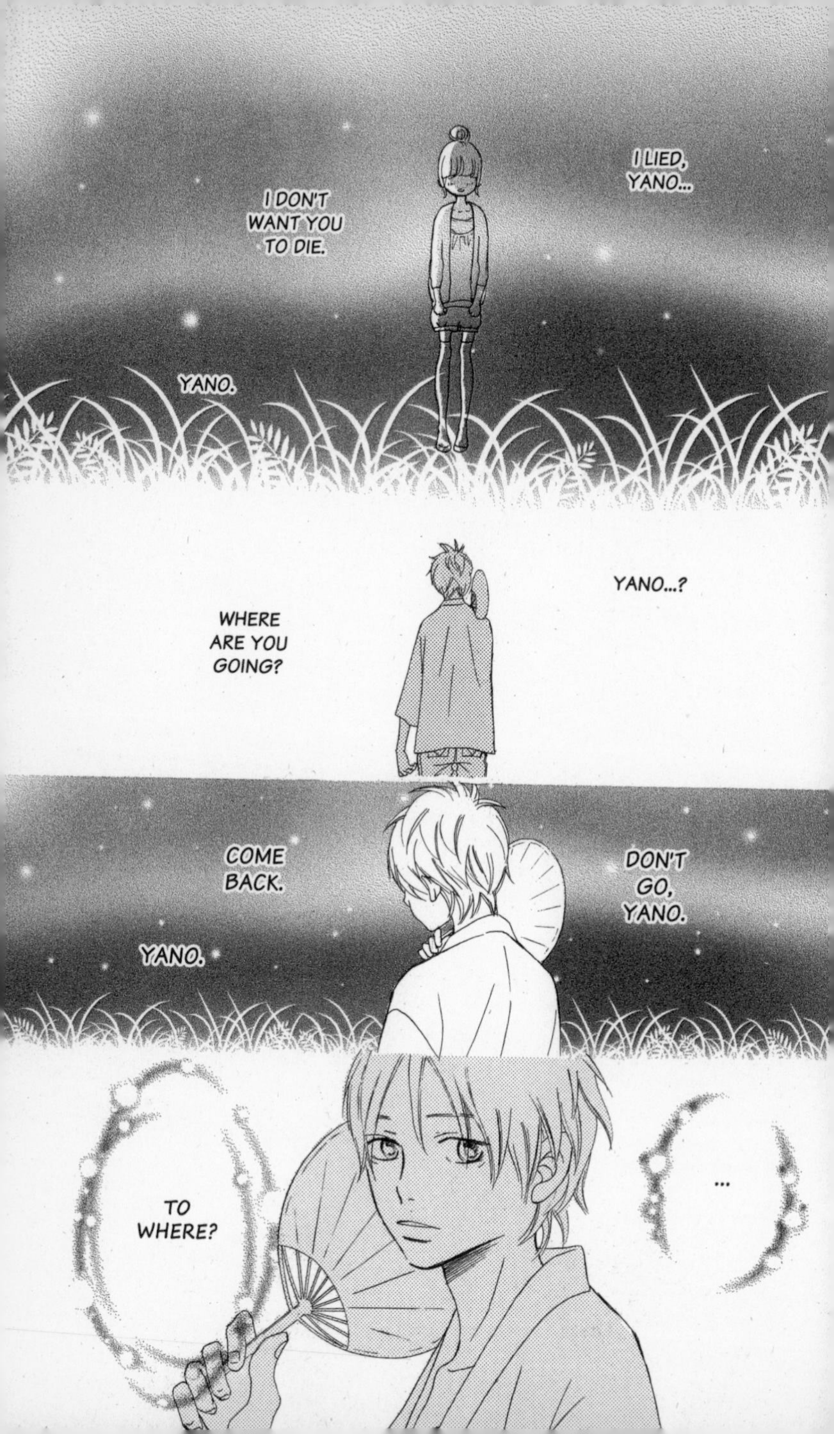
I LIED, YANO...
I DON'T WANT YOU TO DIE.
YANO.
YANO...?
WHERE ARE YOU GOING?
DON'T GO, YANO.
COME BACK.
YANO.
...
TO WHERE?

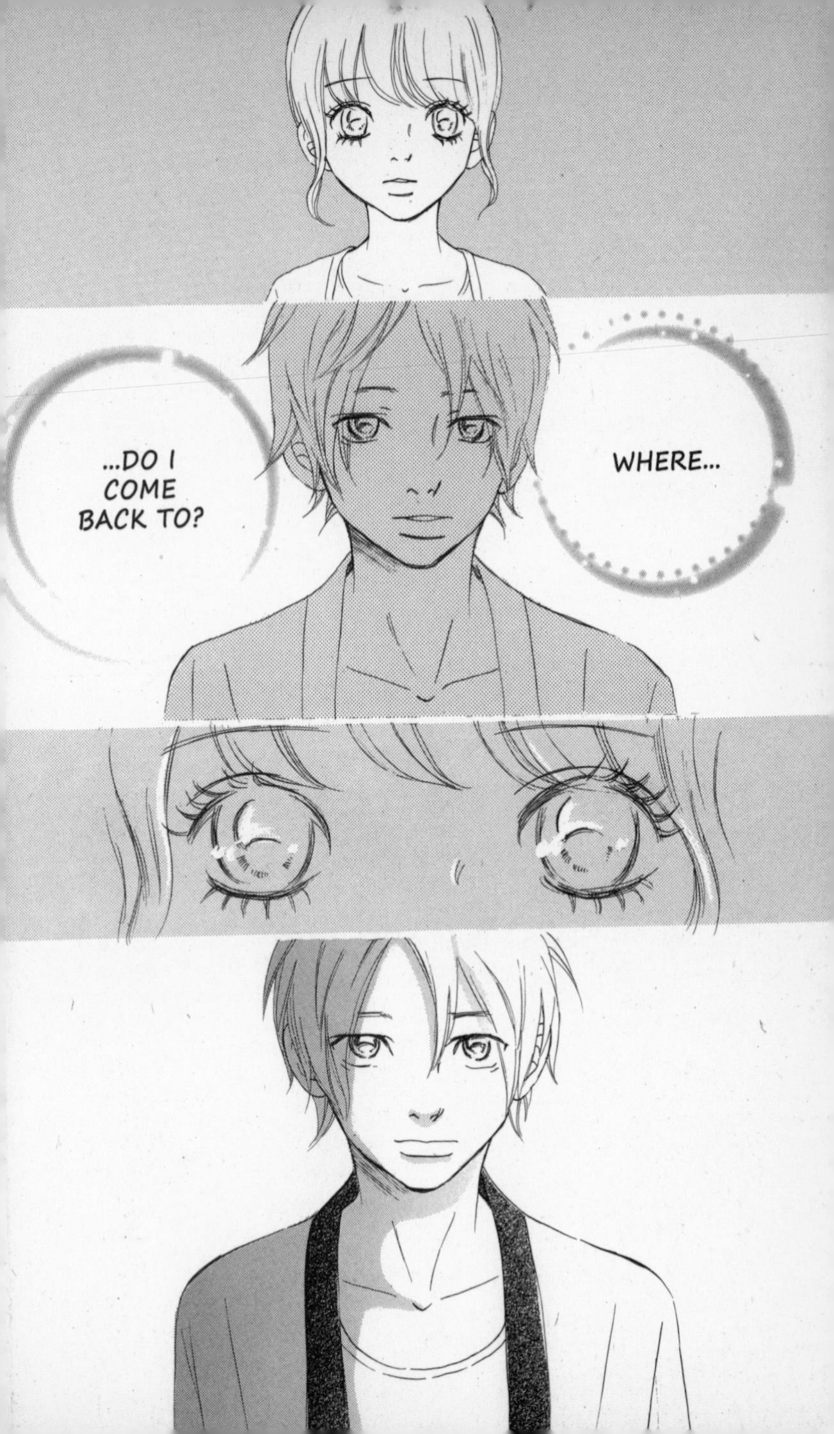
WHERE...
...DO I COME BACK TO?

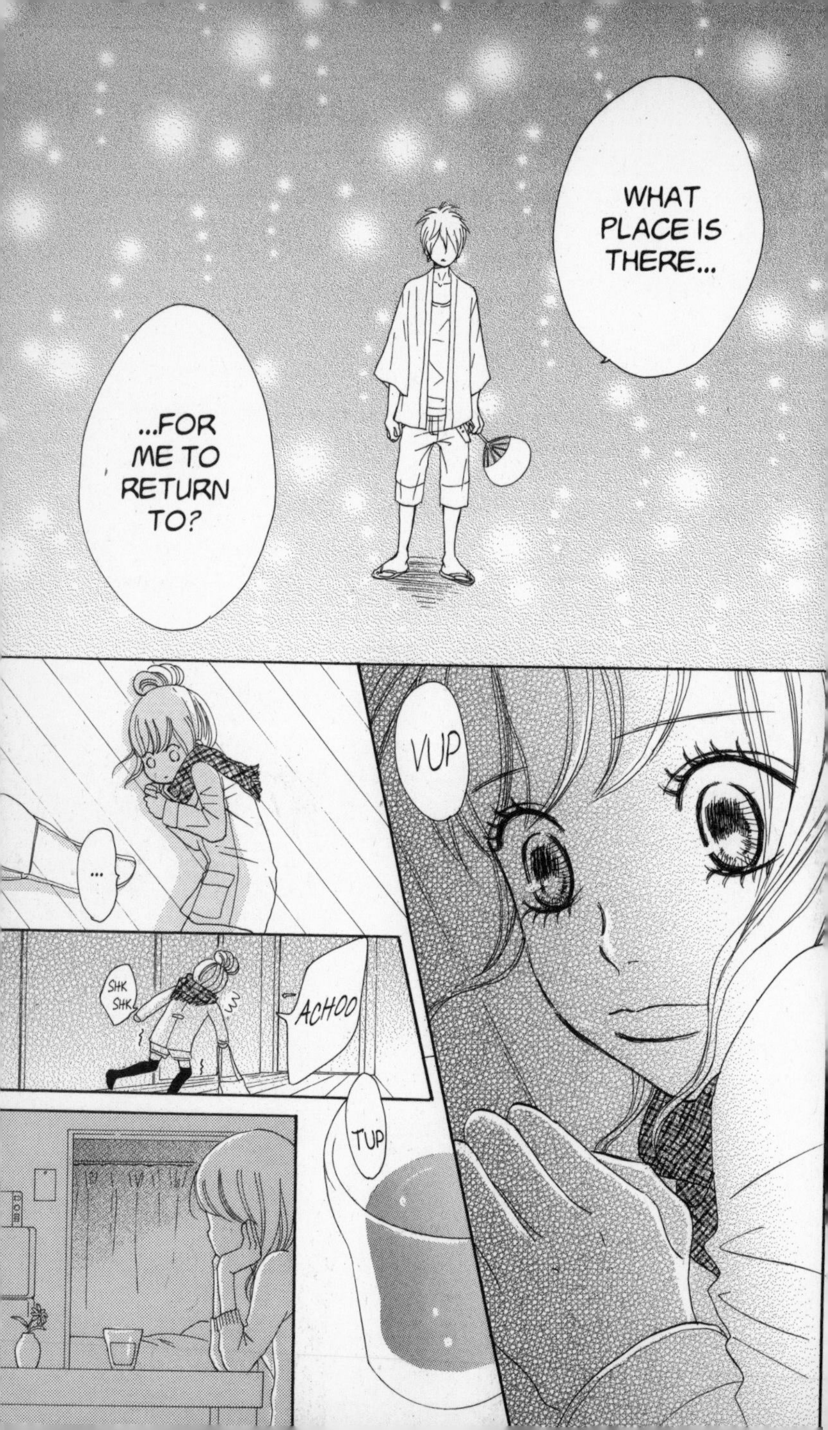
WHAT PLACE IS THERE...
...FOR ME TO RETURN TO?
VUP
TUP
...
SHK SHK
ACHOO

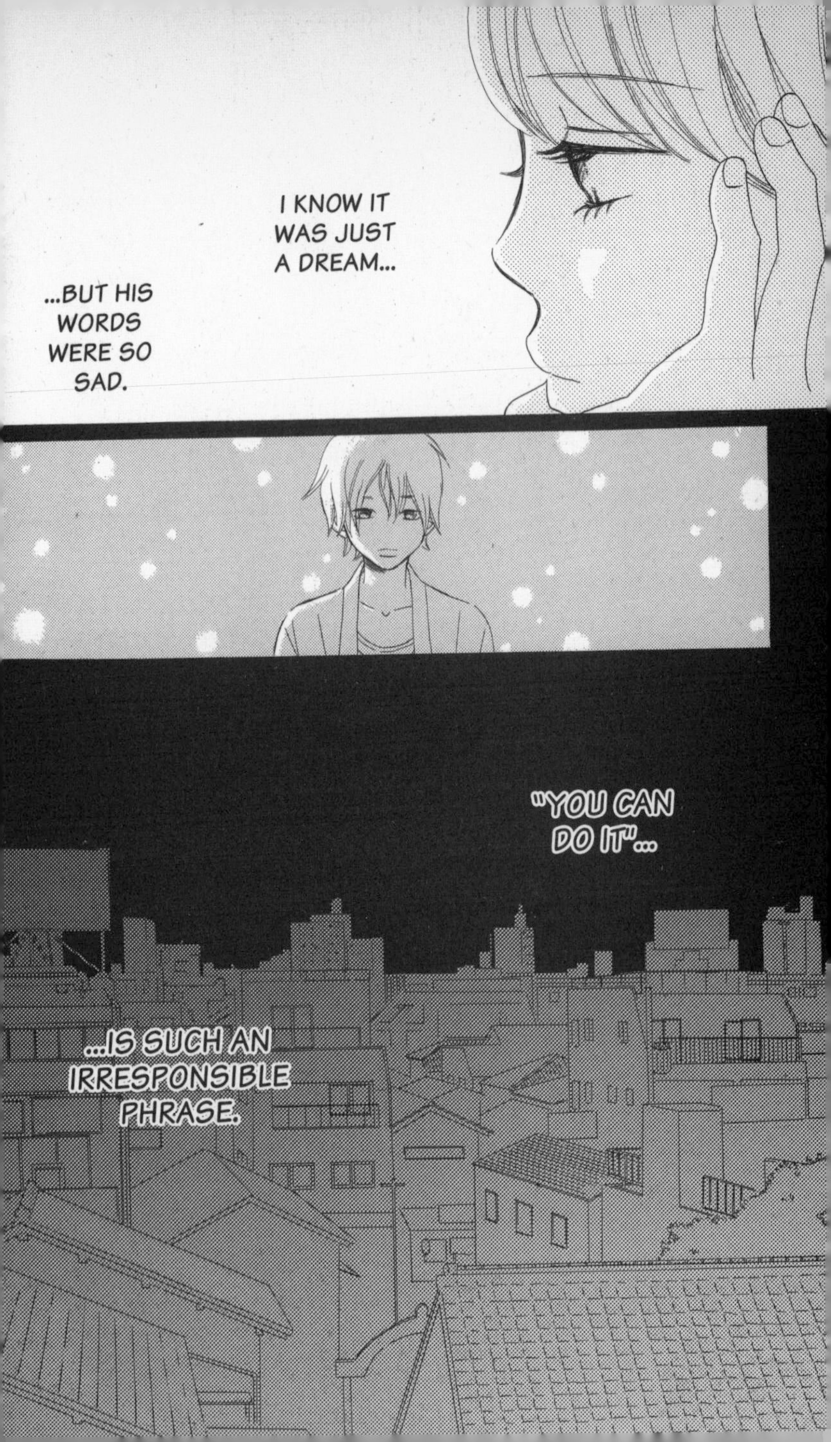
I KNOW IT WAS JUST A DREAM...
...BUT HIS WORDS WERE SO SAD.
"YOU CAN DO IT"...
...IS SUCH AN IRRESPONSIBLE PHRASE.

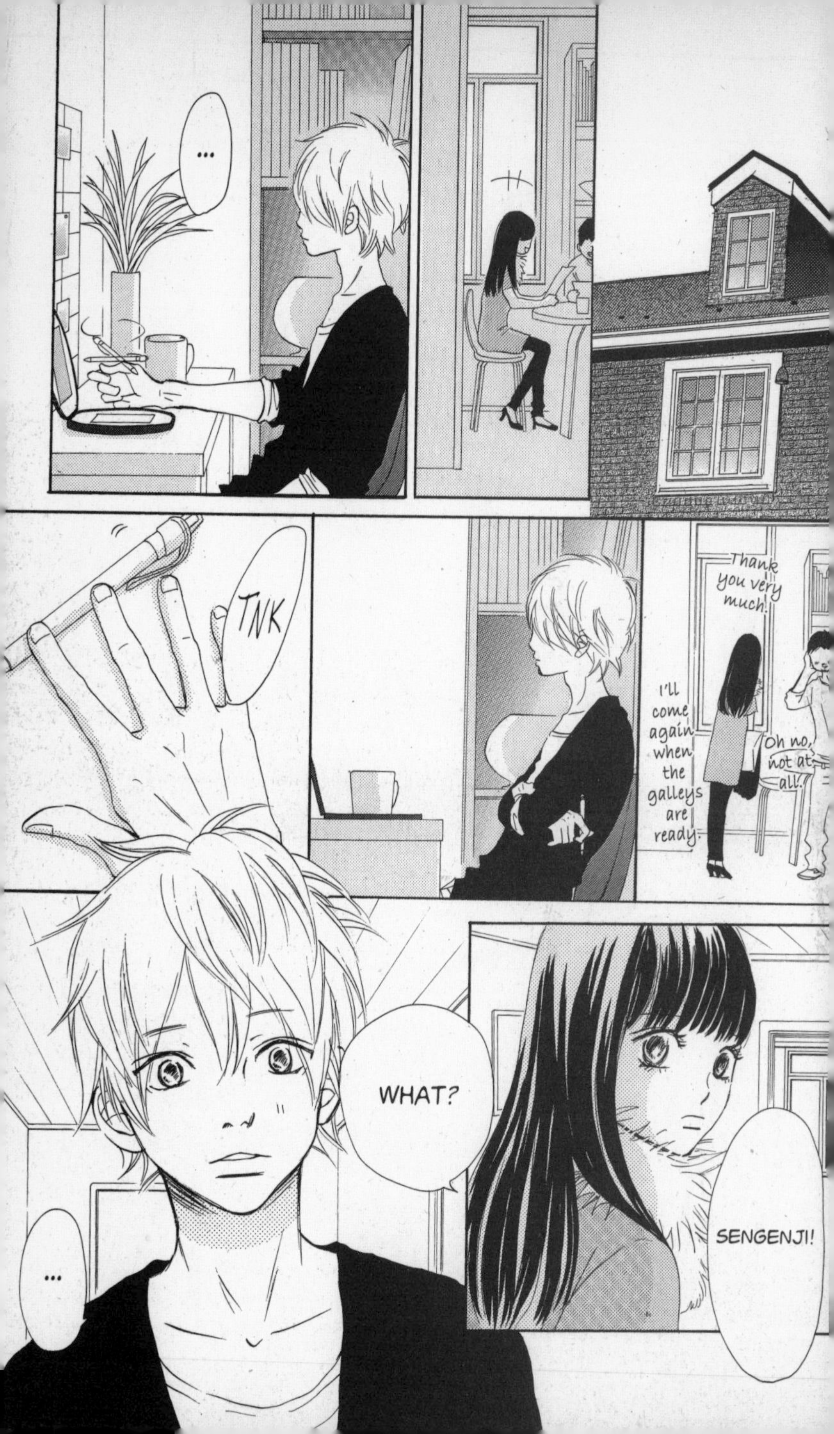
...
Thank you very much.
Oh no, not at all.
I'll come again when the galleys are ready.
TNK
SENGENJI!
WHAT?
...

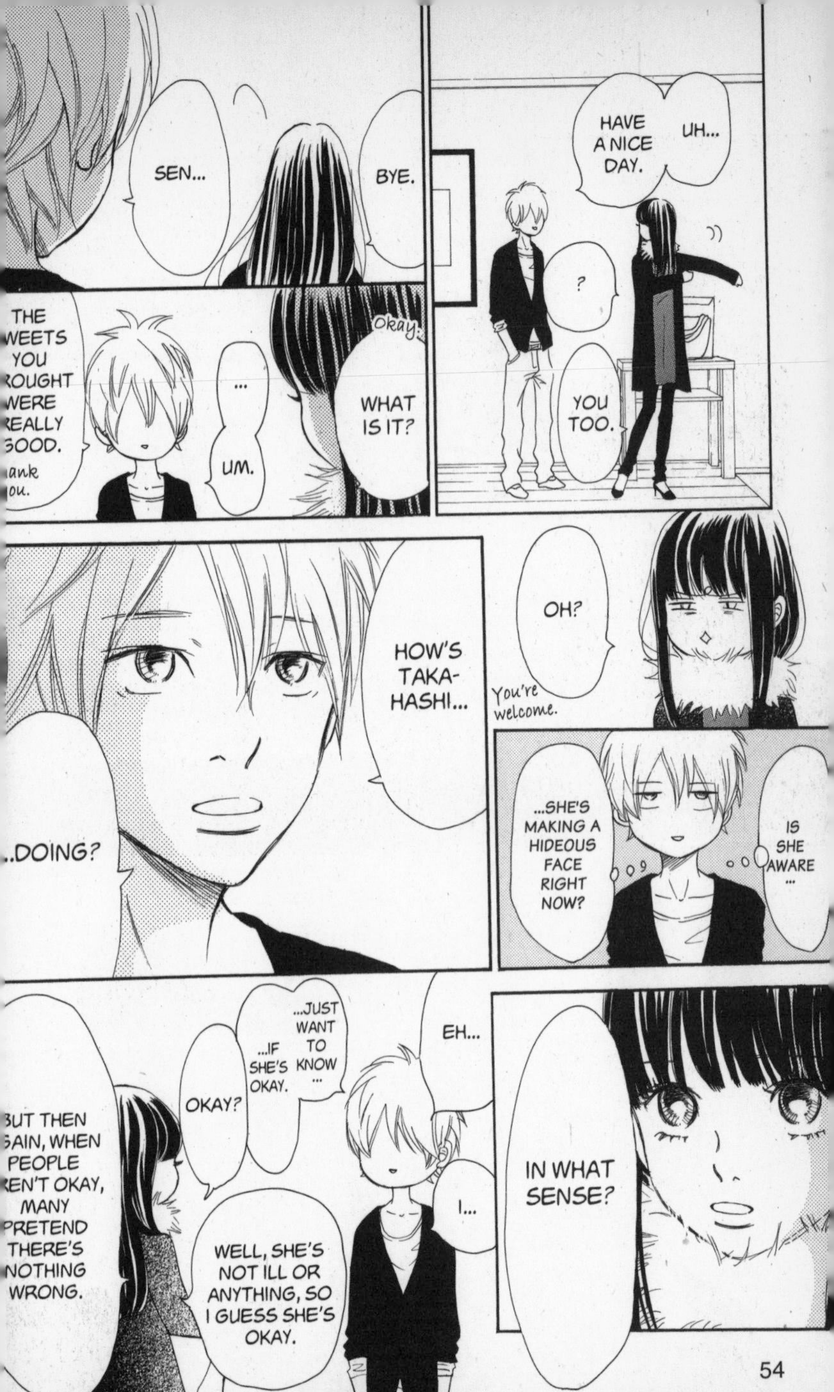
UH...
HAVE A NICE DAY.
?
YOU TOO.
BYE.
SEN...
Okay.
WHAT IS IT?
...
UM.
THE WEETS YOU ROUGHT WERE REALLY GOOD.
ank ou.
OH?
You're welcome.
IS SHE AWARE ...
...SHE'S MAKING A HIDEOUS FACE RIGHT NOW?
HOW'S TAKA-HASHI...
..DOING?
IN WHAT SENSE?
EH...
I...
...JUST WANT TO KNOW ...
...IF SHE'S OKAY.
OKAY?
WELL, SHE'S NOT ILL OR ANYTHING, SO I GUESS SHE'S OKAY.
BUT THEN GAIN, WHEN PEOPLE REN'T OKAY, MANY PRETEND THERE'S NOTHING WRONG.

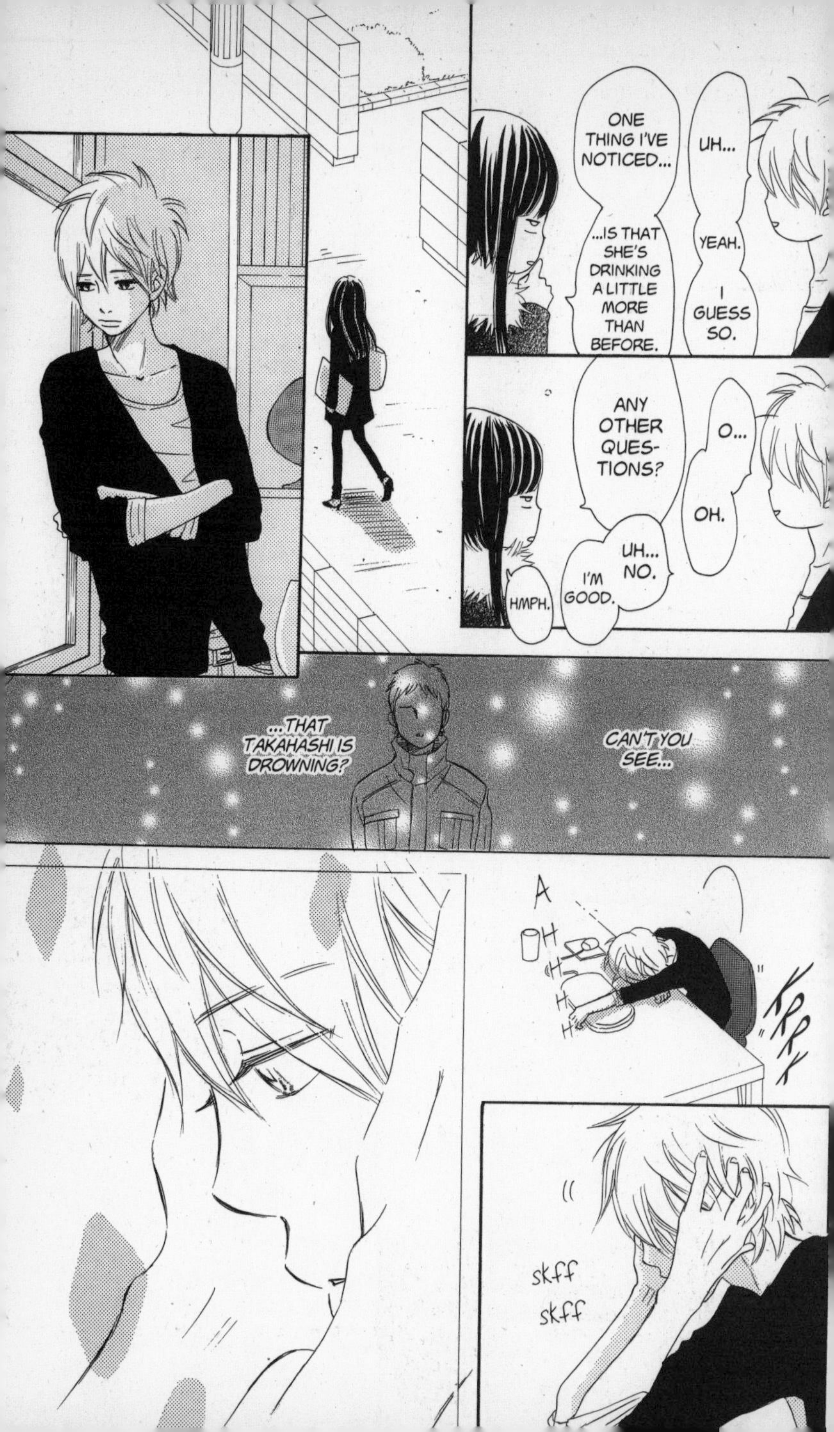
ONE THING I'VE NOTICED...
...IS THAT SHE'S DRINKING A LITTLE MORE THAN BEFORE.
UH... YEAH. I GUESS SO.
ANY OTHER QUESTIONS?
O... OH.
UH... NO. I'M GOOD.
HMPH.
CAN'T YOU SEE...
...THAT TAKAHASHI IS DROWNING?
AHHHHH
KRRK
skff skff

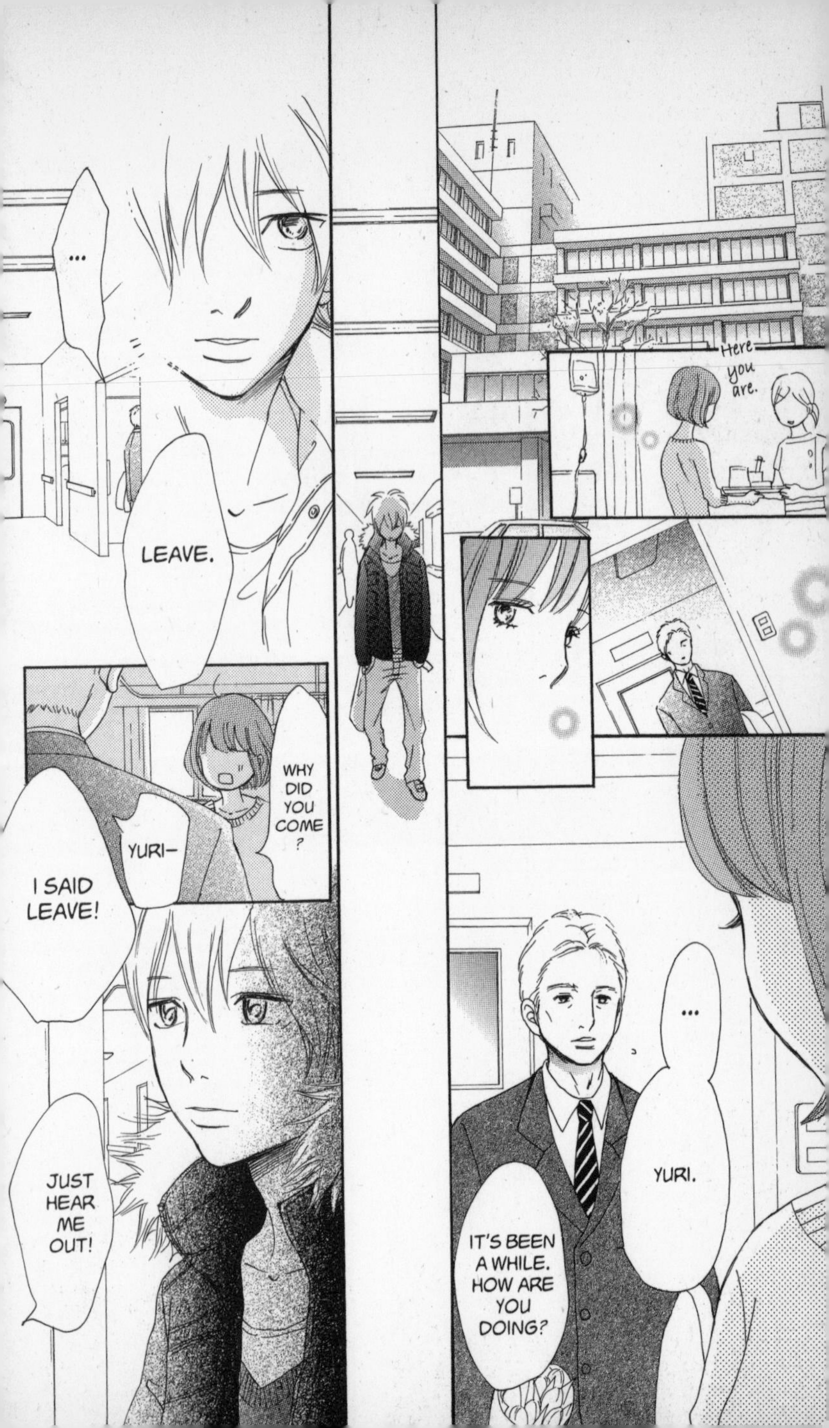
Here you are.
...
YURI.
IT'S BEEN A WHILE. HOW ARE YOU DOING?
...
LEAVE.
WHY DID YOU COME?
YURI—
I SAID LEAVE!
JUST HEAR ME OUT!

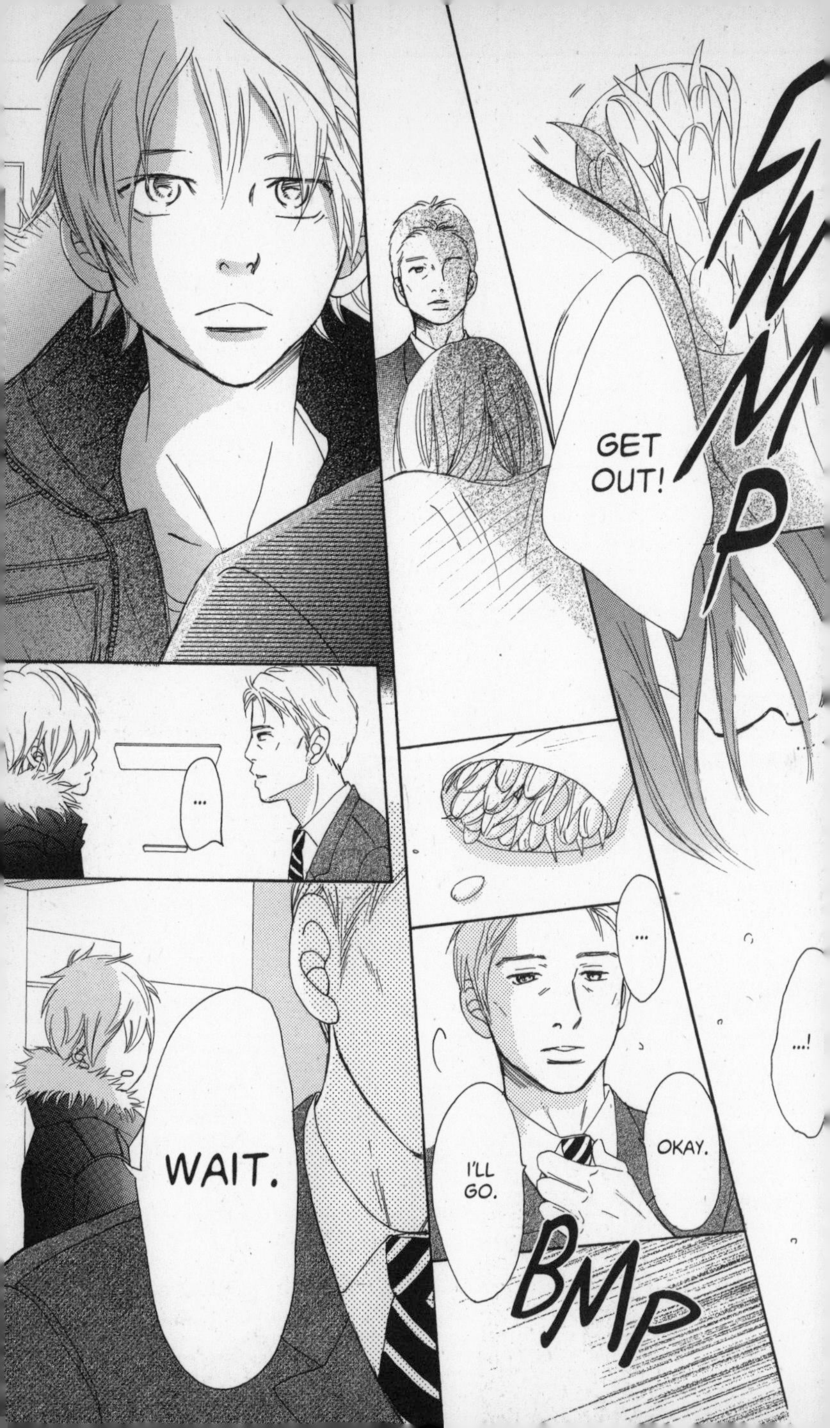

GET OUT!
FWMP
...
...!
OKAY.
I'LL GO.
BMP
...
WAIT.

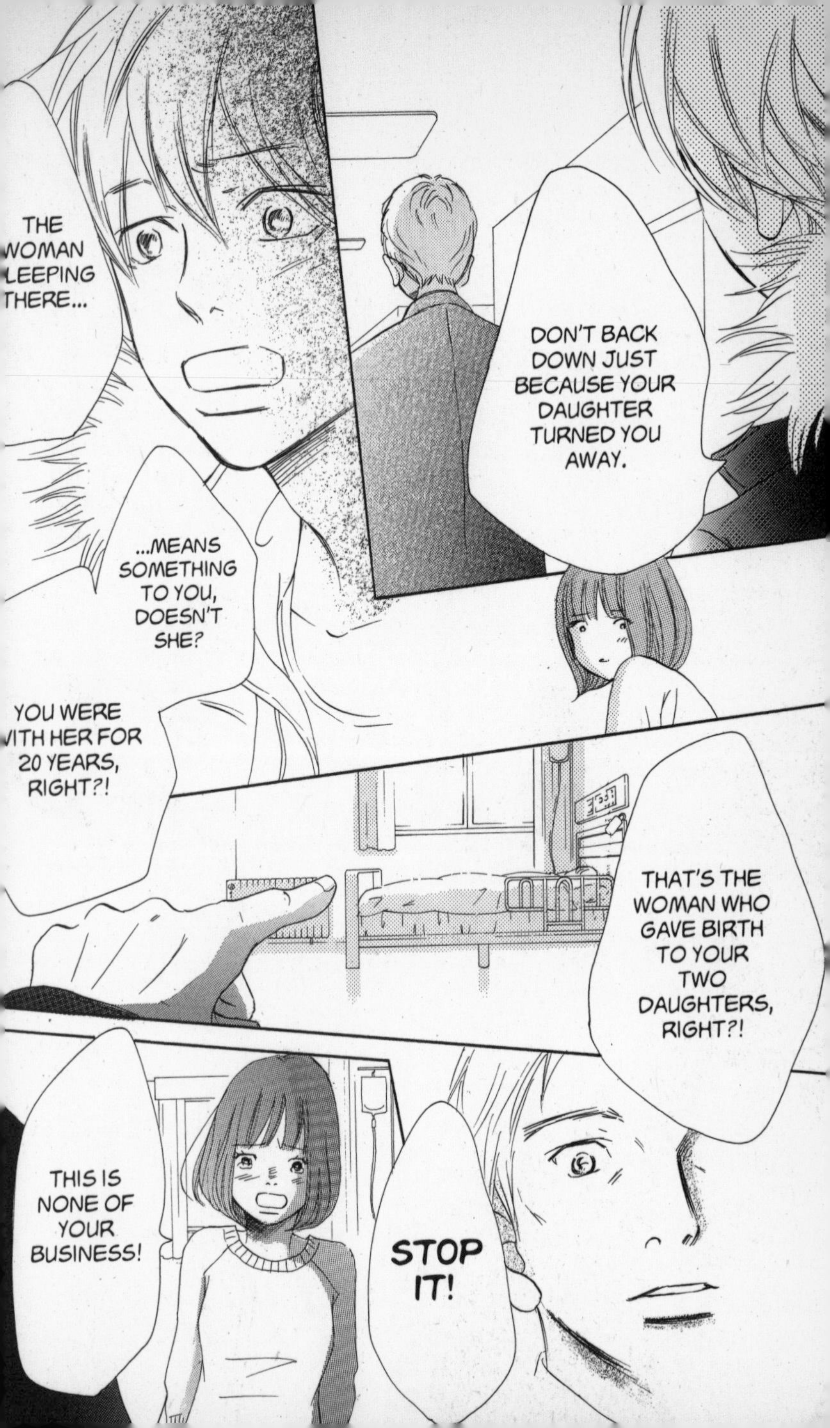
DON'T BACK DOWN JUST BECAUSE YOUR DAUGHTER TURNED YOU AWAY.
THE WOMAN LEEPING THERE...
...MEANS SOMETHING TO YOU, DOESN'T SHE?
YOU WERE WITH HER FOR 20 YEARS, RIGHT?!
THAT'S THE WOMAN WHO GAVE BIRTH TO YOUR TWO DAUGHTERS, RIGHT?!
STOP IT!
THIS IS NONE OF YOUR BUSINESS!

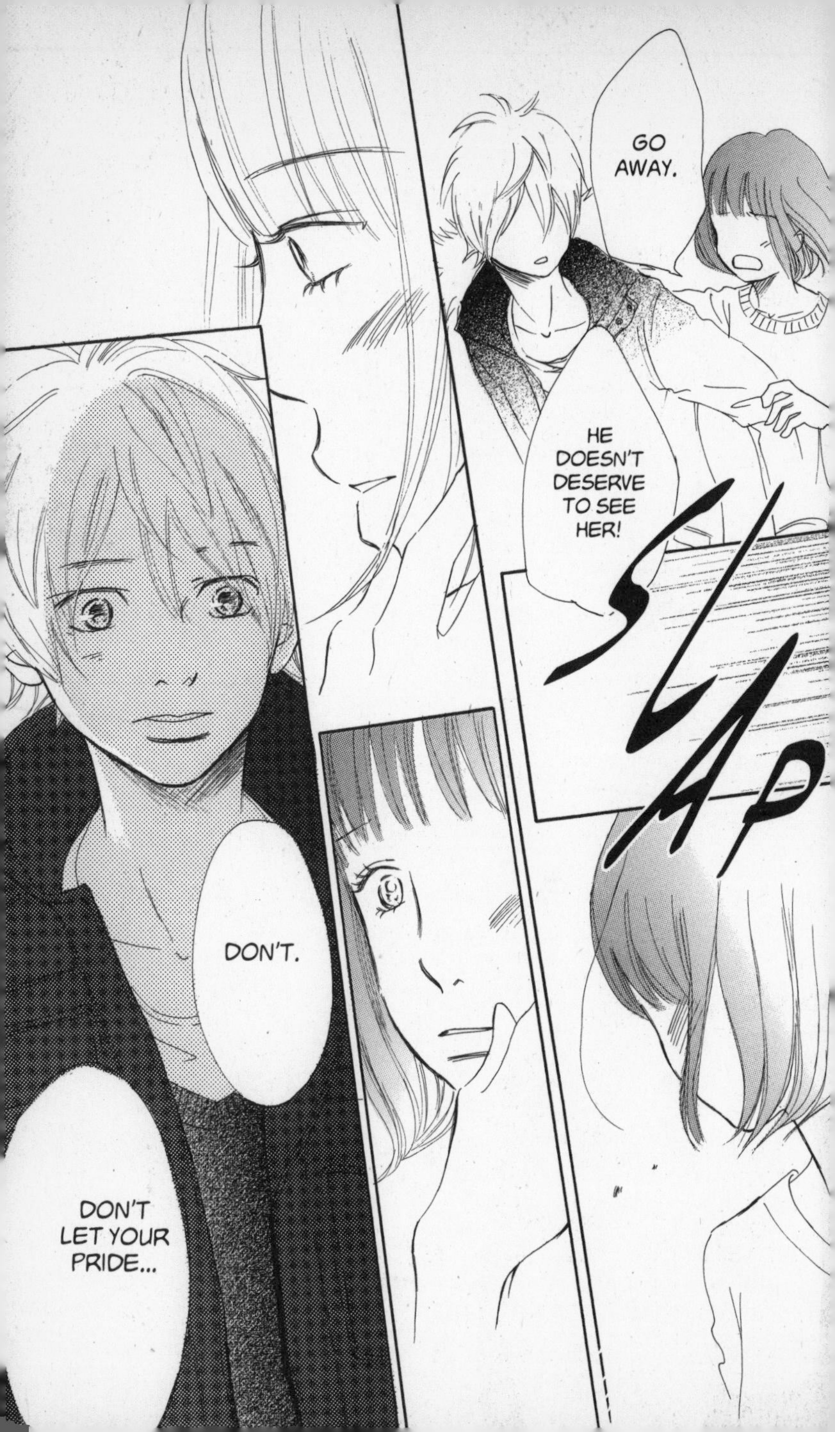
GO AWAY.
HE DOESN'T DESERVE TO SEE HER!
SLAP
DON'T.
DON'T LET YOUR PRIDE...

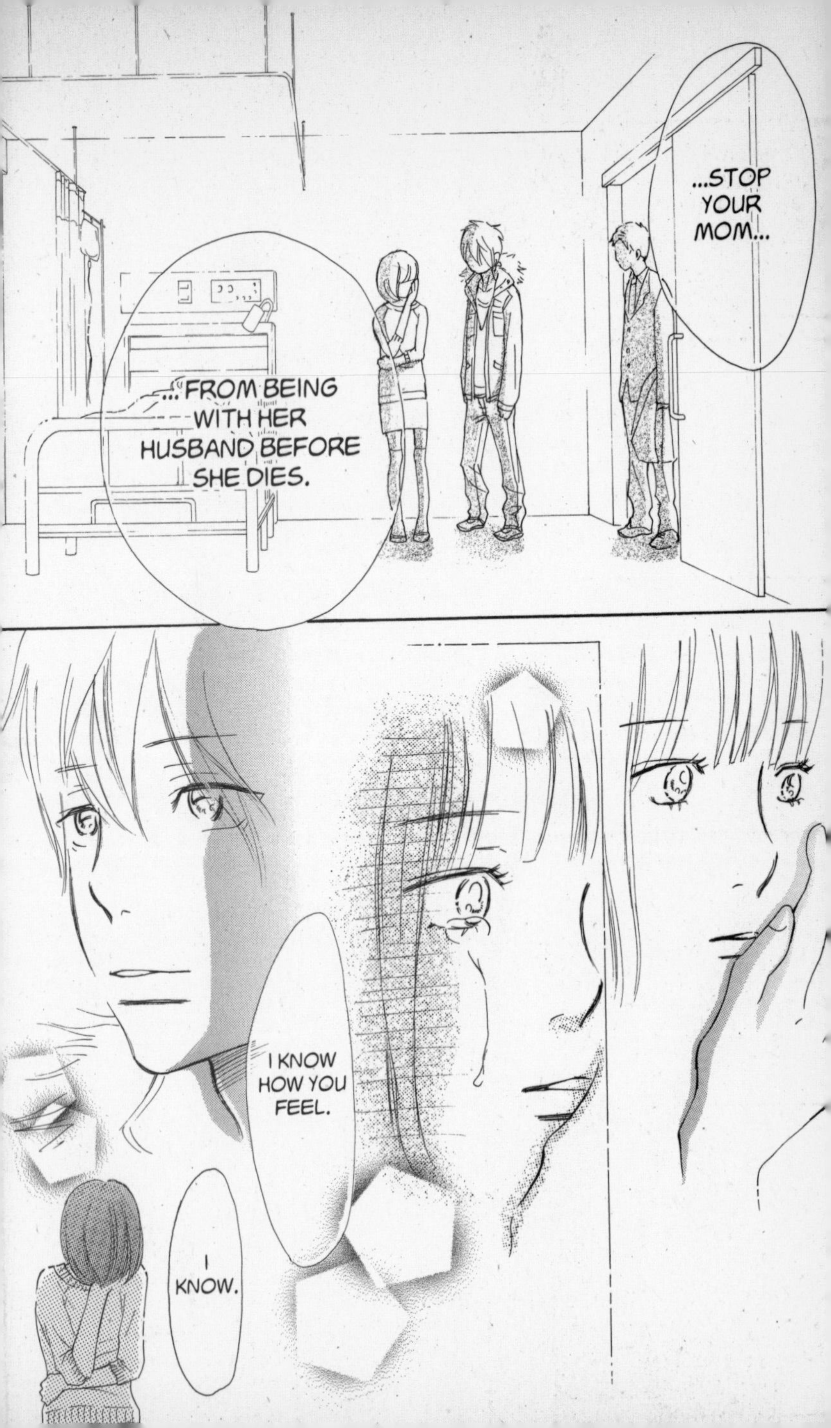
...STOP YOUR MOM...
...FROM BEING WITH HER HUSBAND BEFORE SHE DIES.
I KNOW HOW YOU FEEL.
I KNOW.

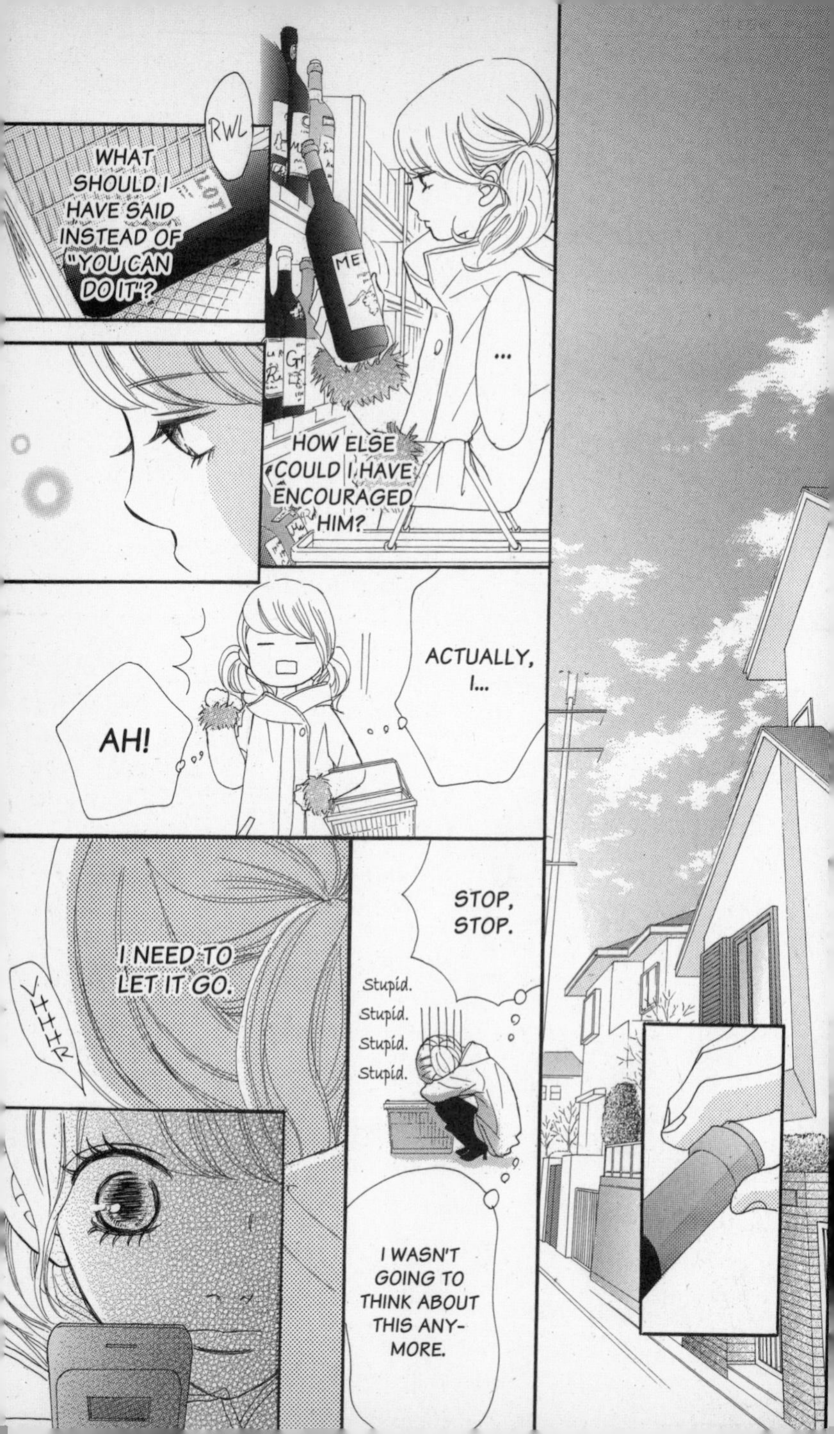
...
HOW ELSE COULD I HAVE ENCOURAGED HIM?
RWL
WHAT SHOULD I HAVE SAID INSTEAD OF "YOU CAN DO IT"?
ACTUALLY, I...
AH!
STOP, STOP.
Stupid.
Stupid.
Stupid.
Stupid.
I WASN'T GOING TO THINK ABOUT THIS ANY-MORE.
I NEED TO LET IT GO.
VHHHR

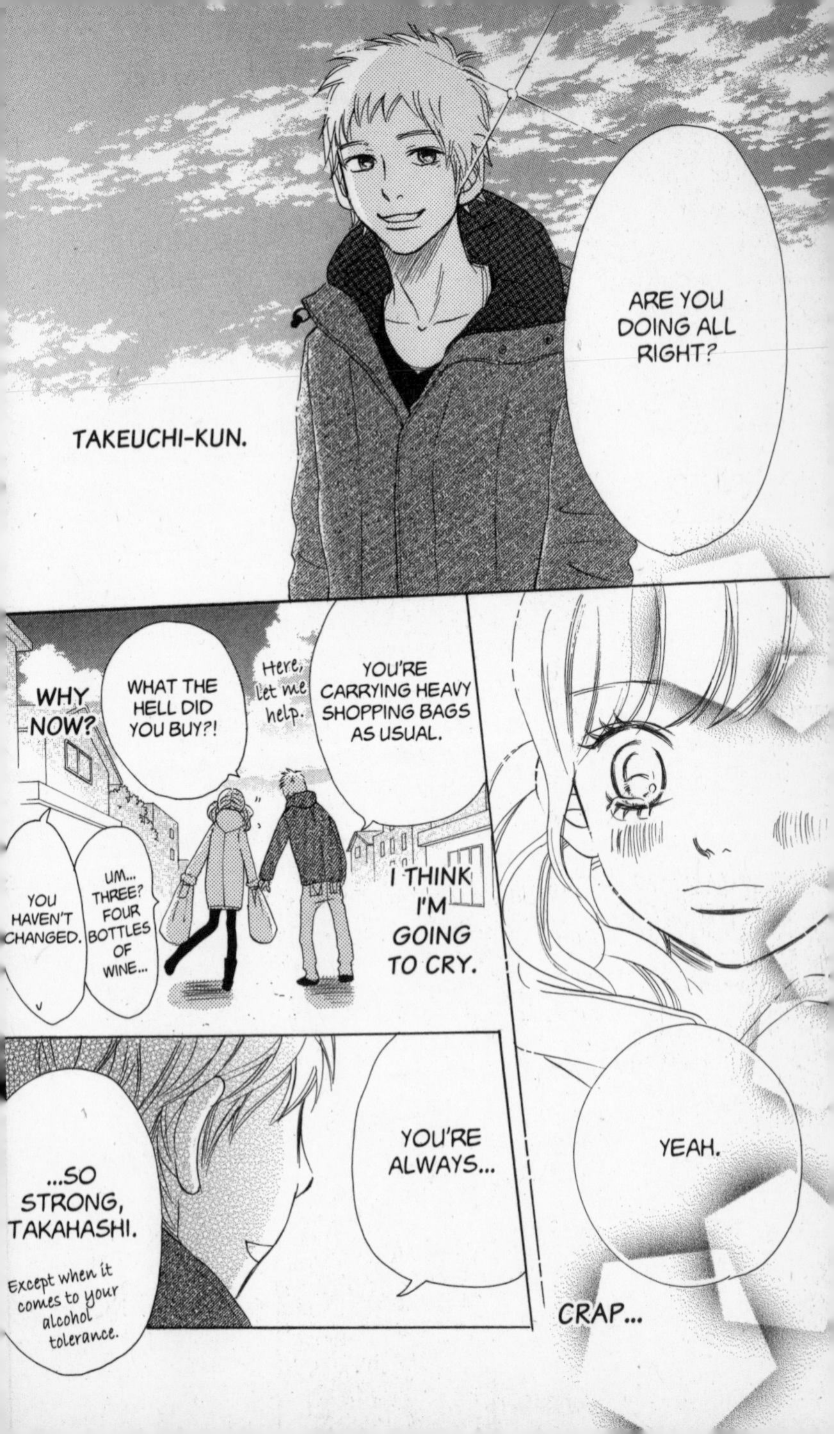
ARE YOU DOING ALL RIGHT?
TAKEUCHI-KUN.
YEAH.
CRAP...
YOU'RE CARRYING HEAVY SHOPPING BAGS AS USUAL.
Here, let me help.
WHAT THE HELL DID YOU BUY?!
WHY NOW?
I THINK I'M GOING TO CRY.
UM... THREE? FOUR BOTTLES OF WINE...
YOU HAVEN'T CHANGED.
YOU'RE ALWAYS...
...SO STRONG, TAKAHASHI.
Except when it comes to your alcohol tolerance.

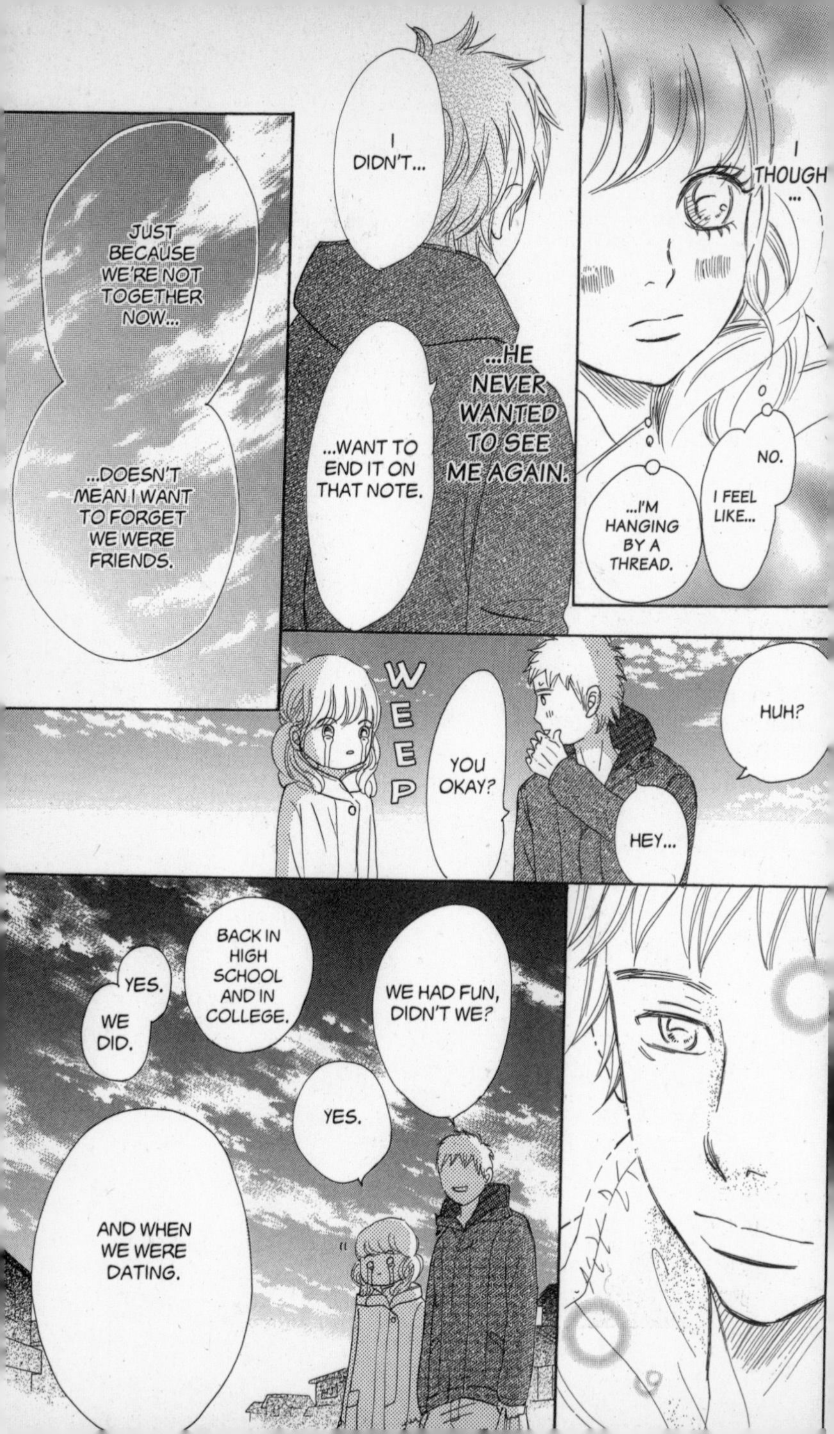
I THOUGH...
NO.
I FEEL LIKE...
...I'M HANGING BY A THREAD.
I DIDN'T...
...HE NEVER WANTED TO SEE ME AGAIN.
...WANT TO END IT ON THAT NOTE.
JUST BECAUSE WE'RE NOT TOGETHER NOW...
...DOESN'T MEAN I WANT TO FORGET WE WERE FRIENDS.
HUH?
HEY...
YOU OKAY?
WEEP
WE HAD FUN, DIDN'T WE?
BACK IN HIGH SCHOOL AND IN COLLEGE.
YES.
WE DID.
YES.
AND WHEN WE WERE DATING.

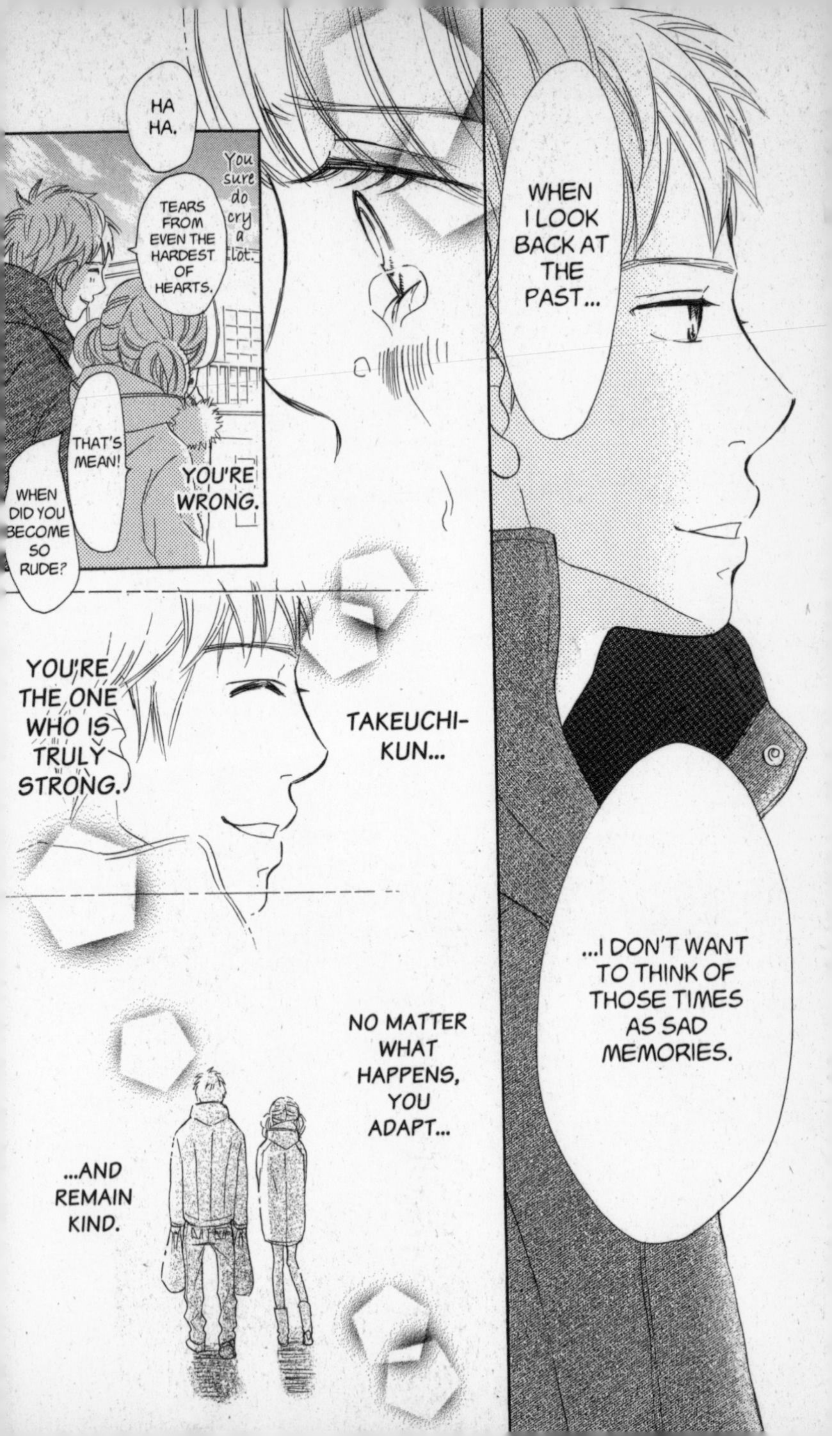
WHEN I LOOK BACK AT THE PAST...
...I DON'T WANT TO THINK OF THOSE TIMES AS SAD MEMORIES.
HA HA.
TEARS FROM EVEN THE HARDEST OF HEARTS.
You sure do cry a lot.
YOU'RE WRONG.
THAT'S MEAN!
WHEN DID YOU BECOME SO RUDE?
TAKEUCHI-KUN...
YOU'RE THE ONE WHO IS TRULY STRONG.
NO MATTER WHAT HAPPENS, YOU ADAPT...
...AND REMAIN KIND.

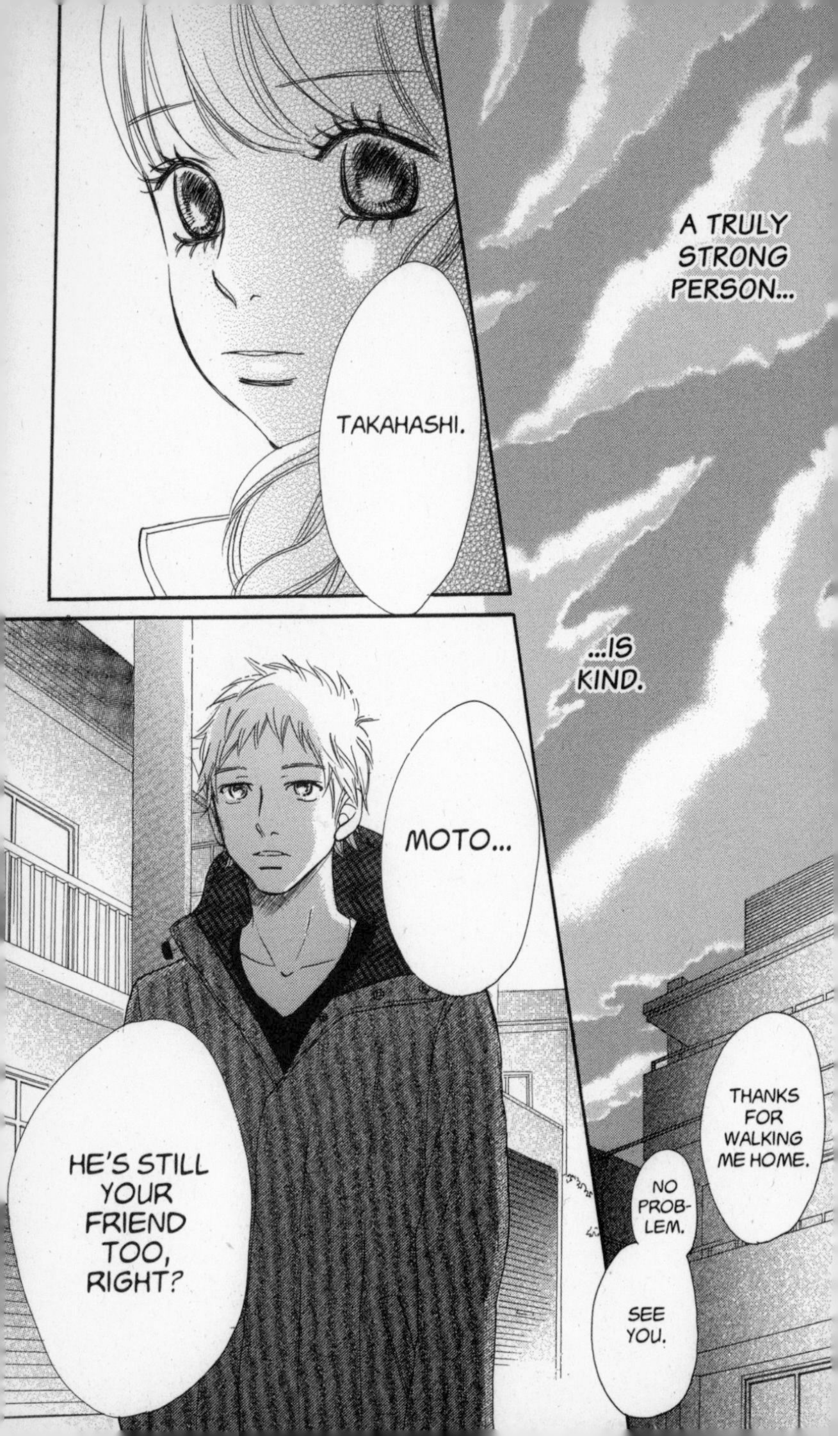
A TRULY STRONG PERSON...
TAKAHASHI.
...IS KIND.
MOTO...
THANKS FOR WALKING ME HOME.
NO PROBLEM.
SEE YOU.
HE'S STILL YOUR FRIEND TOO, RIGHT?

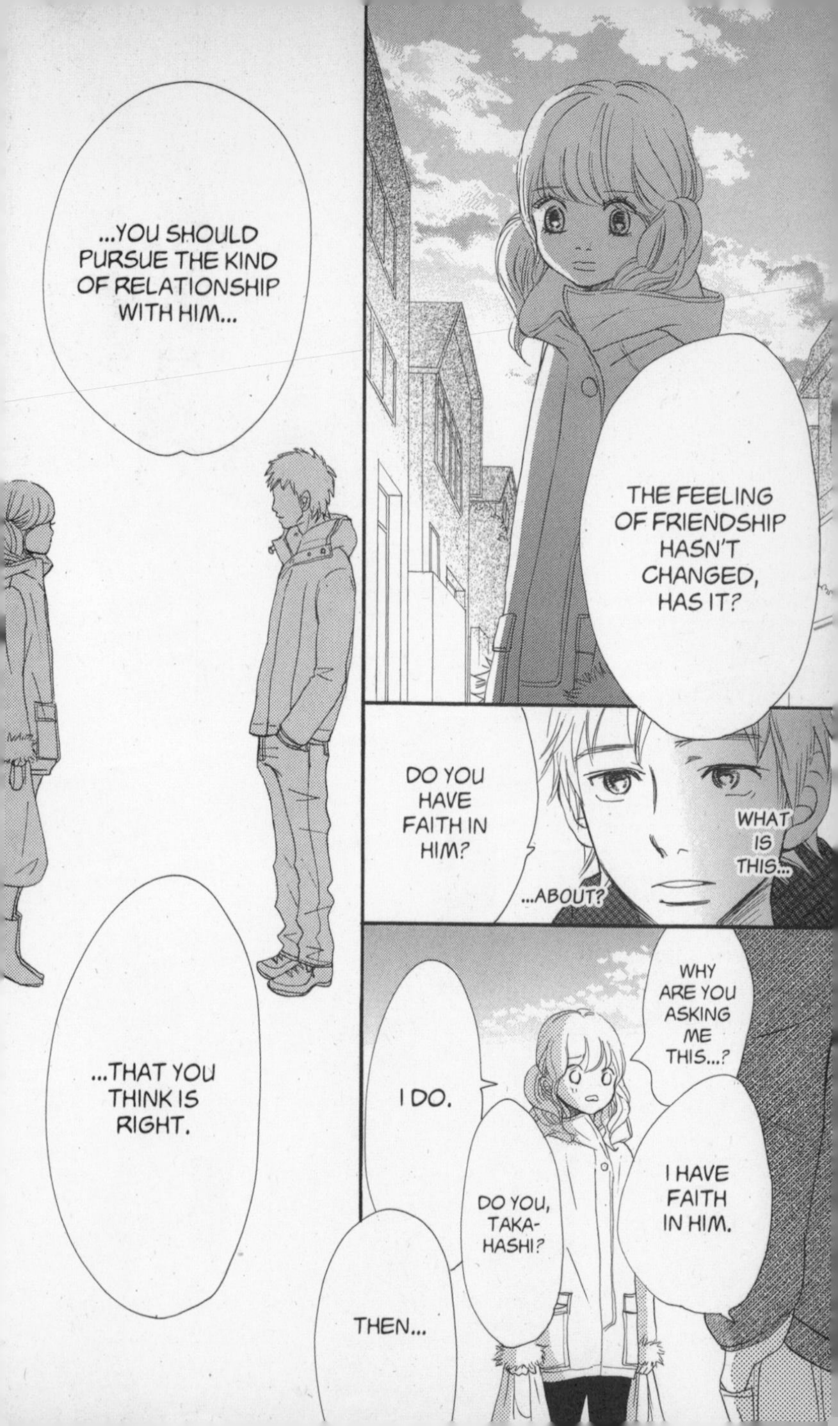
THE FEELING OF FRIENDSHIP HASN'T CHANGED, HAS IT?
DO YOU HAVE FAITH IN HIM?
WHAT IS THIS...
...ABOUT?
WHY ARE YOU ASKING ME THIS...?
I HAVE FAITH IN HIM.
DO YOU, TAKA-HASHI?
I DO.
THEN...
...YOU SHOULD PURSUE THE KIND OF RELATIONSHIP WITH HIM...
...THAT YOU THINK IS RIGHT.

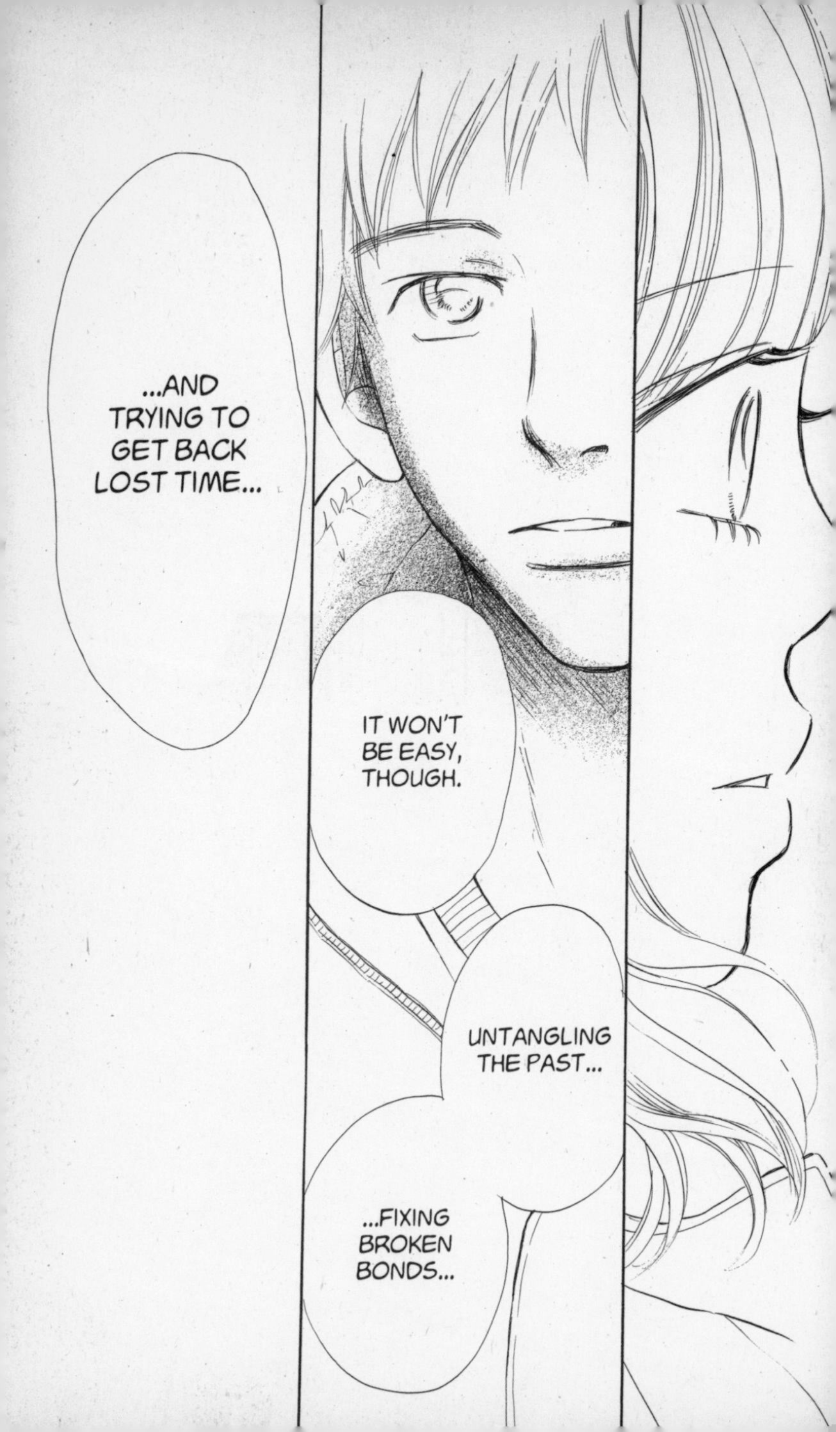
IT WON'T BE EASY, THOUGH.
UNTANGLING THE PAST...
...FIXING BROKEN BONDS...
...AND TRYING TO GET BACK LOST TIME...

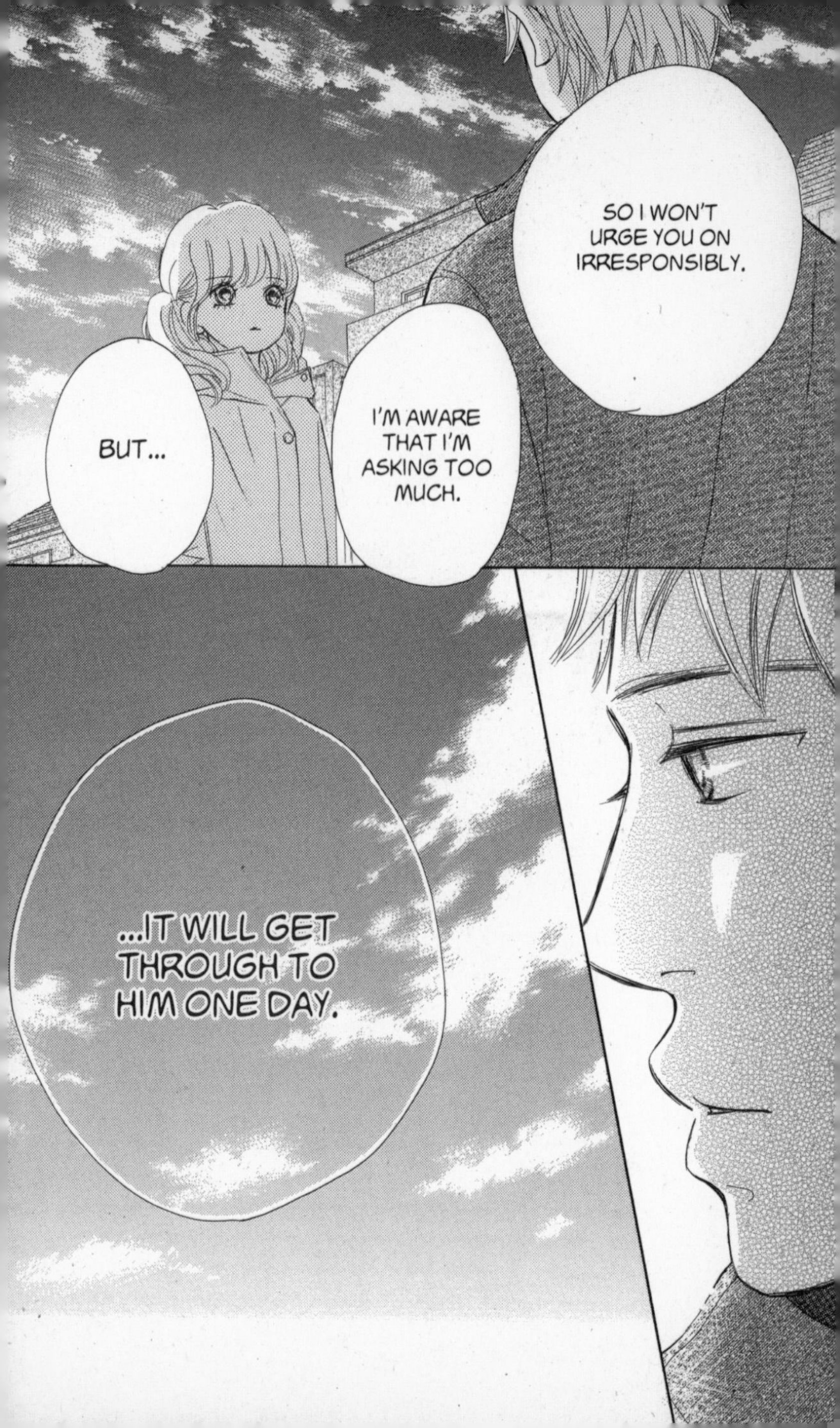
SO I WON'T URGE YOU ON IRRESPONSIBLY.
I'M AWARE THAT I'M ASKING TOO MUCH.
BUT...
...IT WILL GET THROUGH TO HIM ONE DAY.

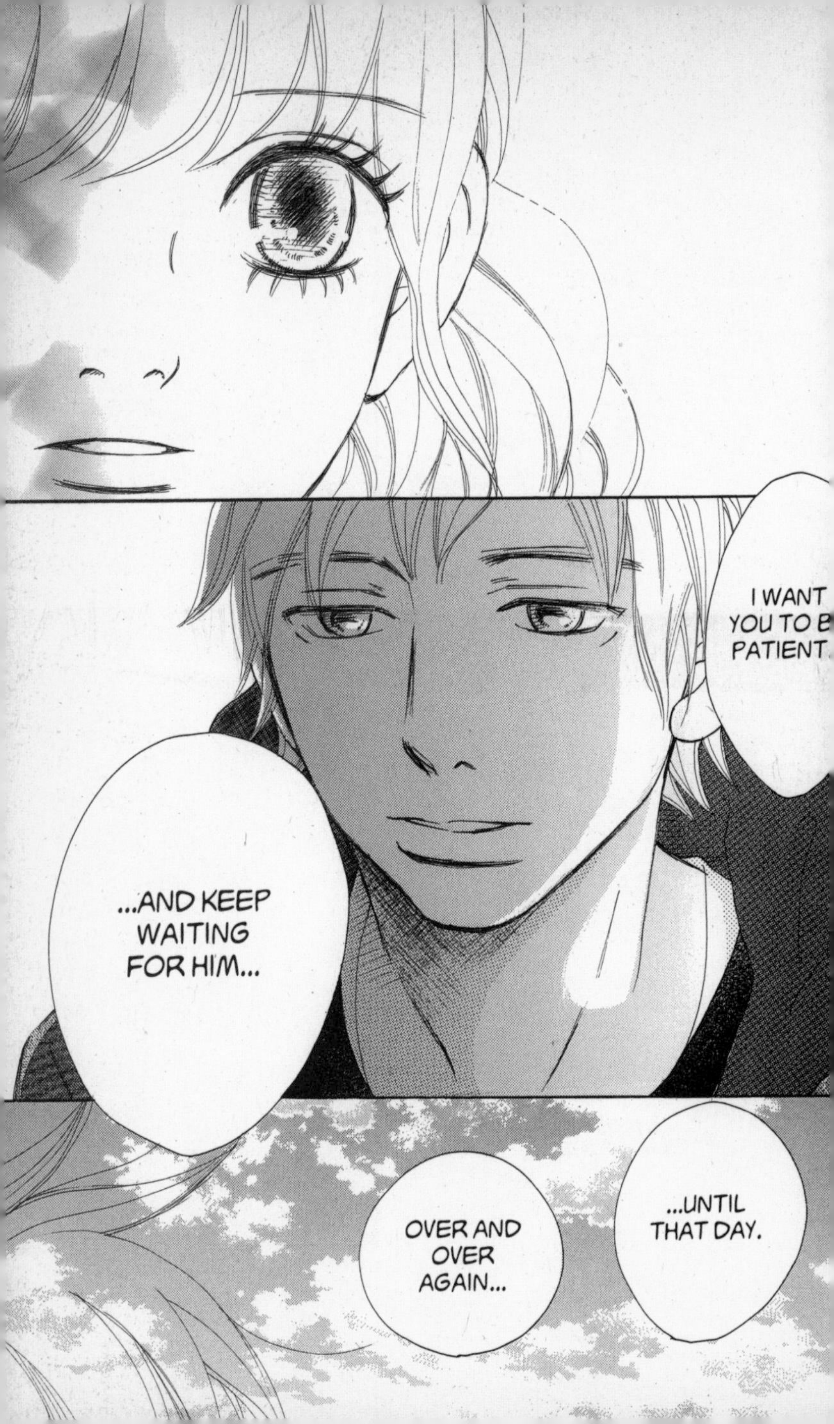
I WANT YOU TO B PATIENT.
...AND KEEP WAITING FOR HIM...
...UNTIL THAT DAY.
OVER AND OVER AGAIN...

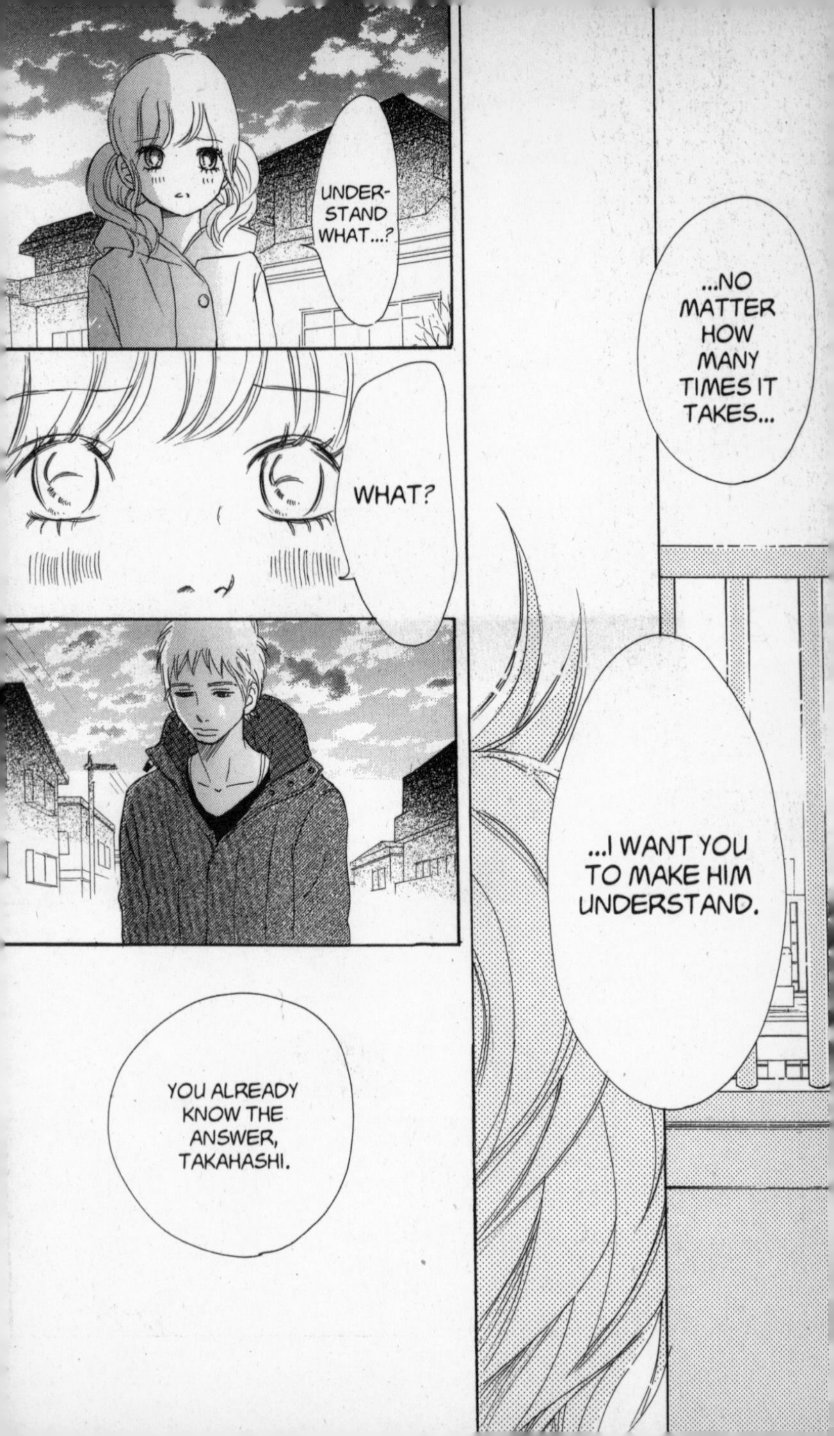
...NO MATTER HOW MANY TIMES IT TAKES...
...I WANT YOU TO MAKE HIM UNDERSTAND.
UNDER-STAND WHAT...?
WHAT?
YOU ALREADY KNOW THE ANSWER, TAKAHASHI.

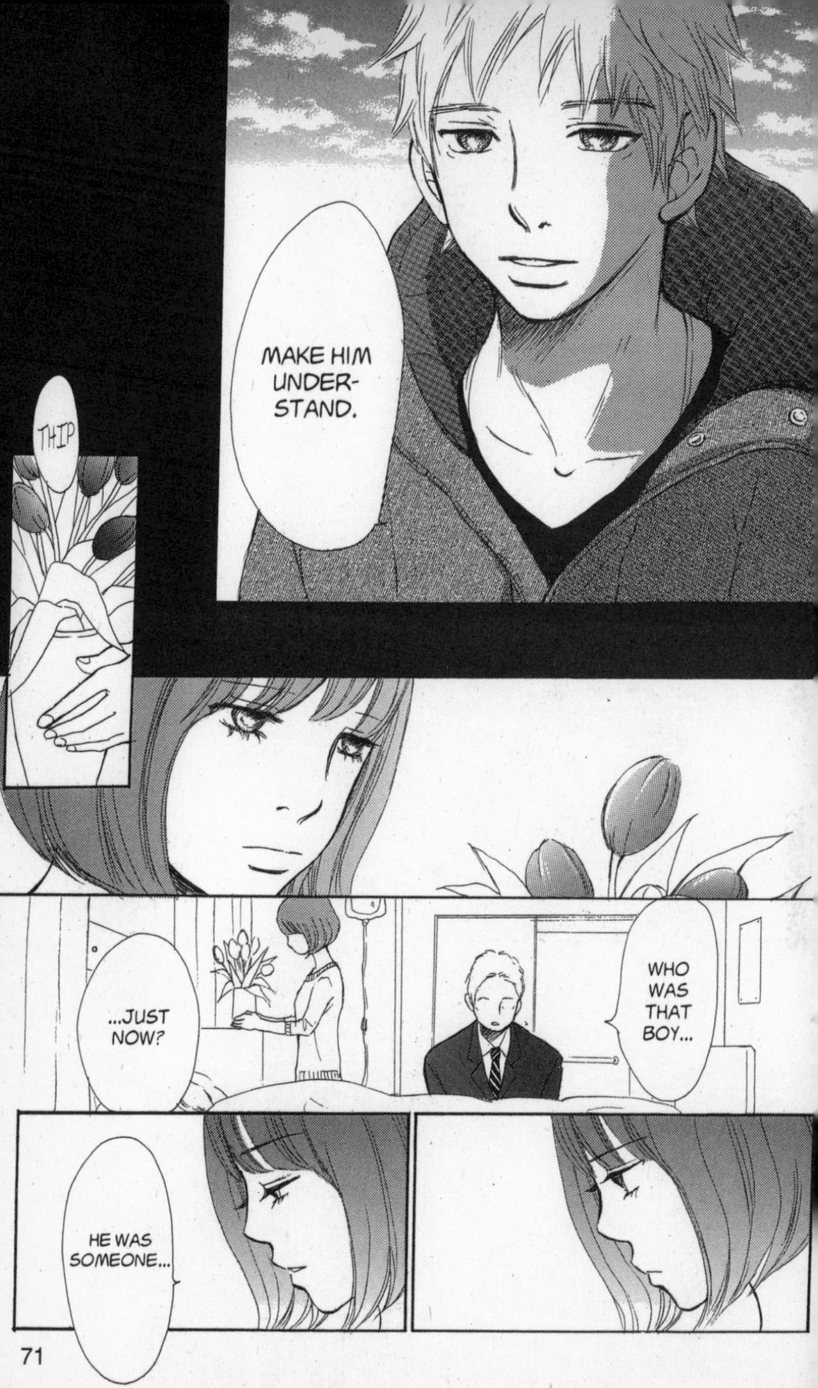
MAKE HIM UNDER-STAND.
THIP
WHO WAS THAT BOY...
...JUST NOW?
HE WAS SOMEONE...

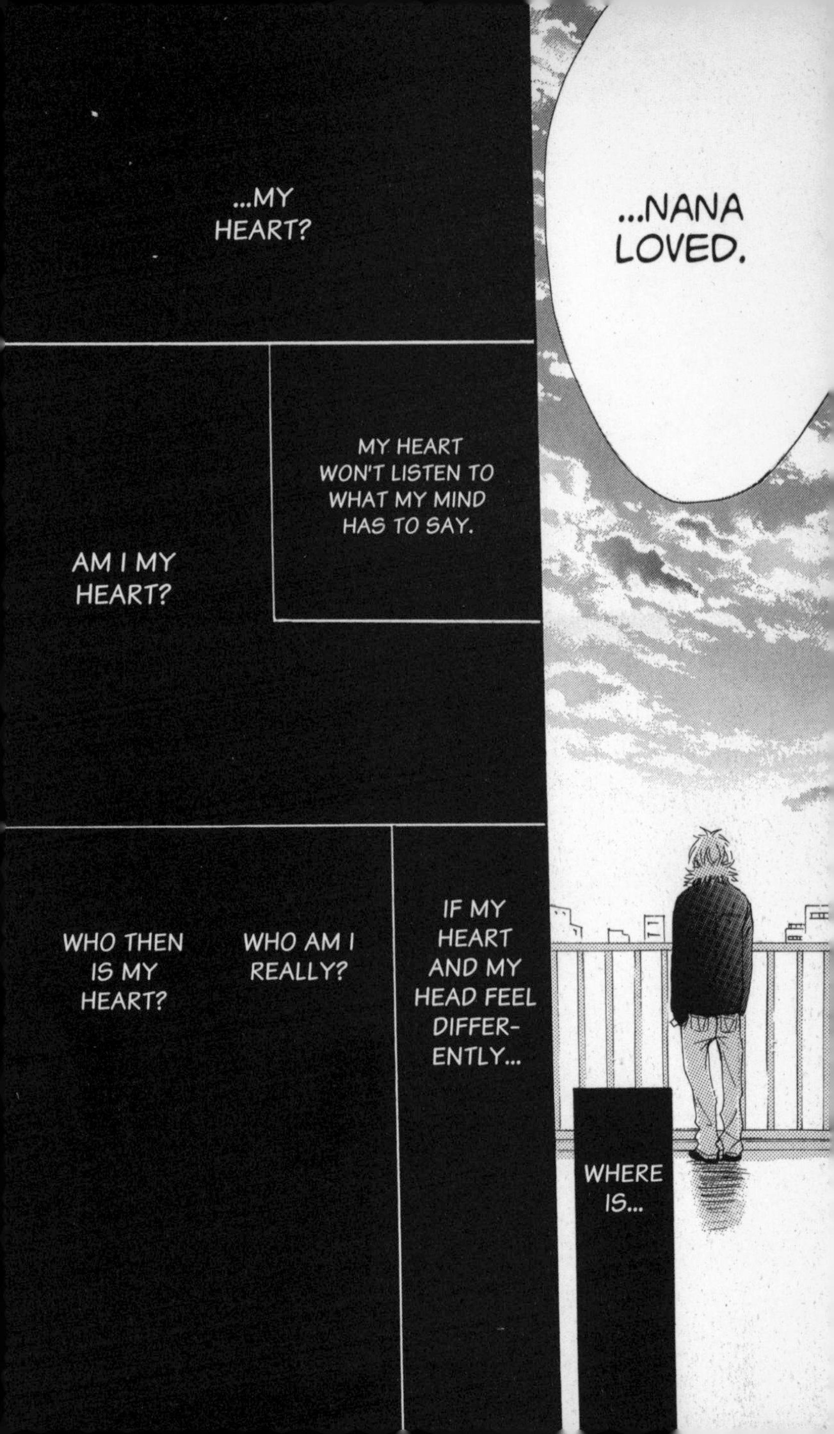
...NANA LOVED.
WHERE IS...
...MY HEART?
MY HEART WON'T LISTEN TO WHAT MY MIND HAS TO SAY.
AM I MY HEART?
IF MY HEART AND MY HEAD FEEL DIFFER-ENTLY...
WHO AM I REALLY?
WHO THEN IS MY HEART?

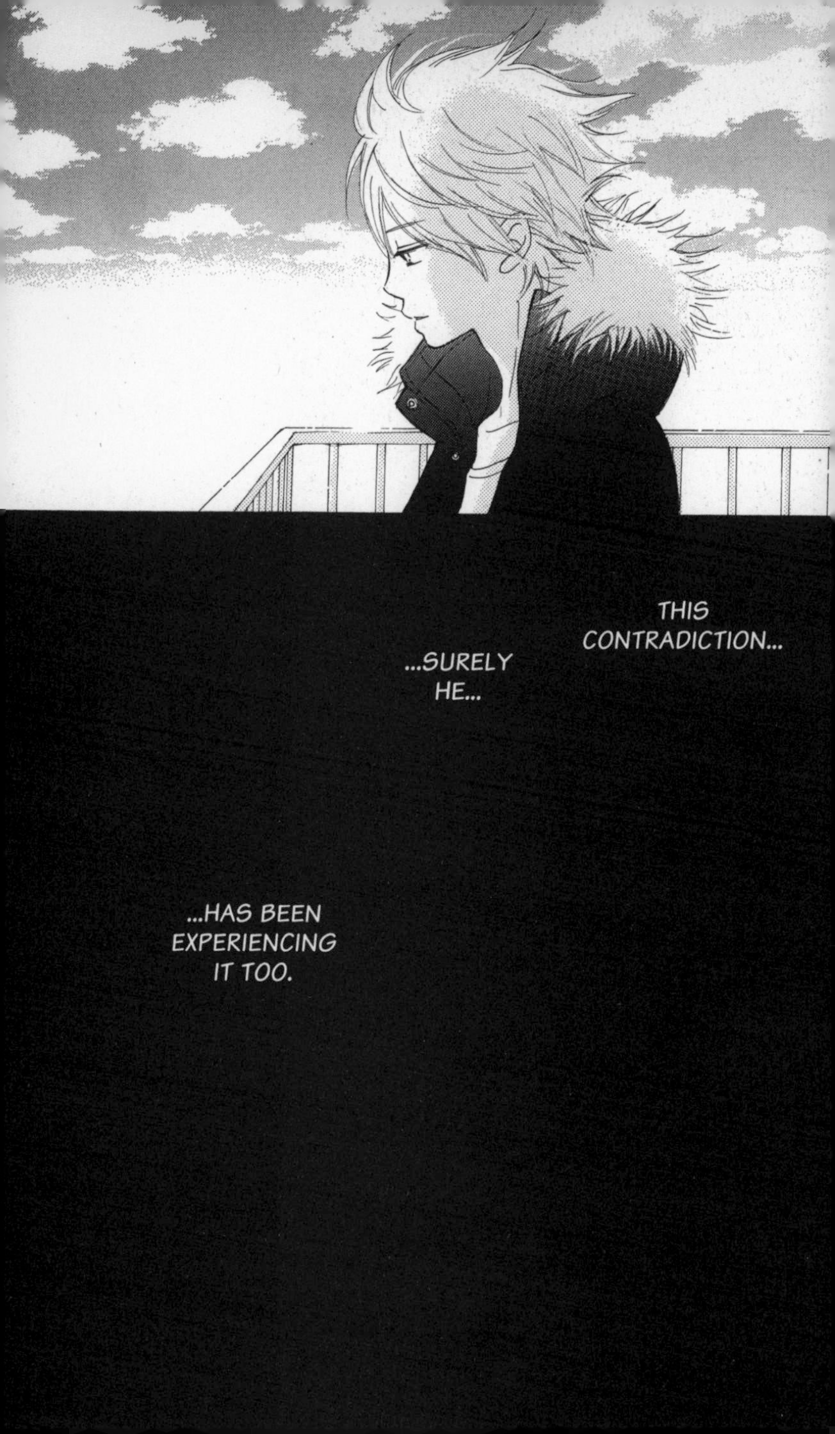
THIS CONTRADICTION...
...SURELY HE...
...HAS BEEN EXPERIENCING IT TOO.

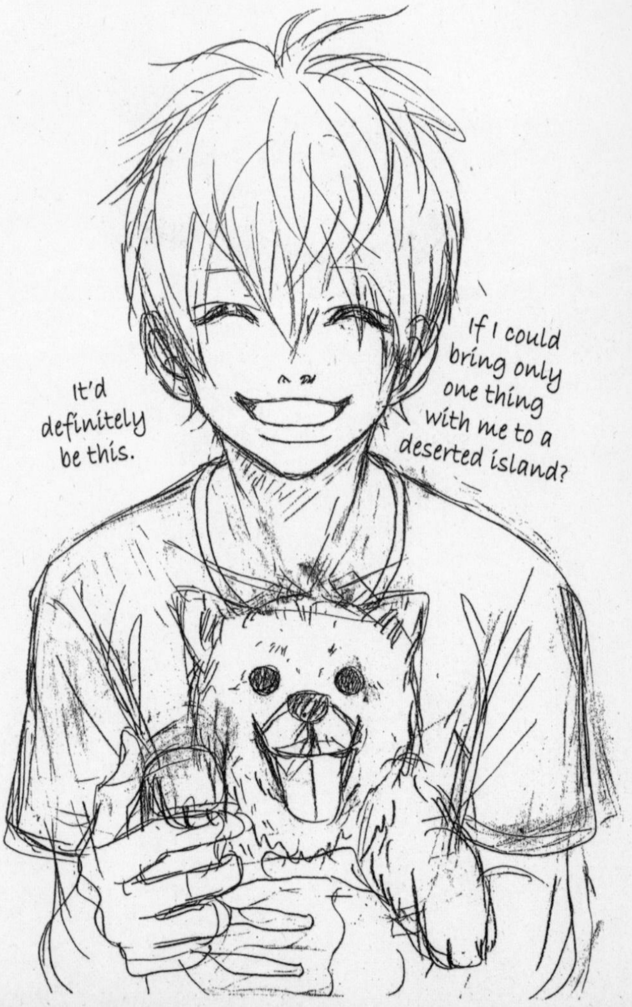
If I could bring only one thing with me to a deserted island?
It'd definitely be this.

THE DARUMA
DOLL...

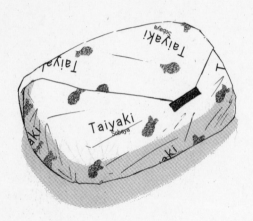

...FELL DOWN.

Chapter 62

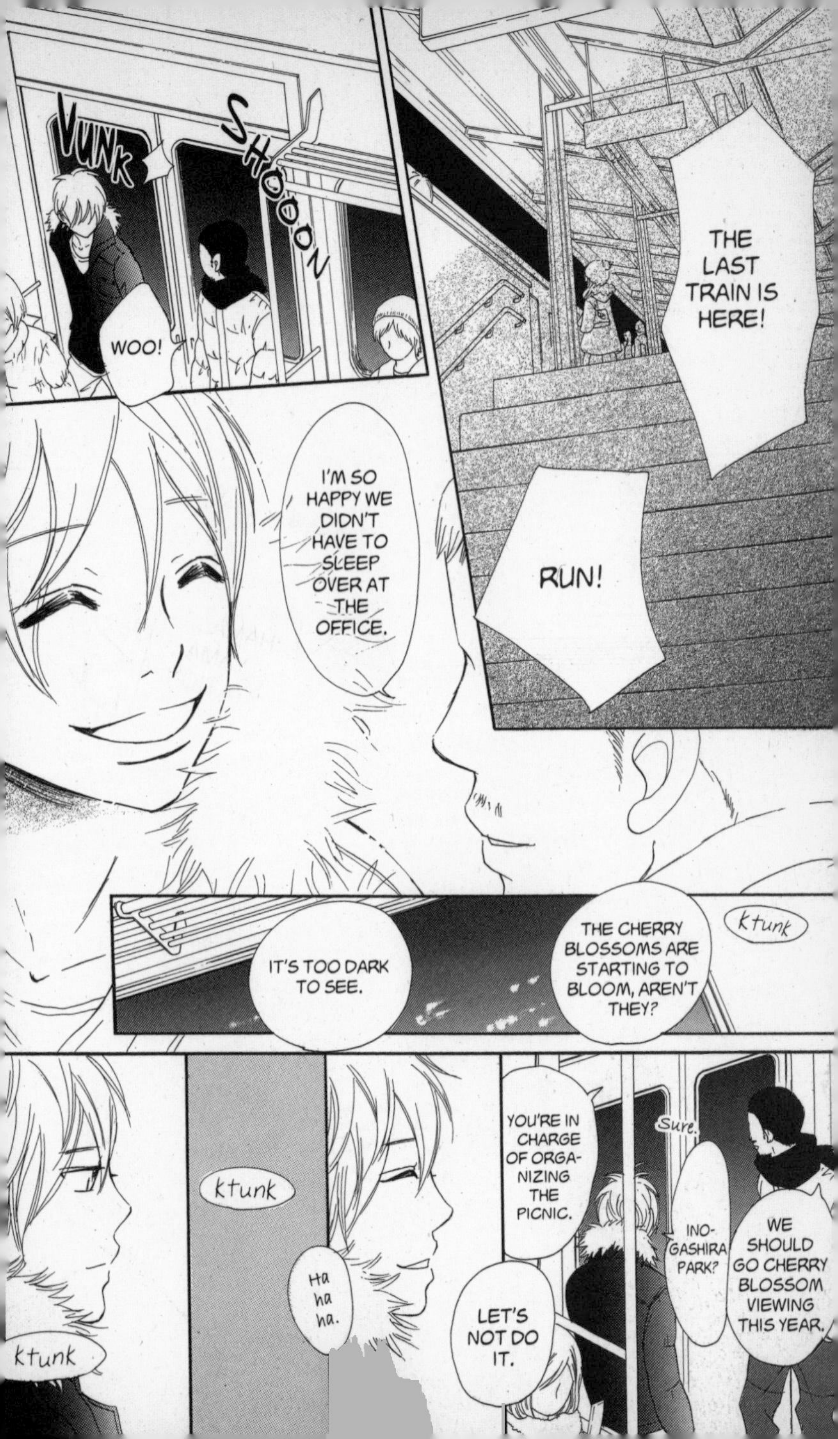
THE LAST TRAIN IS HERE!
RUN!
VUNK
SHOOOON
WOO!
I'M SO HAPPY WE DIDN'T HAVE TO SLEEP OVER AT THE OFFICE.
ktunk
THE CHERRY BLOSSOMS ARE STARTING TO BLOOM, AREN'T THEY?
IT'S TOO DARK TO SEE.
WE SHOULD GO CHERRY BLOSSOM VIEWING THIS YEAR.
INO-GASHIRA PARK?
Sure.
YOU'RE IN CHARGE OF ORGA-NIZING THE PICNIC.
LET'S NOT DO IT.
Ha ha ha.
ktunk
ktunk

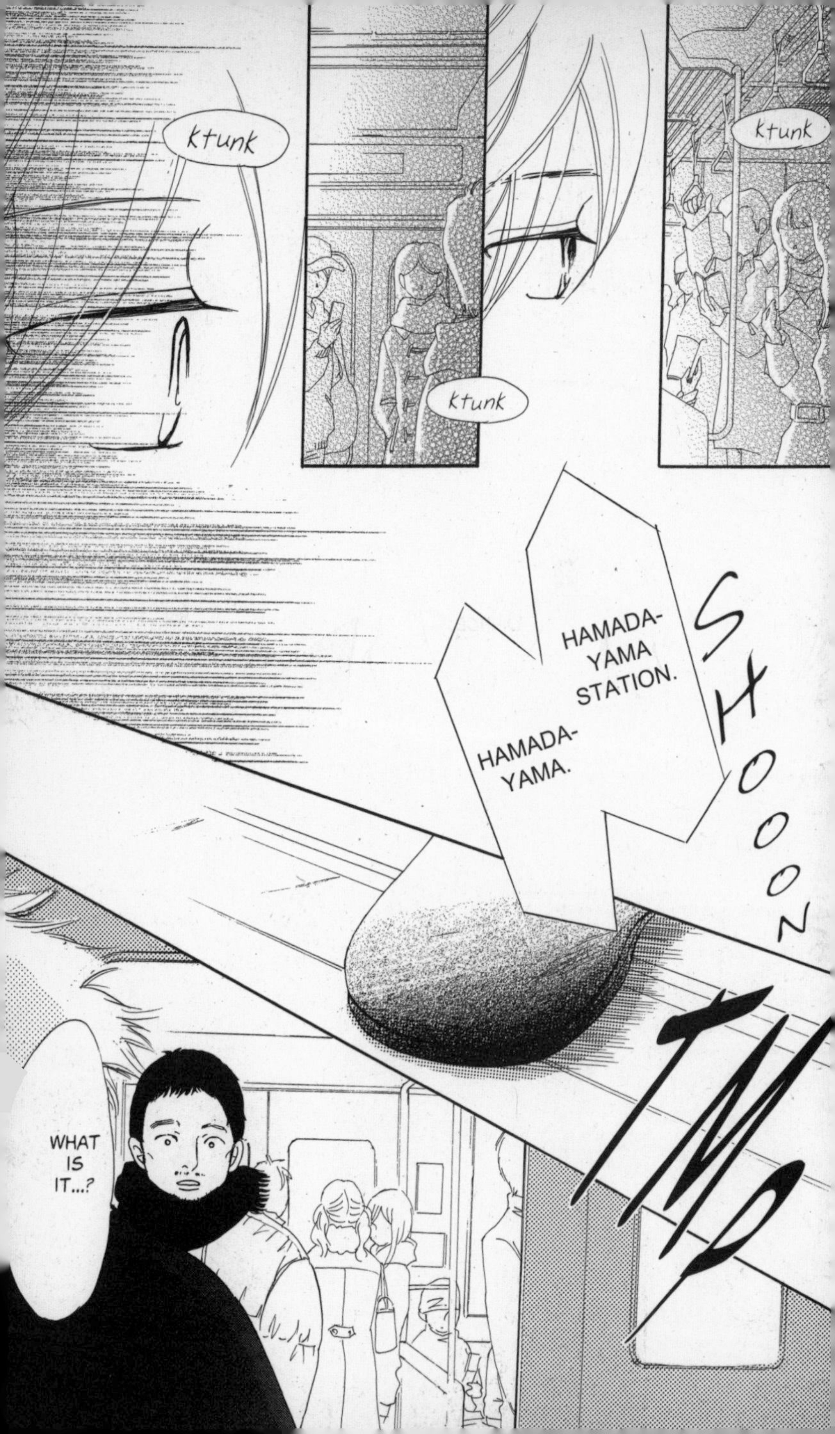
ktunk
ktunk
ktunk
HAMADA-YAMA STATION.
HAMADA-YAMA.
SHOOON
TMP
WHAT IS IT...?

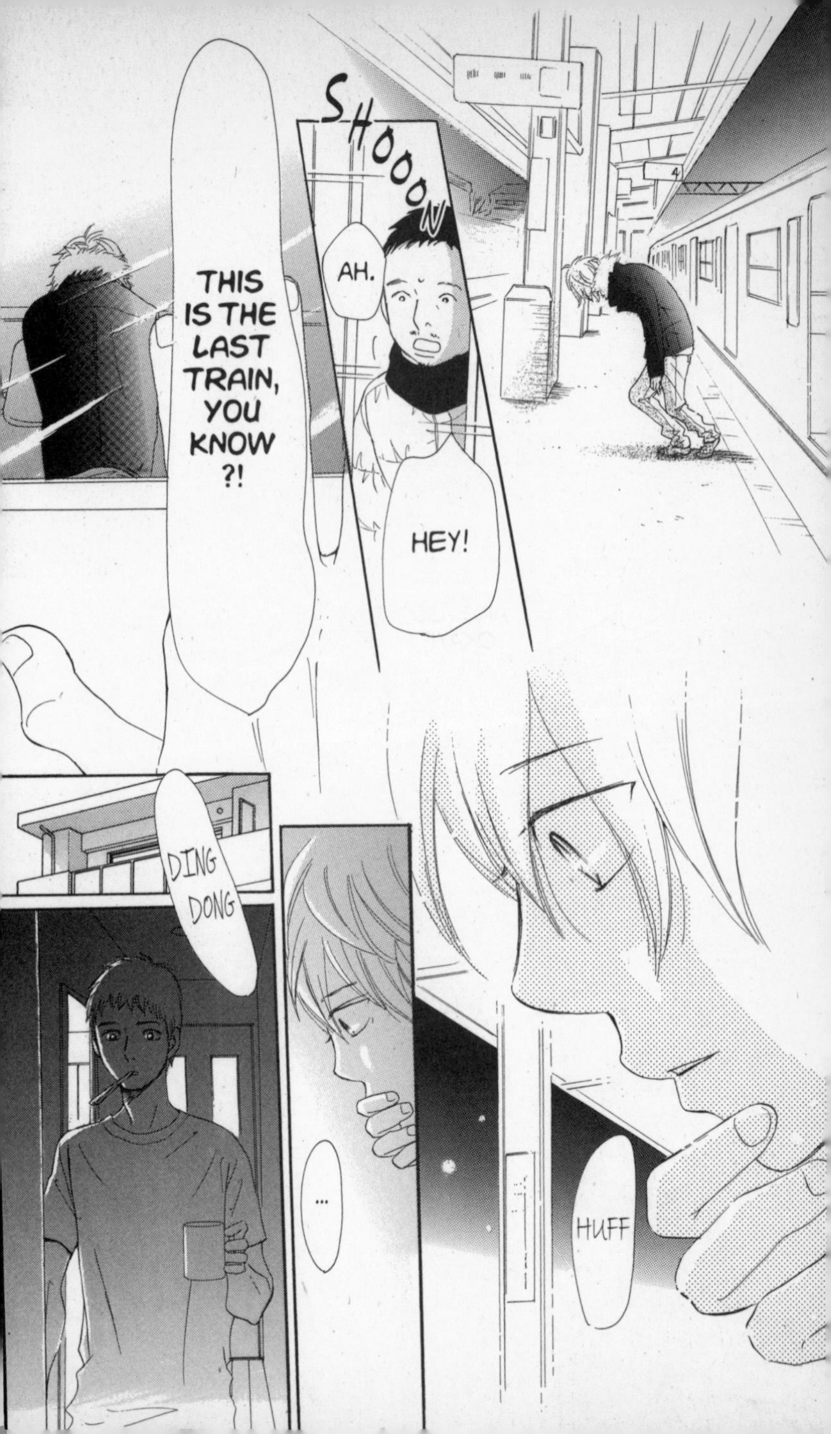
SHOOOON
AH.
HEY!
THIS IS THE LAST TRAIN, YOU KNOW?!
HUFF
...
DING DONG

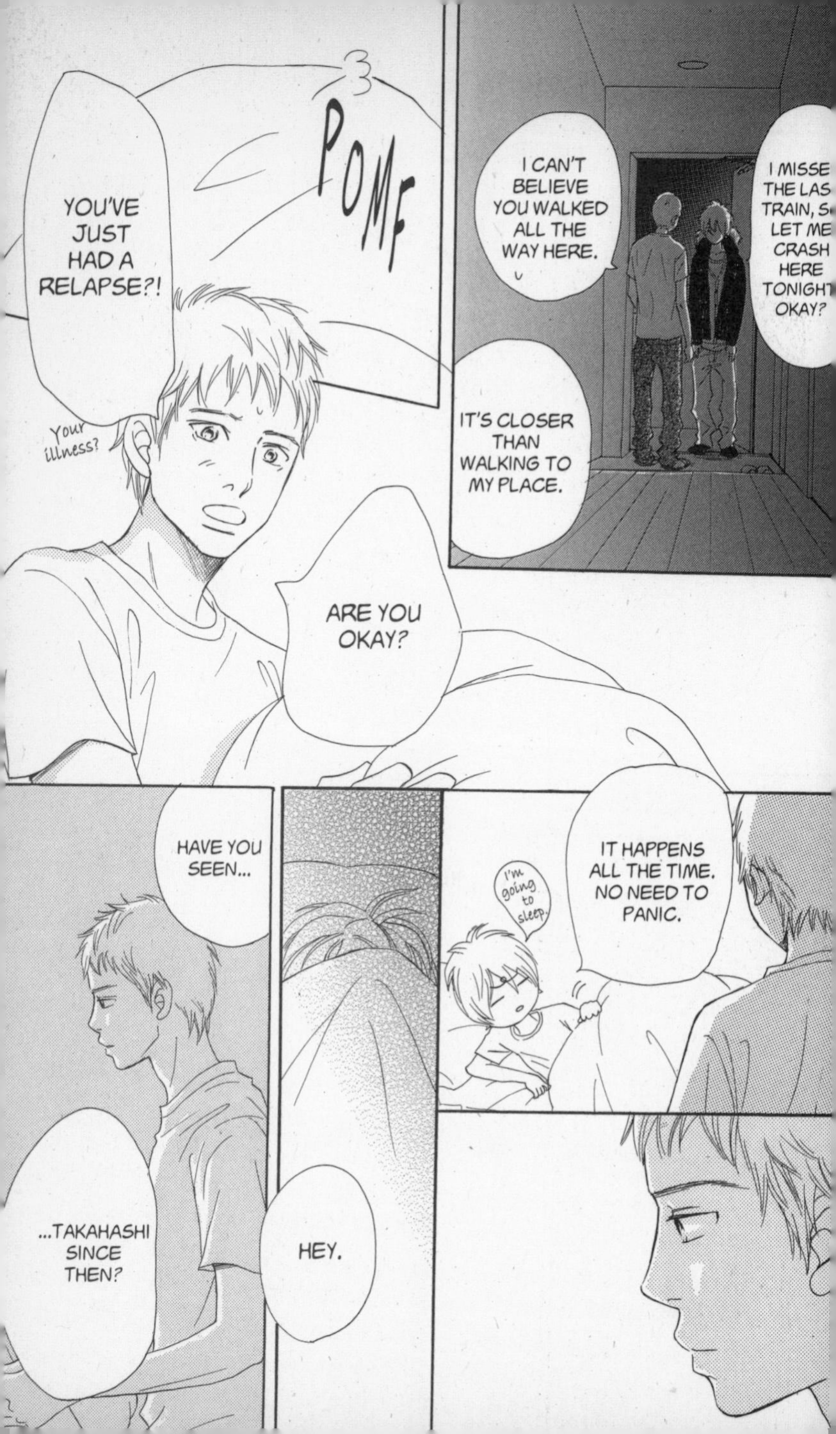
I MISSE THE LAS TRAIN, S LET ME CRASH HERE TONIGHT OKAY?
I CAN'T BELIEVE YOU WALKED ALL THE WAY HERE.
IT'S CLOSER THAN WALKING TO MY PLACE.
POMF
YOU'VE JUST HAD A RELAPSE?!
Your illness?
ARE YOU OKAY?
IT HAPPENS ALL THE TIME. NO NEED TO PANIC.
I'm going to sleep.
HEY.
HAVE YOU SEEN...
...TAKAHASHI SINCE THEN?

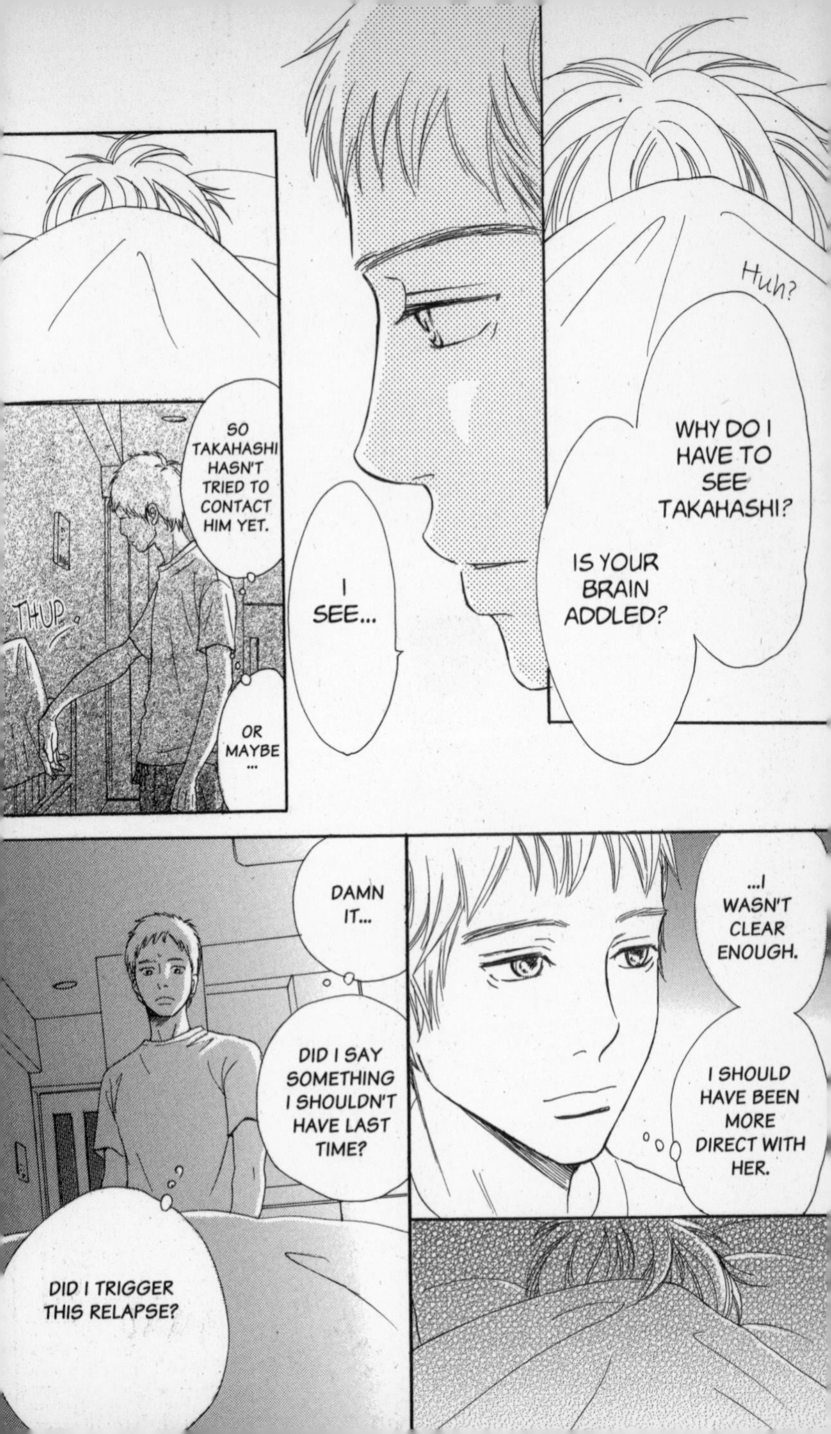
Huh?
WHY DO I HAVE TO SEE TAKAHASHI?
IS YOUR BRAIN ADDLED?
I SEE...
SO TAKAHASHI HASN'T TRIED TO CONTACT HIM YET.
THUP
OR MAYBE ...
...I WASN'T CLEAR ENOUGH.
I SHOULD HAVE BEEN MORE DIRECT WITH HER.
DAMN IT...
DID I SAY SOMETHING I SHOULDN'T HAVE LAST TIME?
DID I TRIGGER THIS RELAPSE?

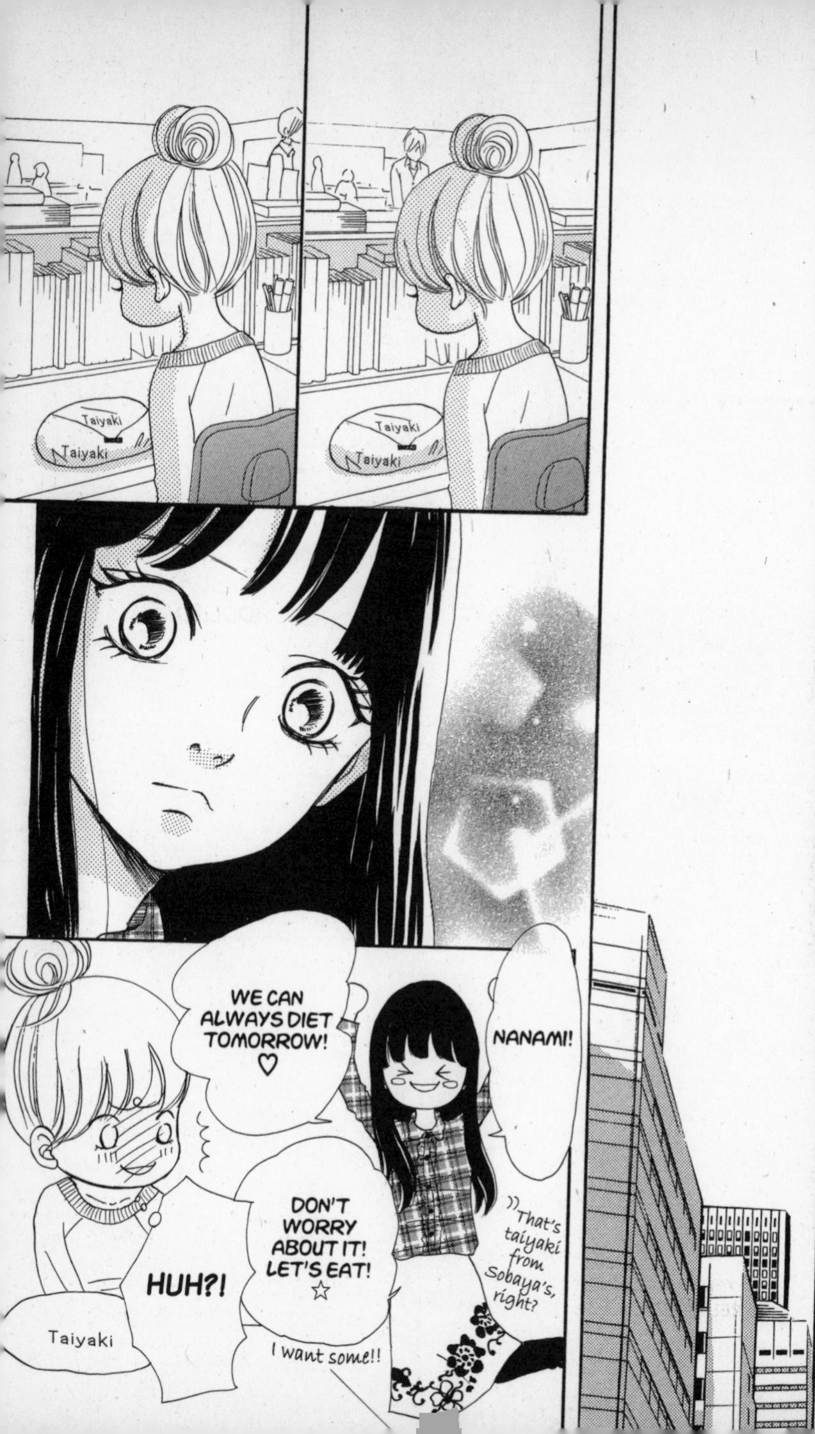
Taiyaki
Taiyaki
Taiyaki
Taiyaki
NANAMI!
That's taiyaki from Sobaya's, right?
WE CAN ALWAYS DIET TOMORROW! ♡
DON'T WORRY ABOUT IT! LET'S EAT! ☆
I want some!!
HUH?!
Taiyaki

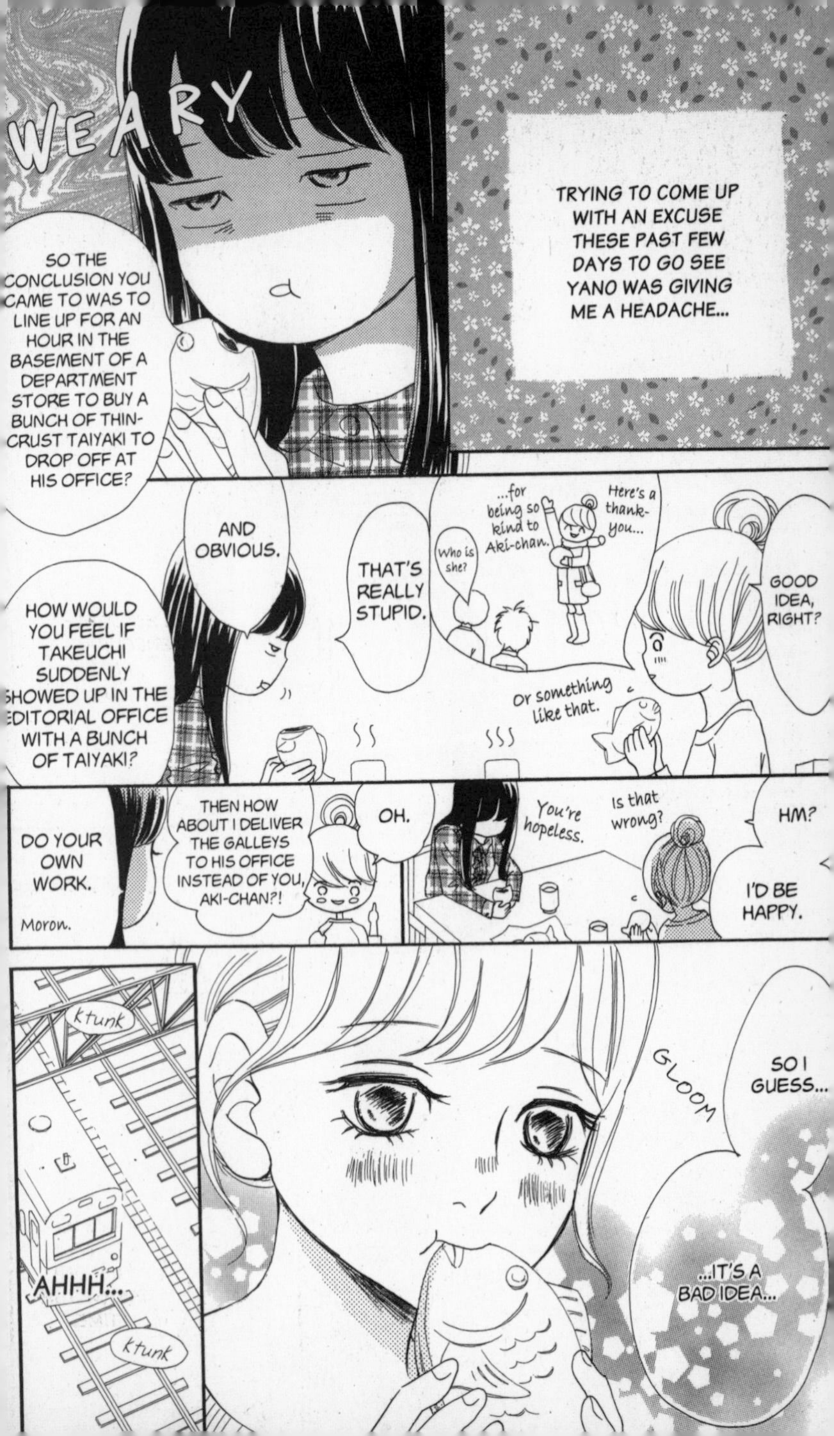
TRYING TO COME UP WITH AN EXCUSE THESE PAST FEW DAYS TO GO SEE YANO WAS GIVING ME A HEADACHE...
WEARY
SO THE CONCLUSION YOU CAME TO WAS TO LINE UP FOR AN HOUR IN THE BASEMENT OF A DEPARTMENT STORE TO BUY A BUNCH OF THIN-CRUST TAIYAKI TO DROP OFF AT HIS OFFICE?
GOOD IDEA, RIGHT?
Here's a thank-you...
...for being so kind to Aki-chan.
Who is she?
Or something like that.
THAT'S REALLY STUPID.
AND OBVIOUS.
HOW WOULD YOU FEEL IF TAKEUCHI SUDDENLY SHOWED UP IN THE EDITORIAL OFFICE WITH A BUNCH OF TAIYAKI?
HM?
I'D BE HAPPY.
Is that wrong?
You're hopeless.
OH.
THEN HOW ABOUT I DELIVER THE GALLEYS TO HIS OFFICE INSTEAD OF YOU, AKI-CHAN?!
DO YOUR OWN WORK.
Moron.
SO I GUESS...
GLOOM
...IT'S A BAD IDEA...
ktunk
AHHH...
ktunk

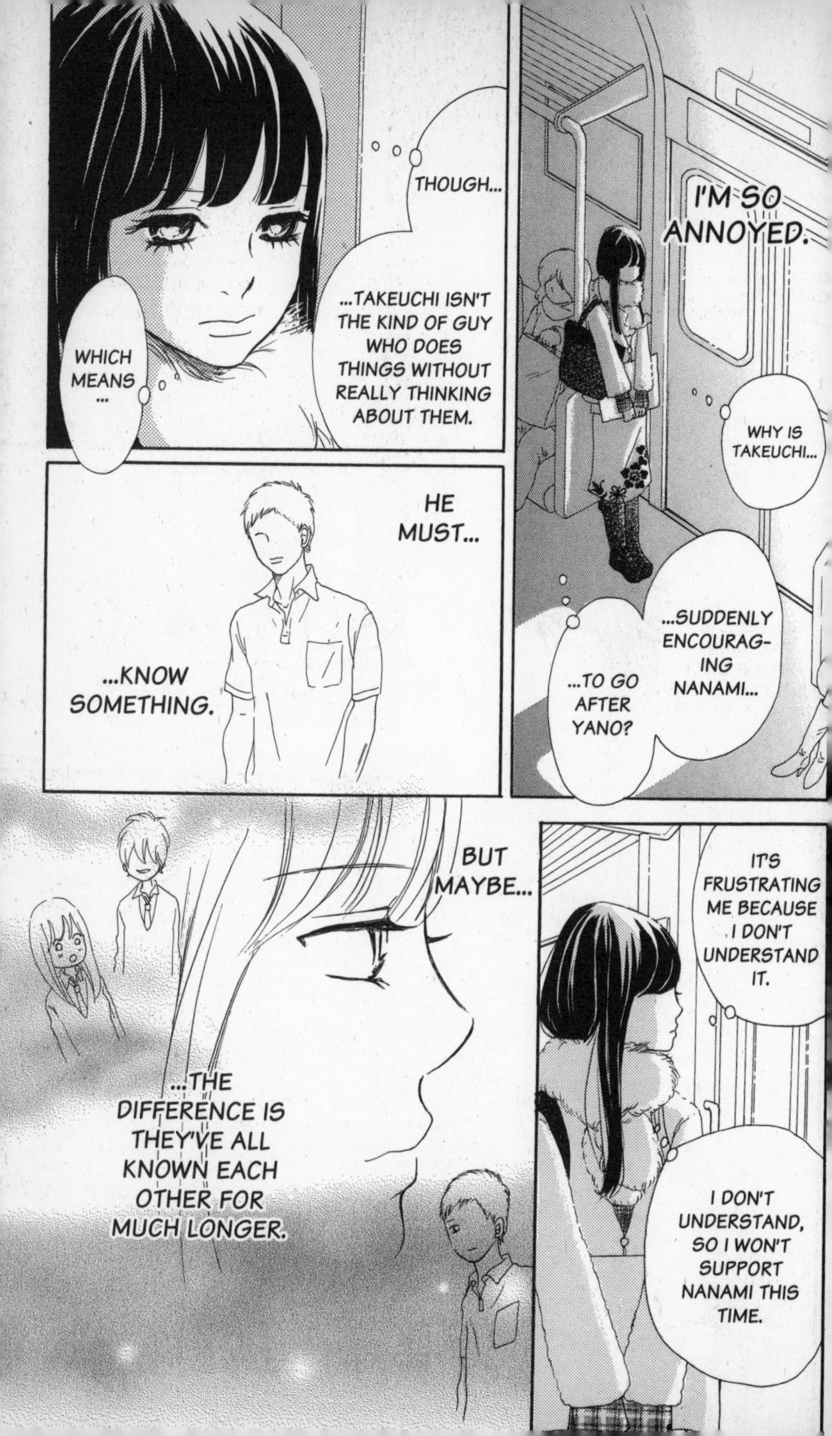
I'M SO ANNOYED.
WHY IS TAKEUCHI...
...SUDDENLY ENCOURAG-ING NANAMI...
...TO GO AFTER YANO?
THOUGH...
...TAKEUCHI ISN'T THE KIND OF GUY WHO DOES THINGS WITHOUT REALLY THINKING ABOUT THEM.
WHICH MEANS...
HE MUST...
...KNOW SOMETHING.
IT'S FRUSTRATING ME BECAUSE I DON'T UNDERSTAND IT.
I DON'T UNDERSTAND, SO I WON'T SUPPORT NANAMI THIS TIME.
BUT MAYBE...
...THE DIFFERENCE IS THEY'VE ALL KNOWN EACH OTHER FOR MUCH LONGER.

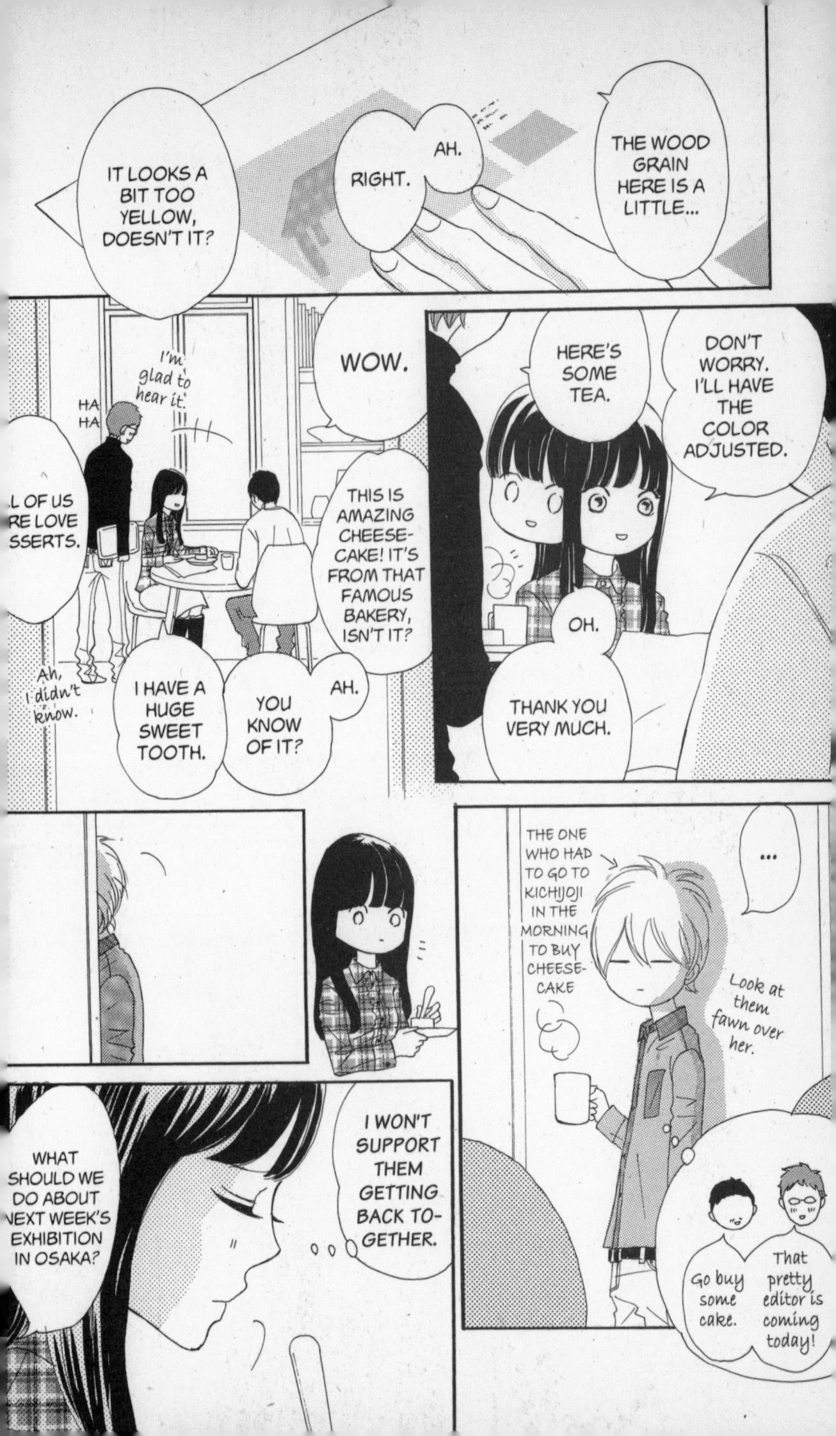
THE WOOD GRAIN HERE IS A LITTLE...
AH.
RIGHT.
IT LOOKS A BIT TOO YELLOW, DOESN'T IT?
DON'T WORRY. I'LL HAVE THE COLOR ADJUSTED.
HERE'S SOME TEA.
OH.
THANK YOU VERY MUCH.
WOW.
THIS IS AMAZING CHEESE-CAKE! IT'S FROM THAT FAMOUS BAKERY, ISN'T IT?
AH.
YOU KNOW OF IT?
I HAVE A HUGE SWEET TOOTH.
I'm glad to hear it.
HA HA
L OF US RE LOVE SSERTS.
Ah, I didn't know.
...
THE ONE WHO HAD TO GO TO KICHIJOJI IN THE MORNING TO BUY CHEESE-CAKE
Look at them fawn over her.
That pretty editor is coming today!
Go buy some cake.
I WON'T SUPPORT THEM GETTING BACK TO-GETHER.
WHAT SHOULD WE DO ABOUT EXT WEEK'S EXHIBITION IN OSAKA?

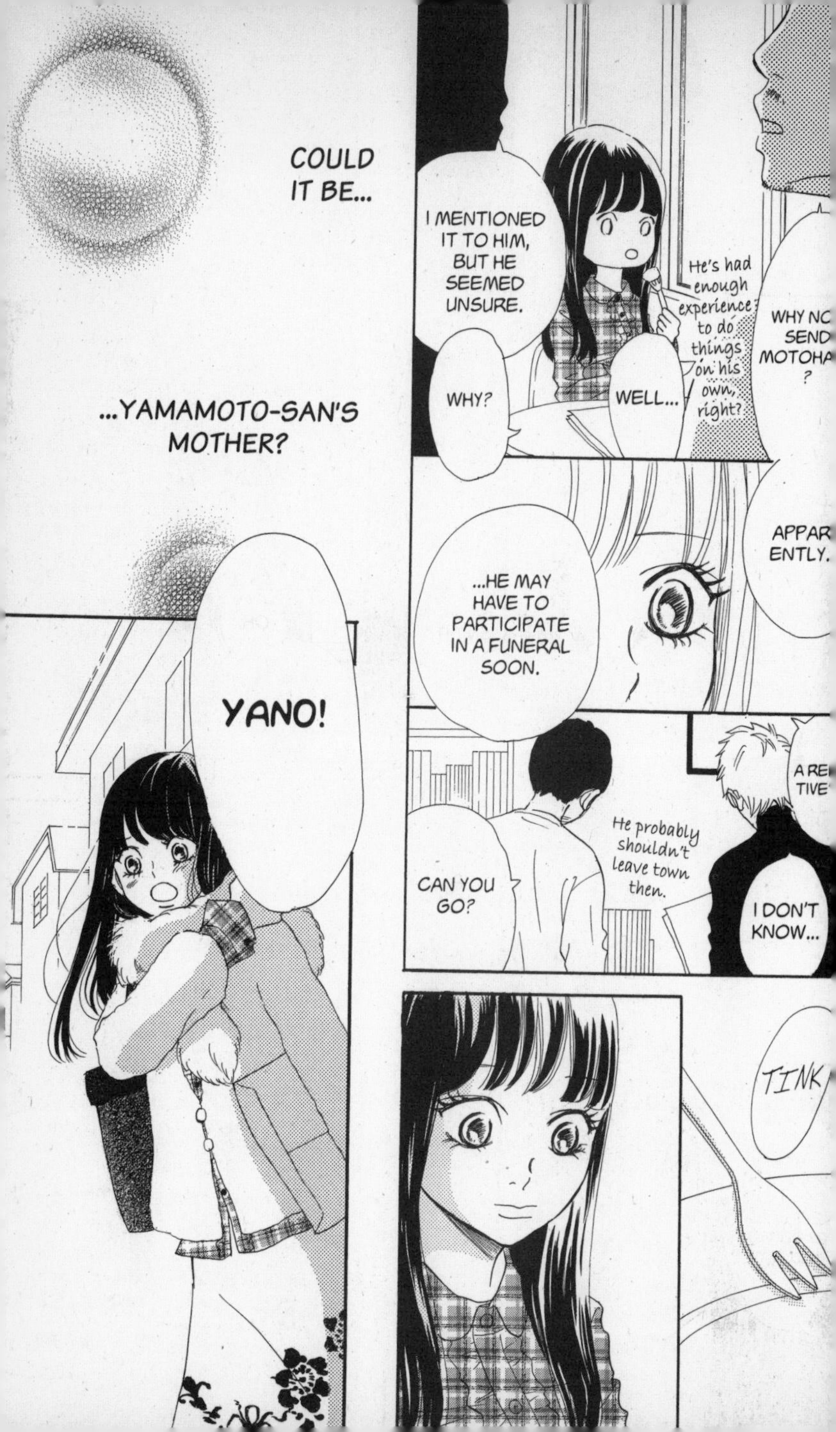

WHY NO SEND MOTOHA ?
He's had enough experience to do things on his own, right?
I MENTIONED IT TO HIM, BUT HE SEEMED UNSURE.
WELL...
WHY?
APPAR ENTLY.
...HE MAY HAVE TO PARTICIPATE IN A FUNERAL SOON.
A RE TIVE
I DON'T KNOW...
He probably shouldn't leave town then.
CAN YOU GO?
TINK
COULD IT BE...
...YAMAMOTO-SAN'S MOTHER?
YANO!

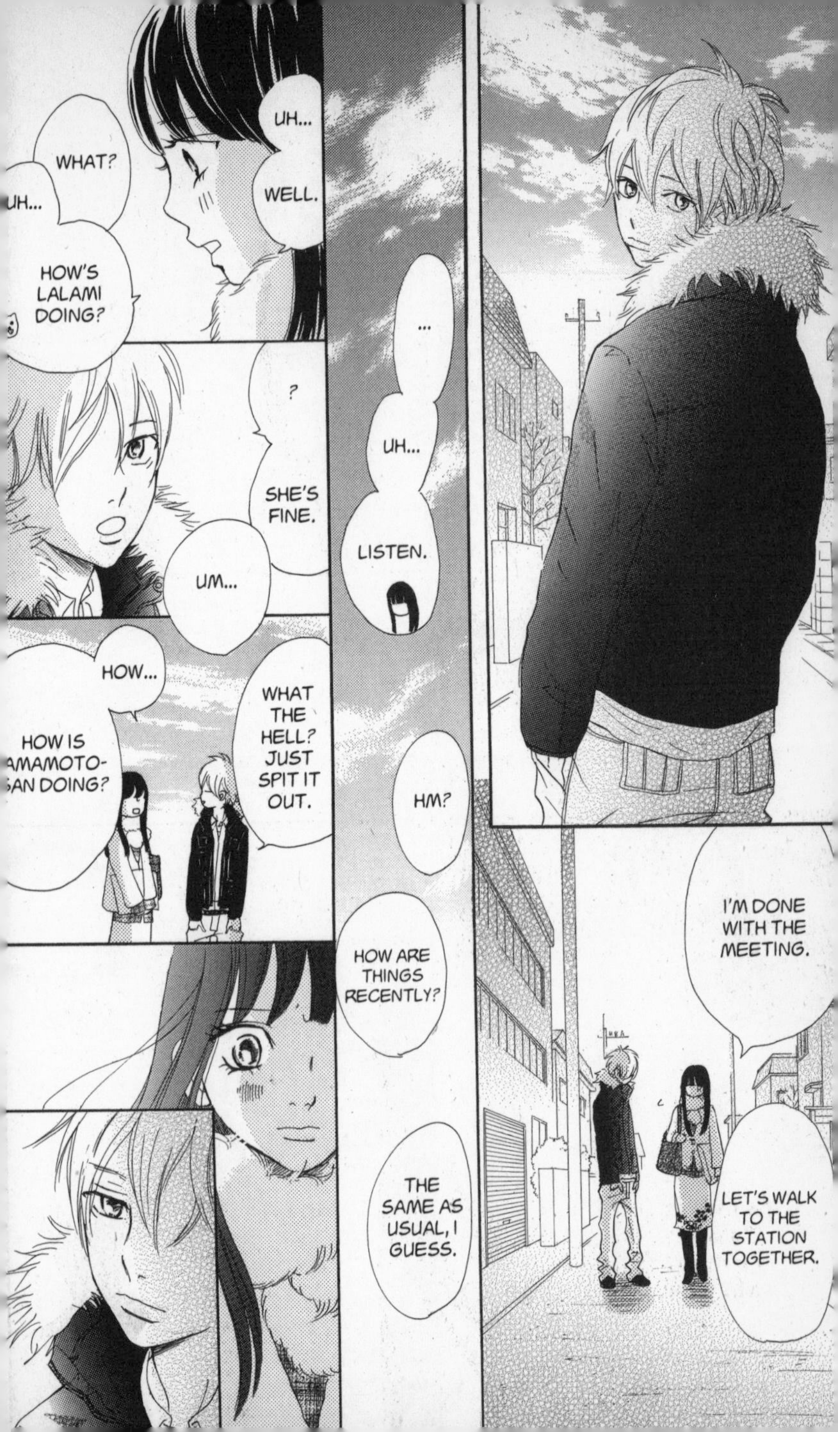
I'M DONE WITH THE MEETING.
LET'S WALK TO THE STATION TOGETHER.
...
UH...
LISTEN.
HM?
HOW ARE THINGS RECENTLY?
THE SAME AS USUAL, I GUESS.
UH...
WELL.
WHAT?
UH...
HOW'S LALAMI DOING?
?
SHE'S FINE.
UM...
WHAT THE HELL? JUST SPIT IT OUT.
HOW...
HOW IS AMAMOTO-SAN DOING?

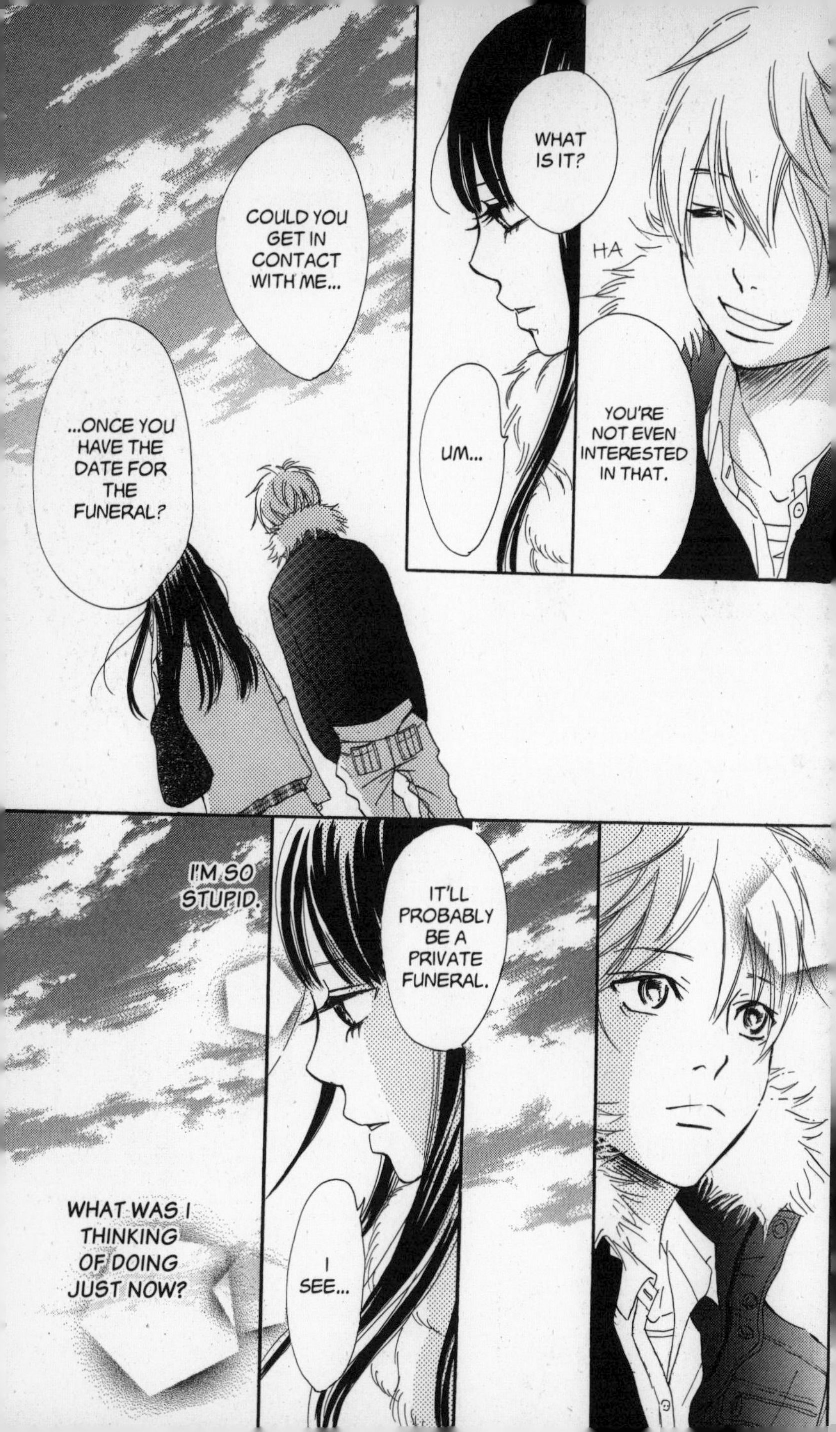
HA
YOU'RE NOT EVEN INTERESTED IN THAT.
WHAT IS IT?
UM...
COULD YOU GET IN CONTACT WITH ME...
...ONCE YOU HAVE THE DATE FOR THE FUNERAL?
IT'LL PROBABLY BE A PRIVATE FUNERAL.
I SEE...
I'M SO STUPID.
WHAT WAS I THINKING OF DOING JUST NOW?

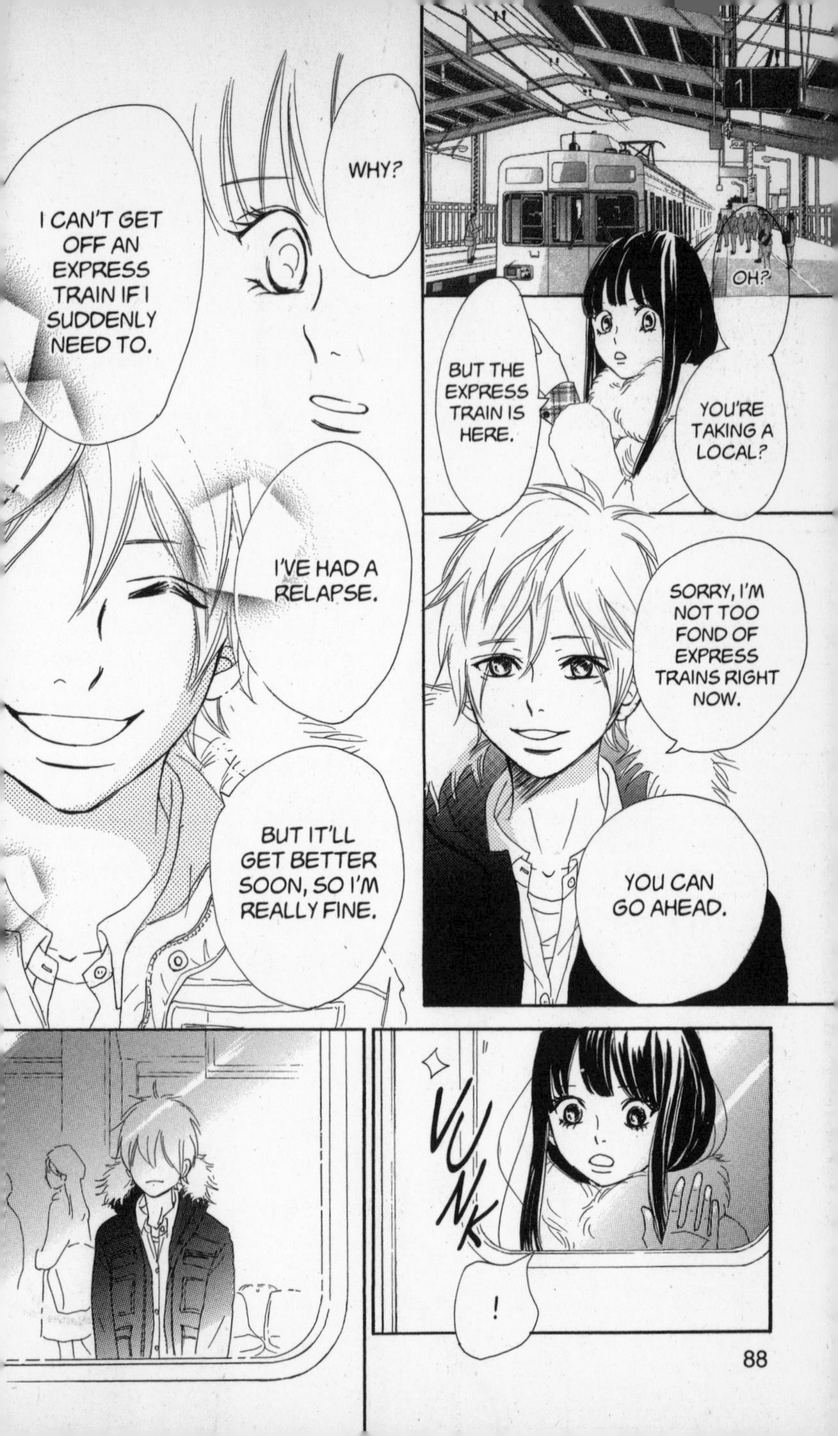
OH?
YOU'RE TAKING A LOCAL?
BUT THE EXPRESS TRAIN IS HERE.
SORRY, I'M NOT TOO FOND OF EXPRESS TRAINS RIGHT NOW.
YOU CAN GO AHEAD.
WHY?
I CAN'T GET OFF AN EXPRESS TRAIN IF I SUDDENLY NEED TO.
I'VE HAD A RELAPSE.
BUT IT'LL GET BETTER SOON, SO I'M REALLY FINE.
VUNK
!

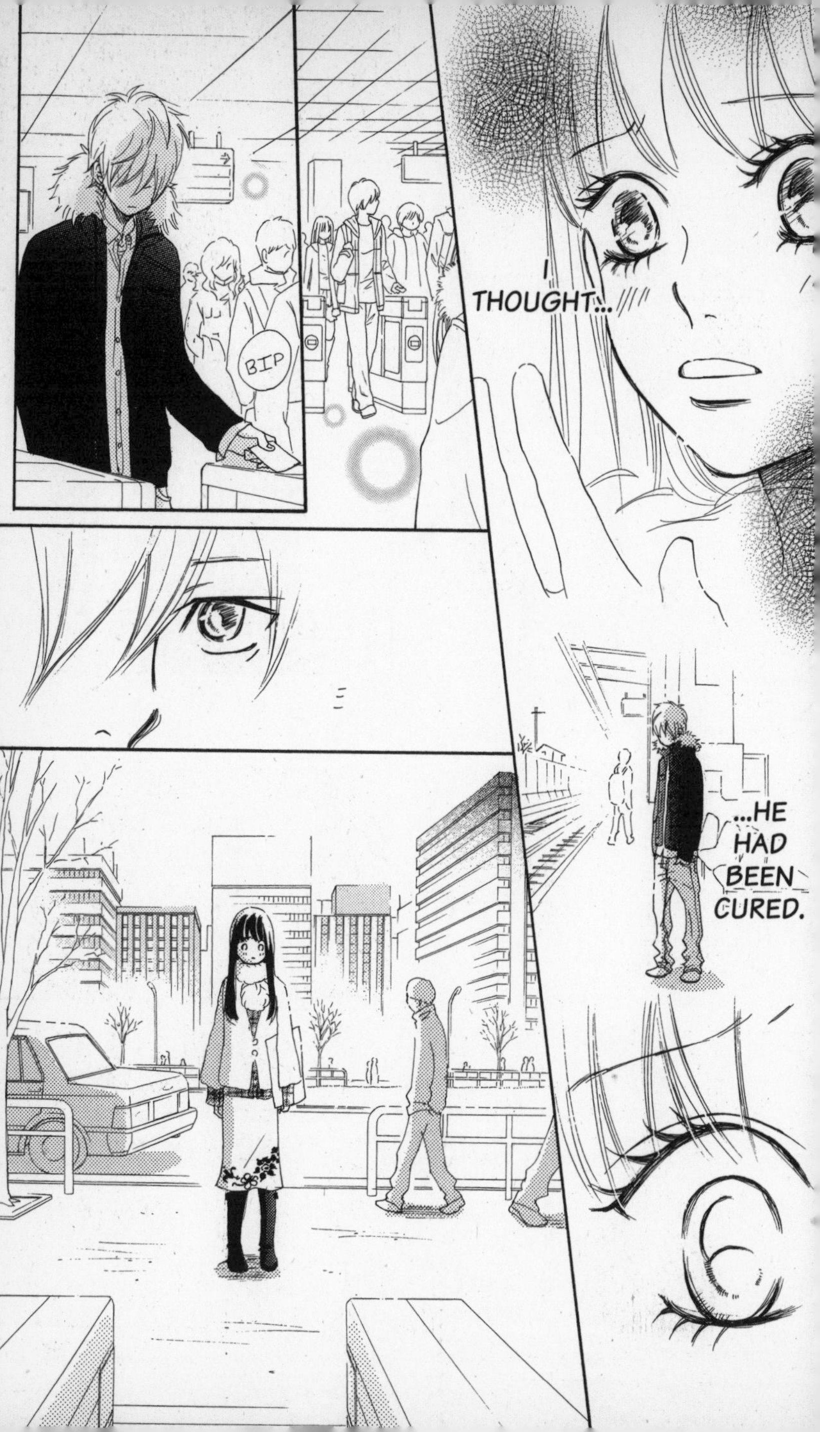
I THOUGHT...
...HE HAD BEEN CURED.
BIP

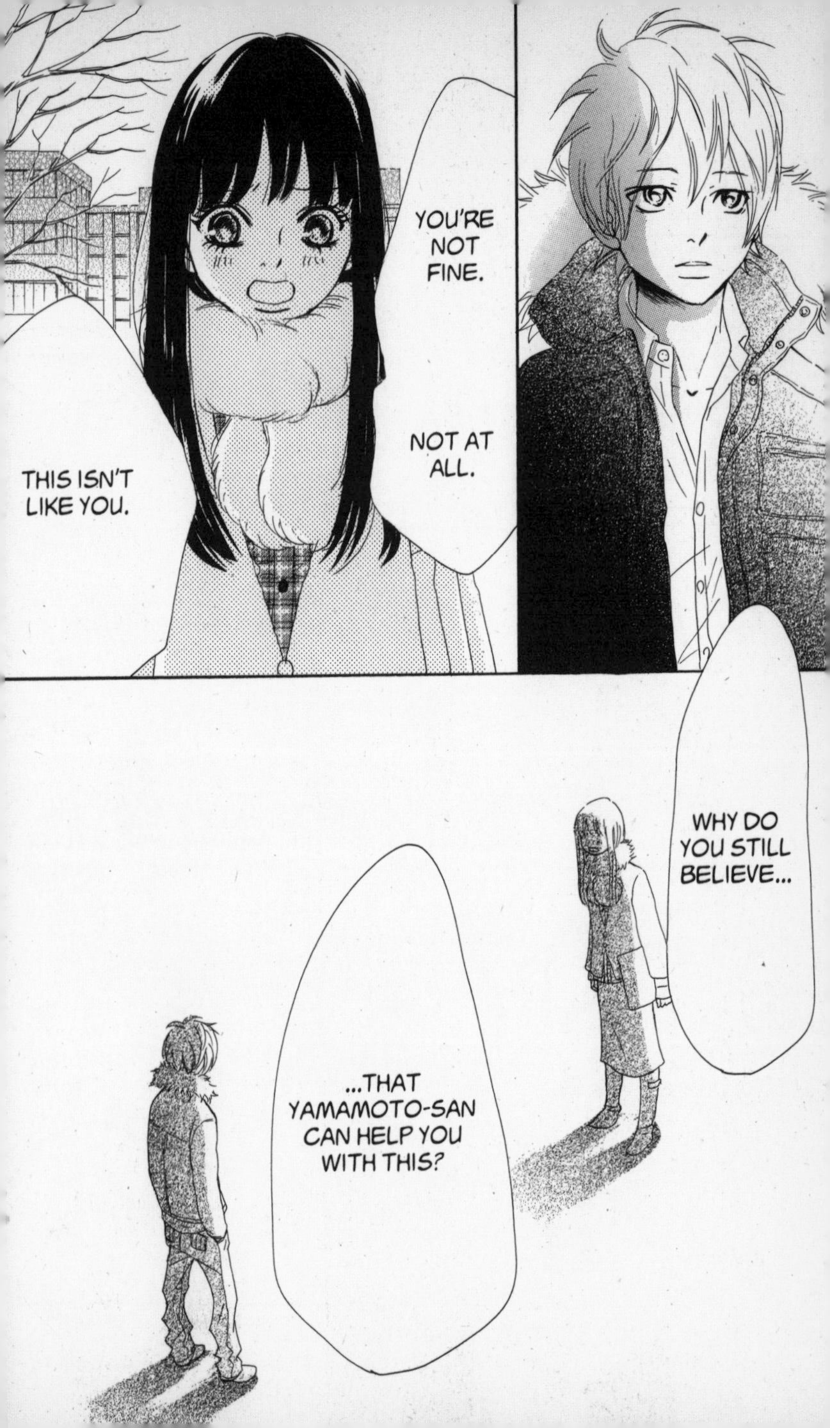
YOU'RE NOT FINE.
NOT AT ALL.
THIS ISN'T LIKE YOU.
WHY DO YOU STILL BELIEVE...
...THAT YAMAMOTO-SAN CAN HELP YOU WITH THIS?

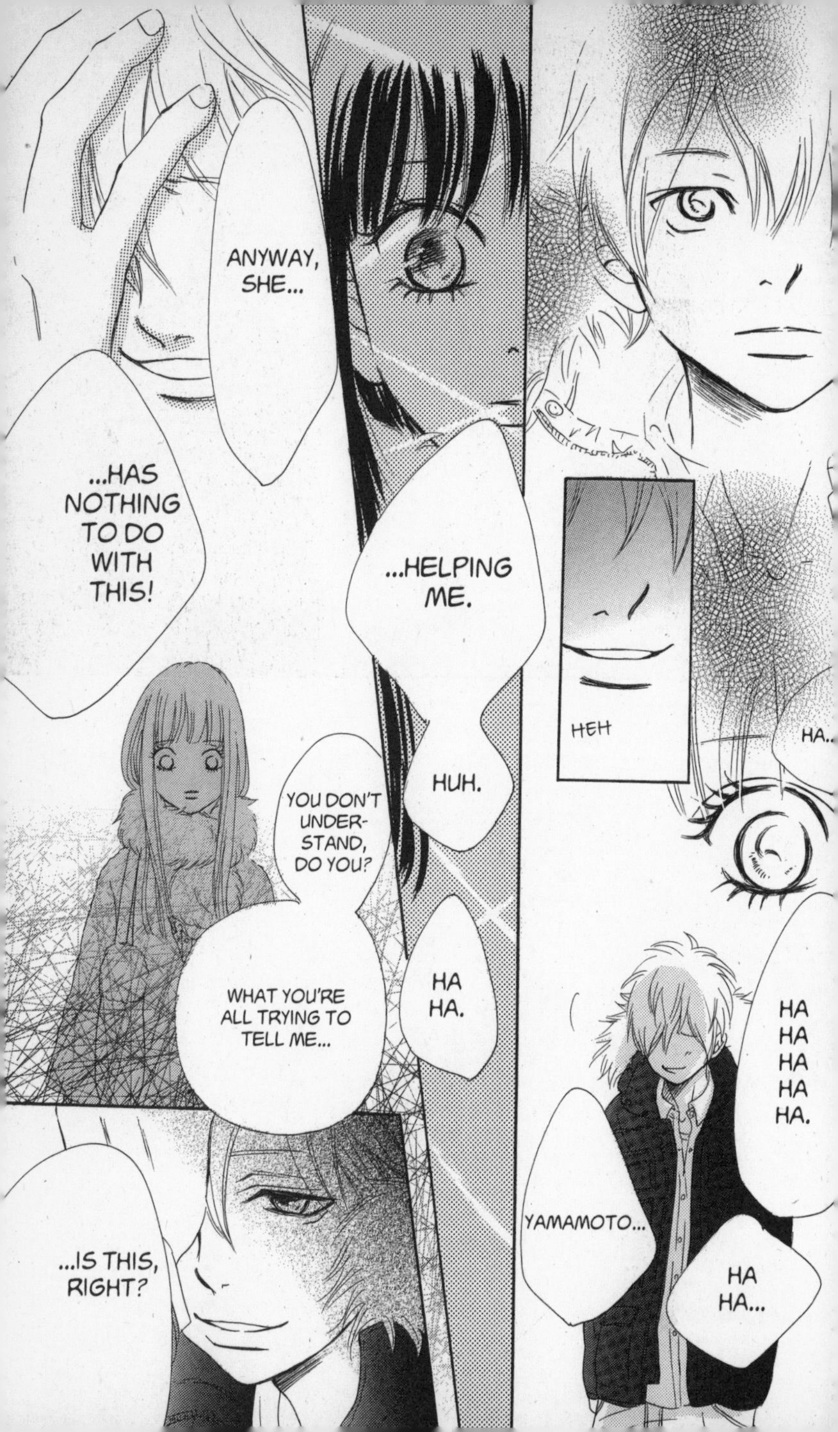
...HELPING ME.
ANYWAY, SHE...
...HAS NOTHING TO DO WITH THIS!
HEH
HA...
HUH.
HA HA.
HA HA HA HA HA.
YAMAMOTO...
HA HA...
YOU DON'T UNDER-STAND, DO YOU?
WHAT YOU'RE ALL TRYING TO TELL ME...
...IS THIS, RIGHT?

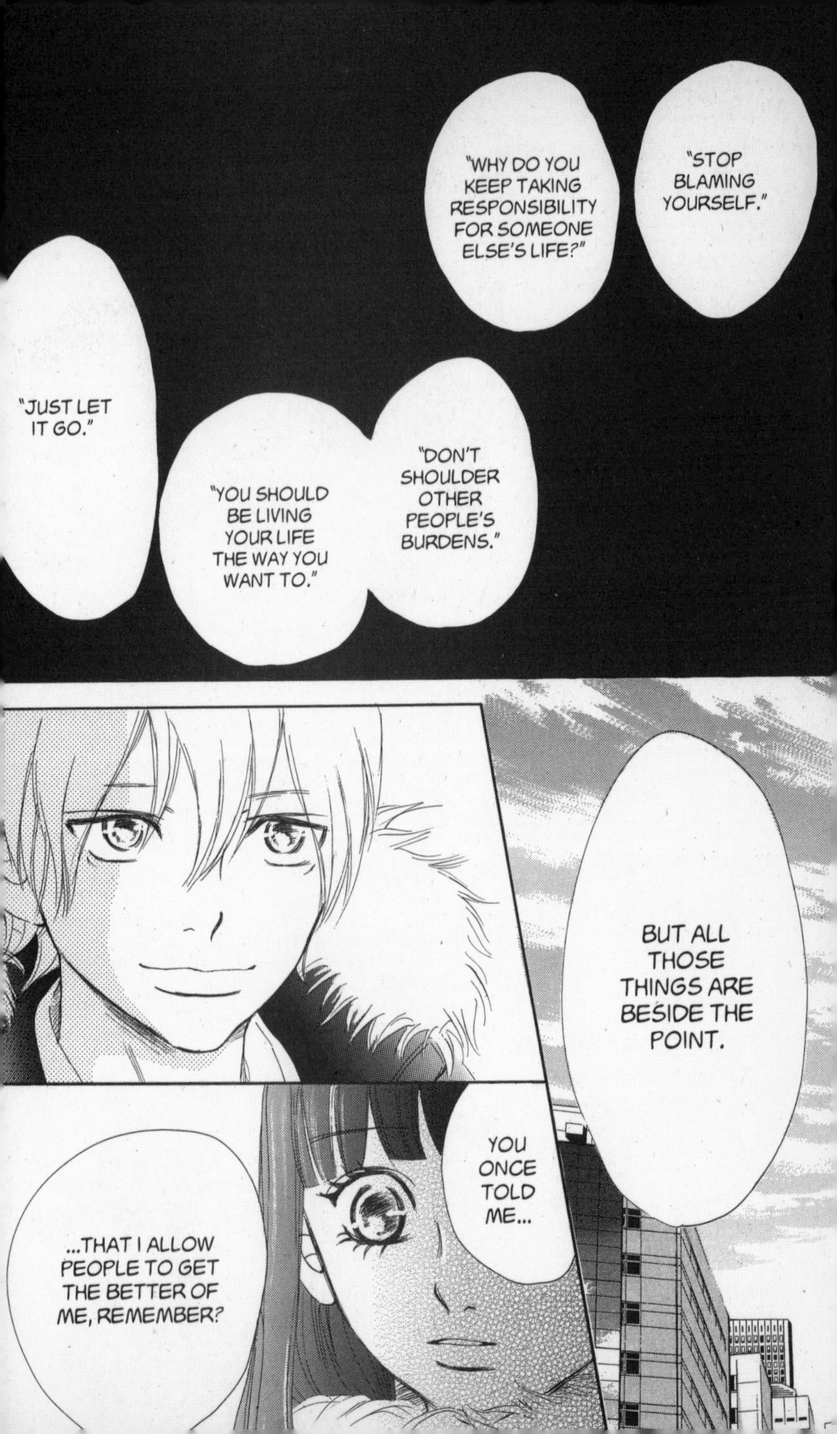
"STOP BLAMING YOURSELF."
"WHY DO YOU KEEP TAKING RESPONSIBILITY FOR SOMEONE ELSE'S LIFE?"
"DON'T SHOULDER OTHER PEOPLE'S BURDENS."
"YOU SHOULD BE LIVING YOUR LIFE THE WAY YOU WANT TO."
"JUST LET IT GO."
BUT ALL THOSE THINGS ARE BESIDE THE POINT.
YOU ONCE TOLD ME...
...THAT I ALLOW PEOPLE TO GET THE BETTER OF ME, REMEMBER?

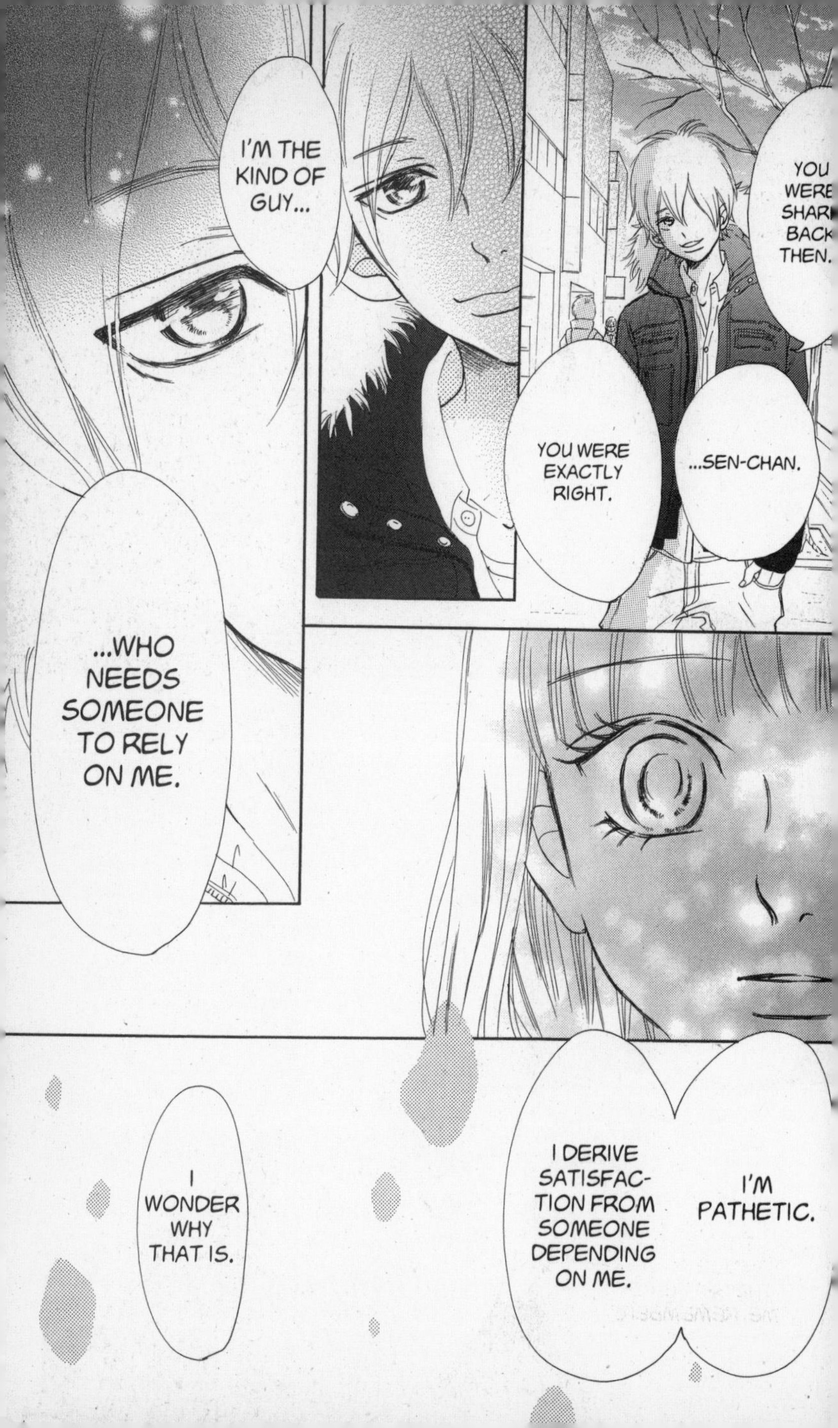
YOU WERE SHARP BACK THEN.
...SEN-CHAN.
YOU WERE EXACTLY RIGHT.
I'M THE KIND OF GUY...
...WHO NEEDS SOMEONE TO RELY ON ME.
I'M PATHETIC.
I DERIVE SATISFAC-TION FROM SOMEONE DEPENDING ON ME.
I WONDER WHY THAT IS.

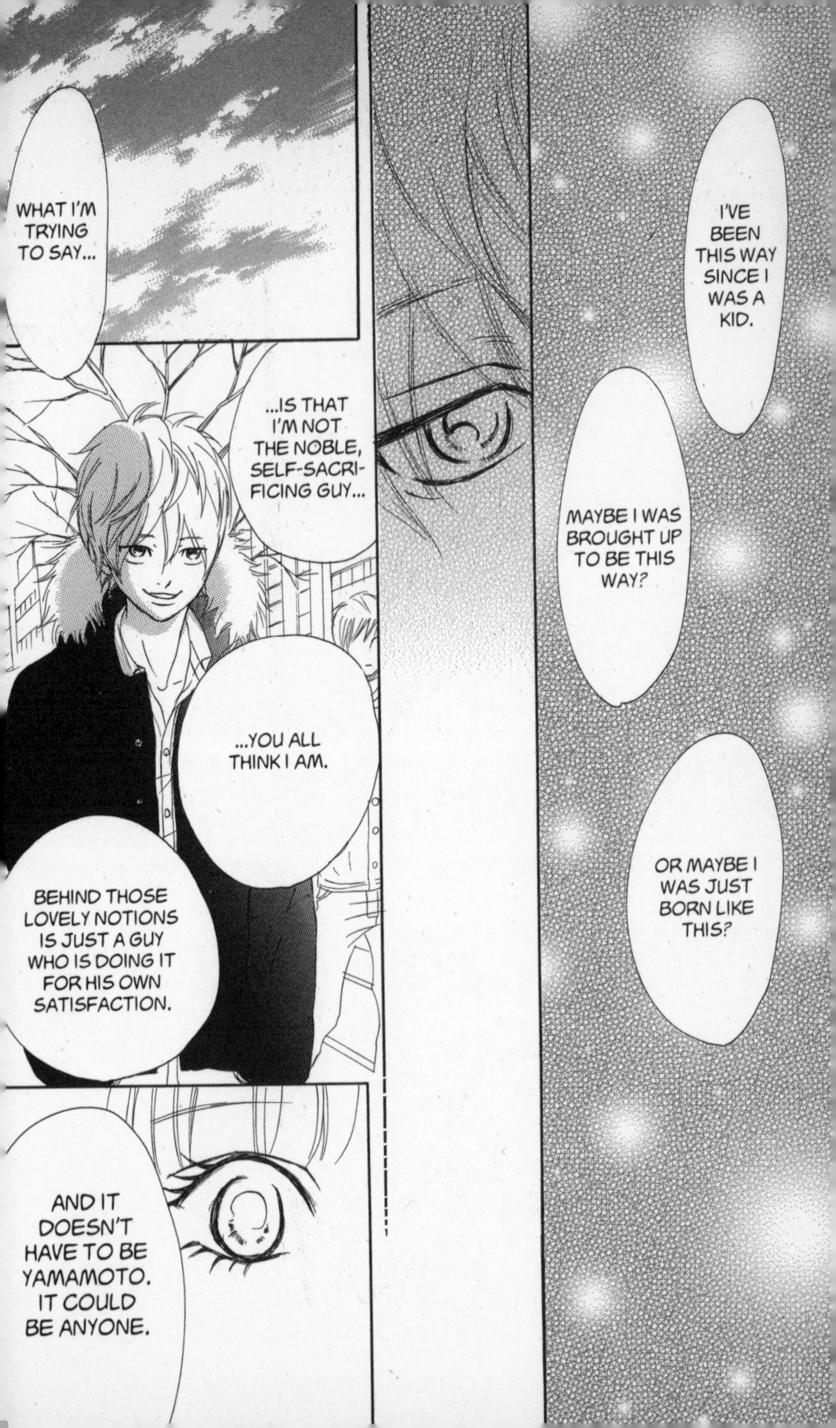
I'VE BEEN THIS WAY SINCE I WAS A KID.
MAYBE I WAS BROUGHT UP TO BE THIS WAY?
OR MAYBE I WAS JUST BORN LIKE THIS?
WHAT I'M TRYING TO SAY...
...IS THAT I'M NOT THE NOBLE, SELF-SACRIFICING GUY...
...YOU ALL THINK I AM.
BEHIND THOSE LOVELY NOTIONS IS JUST A GUY WHO IS DOING IT FOR HIS OWN SATISFACTION.
AND IT DOESN'T HAVE TO BE YAMAMOTO. IT COULD BE ANYONE.

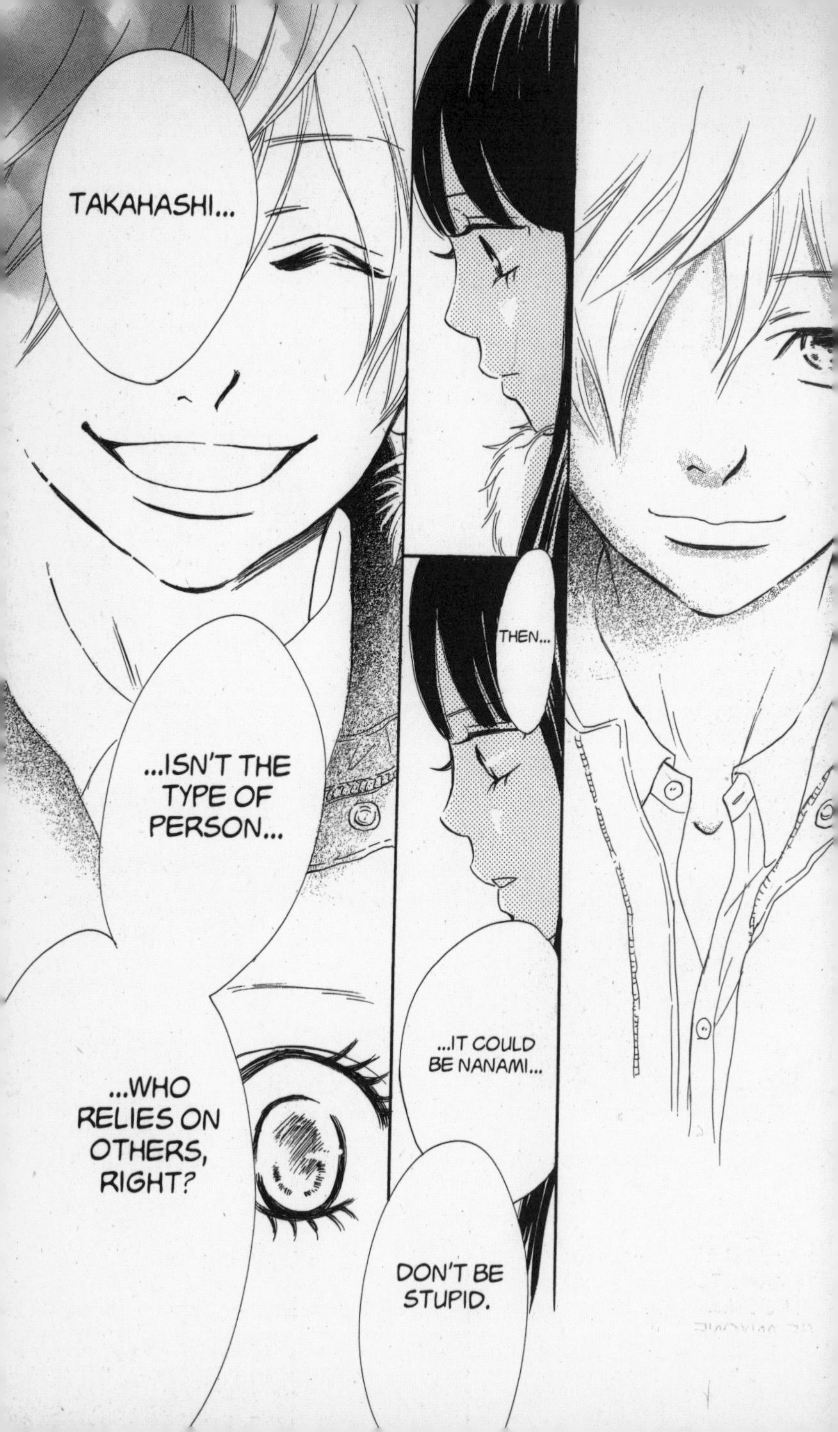
THEN...
...IT COULD BE NANAMI...
DON'T BE STUPID.
TAKAHASHI...
...ISN'T THE TYPE OF PERSON...
...WHO RELIES ON OTHERS, RIGHT?

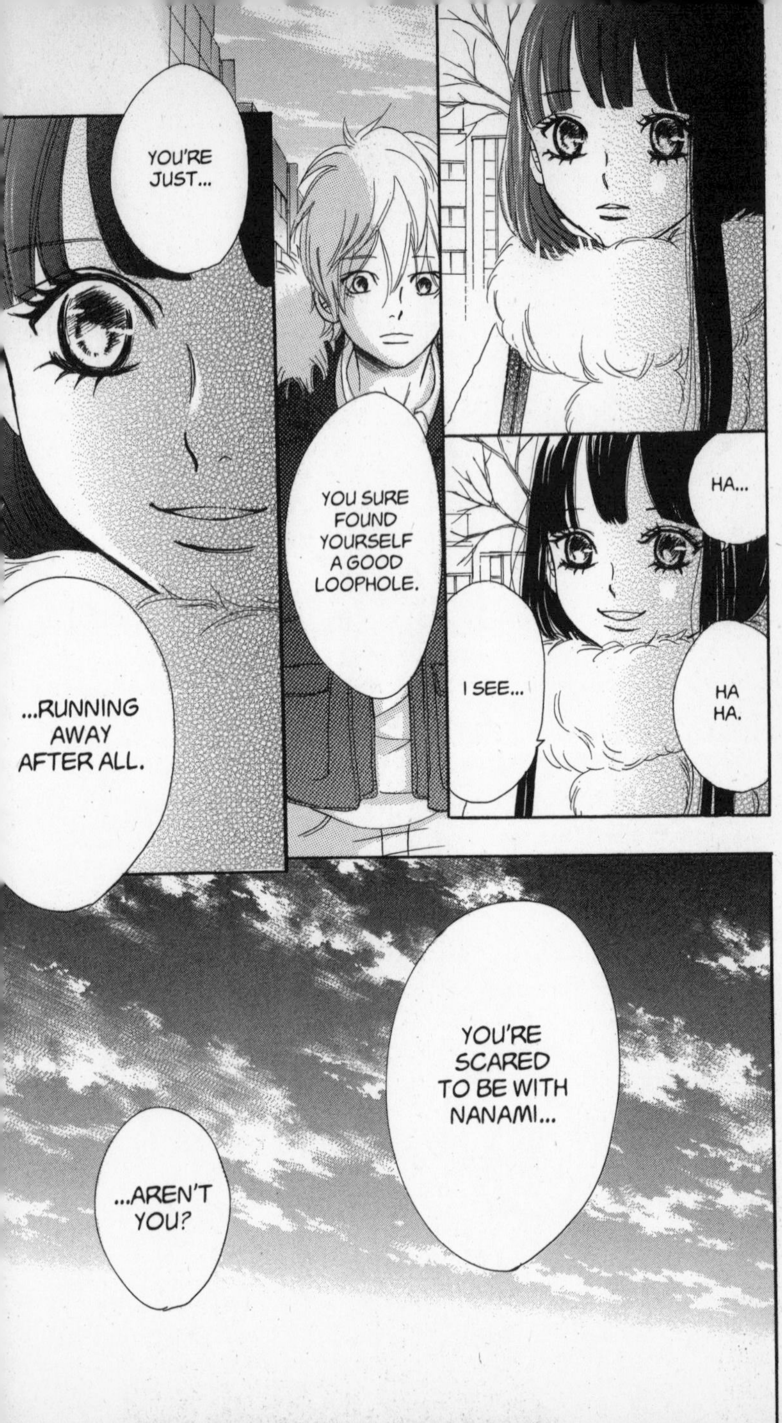
HA...
HA HA.
I SEE...
YOU SURE FOUND YOURSELF A GOOD LOOPHOLE.
YOU'RE JUST...
...RUNNING AWAY AFTER ALL.
YOU'RE SCARED TO BE WITH NANAMI...
...AREN'T YOU?

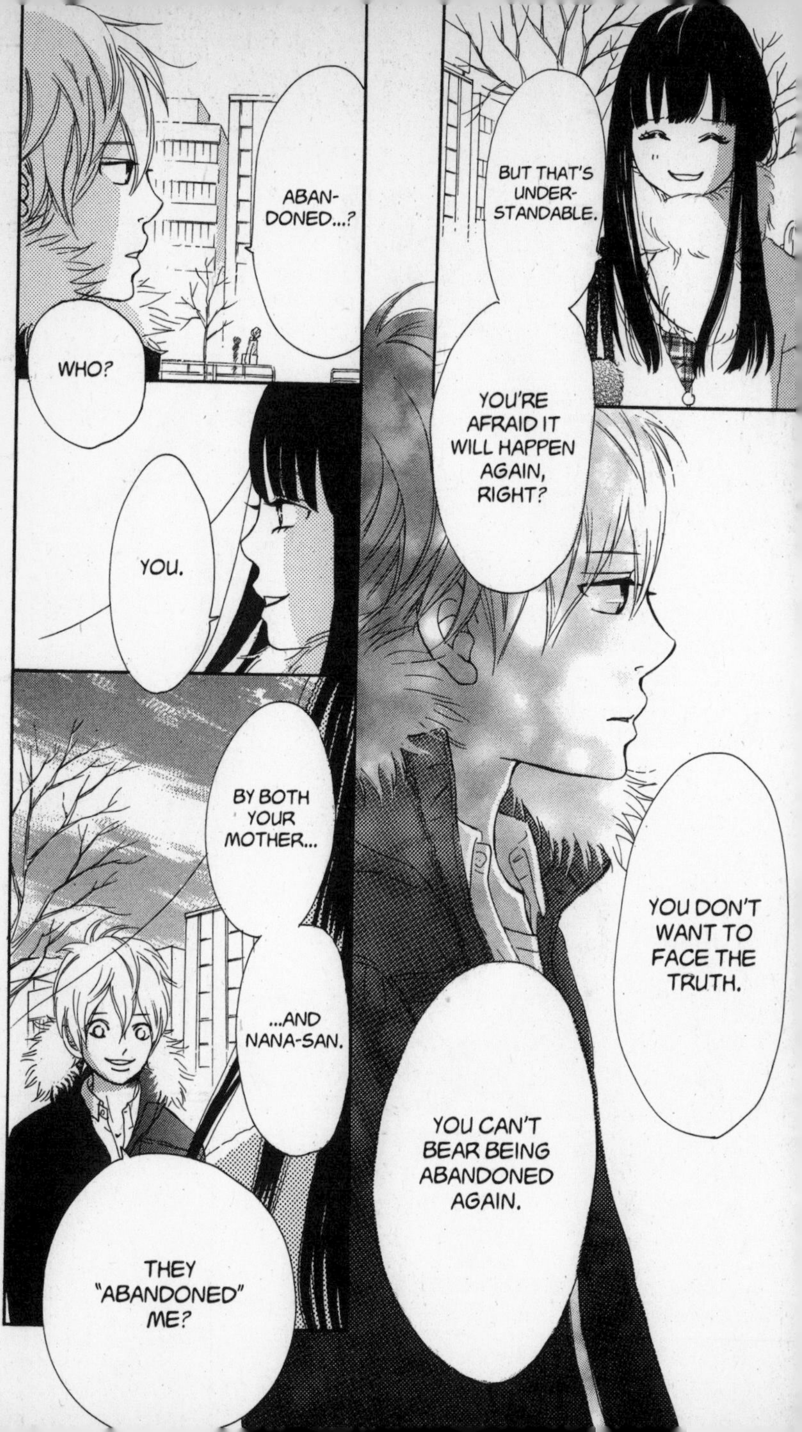
ABAN-
DONED...?
WHO?
YOU.
BY BOTH YOUR MOTHER...
...AND NANA-SAN.
THEY "ABANDONED" ME?
BUT THAT'S UNDER-STANDABLE.
YOU'RE AFRAID IT WILL HAPPEN AGAIN, RIGHT?
YOU DON'T WANT TO FACE THE TRUTH.
YOU CAN'T BEAR BEING ABANDONED AGAIN.

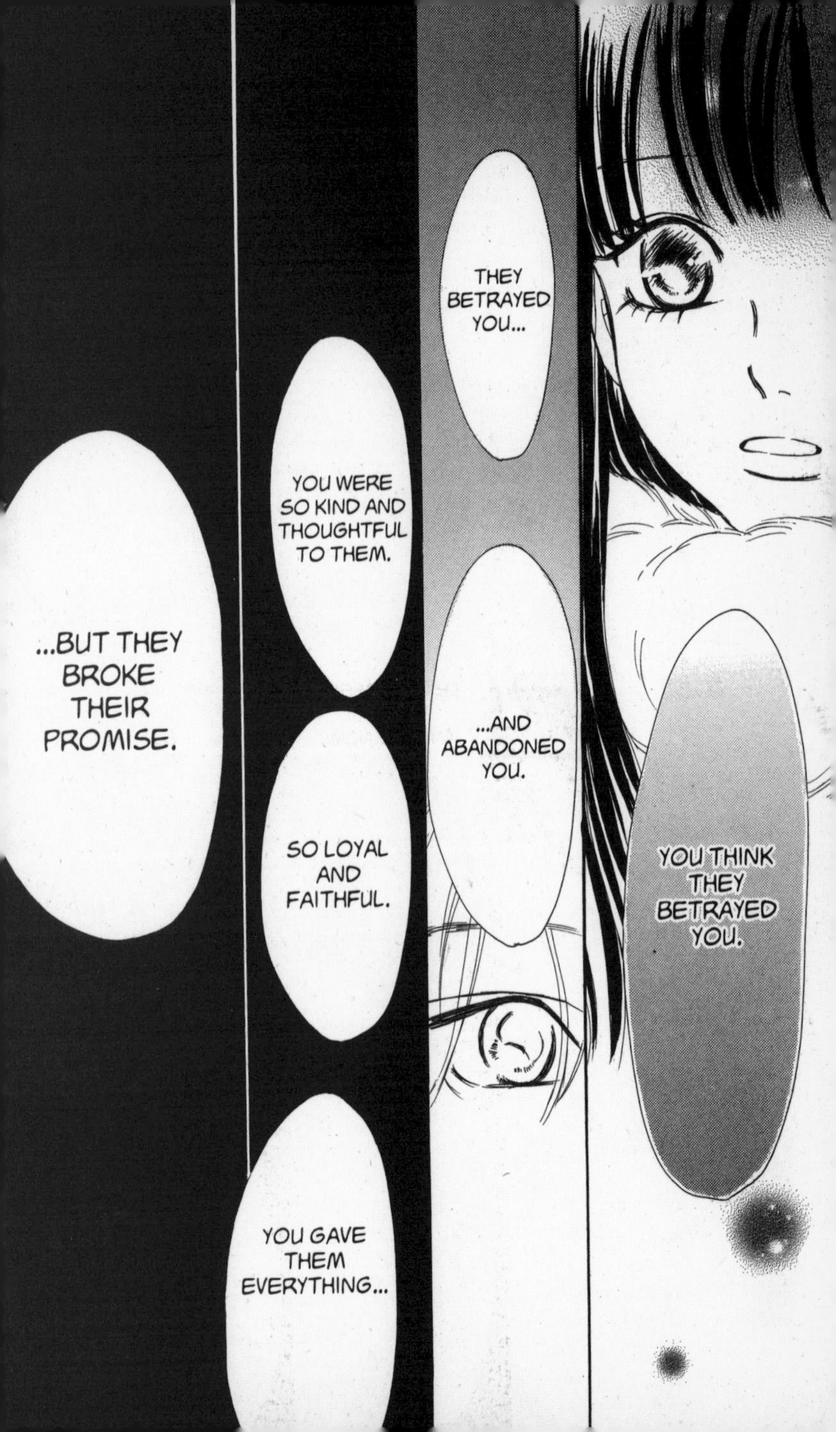
YOU THINK THEY BETRAYED YOU.
THEY BETRAYED YOU...
...AND ABANDONED YOU.
YOU WERE SO KIND AND THOUGHTFUL TO THEM.
SO LOYAL AND FAITHFUL.
YOU GAVE THEM EVERYTHING...
...BUT THEY BROKE THEIR PROMISE.

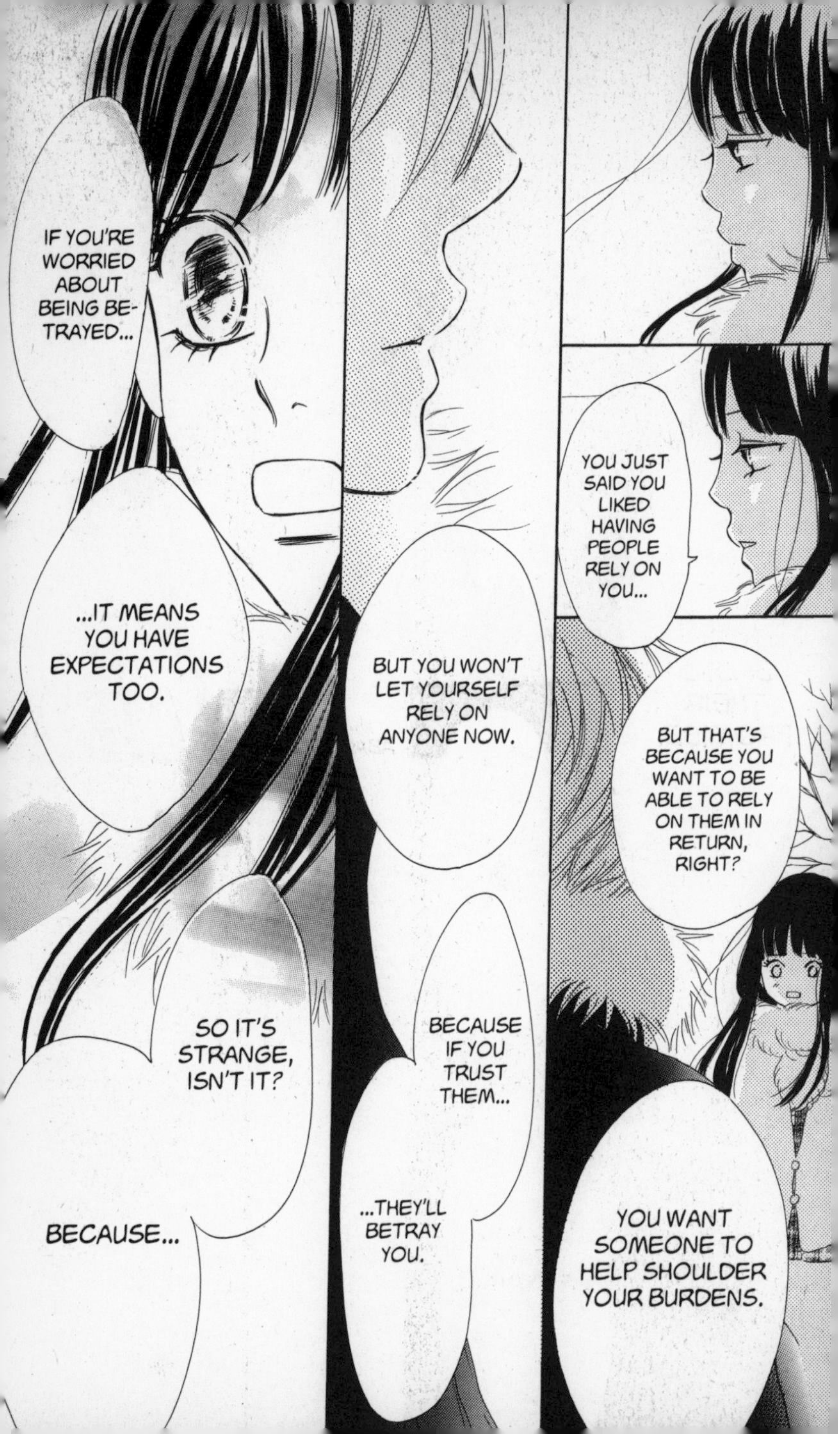
YOU JUST SAID YOU LIKED HAVING PEOPLE RELY ON YOU...
BUT THAT'S BECAUSE YOU WANT TO BE ABLE TO RELY ON THEM IN RETURN, RIGHT?
YOU WANT SOMEONE TO HELP SHOULDER YOUR BURDENS.
BUT YOU WON'T LET YOURSELF RELY ON ANYONE NOW.
BECAUSE IF YOU TRUST THEM...
...THEY'LL BETRAY YOU.
IF YOU'RE WORRIED ABOUT BEING BE-TRAYED...
...IT MEANS YOU HAVE EXPECTATIONS TOO.
SO IT'S STRANGE, ISN'T IT?
BECAUSE...

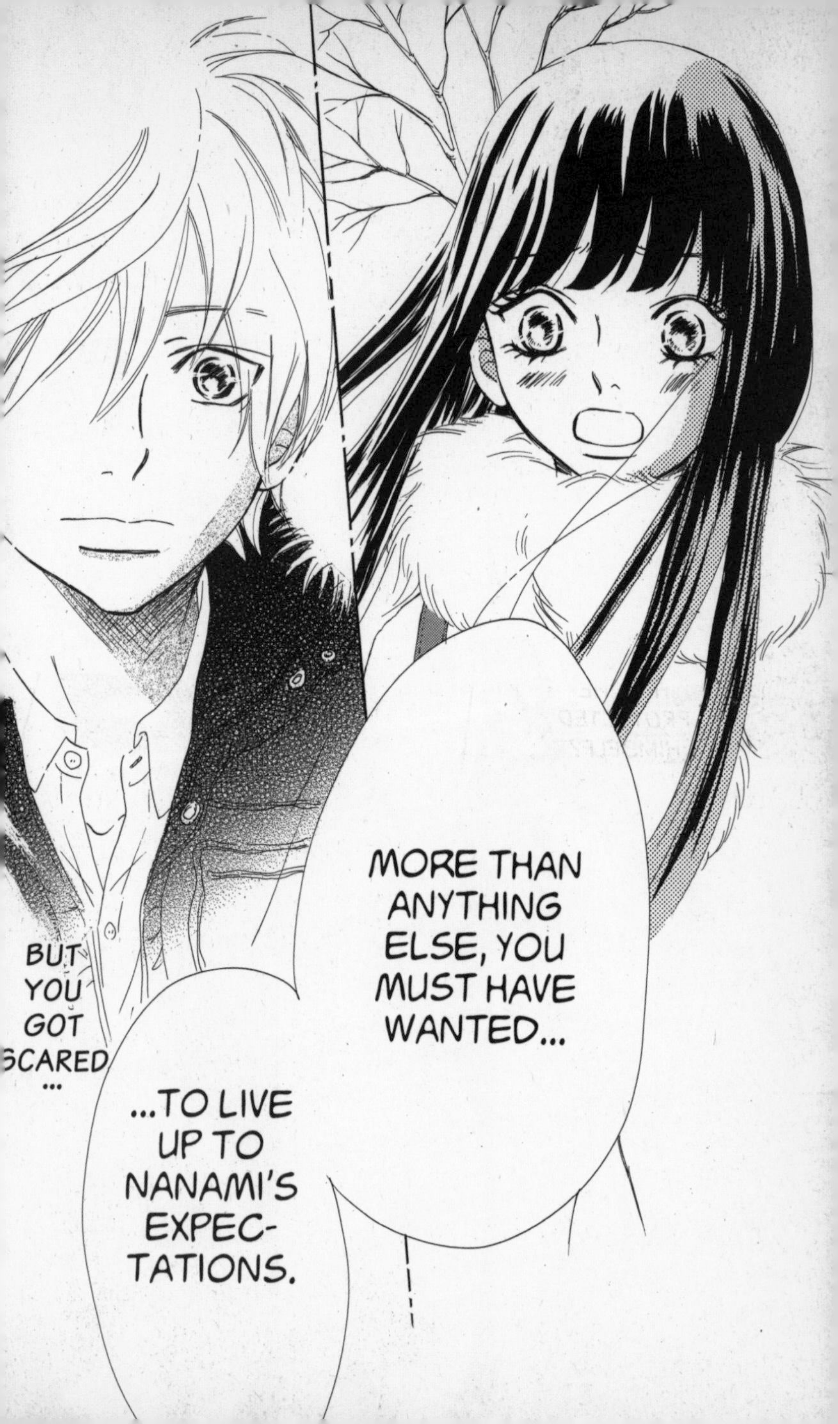
MORE THAN ANYTHING ELSE, YOU MUST HAVE WANTED...
...TO LIVE UP TO NANAMI'S EXPECTATIONS.
BUT YOU GOT SCARED...

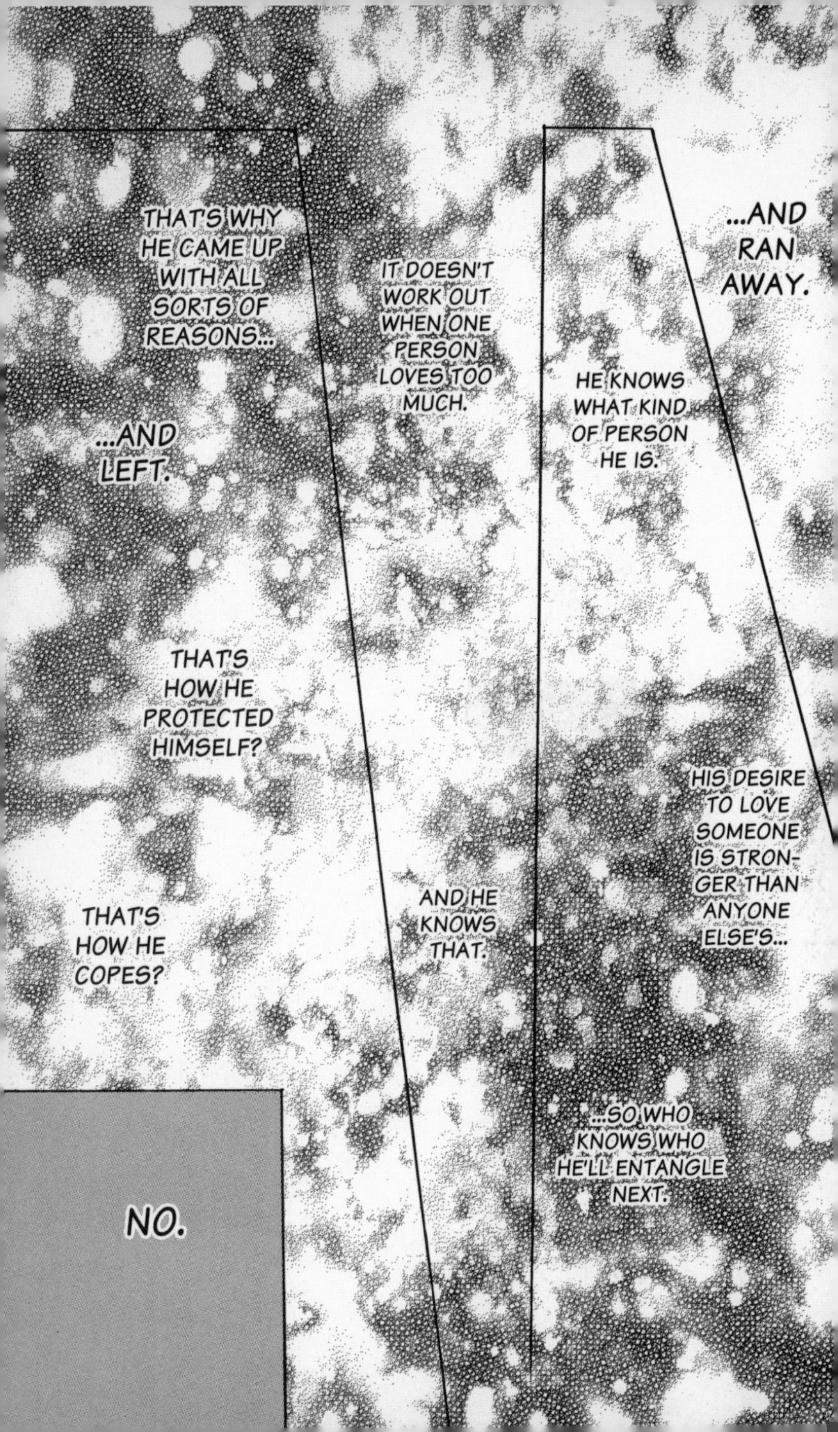
...AND RAN AWAY.
HE KNOWS WHAT KIND OF PERSON HE IS.
HIS DESIRE TO LOVE SOMEONE IS STRONGER THAN ANYONE ELSE'S...
...SO WHO KNOWS WHO HE'LL ENTANGLE NEXT.
IT DOESN'T WORK OUT WHEN ONE PERSON LOVES TOO MUCH.
AND HE KNOWS THAT.
THAT'S WHY HE CAME UP WITH ALL SORTS OF REASONS...
...AND LEFT.
THAT'S HOW HE PROTECTED HIMSELF?
THAT'S HOW HE COPES?
NO.

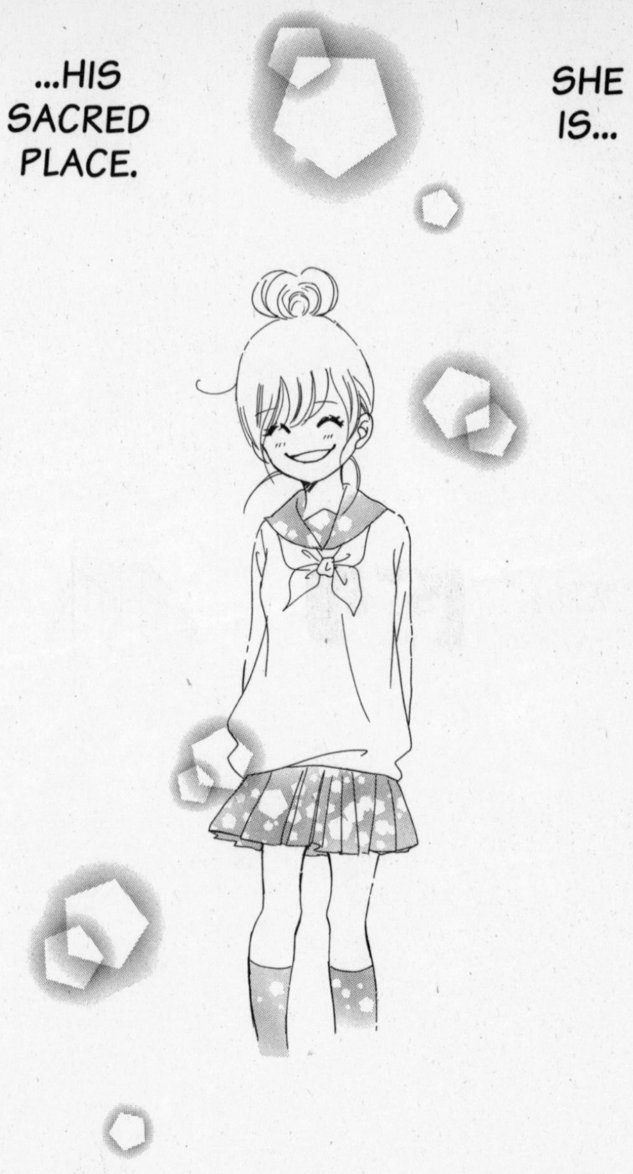
SHE IS...
...HIS SACRED PLACE.

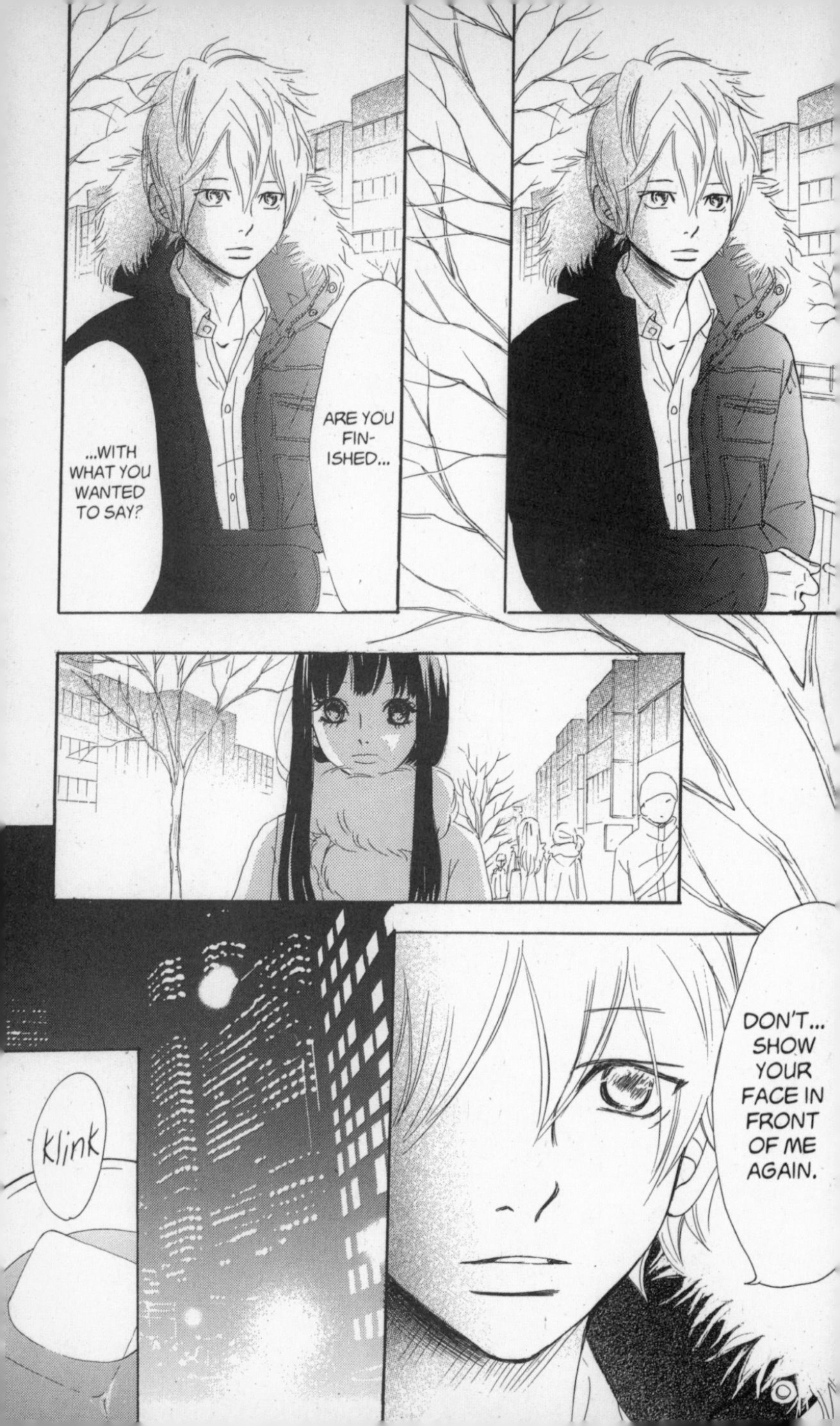
ARE YOU FIN-ISHED...
...WITH WHAT YOU WANTED TO SAY?
DON'T... SHOW YOUR FACE IN FRONT OF ME AGAIN.
klink

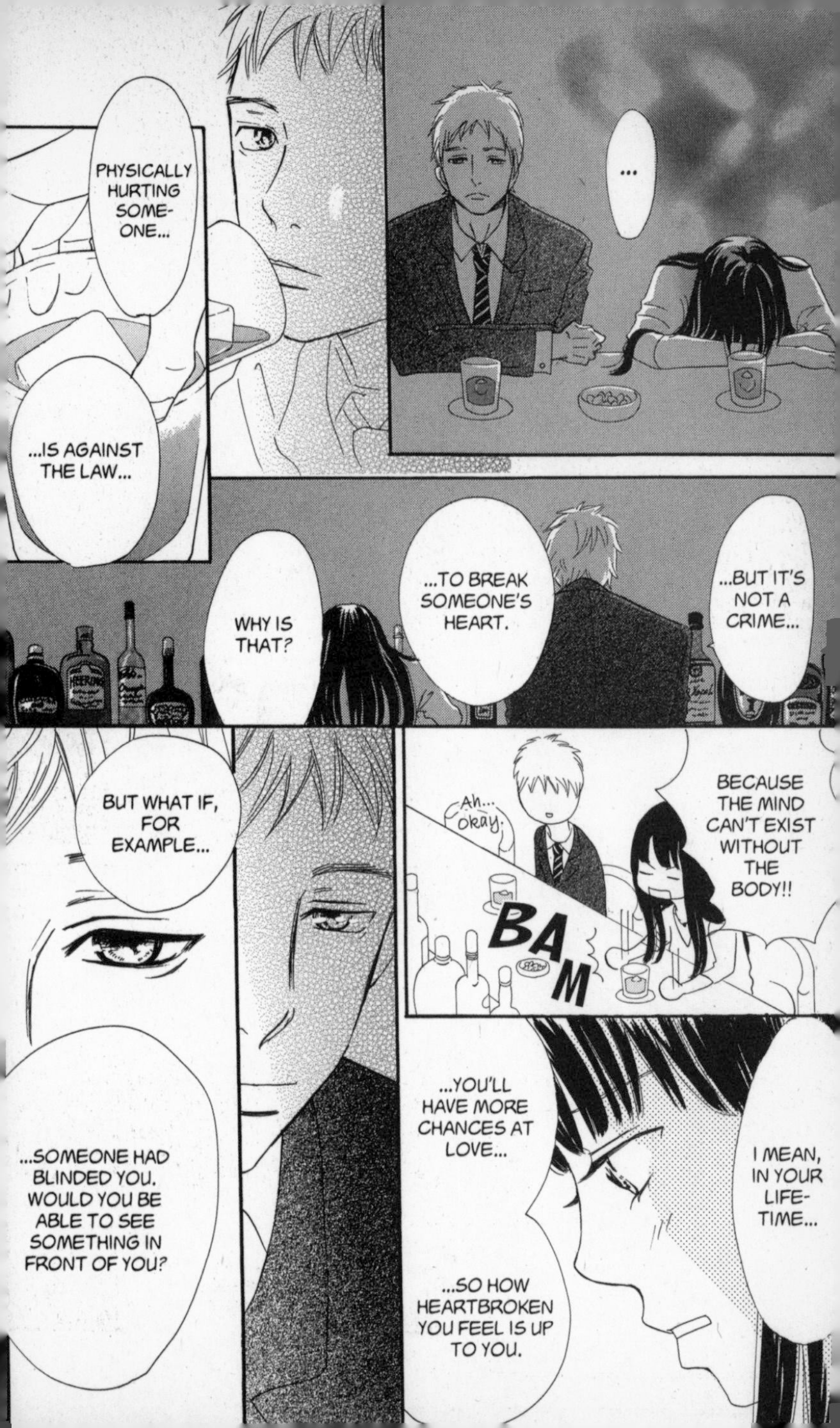
...
PHYSICALLY HURTING SOME-ONE...
...IS AGAINST THE LAW...
...BUT IT'S NOT A CRIME...
...TO BREAK SOMEONE'S HEART.
WHY IS THAT?
BECAUSE THE MIND CAN'T EXIST WITHOUT THE BODY!!
Ah... okay.
BAM
I MEAN, IN YOUR LIFE-TIME...
...YOU'LL HAVE MORE CHANCES AT LOVE...
...SO HOW HEARTBROKEN YOU FEEL IS UP TO YOU.
BUT WHAT IF, FOR EXAMPLE...
...SOMEONE HAD BLINDED YOU. WOULD YOU BE ABLE TO SEE SOMETHING IN FRONT OF YOU?

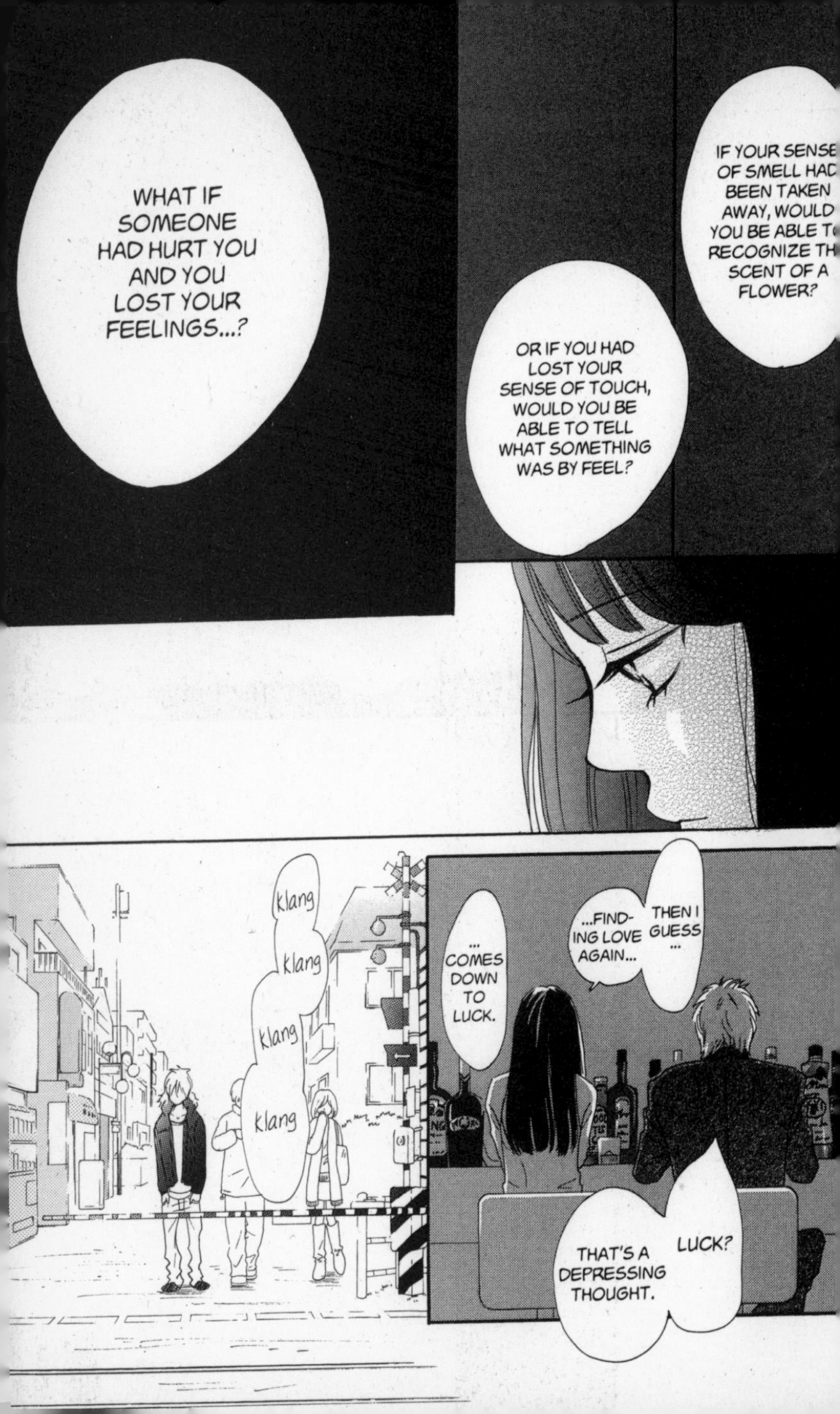
IF YOUR SENSE OF SMELL HAD BEEN TAKEN AWAY, WOULD YOU BE ABLE TO RECOGNIZE THE SCENT OF A FLOWER?
OR IF YOU HAD LOST YOUR SENSE OF TOUCH, WOULD YOU BE ABLE TO TELL WHAT SOMETHING WAS BY FEEL?
WHAT IF SOMEONE HAD HURT YOU AND YOU LOST YOUR FEELINGS...?
THEN I GUESS ...
...FIND-ING LOVE AGAIN...
... COMES DOWN TO LUCK.
LUCK?
THAT'S A DEPRESSING THOUGHT.
klang
klang
klang
klang

MORE THAN ANYTHING ELSE,
YOU MUST HAVE WANTED...

...TO LIVE UP TO NANAMI'S
EXPECTATIONS.

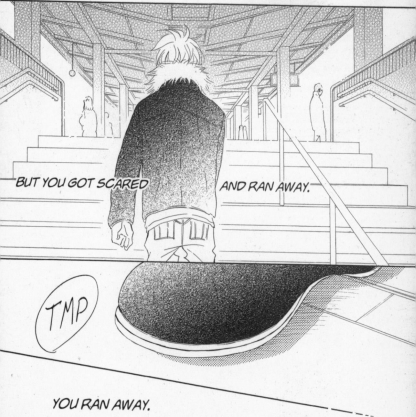

BUT YOU GOT SCARED   AND RAN AWAY.

TMP

YOU RAN AWAY.

HA HA HA
THIS TRAIN WILL BE DEPARTING SHORTLY.
YOU RAN AWAY.
SHOOOON
DASH
VUNK

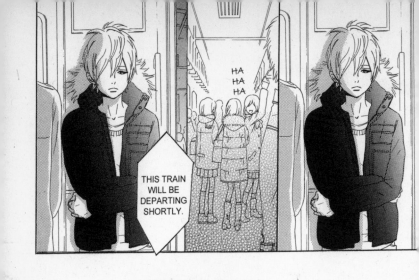

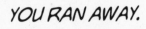

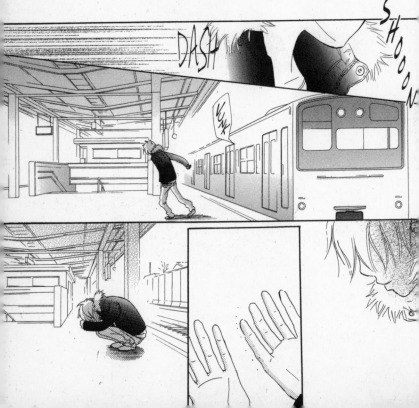

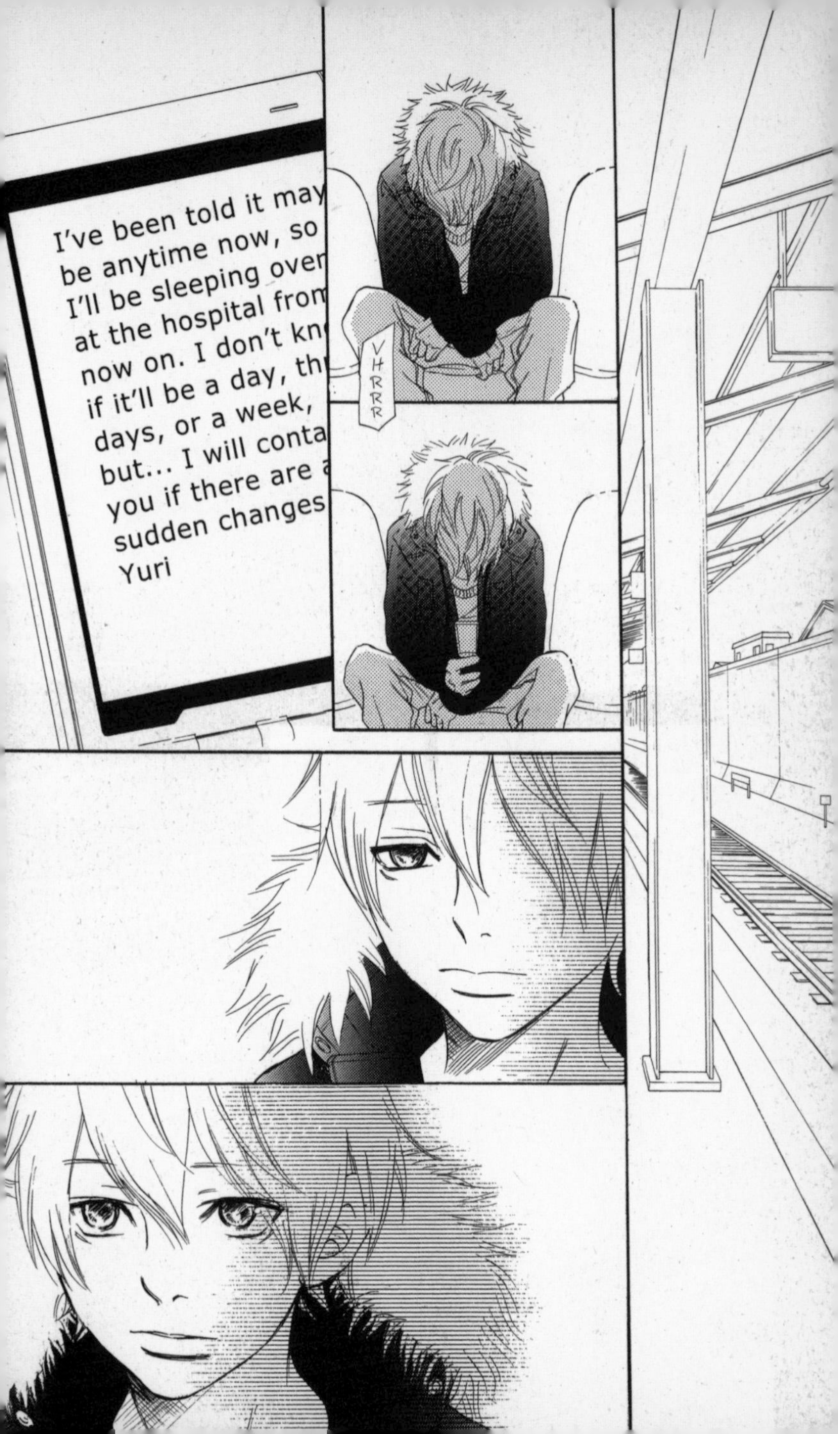
VHRRR
I've been told it may be anytime now, so I'll be sleeping over at the hospital from now on. I don't kn if it'll be a day, th days, or a week, but... I will conta you if there are a sudden changes Yuri

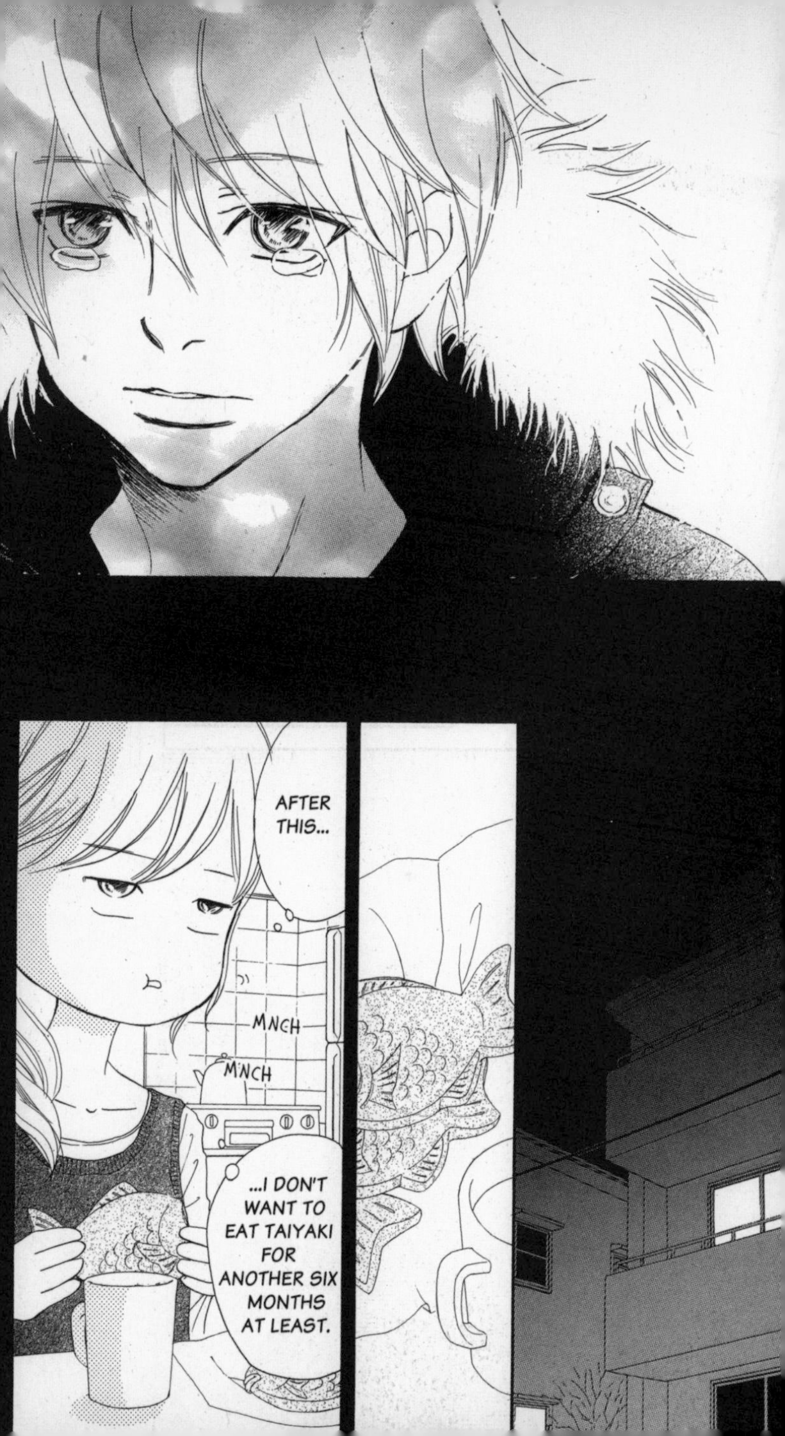
AFTER THIS...
MNCH
MNCH
...I DON'T WANT TO EAT TAIYAKI FOR ANOTHER SIX MONTHS AT LEAST.

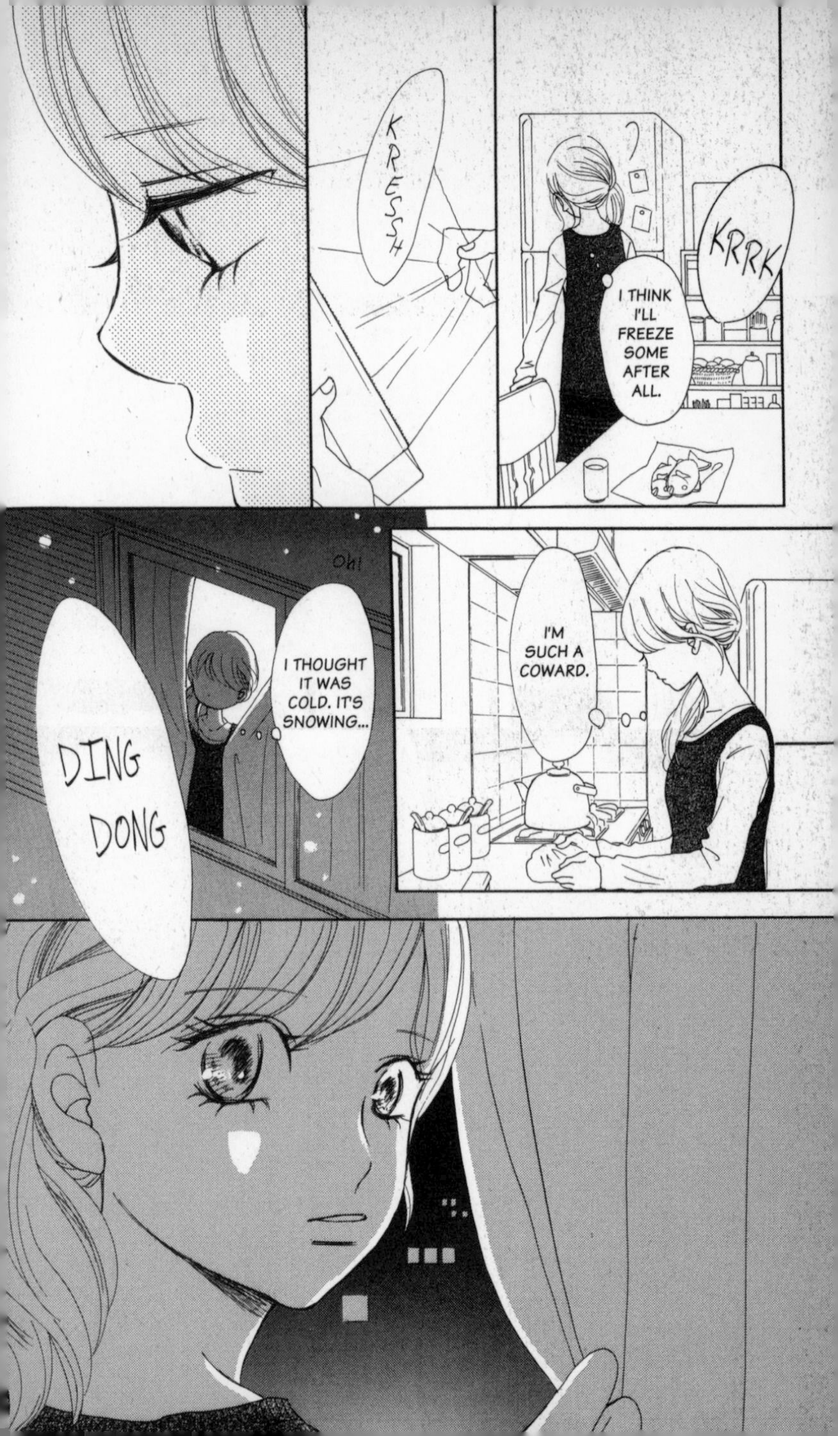
KRRK
I THINK I'LL FREEZE SOME AFTER ALL.
KRESSH
I'M SUCH A COWARD.
Oh!
I THOUGHT IT WAS COLD. IT'S SNOWING...
DING DONG

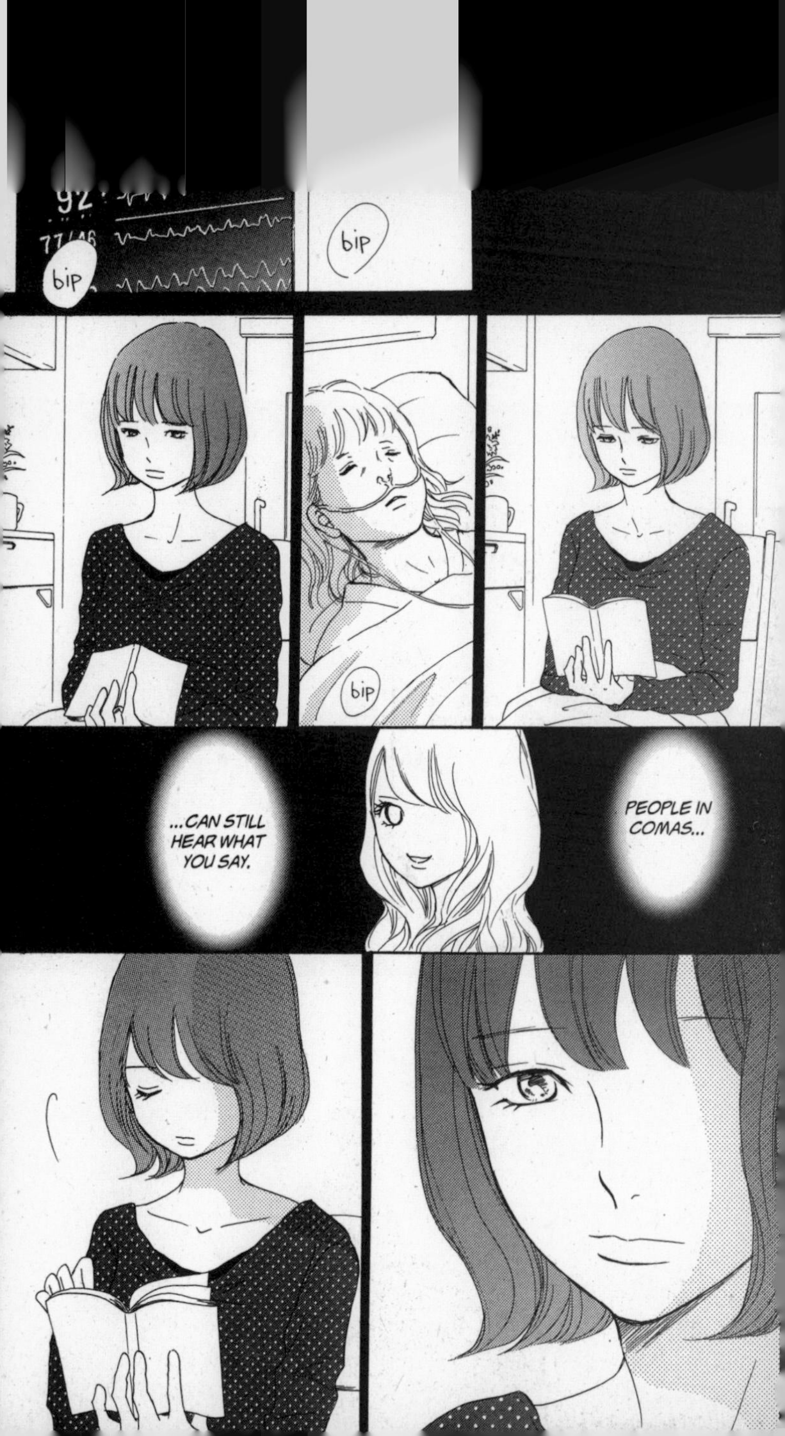
bip
92
77/46
bip
bip
PEOPLE IN COMAS...
...CAN STILL HEAR WHAT YOU SAY.

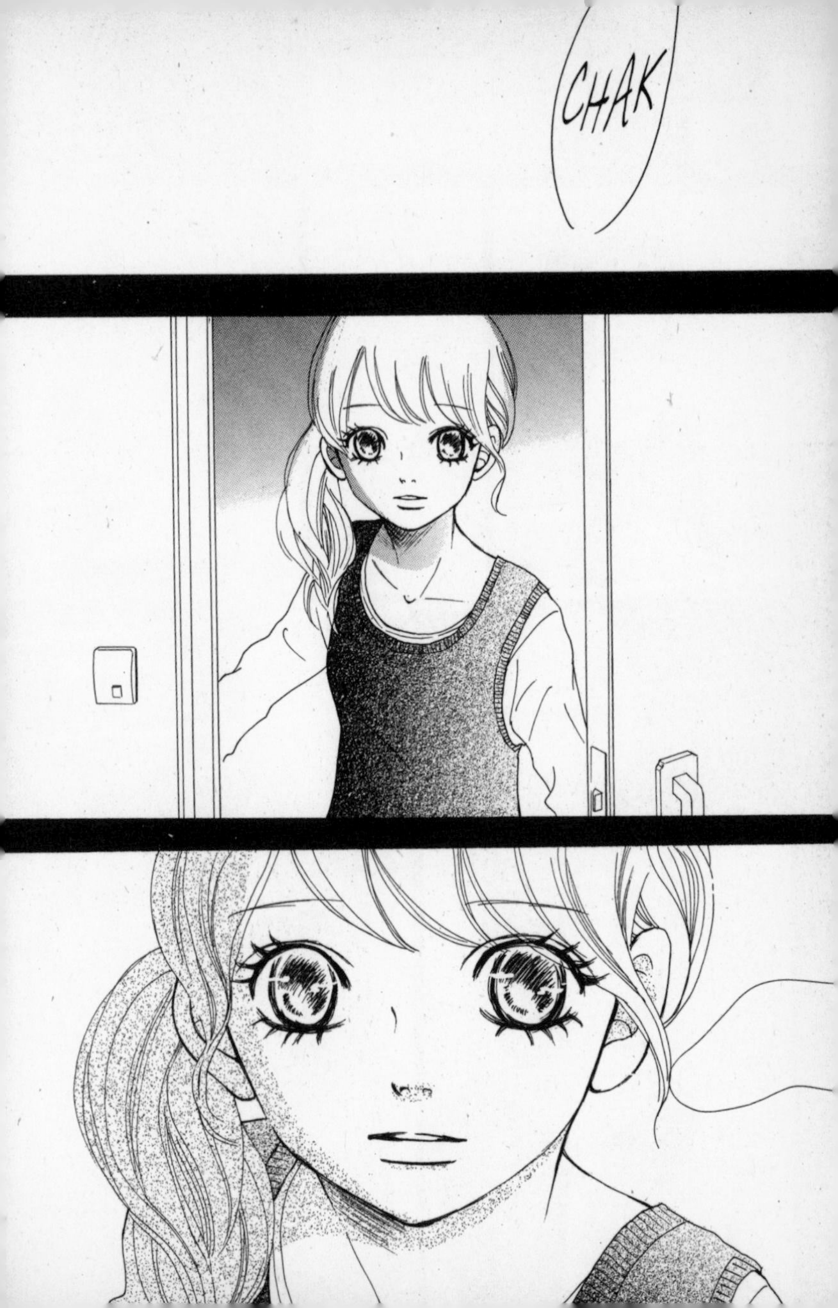
CHAK

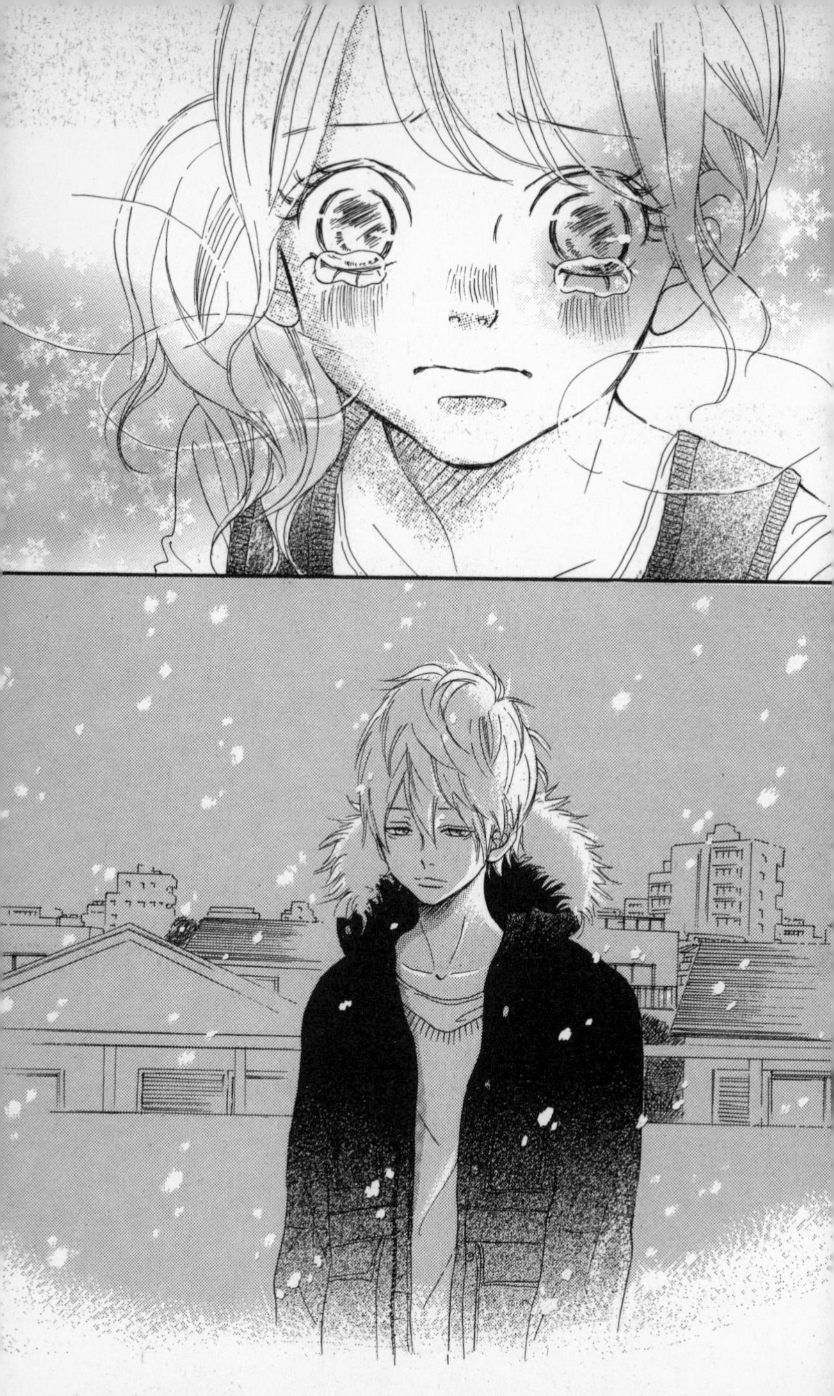

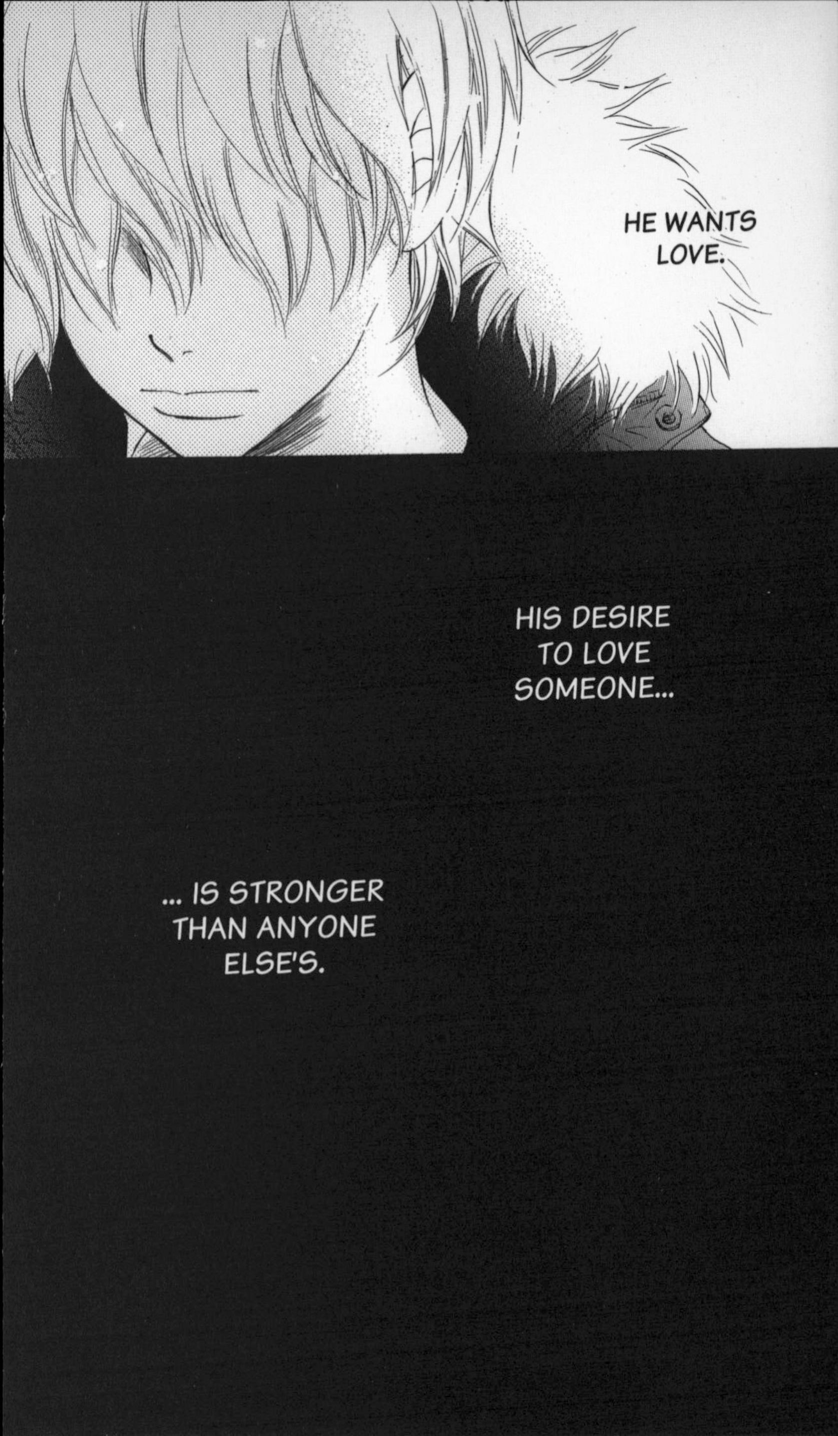
HE WANTS LOVE.
HIS DESIRE TO LOVE SOMEONE...
... IS STRONGER THAN ANYONE ELSE'S.

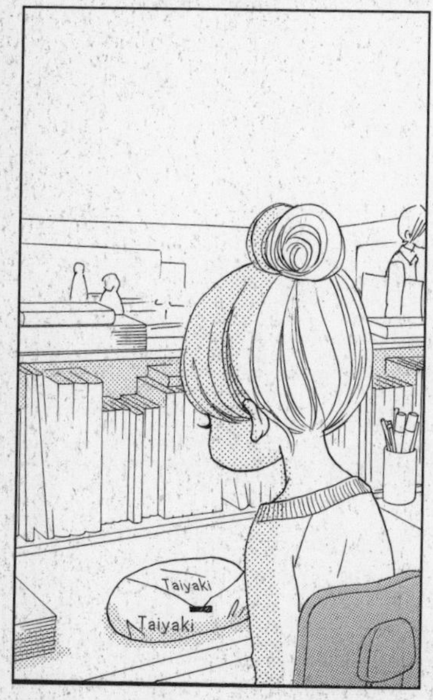
Taiyaki
Taiyaki

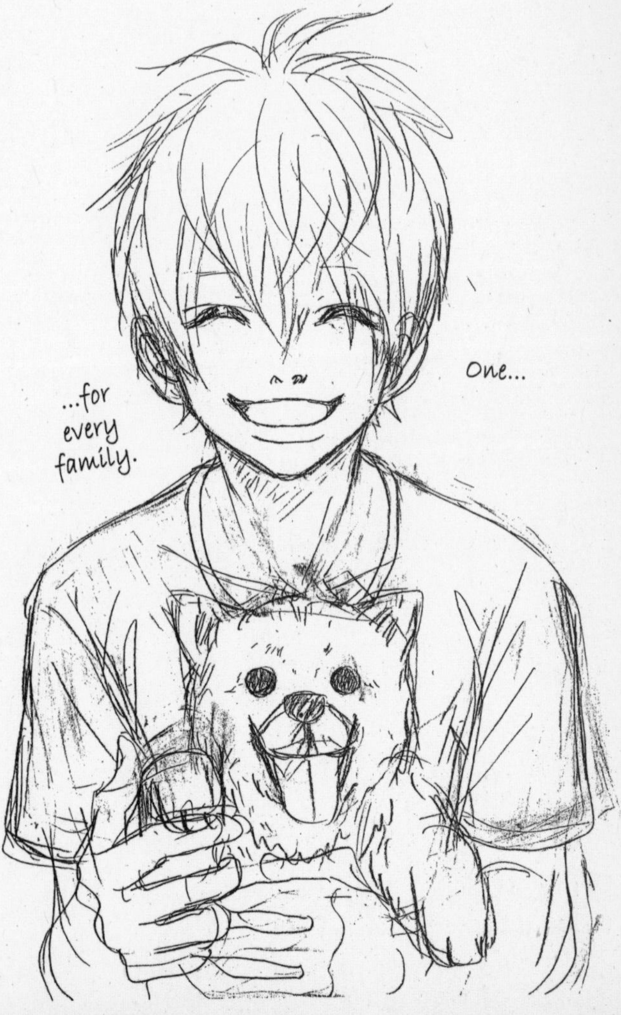
One...
...for every family.

Chapter 63

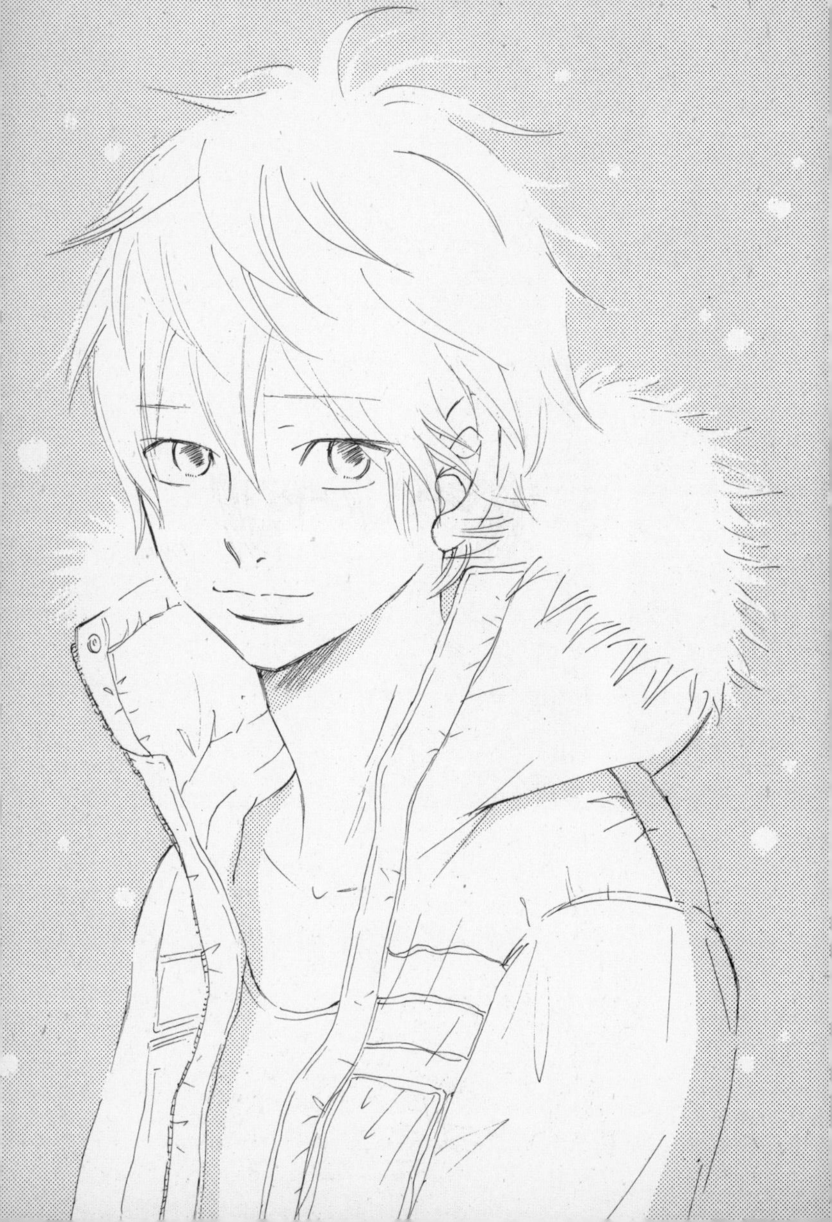

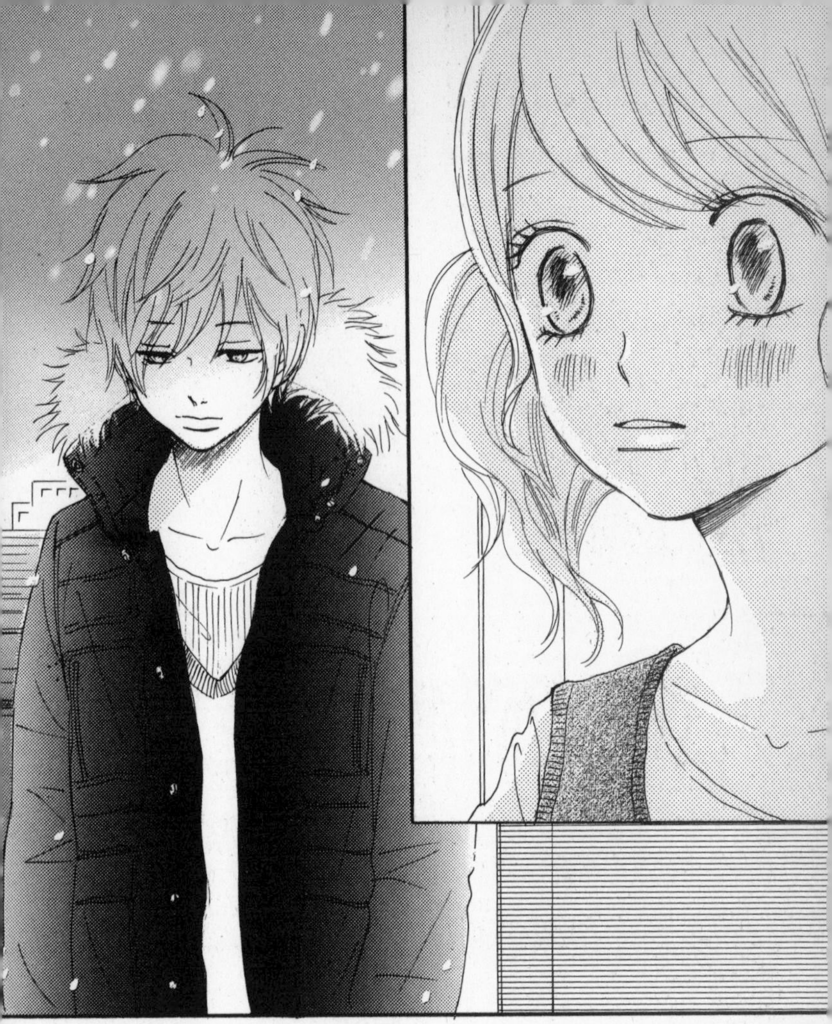

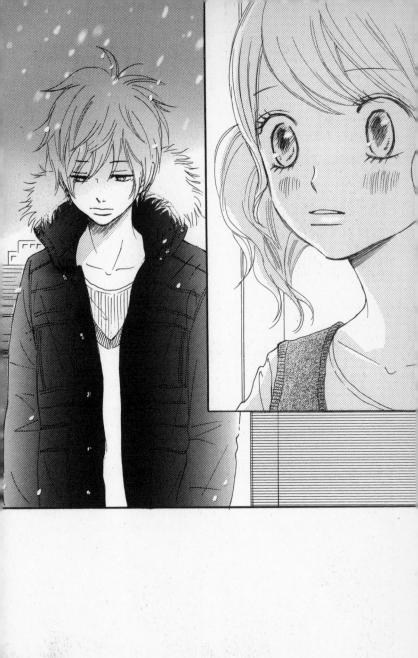

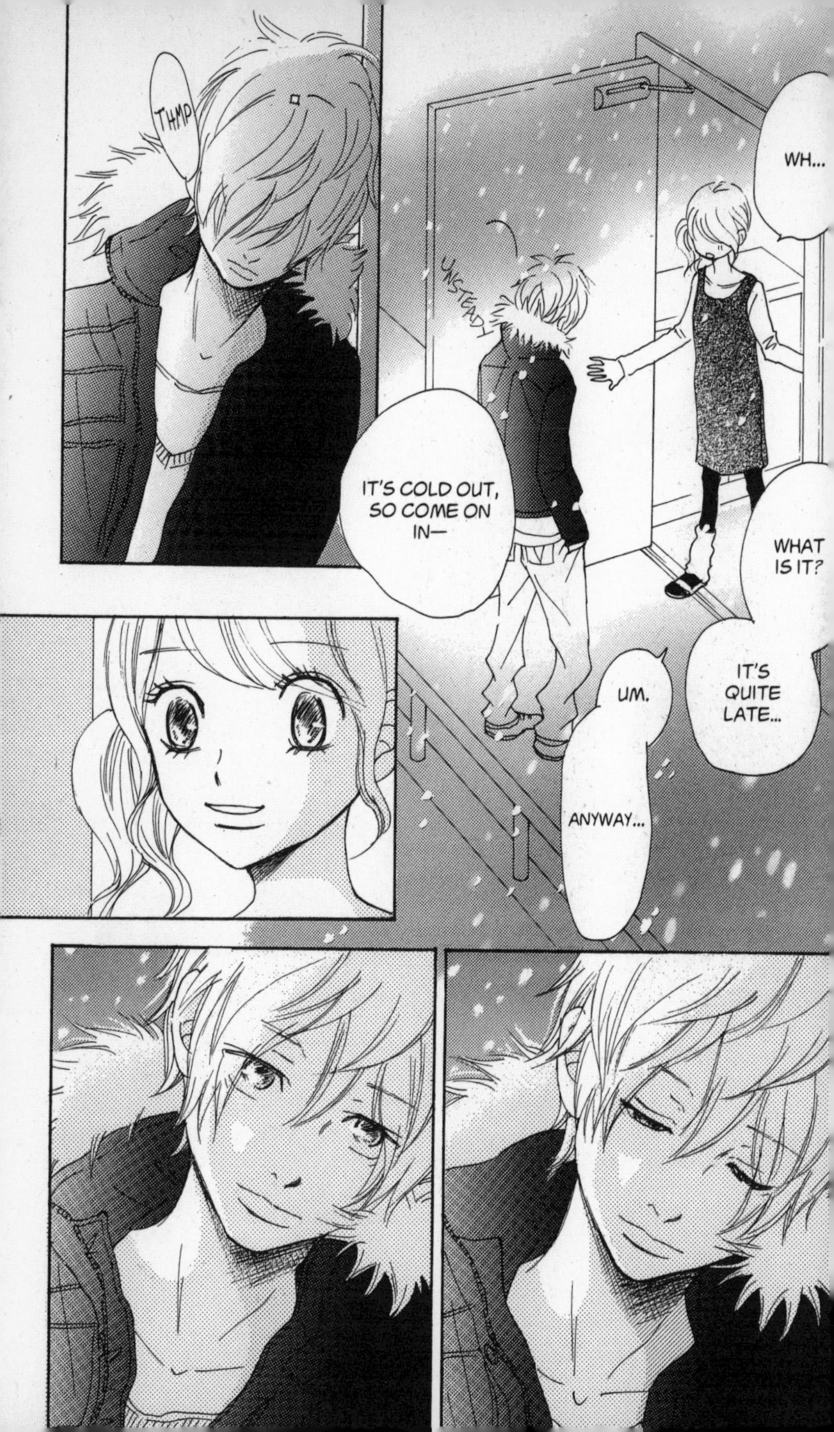
WH...
UNSTEADY
WHAT IS IT?
IT'S COLD OUT, SO COME ON IN—
IT'S QUITE LATE...
UM.
ANYWAY...
THMP

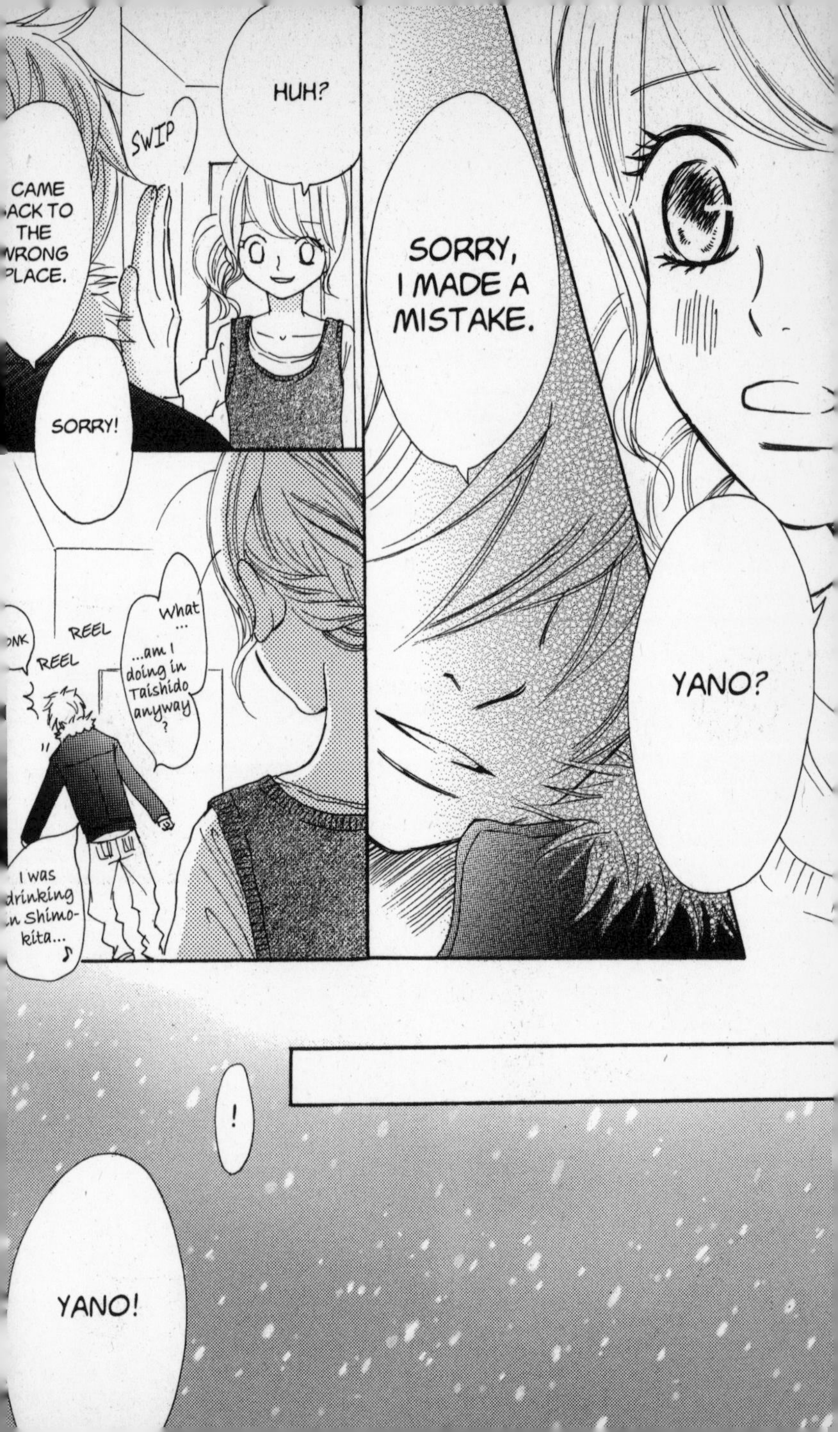
SORRY, I MADE A MISTAKE.
YANO?
HUH?
SWIP
CAME ACK TO THE VRONG PLACE.
SORRY!
What... ...am I doing in Taishido anyway?
REEL
ONK
REEL
I was drinking n Shimo-kita... ♪
!
YANO!

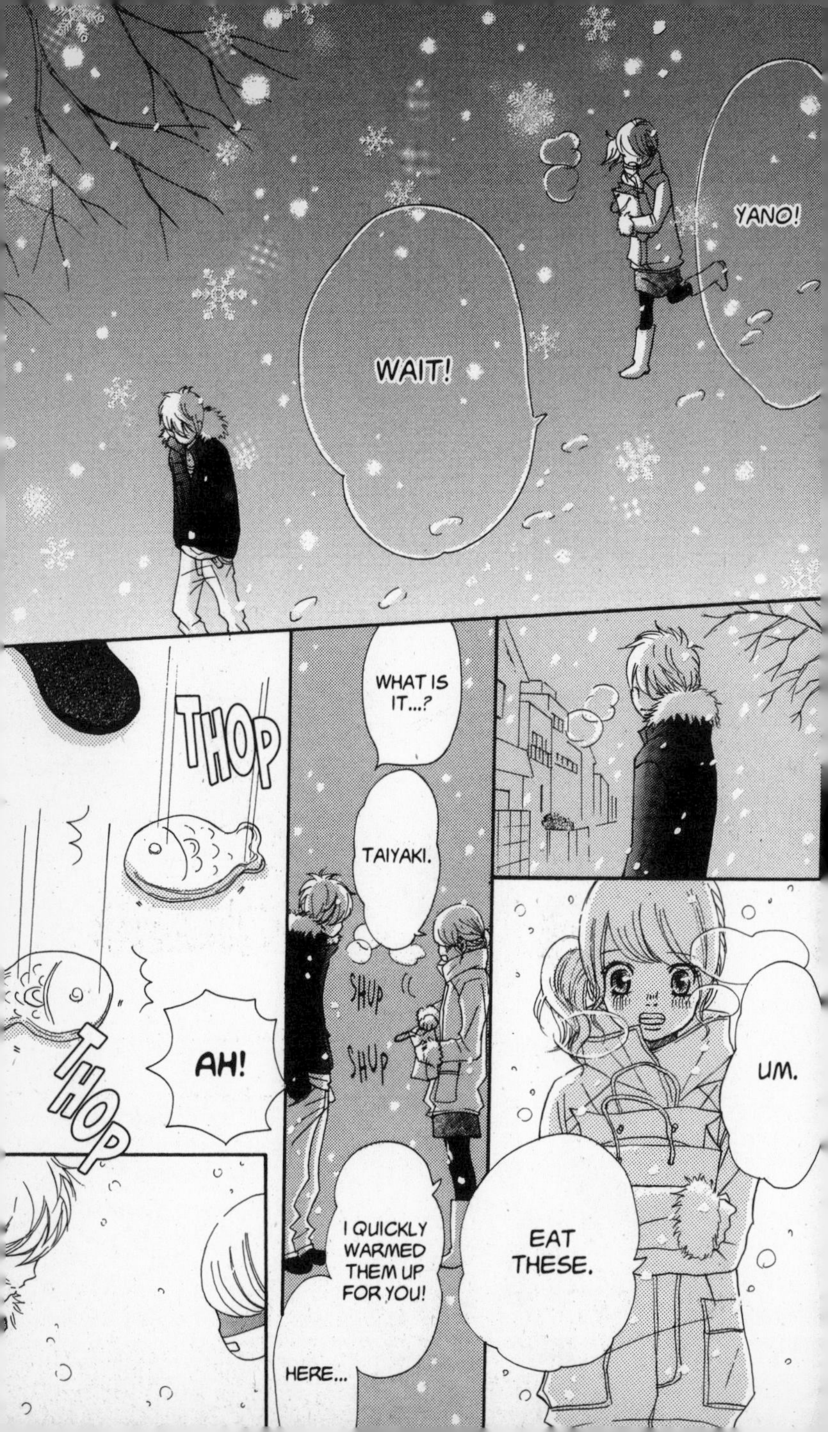
YANO!
WAIT!
UM.
EAT THESE.
WHAT IS IT...?
TAIYAKI.
SHUP
SHUP
I QUICKLY WARMED THEM UP FOR YOU!
HERE...
THOP
THOP
AH!

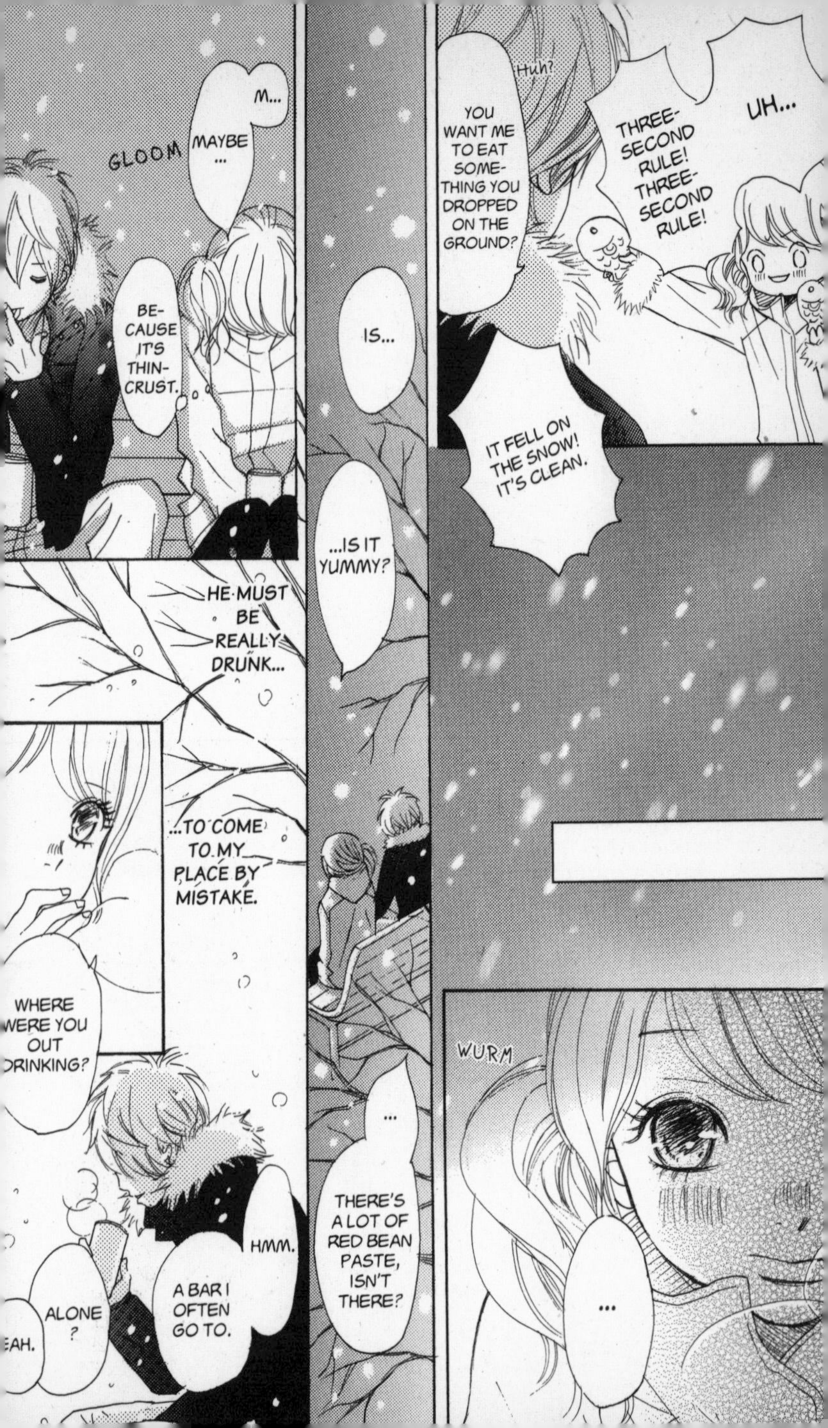
UH...
THREE-SECOND RULE! THREE-SECOND RULE!
Huh?
YOU WANT ME TO EAT SOME-THING YOU DROPPED ON THE GROUND?
IT FELL ON THE SNOW! IT'S CLEAN.
WURM
...
IS...
...IS IT YUMMY?
...
THERE'S A LOT OF RED BEAN PASTE, ISN'T THERE?
M...
MAYBE ...
GLOOM
BE-CAUSE IT'S THIN-CRUST.
HE MUST BE REALLY DRUNK...
...TO COME TO MY PLACE BY MISTAKE.
WHERE WERE YOU OUT DRINKING?
HMM.
A BAR I OFTEN GO TO.
ALONE?
EAH.

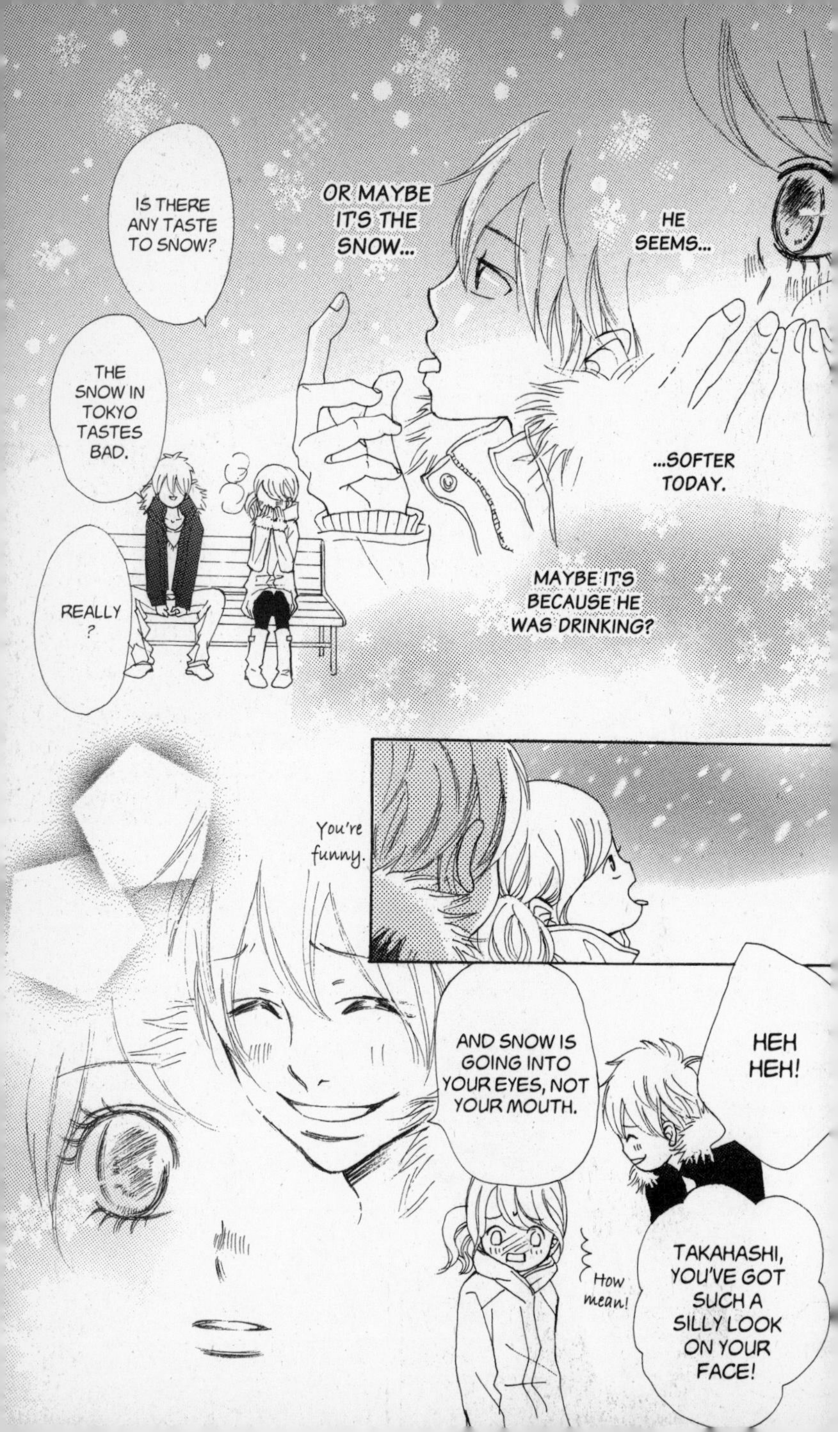
HE SEEMS...
...SOFTER TODAY.
MAYBE IT'S BECAUSE HE WAS DRINKING?
OR MAYBE IT'S THE SNOW...
IS THERE ANY TASTE TO SNOW?
THE SNOW IN TOKYO TASTES BAD.
REALLY?
HEH HEH!
TAKAHASHI, YOU'VE GOT SUCH A SILLY LOOK ON YOUR FACE!
How mean!
AND SNOW IS GOING INTO YOUR EYES, NOT YOUR MOUTH.
You're funny.

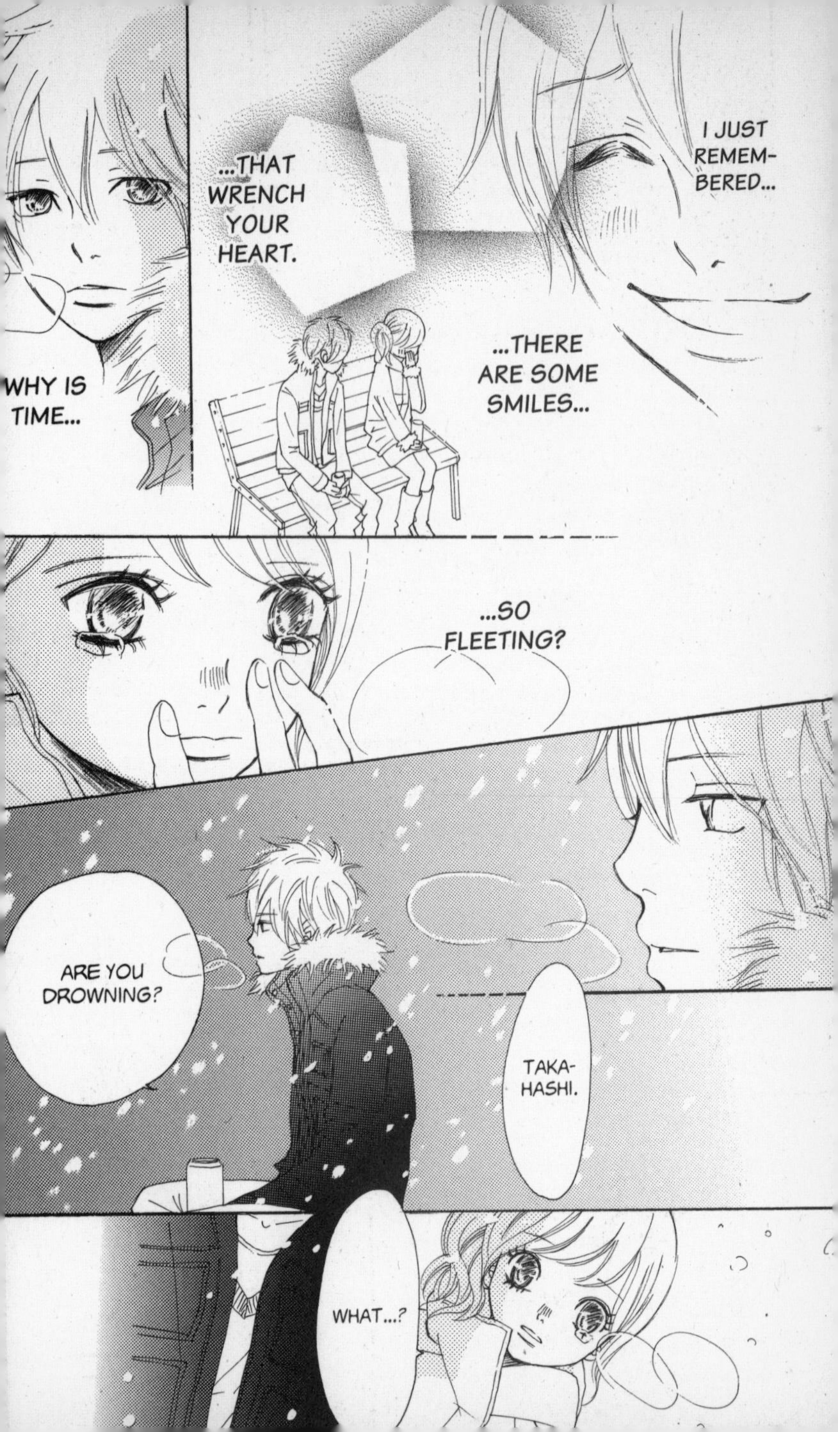
I JUST REMEMBERED...
...THERE ARE SOME SMILES...
...THAT WRENCH YOUR HEART.
WHY IS TIME...
...SO FLEETING?
TAKAHASHI.
ARE YOU DROWNING?
WHAT...?

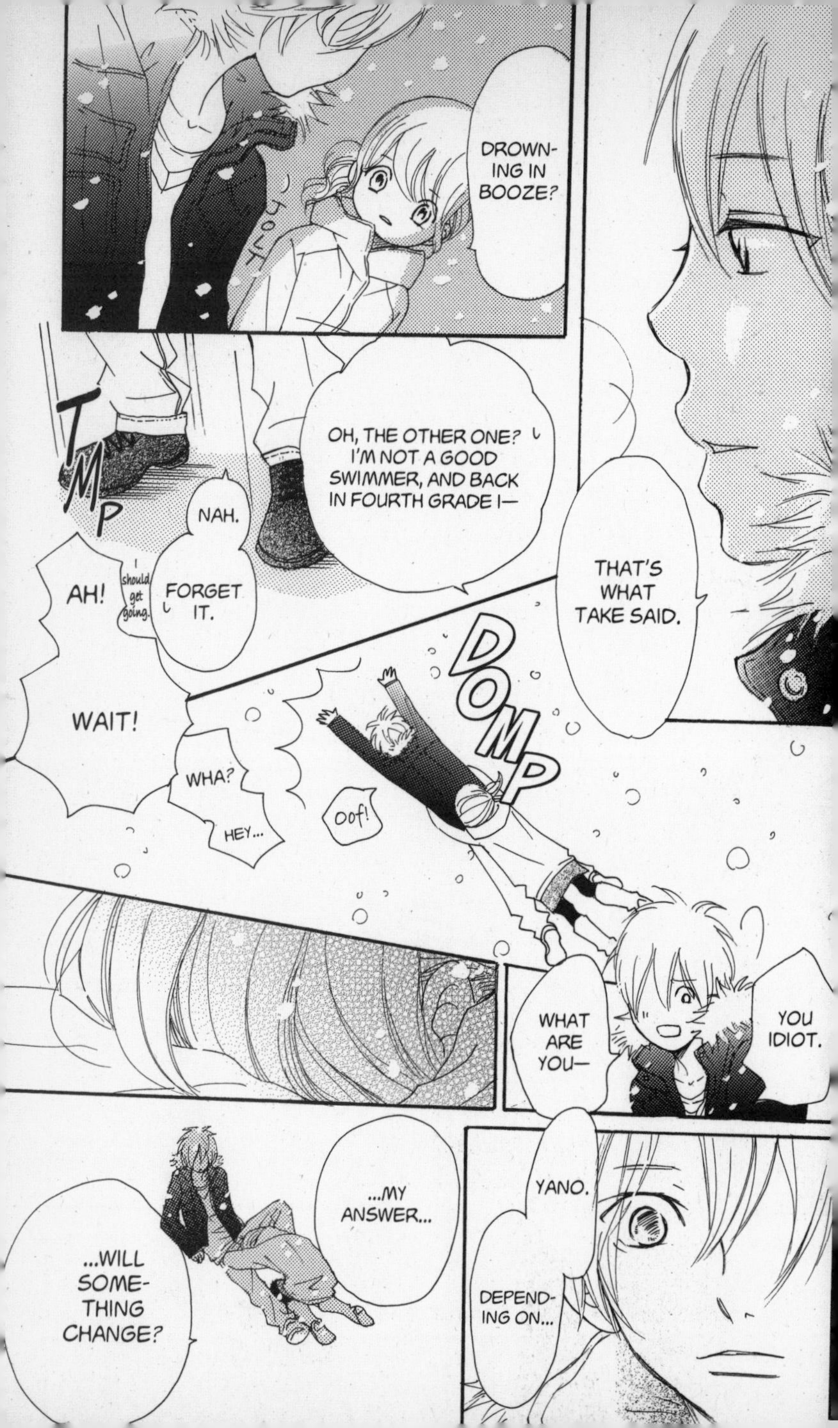
THAT'S WHAT TAKE SAID.
DROWNING-ING IN BOOZE?
JOLT
OH, THE OTHER ONE? I'M NOT A GOOD SWIMMER, AND BACK IN FOURTH GRADE I—
NAH. FORGET IT.
I should get going.
TMP
AH!
WAIT!
DOMP
Oof!
WHA?
HEY...
WHAT ARE YOU—
YOU IDIOT.
YANO.
DEPENDING ON...
...MY ANSWER...
...WILL SOMETHING CHANGE?

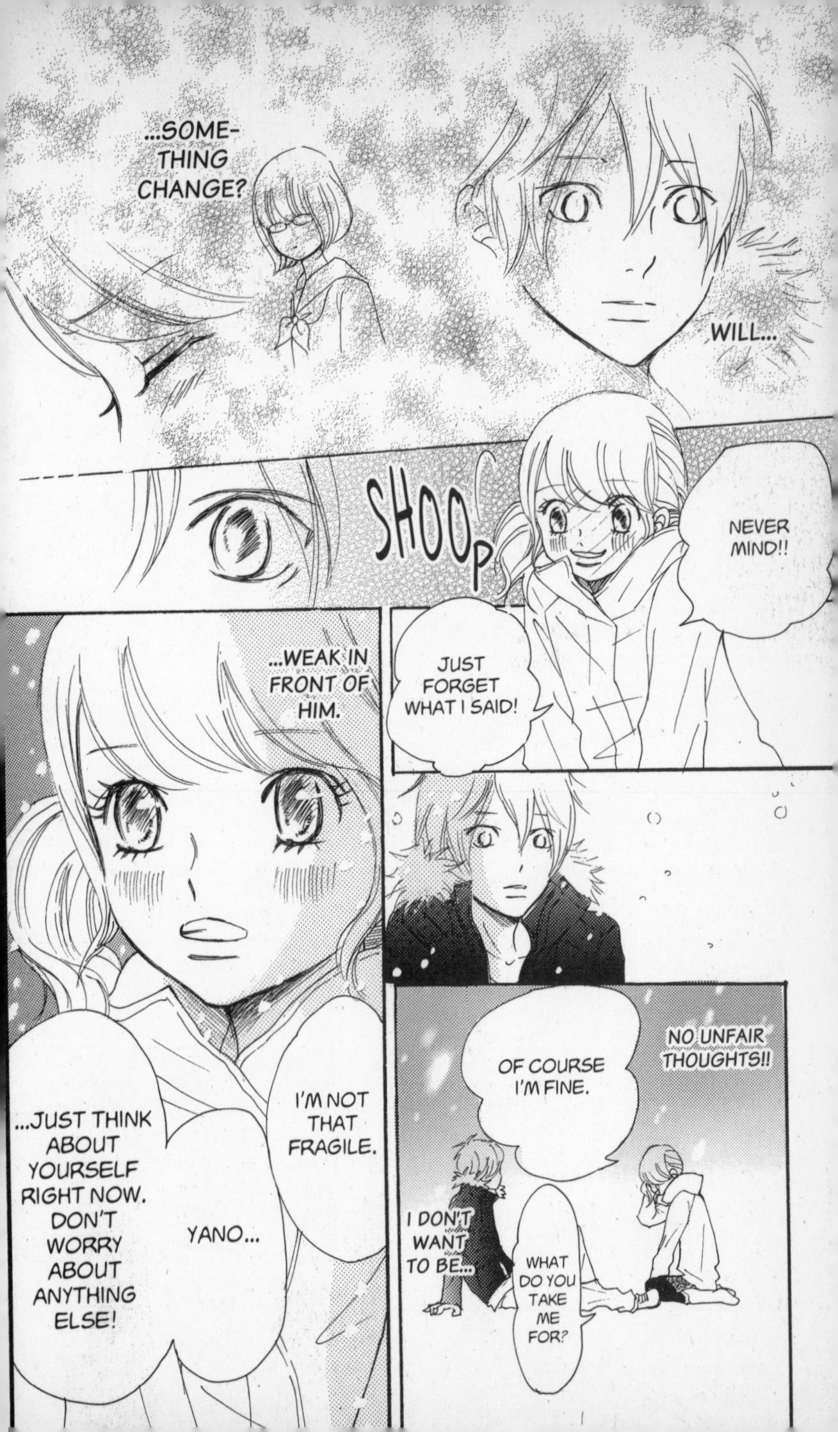
WILL...
...SOMETHING CHANGE?
NEVER MIND!!
SHOOP
JUST FORGET WHAT I SAID!
NO UNFAIR THOUGHTS!!
OF COURSE I'M FINE.
WHAT DO YOU TAKE ME FOR?
I DON'T WANT TO BE...
...WEAK IN FRONT OF HIM.
I'M NOT THAT FRAGILE.
YANO...
...JUST THINK ABOUT YOURSELF RIGHT NOW. DON'T WORRY ABOUT ANYTHING ELSE!

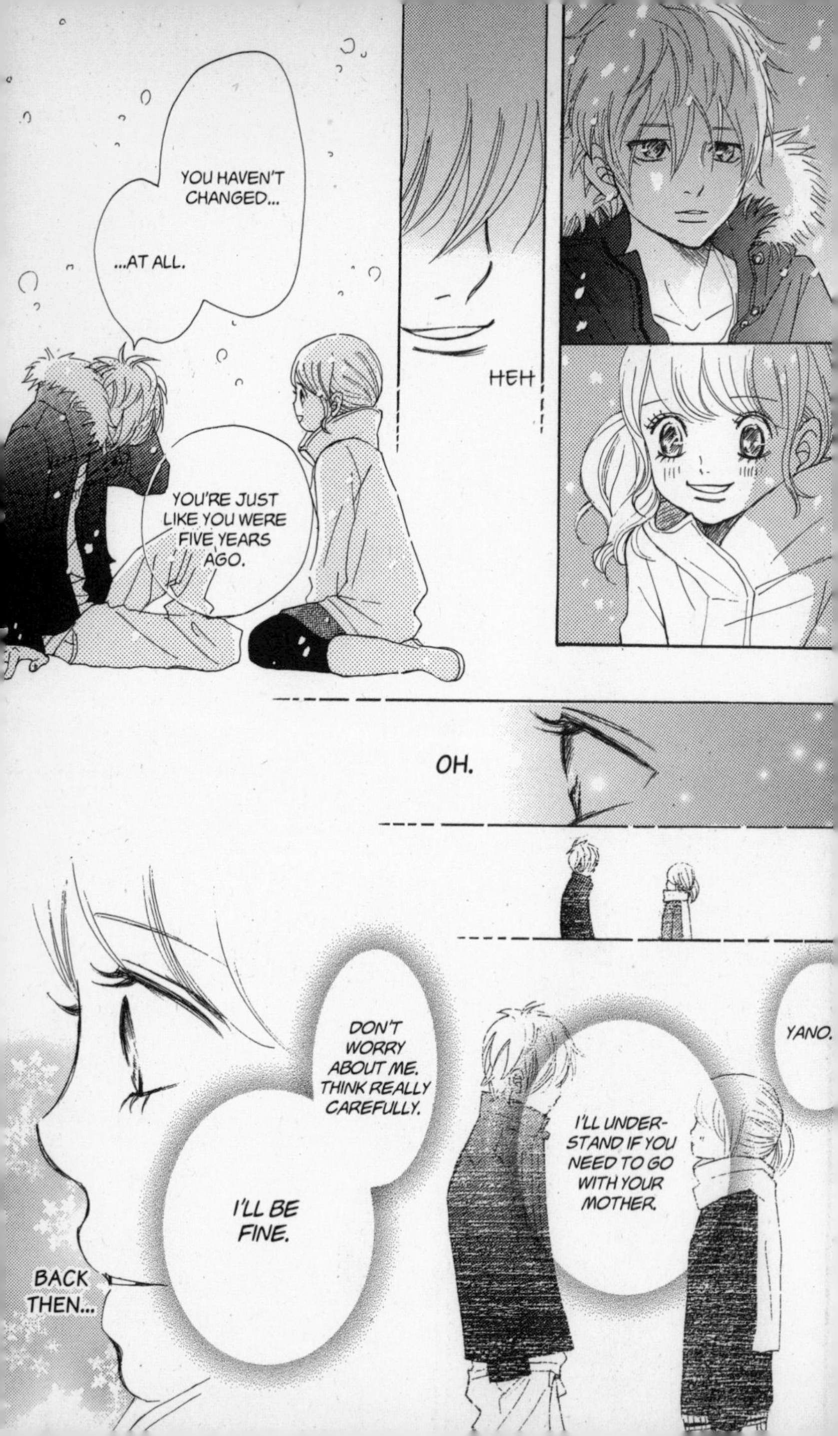
HEH
YOU HAVEN'T CHANGED...
...AT ALL.
YOU'RE JUST LIKE YOU WERE FIVE YEARS AGO.
OH.
YANO.
I'LL UNDER-STAND IF YOU NEED TO GO WITH YOUR MOTHER.
DON'T WORRY ABOUT ME. THINK REALLY CAREFULLY.
I'LL BE FINE.
BACK THEN...

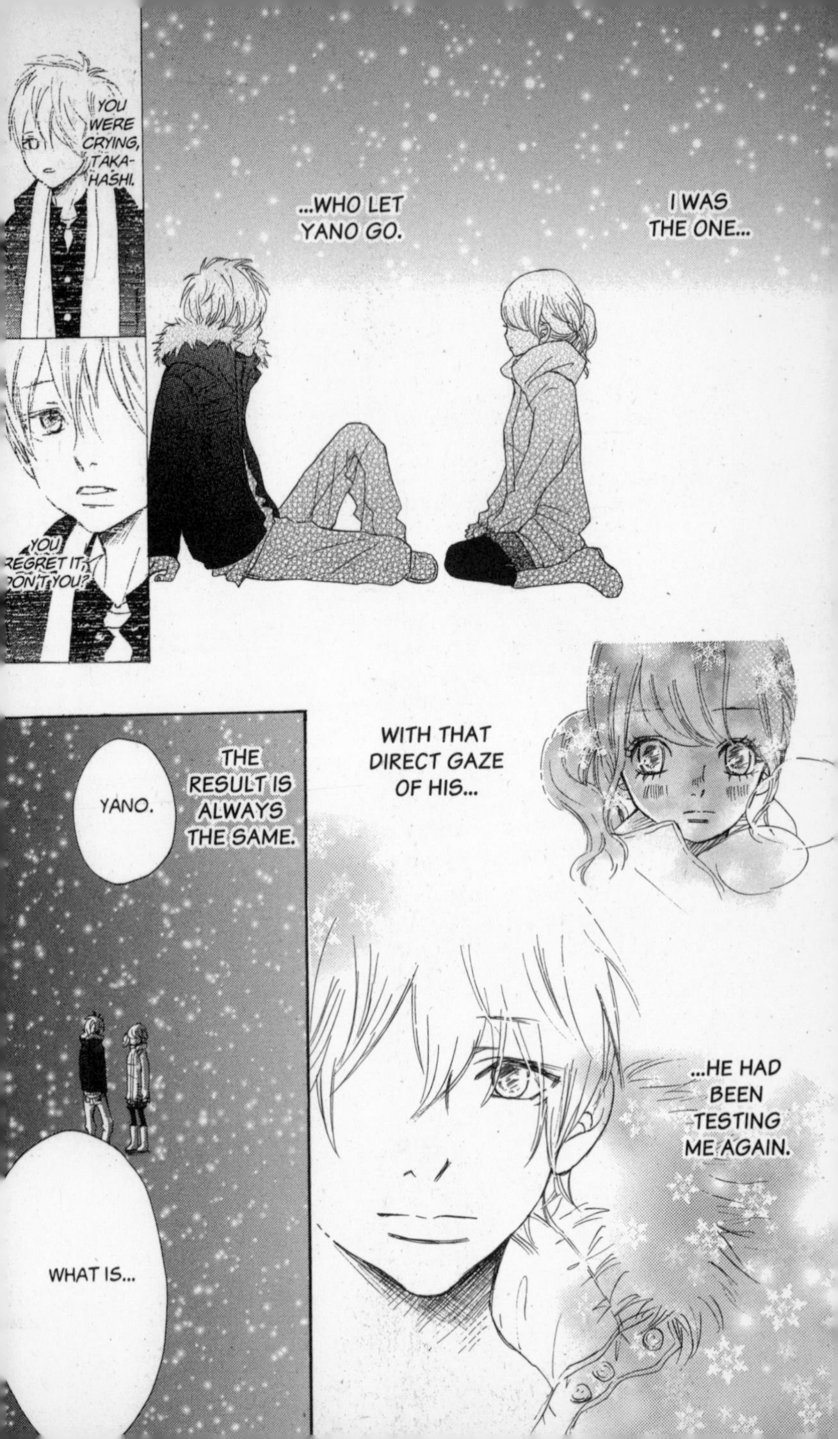
I WAS THE ONE...
...WHO LET YANO GO.
YOU WERE CRYING, TAKAHASHI.
YOU REGRET IT, DON'T YOU?
WITH THAT DIRECT GAZE OF HIS...
...HE HAD BEEN TESTING ME AGAIN.
THE RESULT IS ALWAYS THE SAME.
YANO.
WHAT IS...

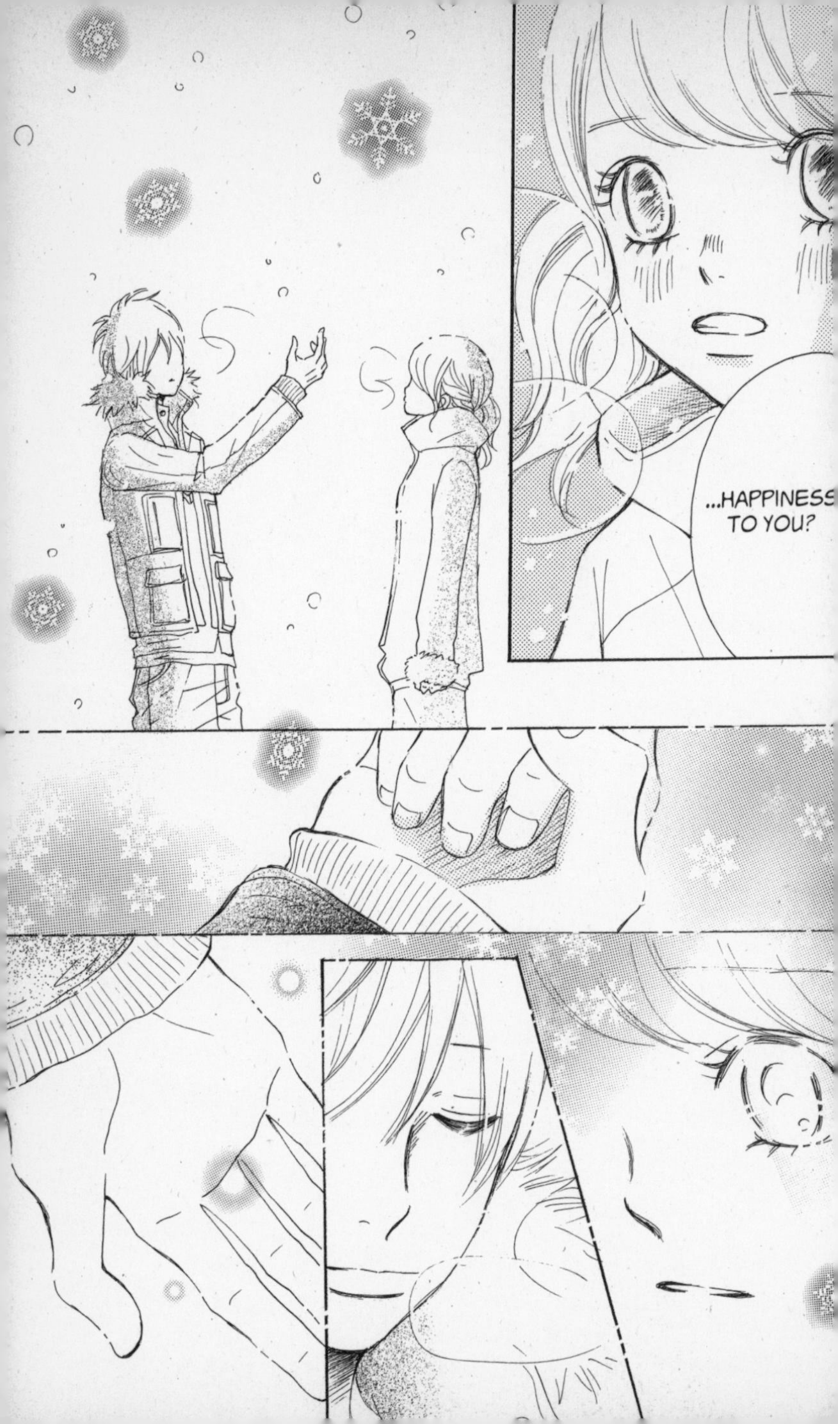
...HAPPINESS TO YOU?

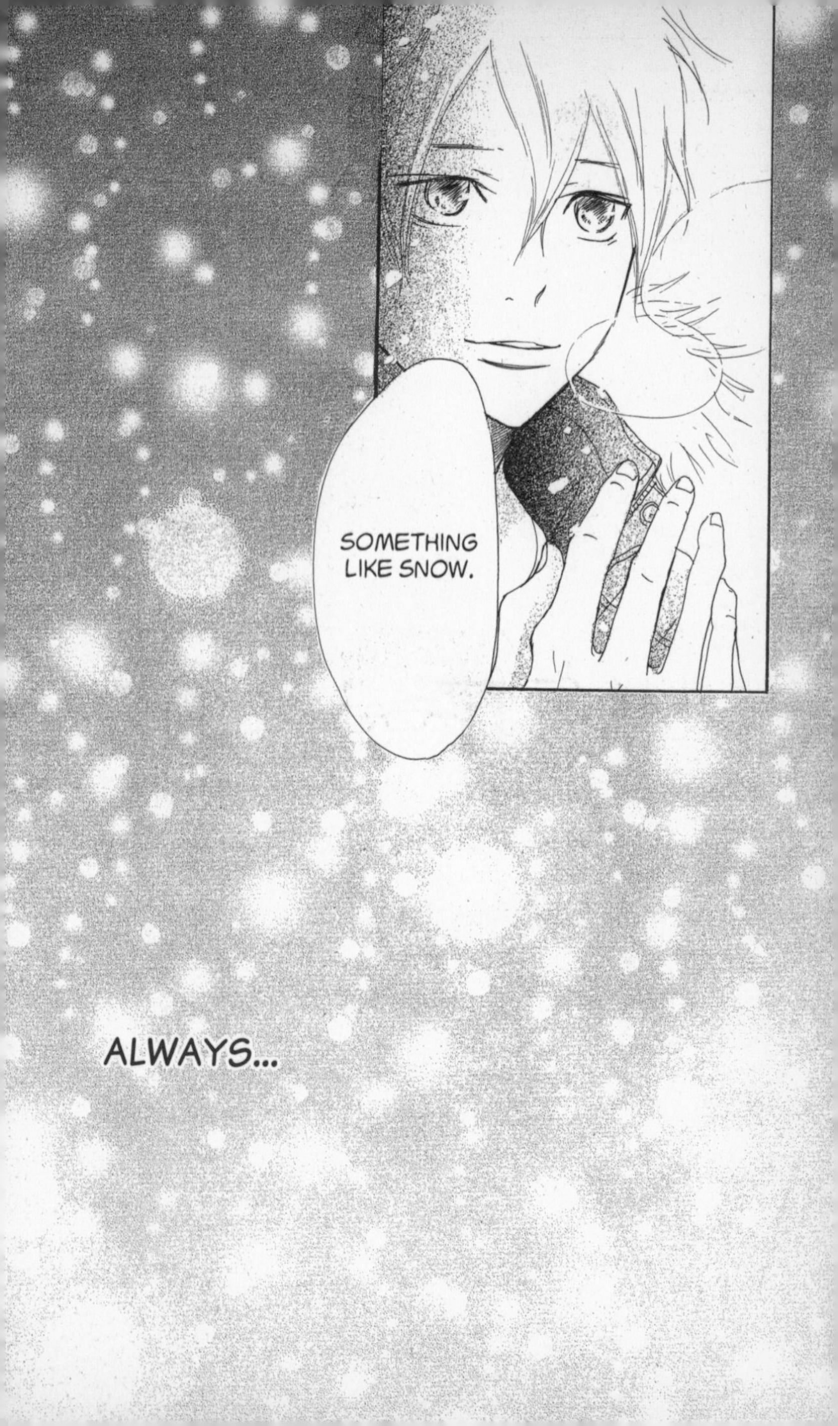
SOMETHING LIKE SNOW.
ALWAYS...

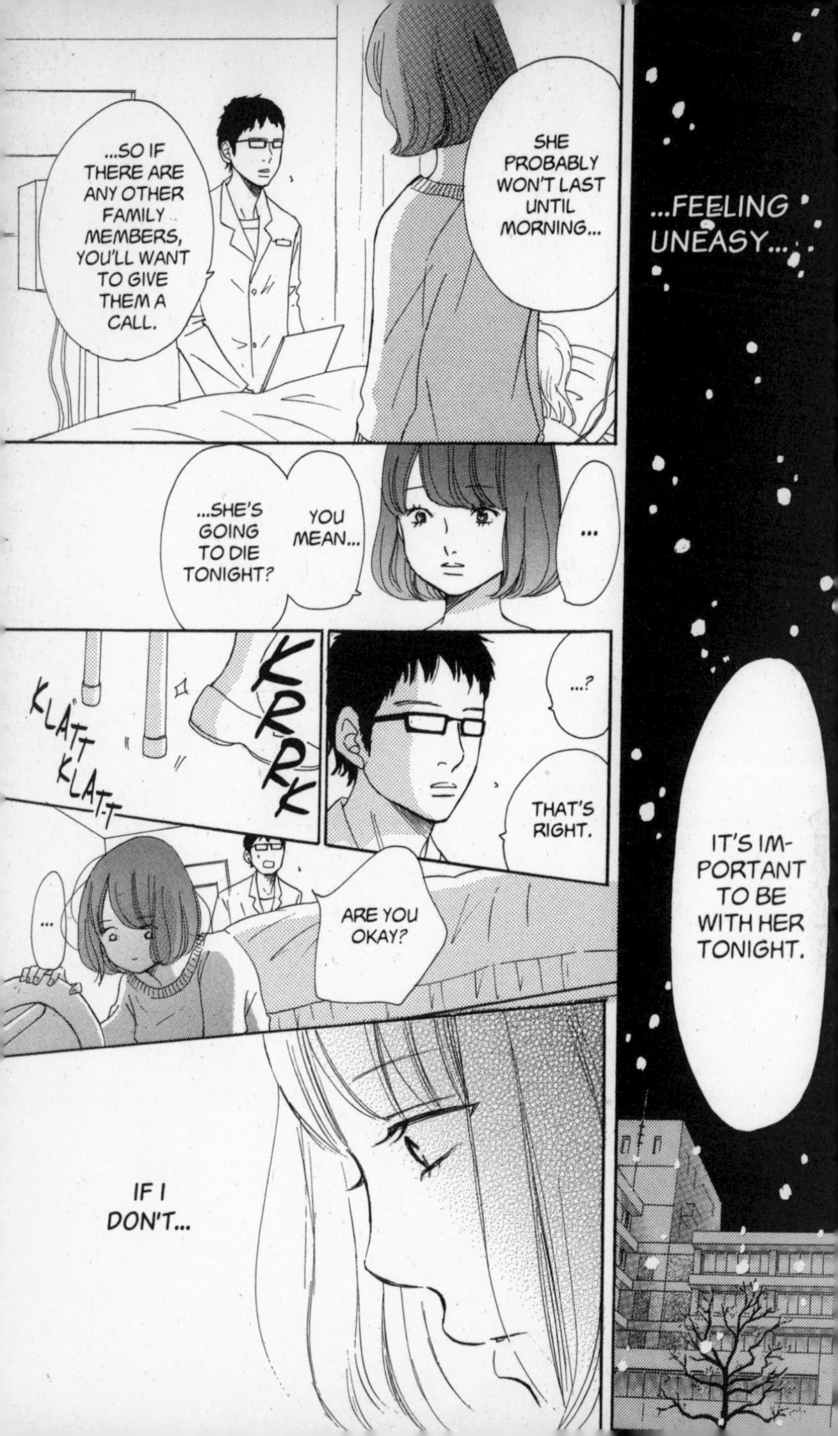
...FEELING UNEASY...
IT'S IMPORTANT TO BE WITH HER TONIGHT.
SHE PROBABLY WON'T LAST UNTIL MORNING...
...SO IF THERE ARE ANY OTHER FAMILY MEMBERS, YOU'LL WANT TO GIVE THEM A CALL.
...
YOU MEAN...
...SHE'S GOING TO DIE TONIGHT?
...?
THAT'S RIGHT.
KRRK
KLATT KLATT
ARE YOU OKAY?
...
IF I DON'T...

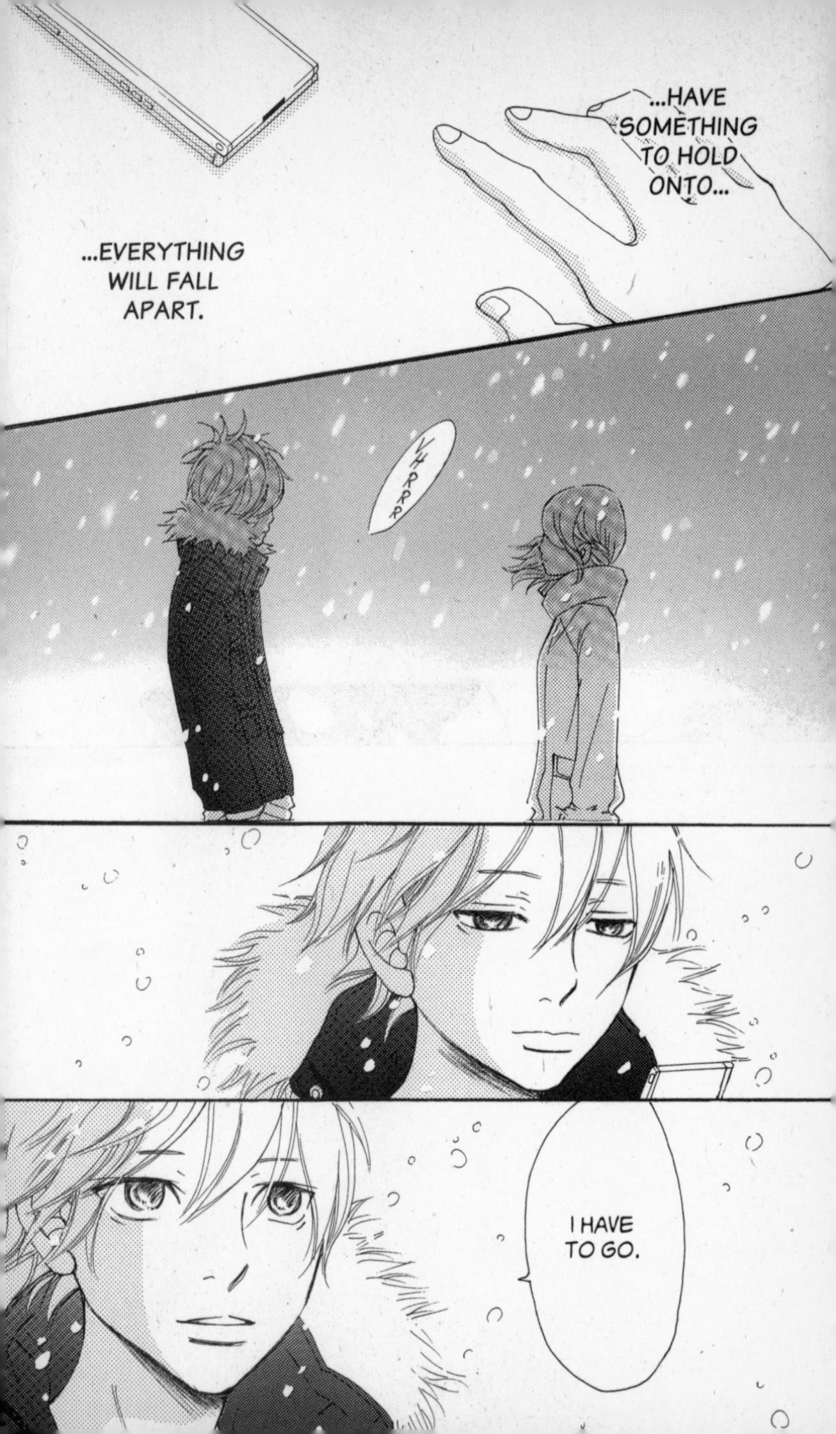
...HAVE SOMETHING TO HOLD ONTO...
...EVERYTHING WILL FALL APART.
VHRRR
I HAVE TO GO.

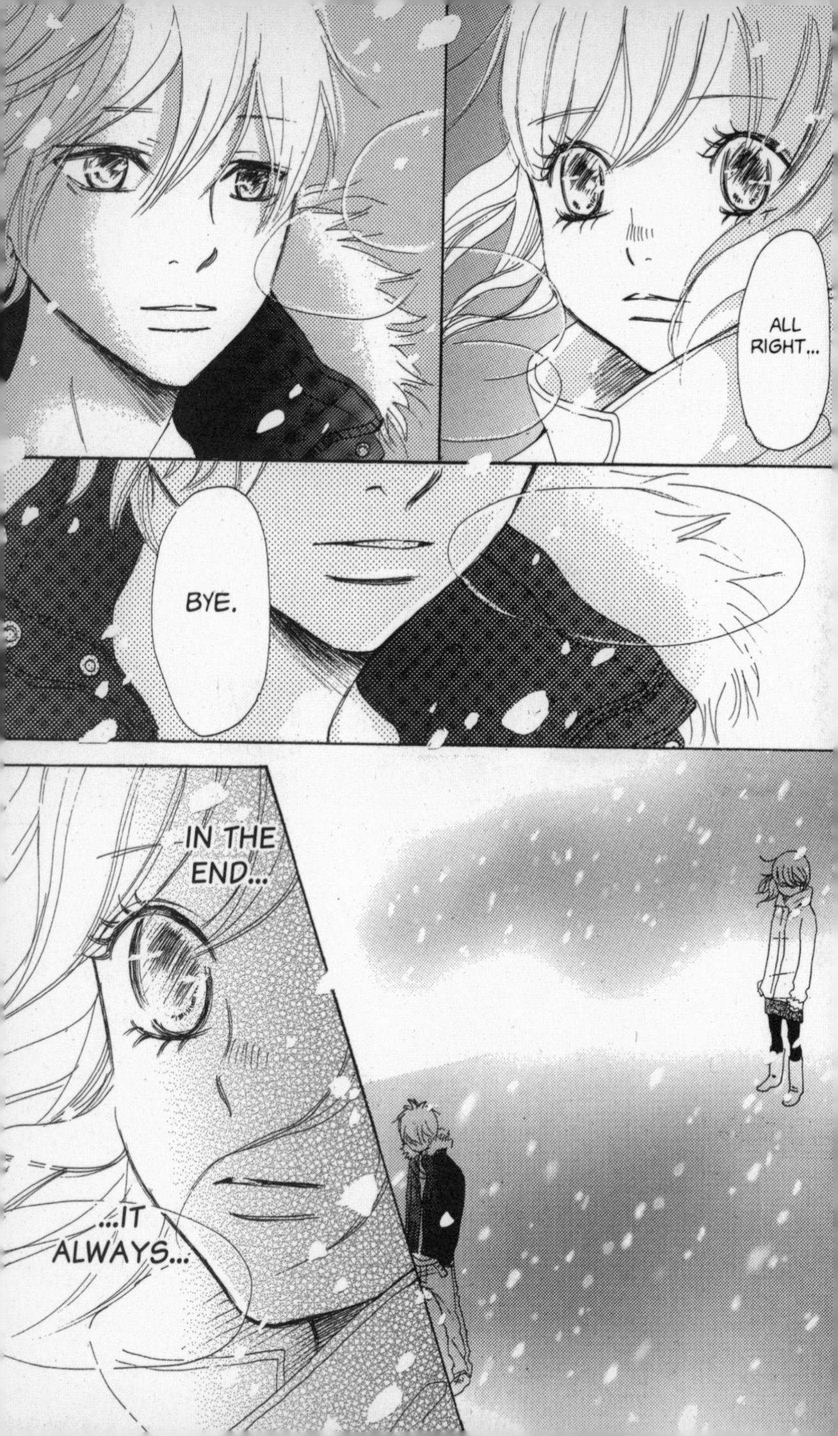
ALL RIGHT...
BYE.
IN THE END...
...IT ALWAYS...

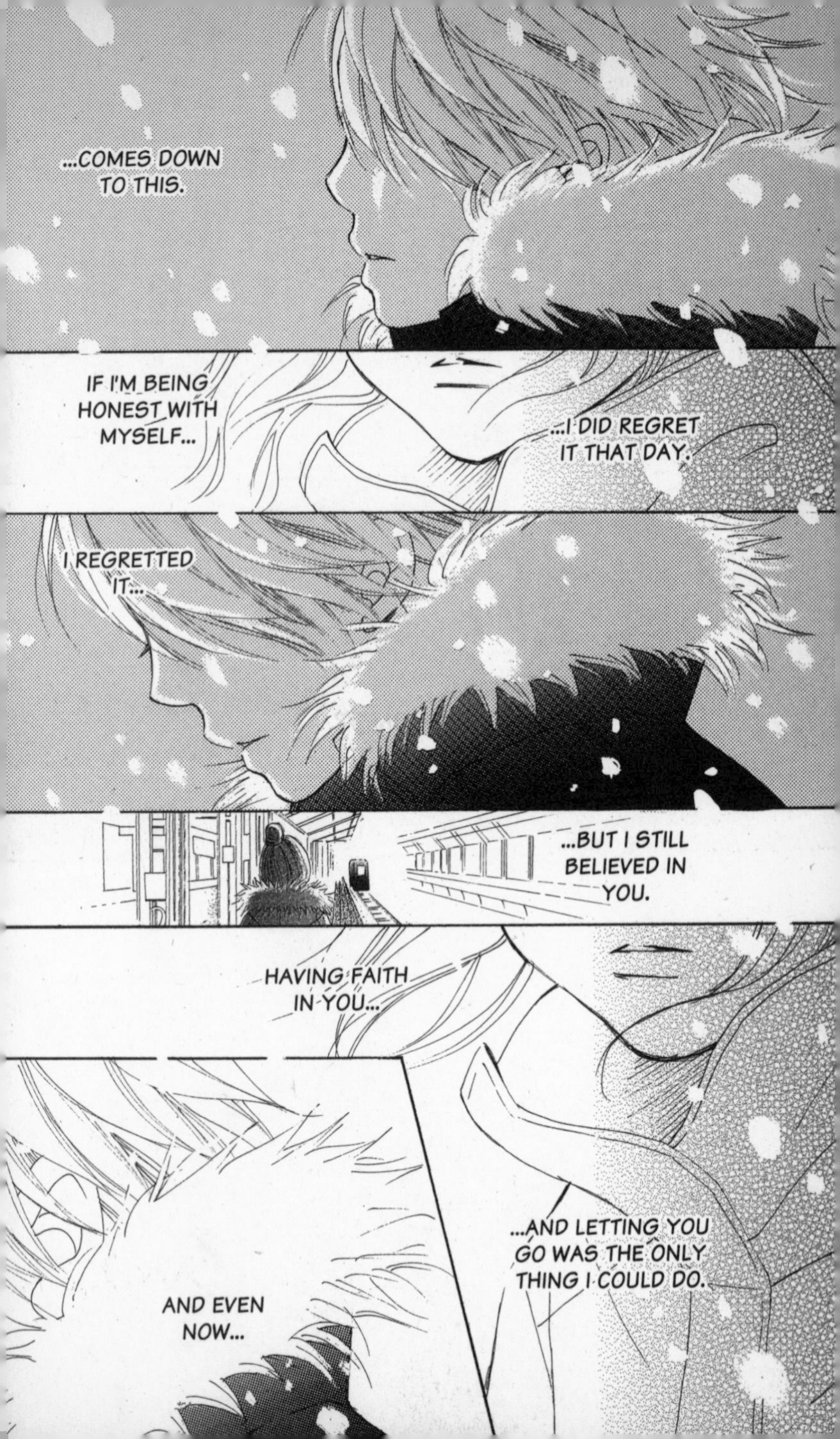
...COMES DOWN TO THIS.
IF I'M BEING HONEST WITH MYSELF...
...I DID REGRET IT THAT DAY.
I REGRETTED IT...
...BUT I STILL BELIEVED IN YOU.
HAVING FAITH IN YOU...
...AND LETTING YOU GO WAS THE ONLY THING I COULD DO.
AND EVEN NOW...

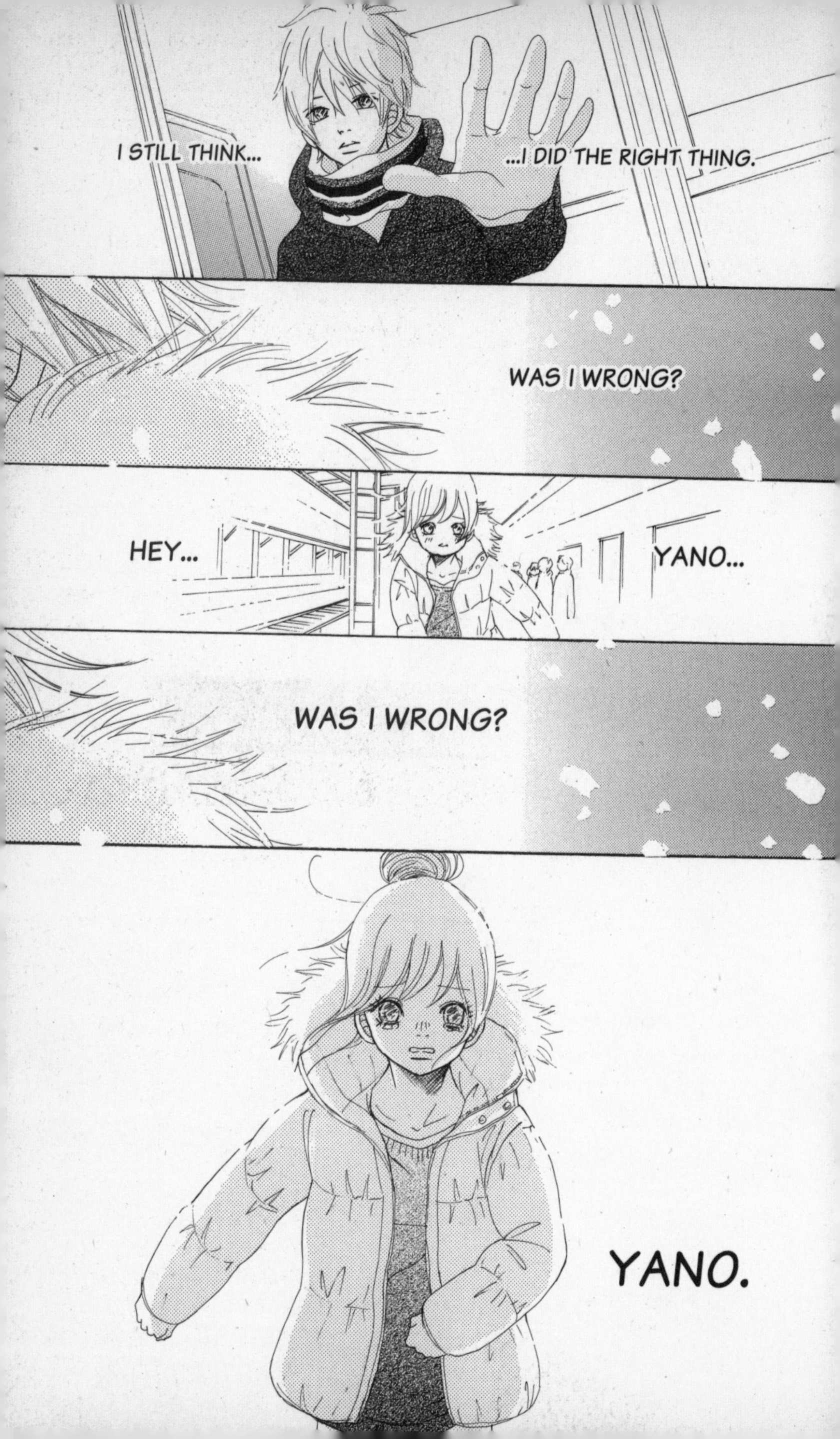
I STILL THINK...
...I DID THE RIGHT THING.
WAS I WRONG?
HEY...
YANO...
WAS I WRONG?
YANO.

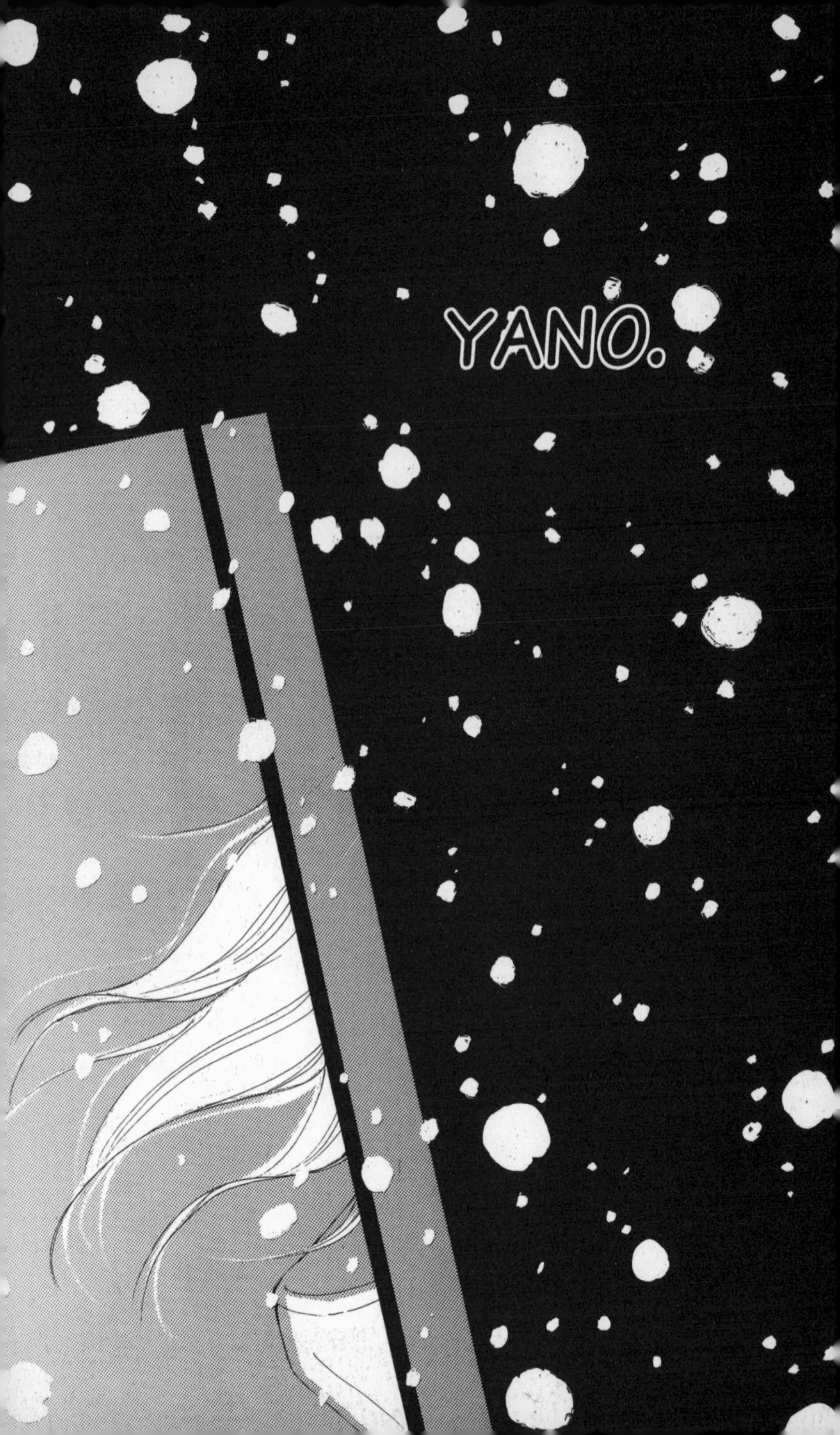
YANO.

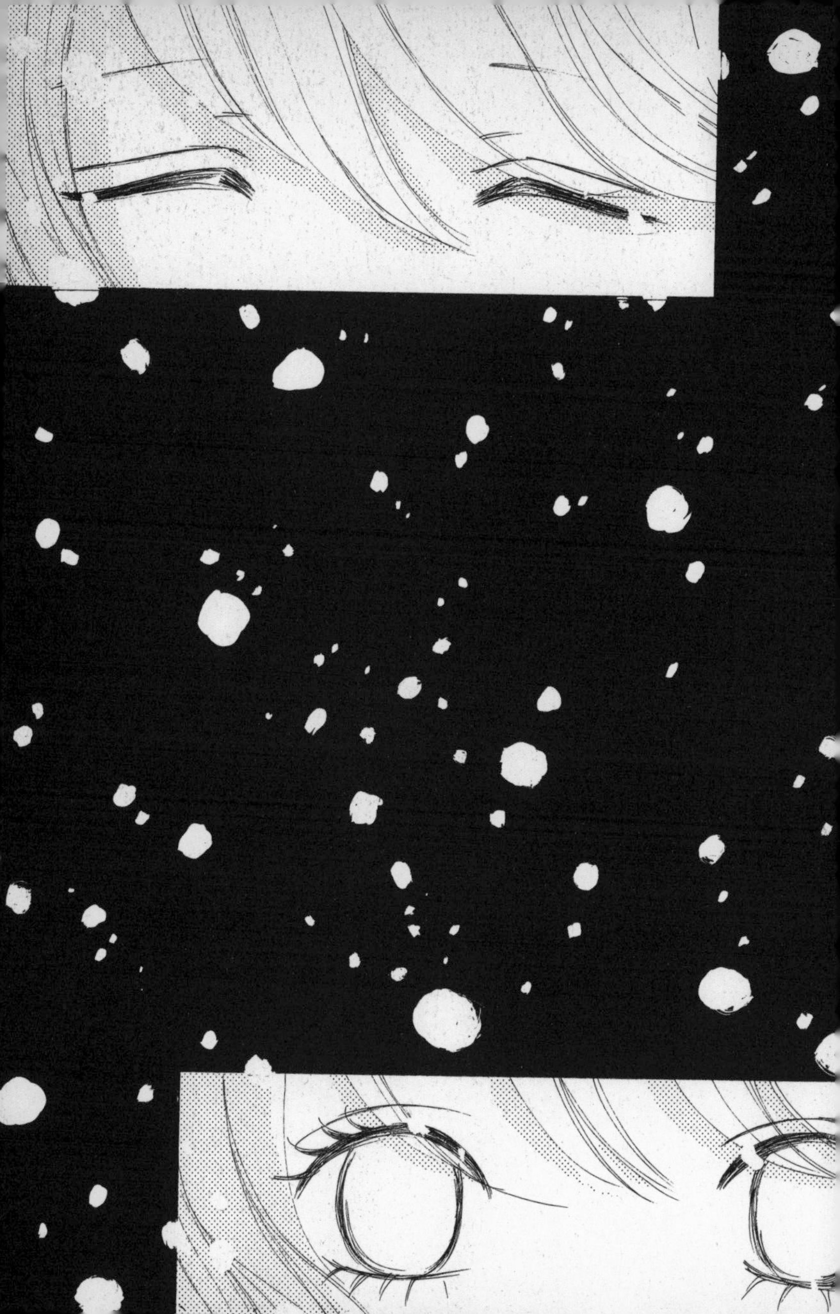

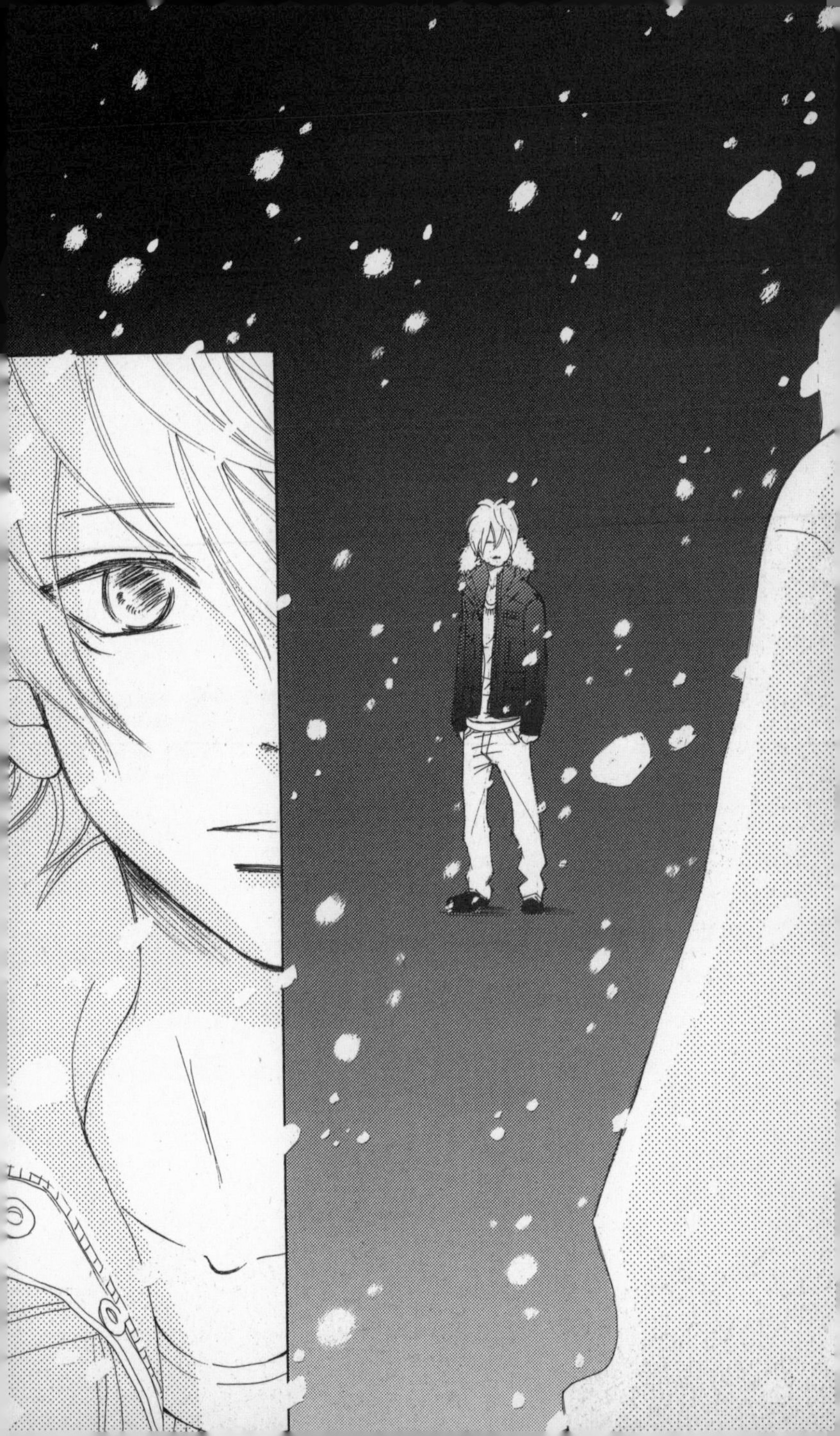

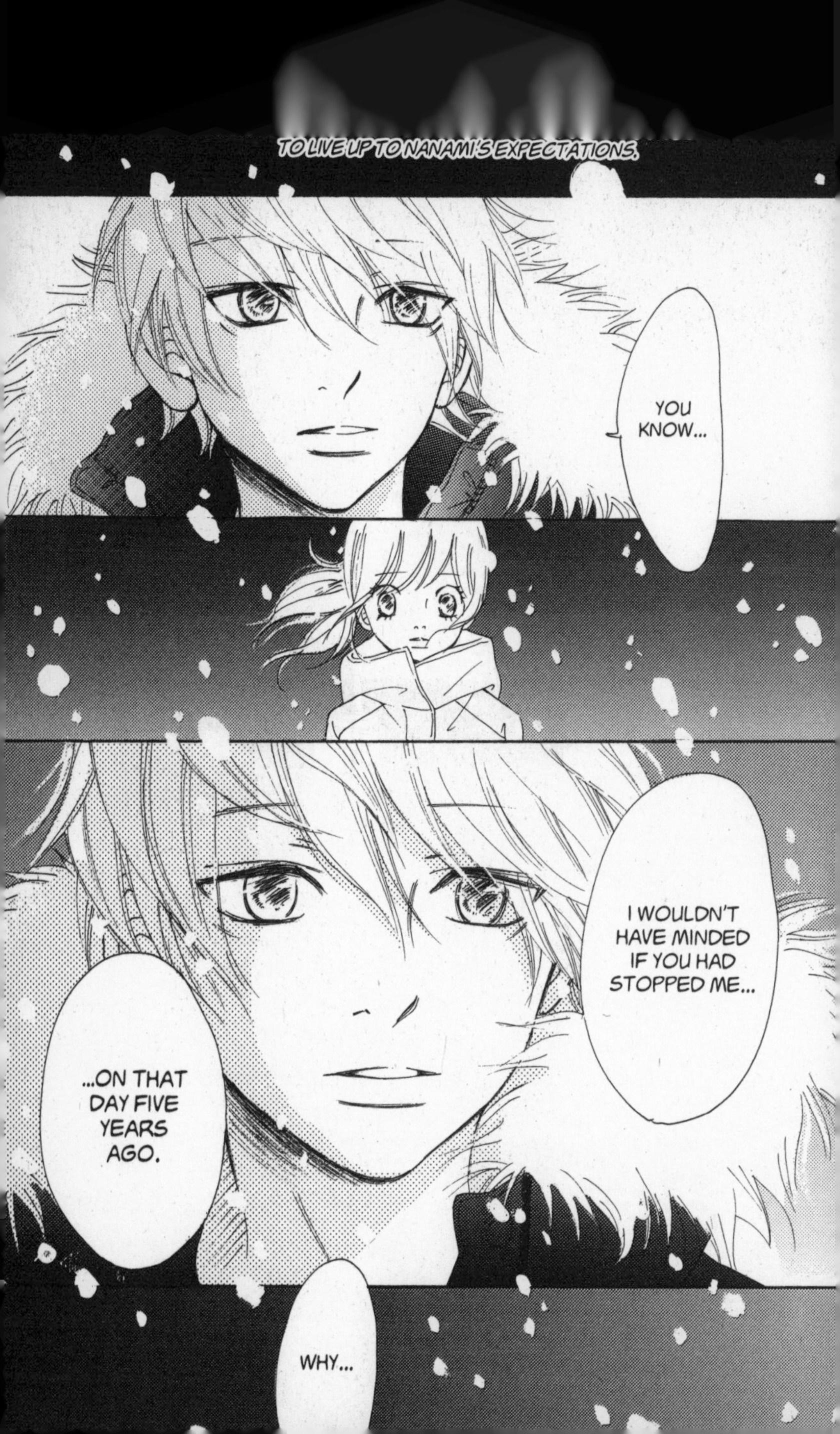
TO LIVE UP TO NANAMI'S EXPECTATIONS.
YOU KNOW...
I WOULDN'T HAVE MINDED IF YOU HAD STOPPED ME...
...ON THAT DAY FIVE YEARS AGO.
WHY...

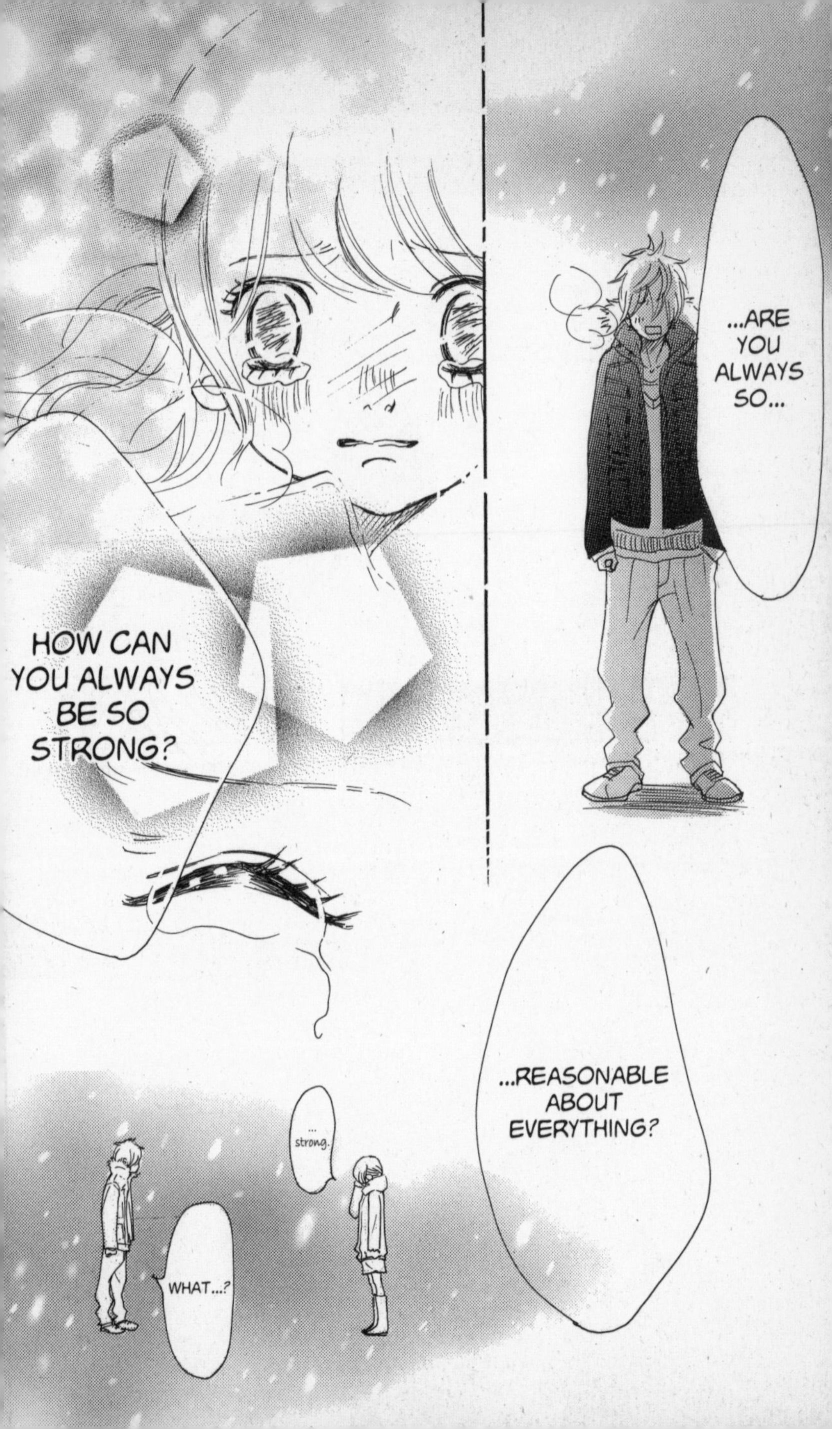
...ARE YOU ALWAYS SO...
...REASONABLE ABOUT EVERYTHING?
HOW CAN YOU ALWAYS BE SO STRONG?
... strong.
WHAT...?

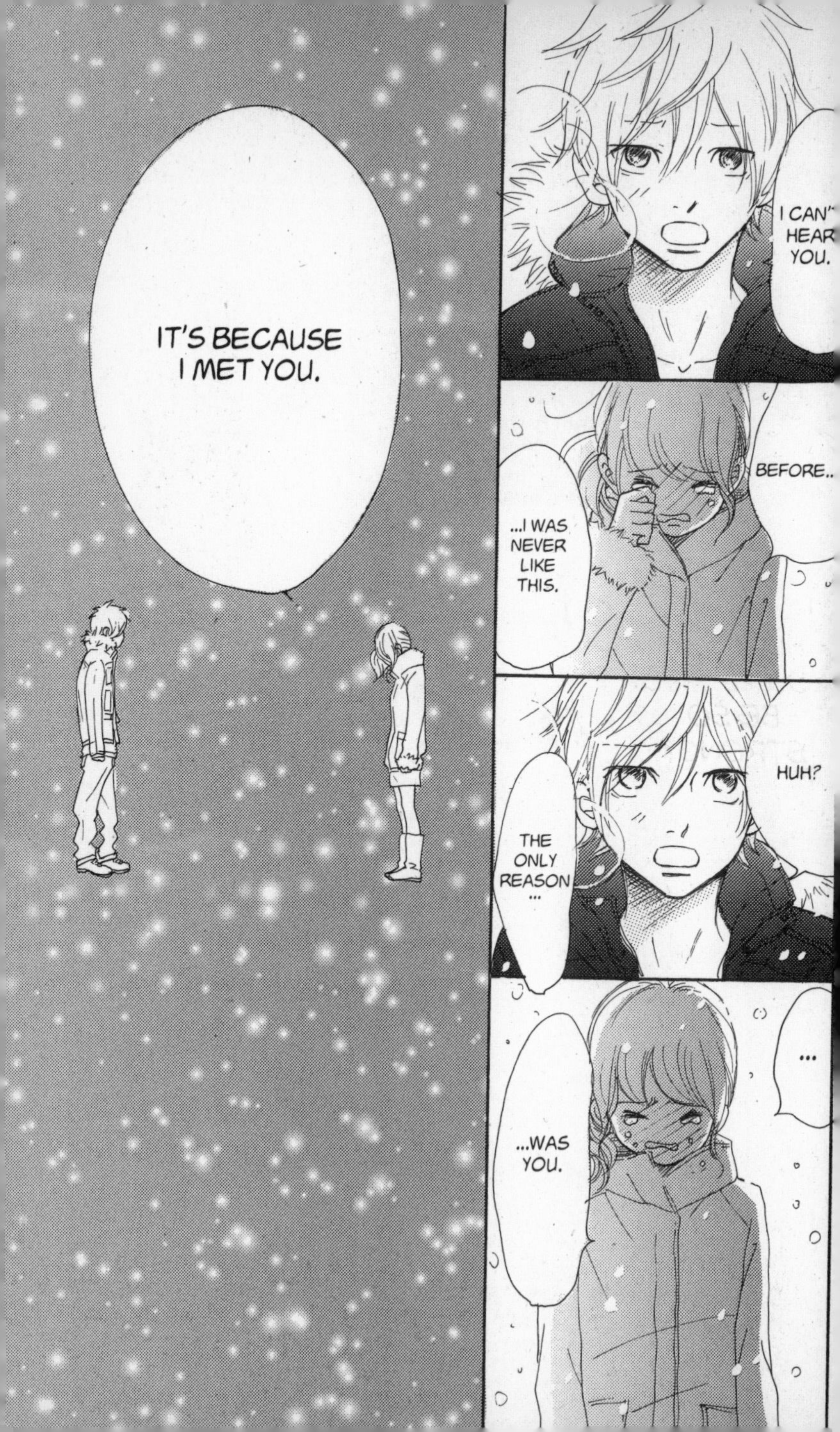
I CAN' HEAR YOU.
BEFORE..
...I WAS NEVER LIKE THIS.
HUH?
THE ONLY REASON ...
...
...WAS YOU.
IT'S BECAUSE I MET YOU.

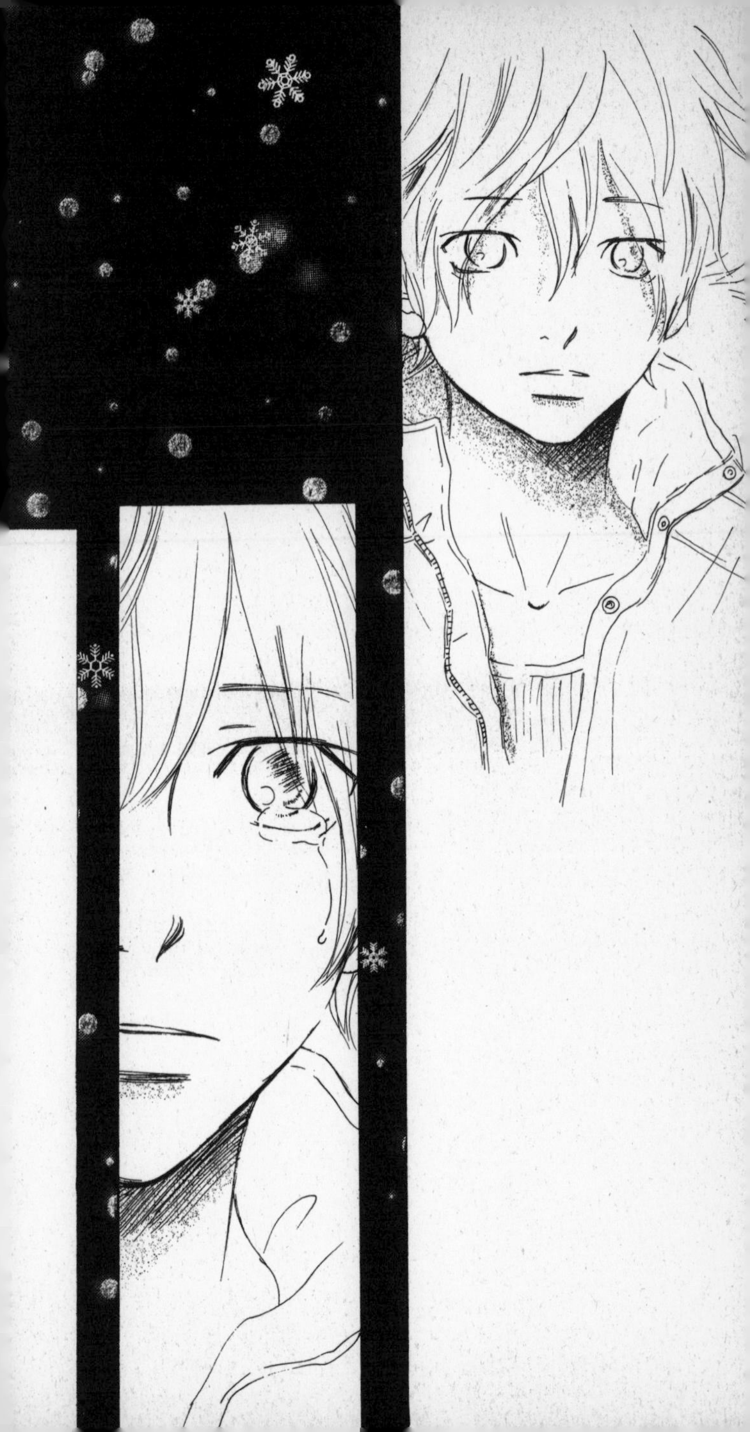

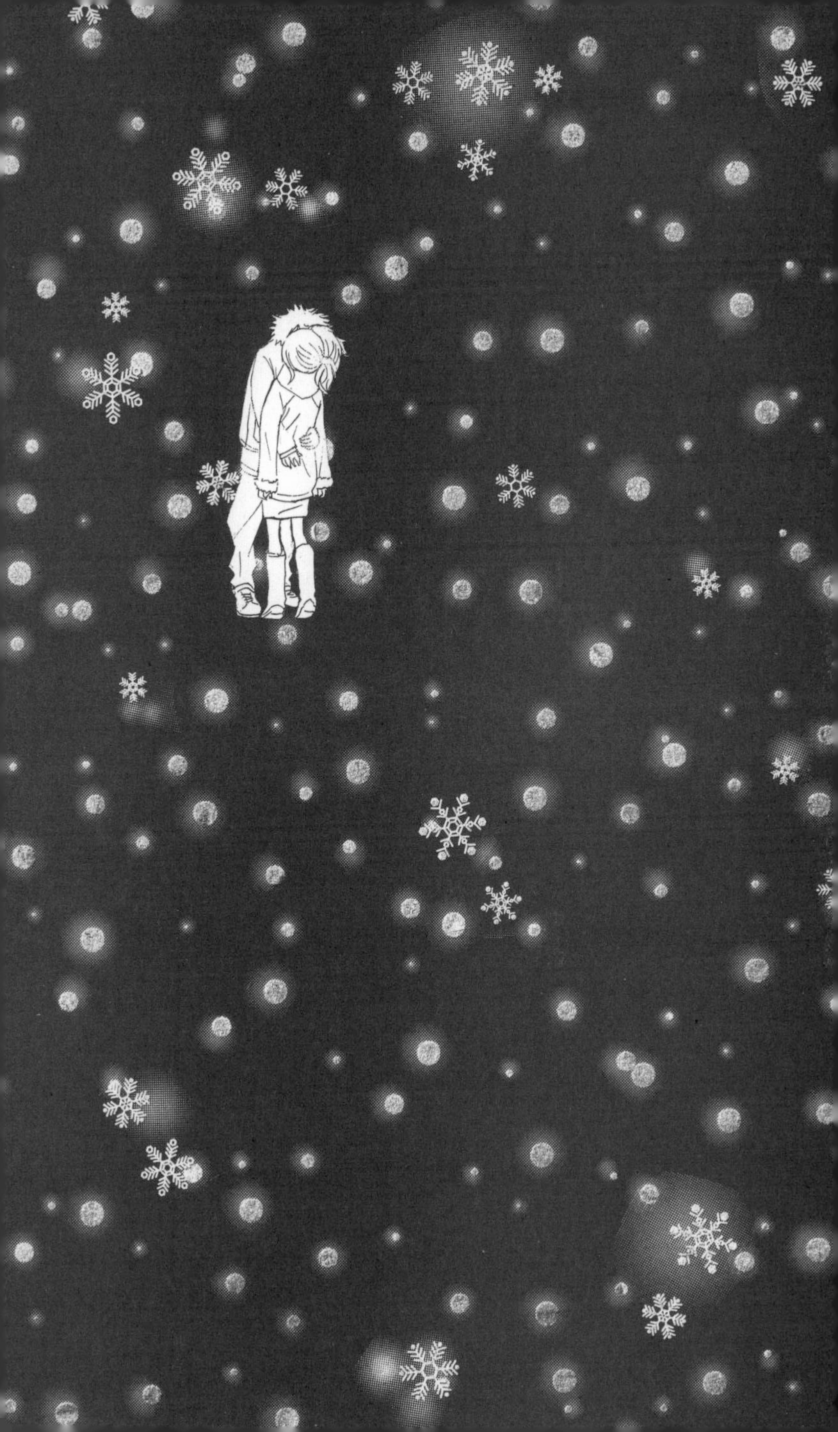

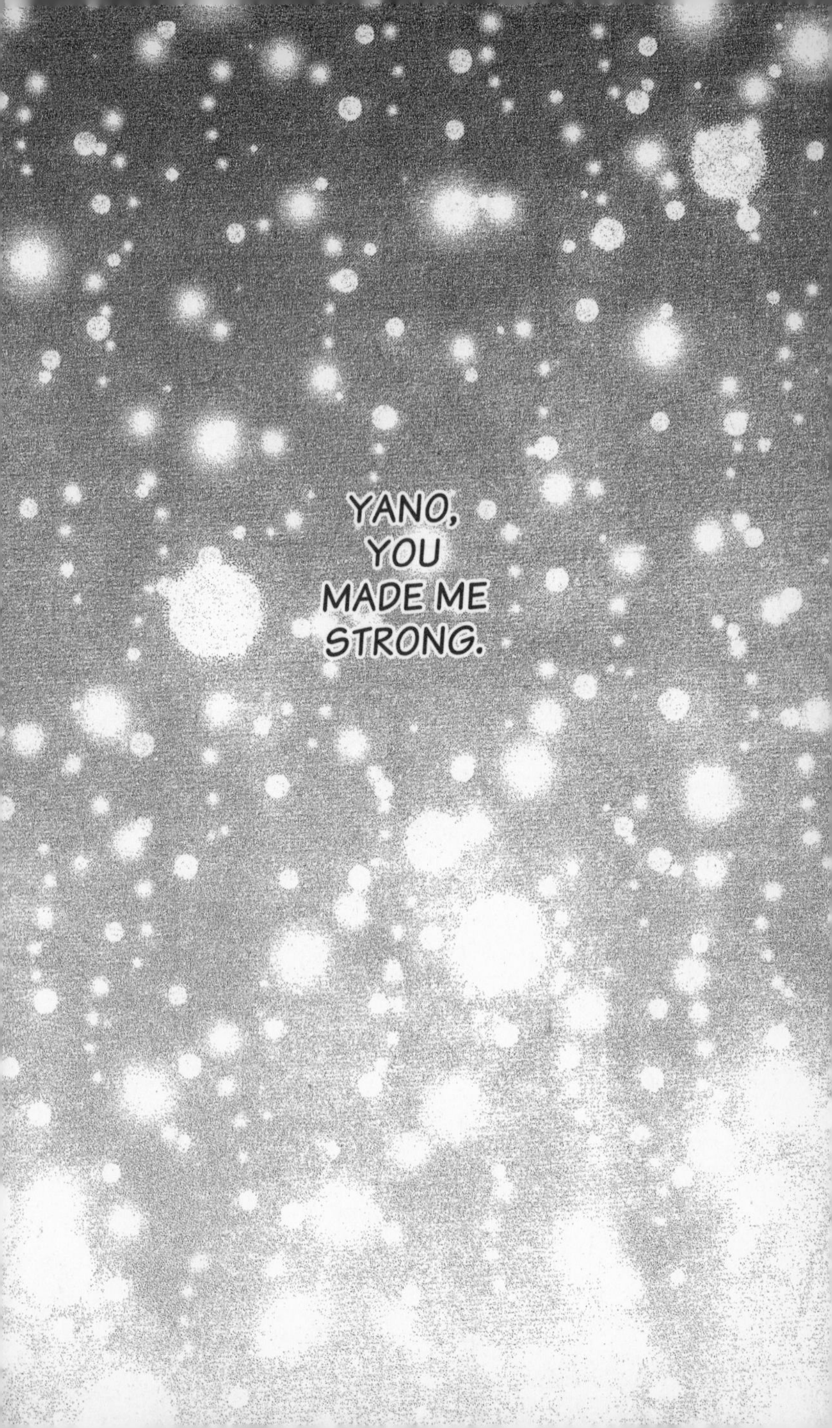
YANO, YOU MADE ME STRONG.

Chapter 64

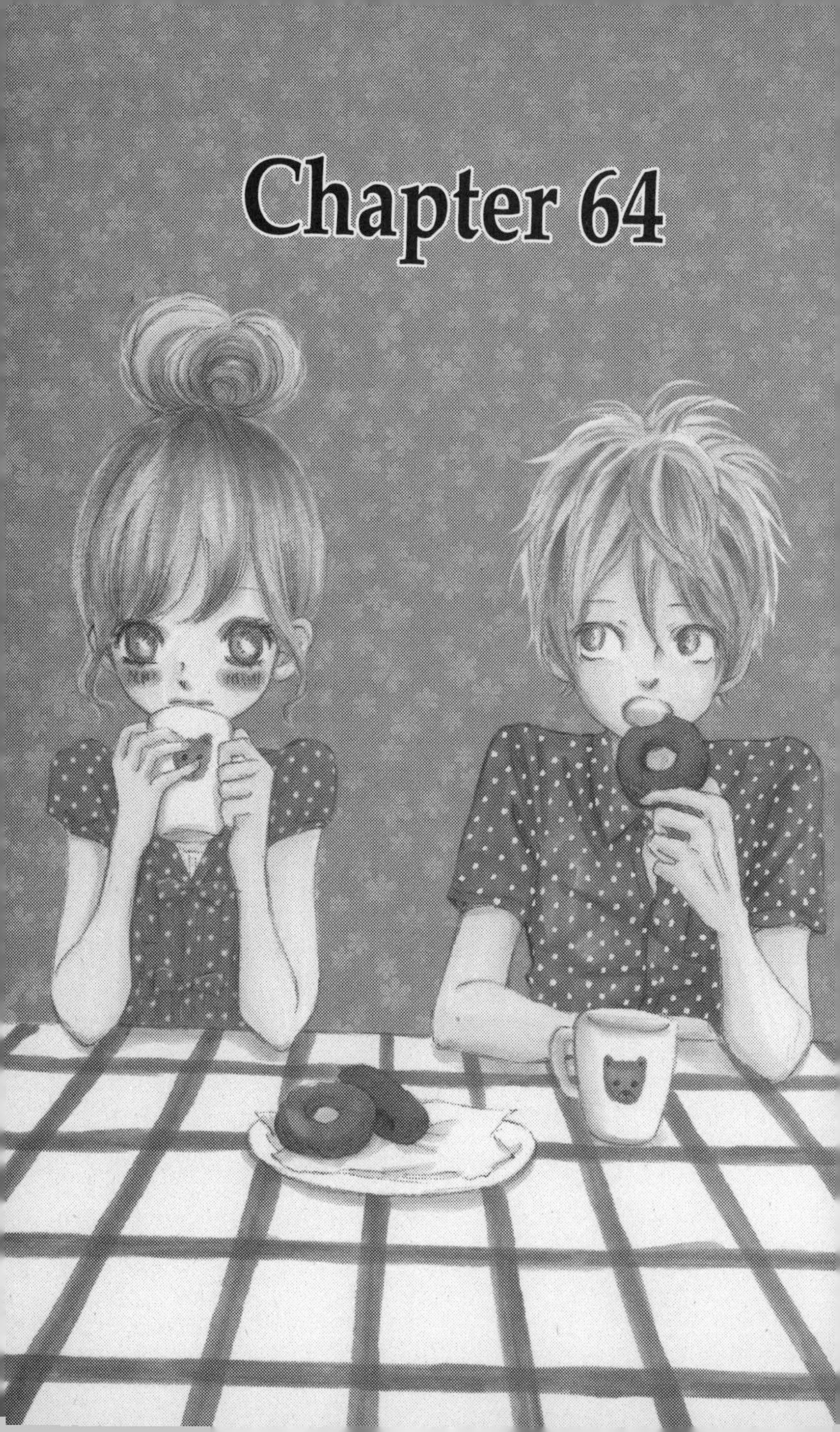

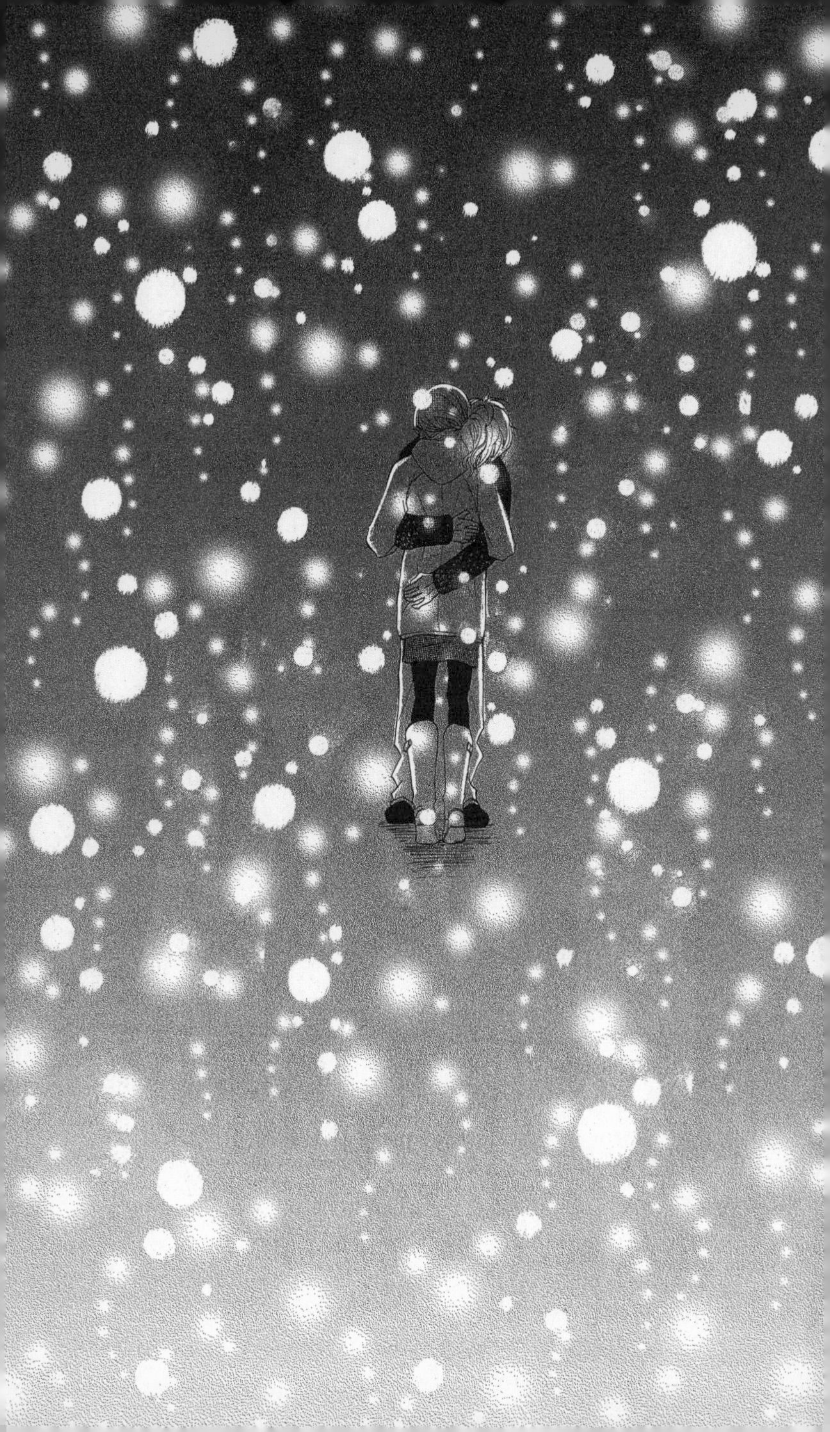

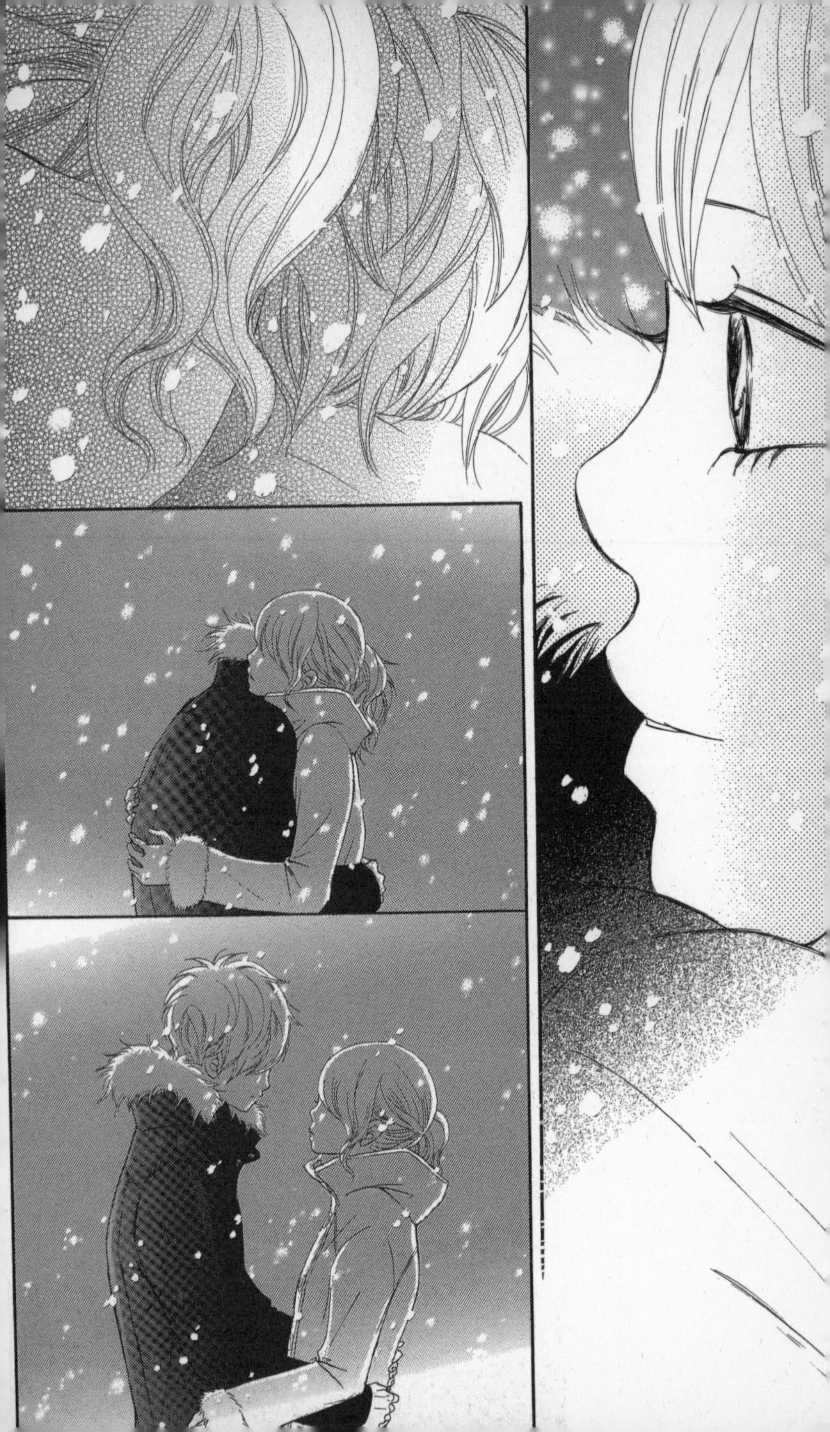

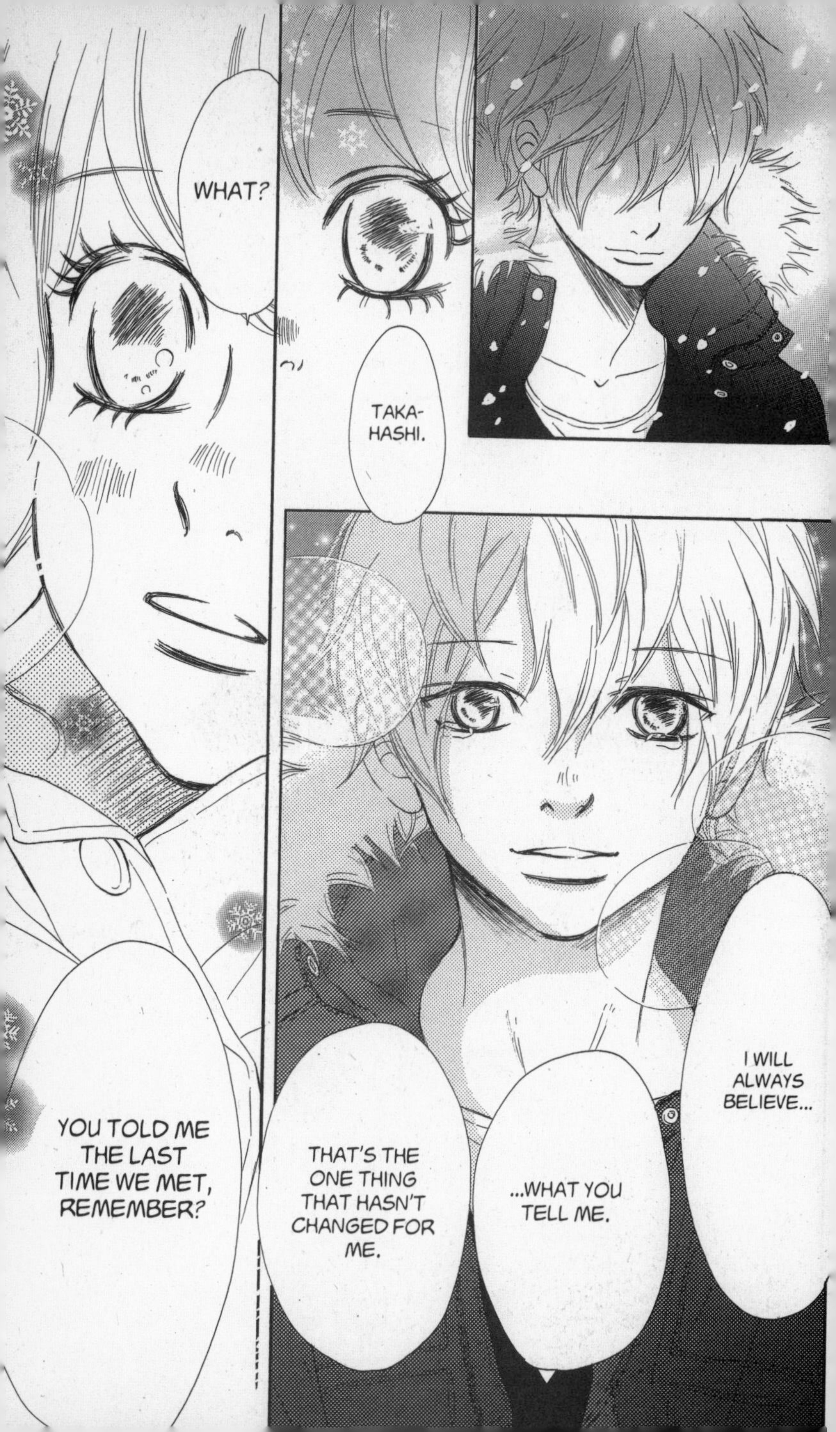
TAKA-HASHI.
I WILL ALWAYS BELIEVE...
...WHAT YOU TELL ME.
THAT'S THE ONE THING THAT HASN'T CHANGED FOR ME.
WHAT?
YOU TOLD ME THE LAST TIME WE MET, REMEMBER?

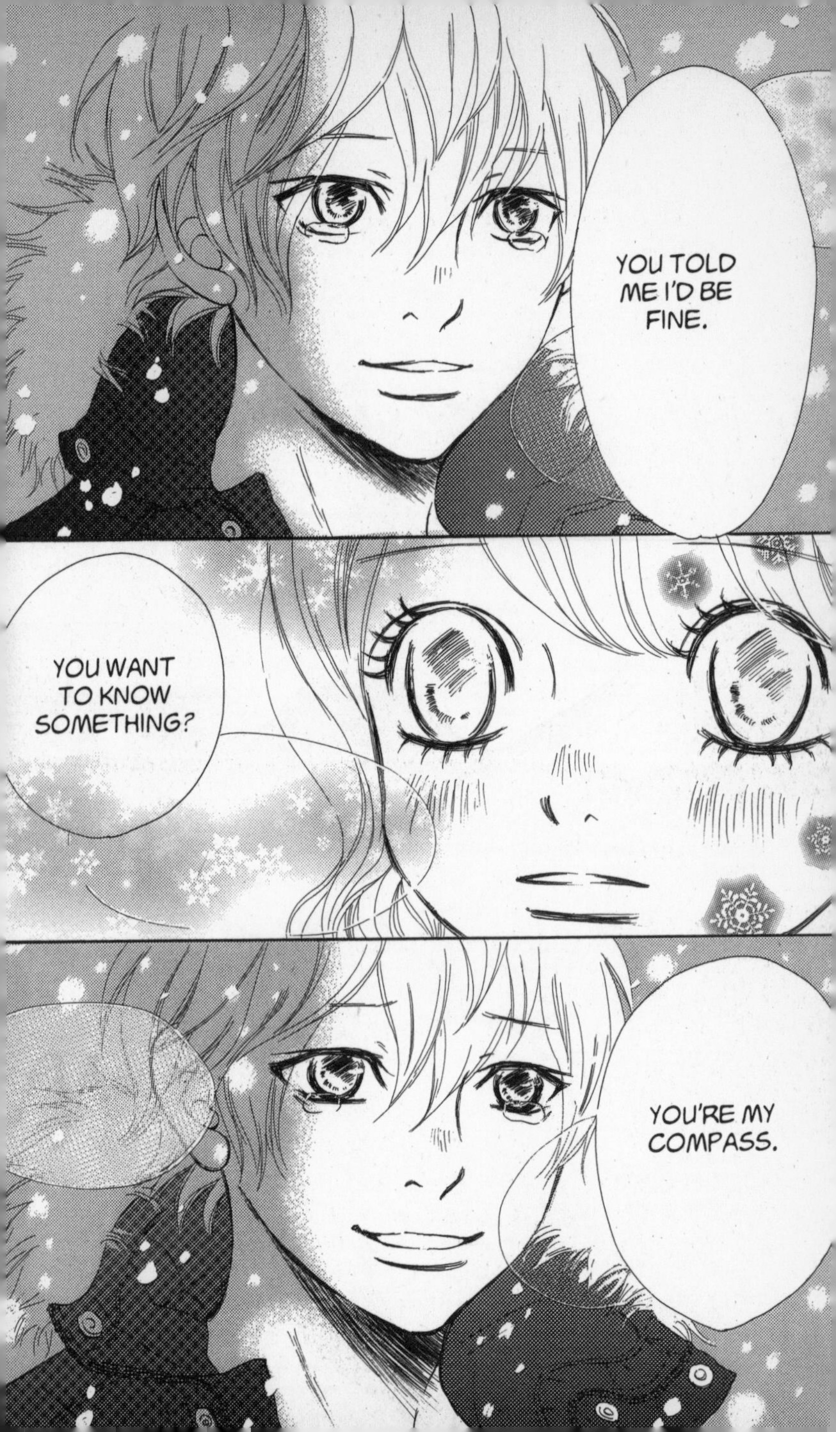
YOU TOLD ME I'D BE FINE.
YOU WANT TO KNOW SOMETHING?
YOU'RE MY COMPASS.

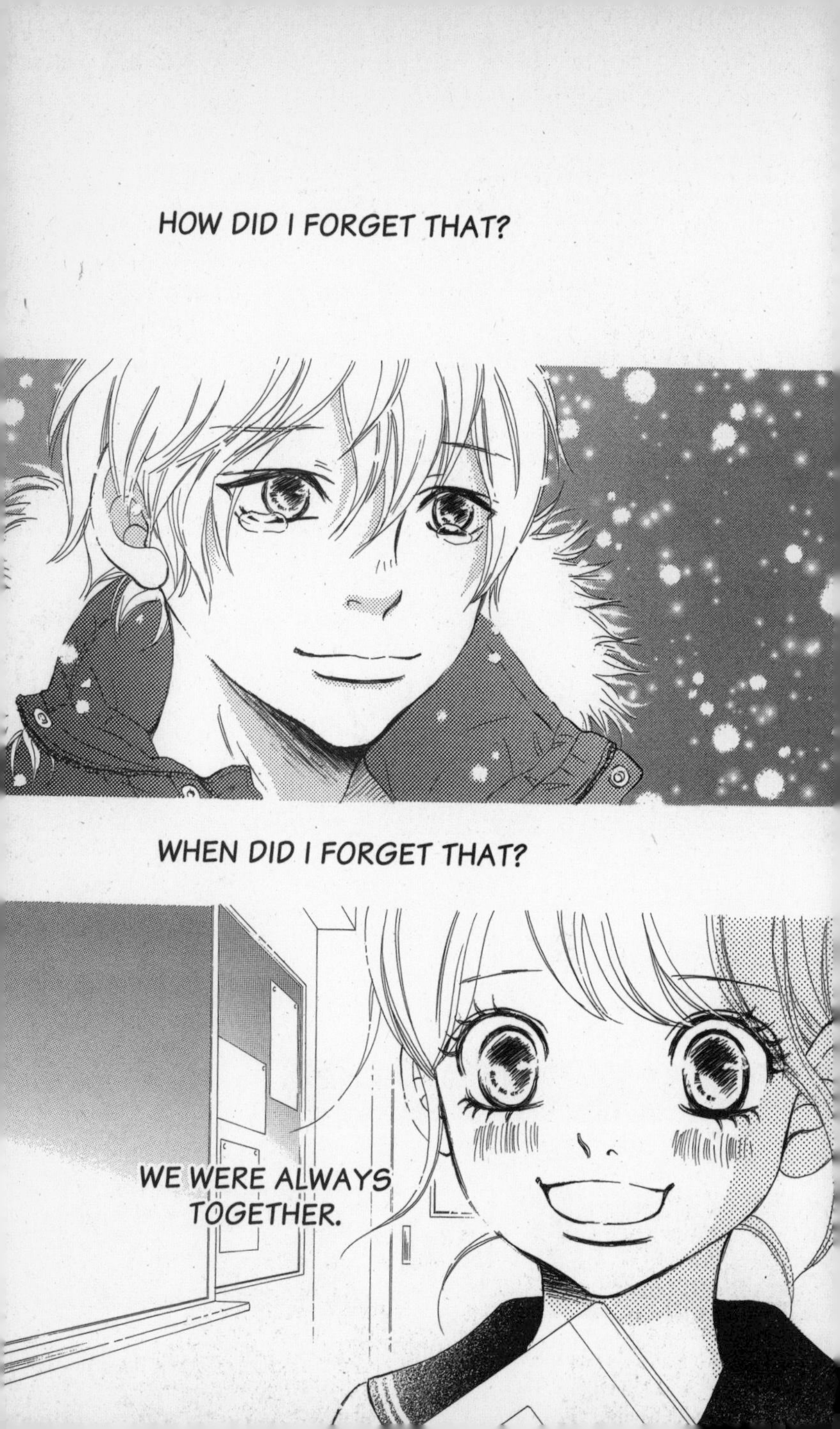
HOW DID I FORGET THAT?
WHEN DID I FORGET THAT?
WE WERE ALWAYS TOGETHER.

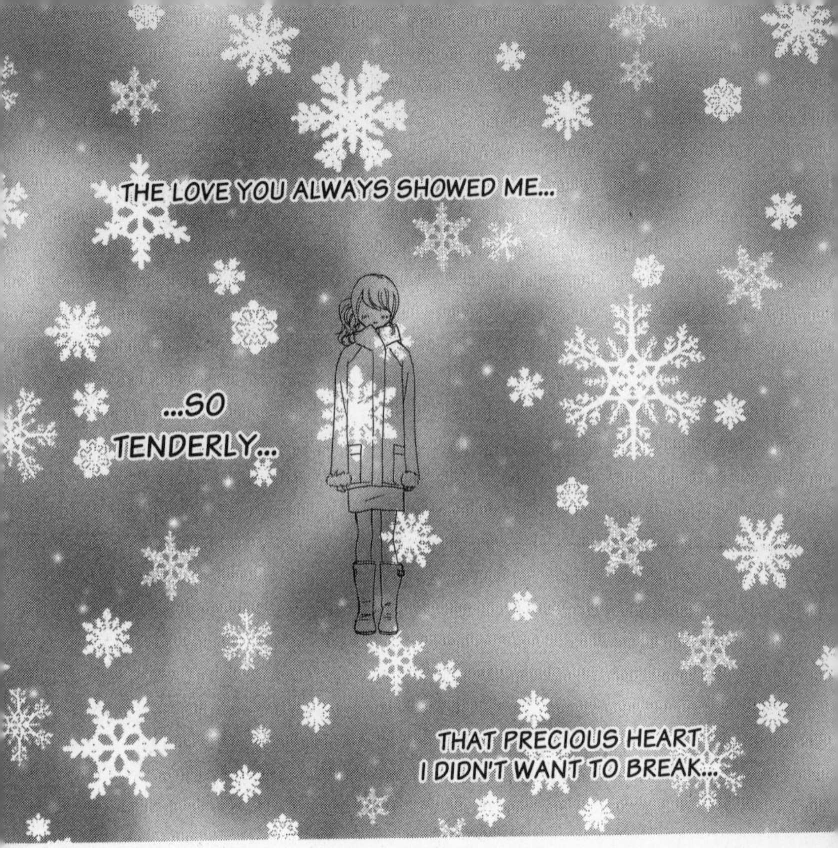
THE LOVE YOU ALWAYS SHOWED ME...
...SO TENDERLY...
THAT PRECIOUS HEART I DIDN'T WANT TO BREAK...

WHEN DID I...?

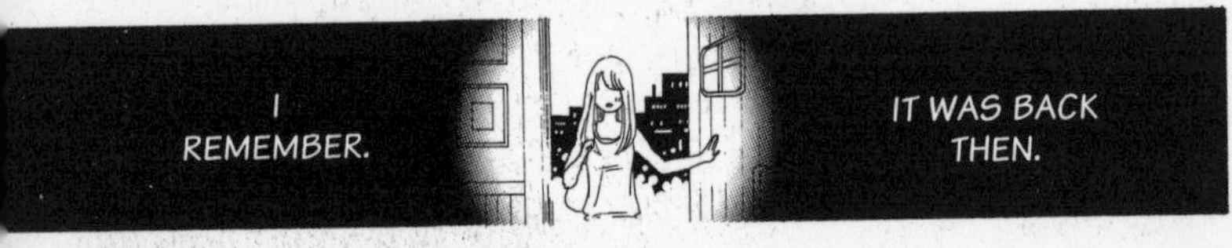
IT WAS BACK THEN.
I REMEMBER.

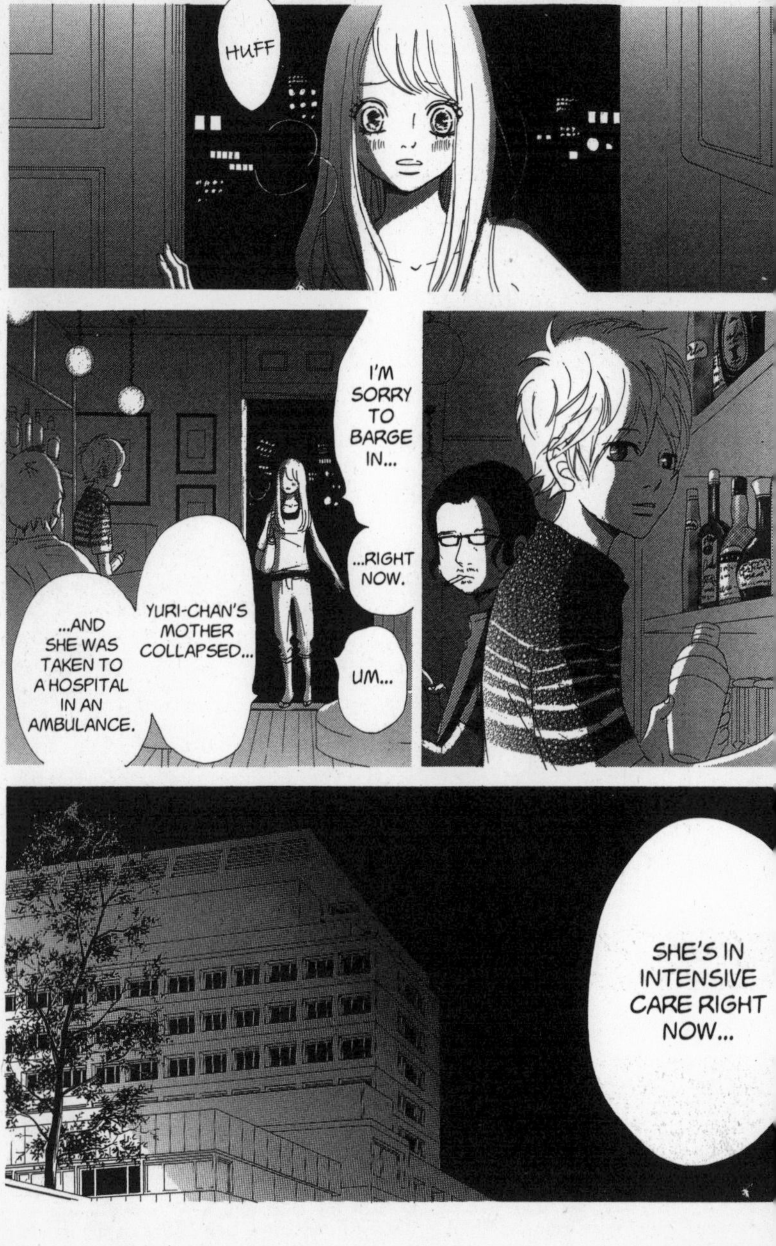
HUFF
I'M SORRY TO BARGE IN...
...RIGHT NOW.
UM...
YURI-CHAN'S MOTHER COLLAPSED...
...AND SHE WAS TAKEN TO A HOSPITAL IN AN AMBULANCE.
SHE'S IN INTENSIVE CARE RIGHT NOW...

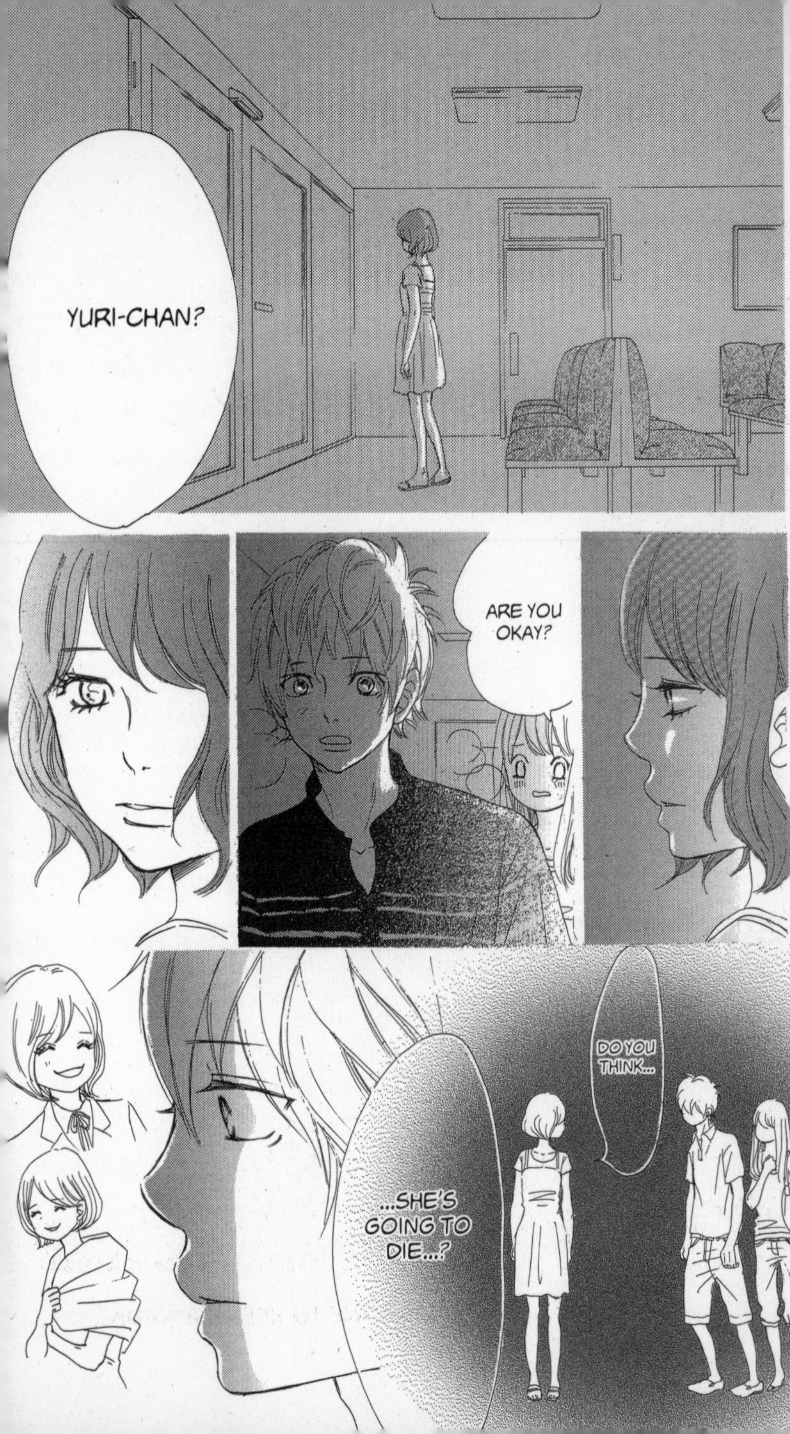
YURI-CHAN?
ARE YOU OKAY?
DO YOU THINK...
...SHE'S GOING TO DIE...?

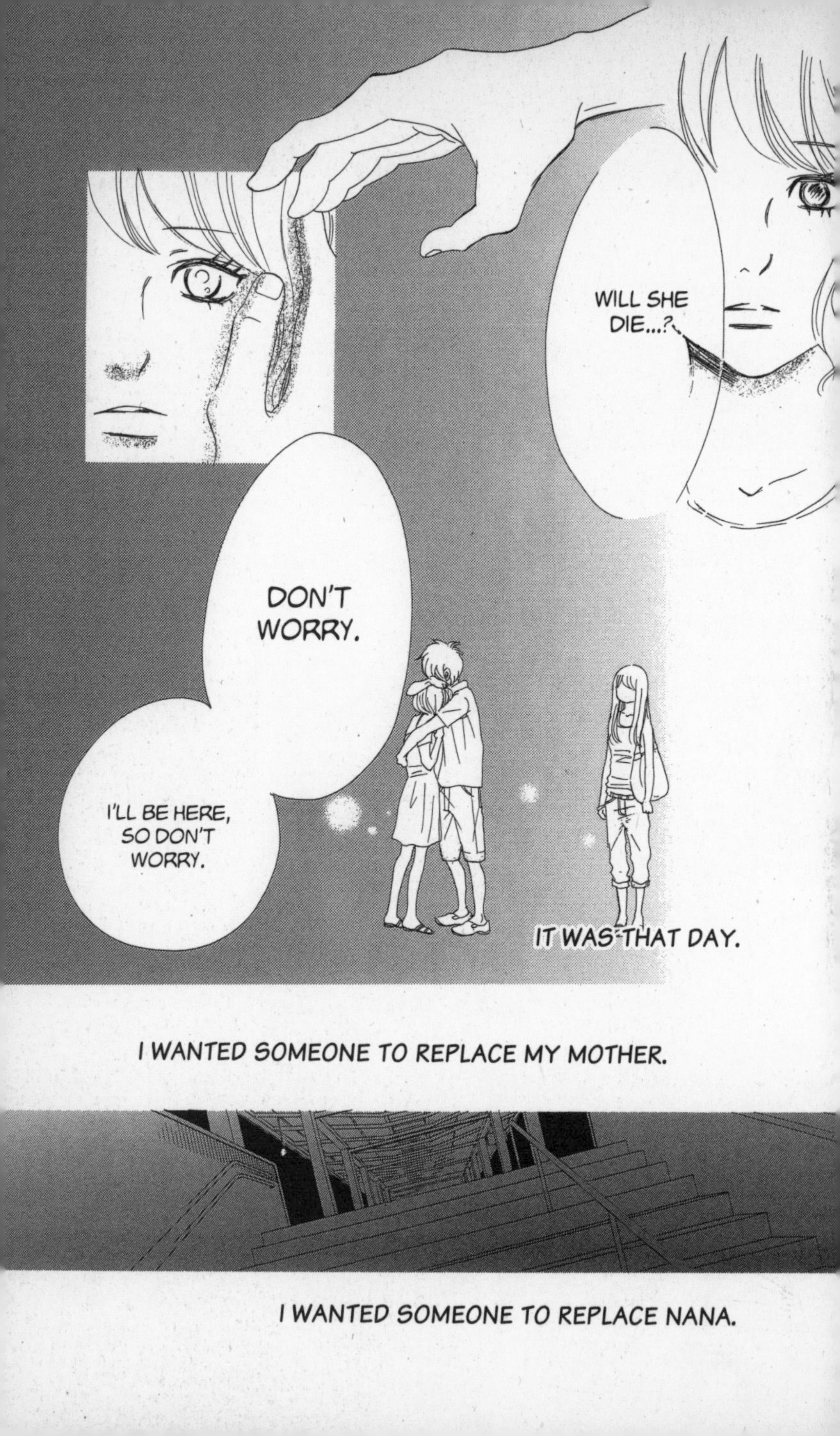
WILL SHE DIE...?
DON'T WORRY.
I'LL BE HERE, SO DON'T WORRY.
IT WAS THAT DAY.
I WANTED SOMEONE TO REPLACE MY MOTHER.
I WANTED SOMEONE TO REPLACE NANA.

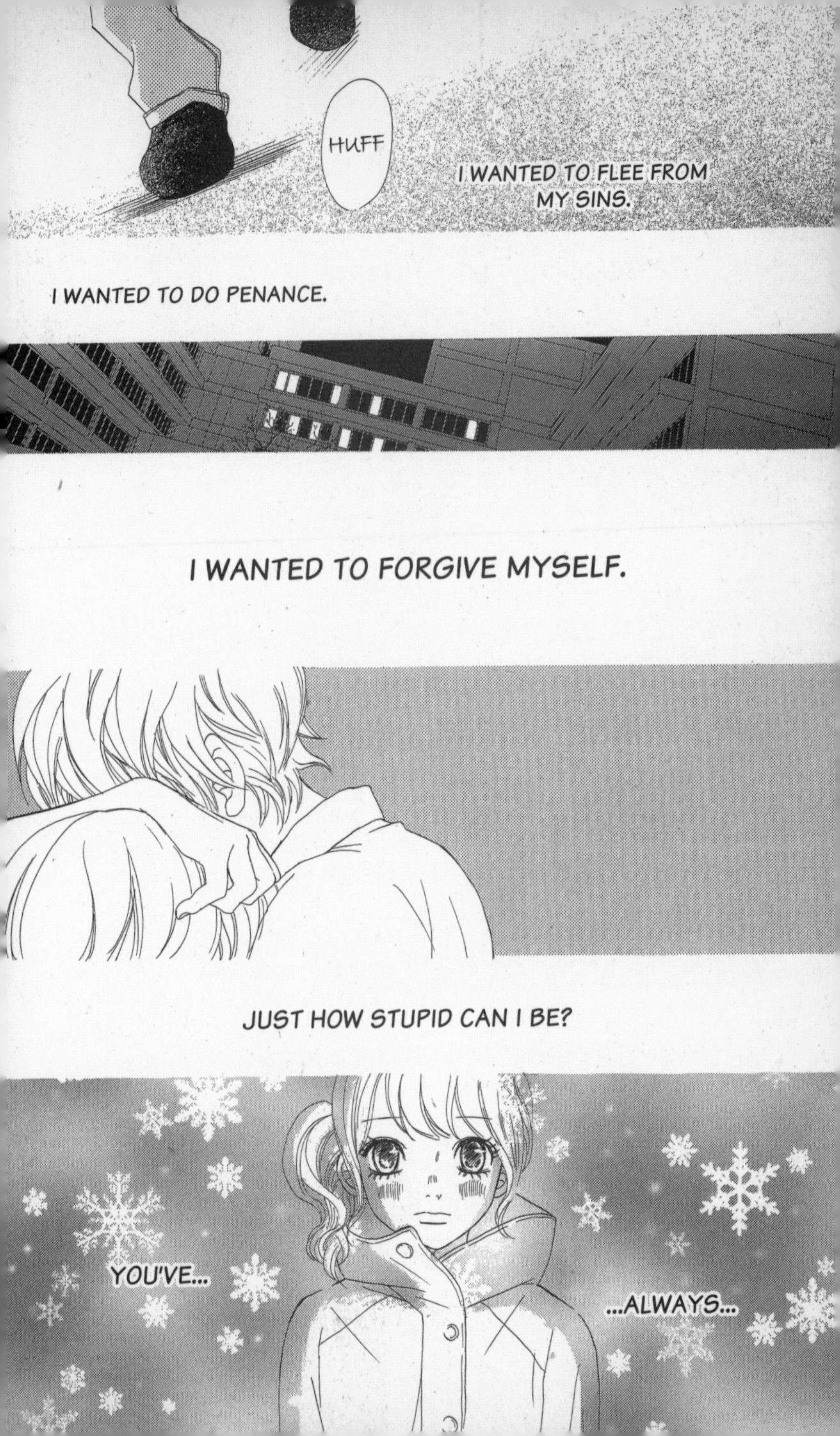
I WANTED TO FLEE FROM MY SINS.
HUFF
I WANTED TO DO PENANCE.
I WANTED TO FORGIVE MYSELF.
JUST HOW STUPID CAN I BE?
YOU'VE...
...ALWAYS...

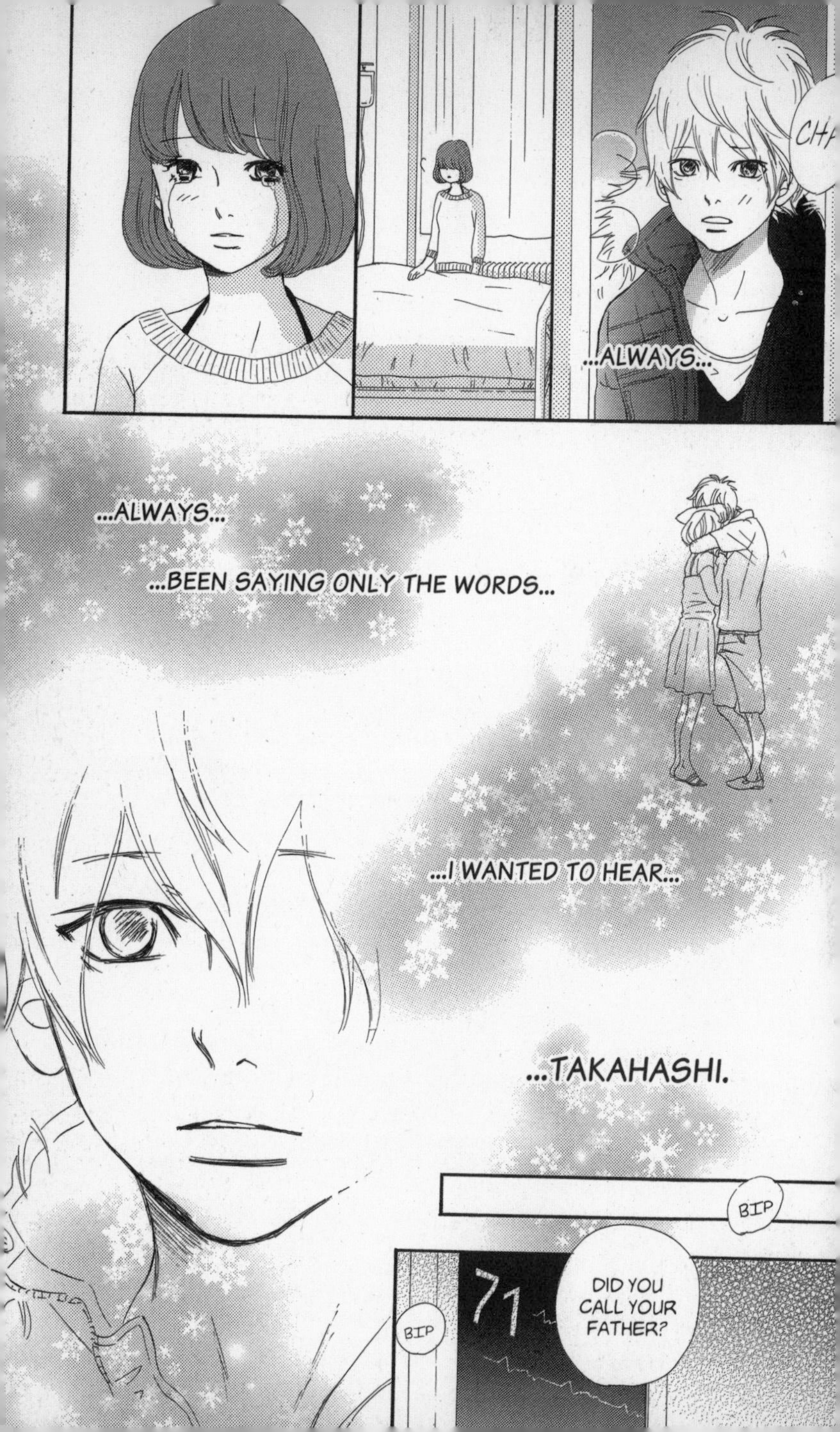
CH
...ALWAYS...
...ALWAYS...
...BEEN SAYING ONLY THE WORDS...
...I WANTED TO HEAR...
...TAKAHASHI.
BIP
DID YOU CALL YOUR FATHER?
BIP
71

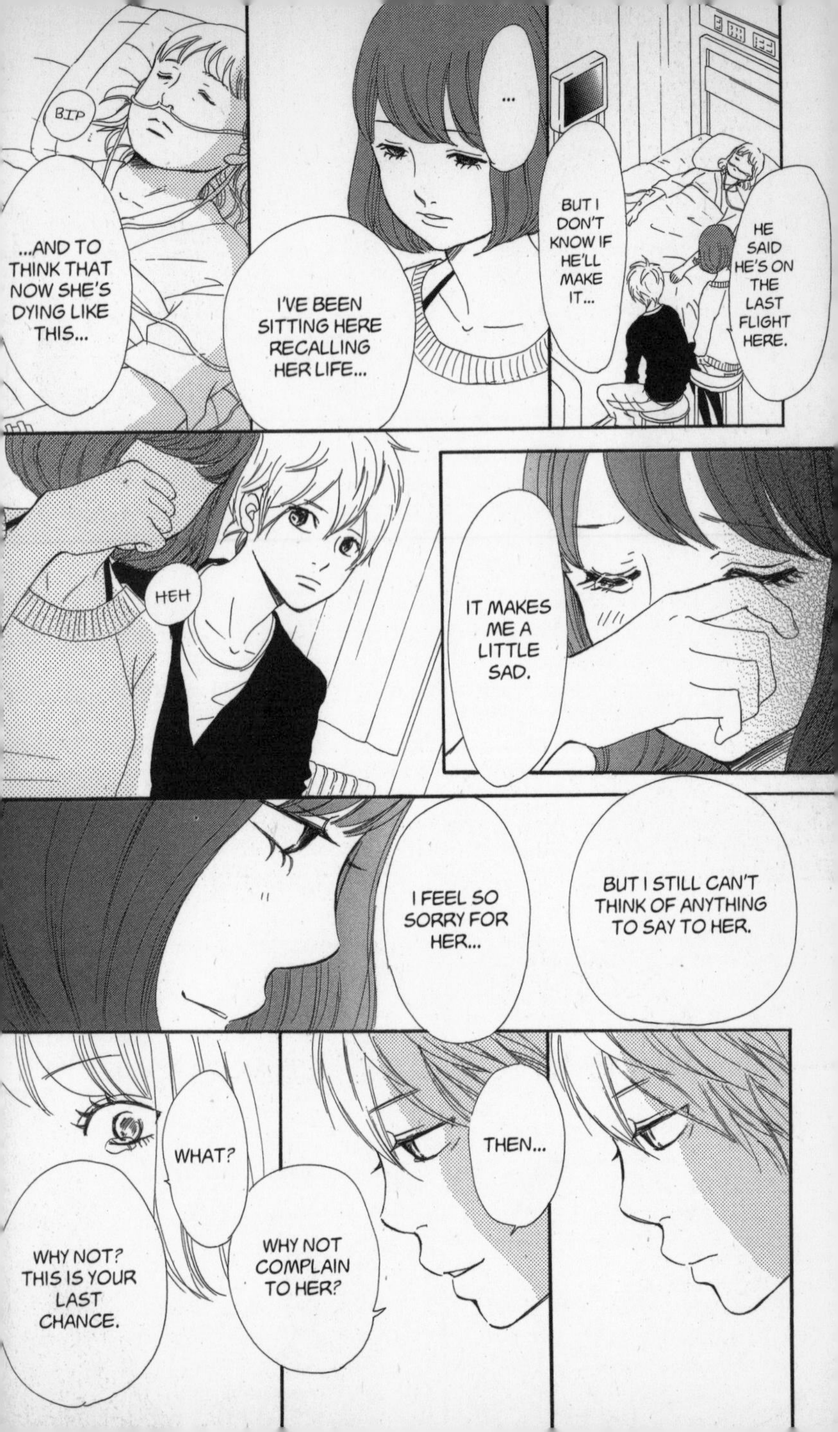
HE SAID HE'S ON THE LAST FLIGHT HERE.
BUT I DON'T KNOW IF HE'LL MAKE IT...
...
I'VE BEEN SITTING HERE RECALLING HER LIFE...
BIP
...AND TO THINK THAT NOW SHE'S DYING LIKE THIS...
IT MAKES ME A LITTLE SAD.
HEH
BUT I STILL CAN'T THINK OF ANYTHING TO SAY TO HER.
I FEEL SO SORRY FOR HER...
THEN...
WHY NOT COMPLAIN TO HER?
WHAT?
WHY NOT? THIS IS YOUR LAST CHANCE.

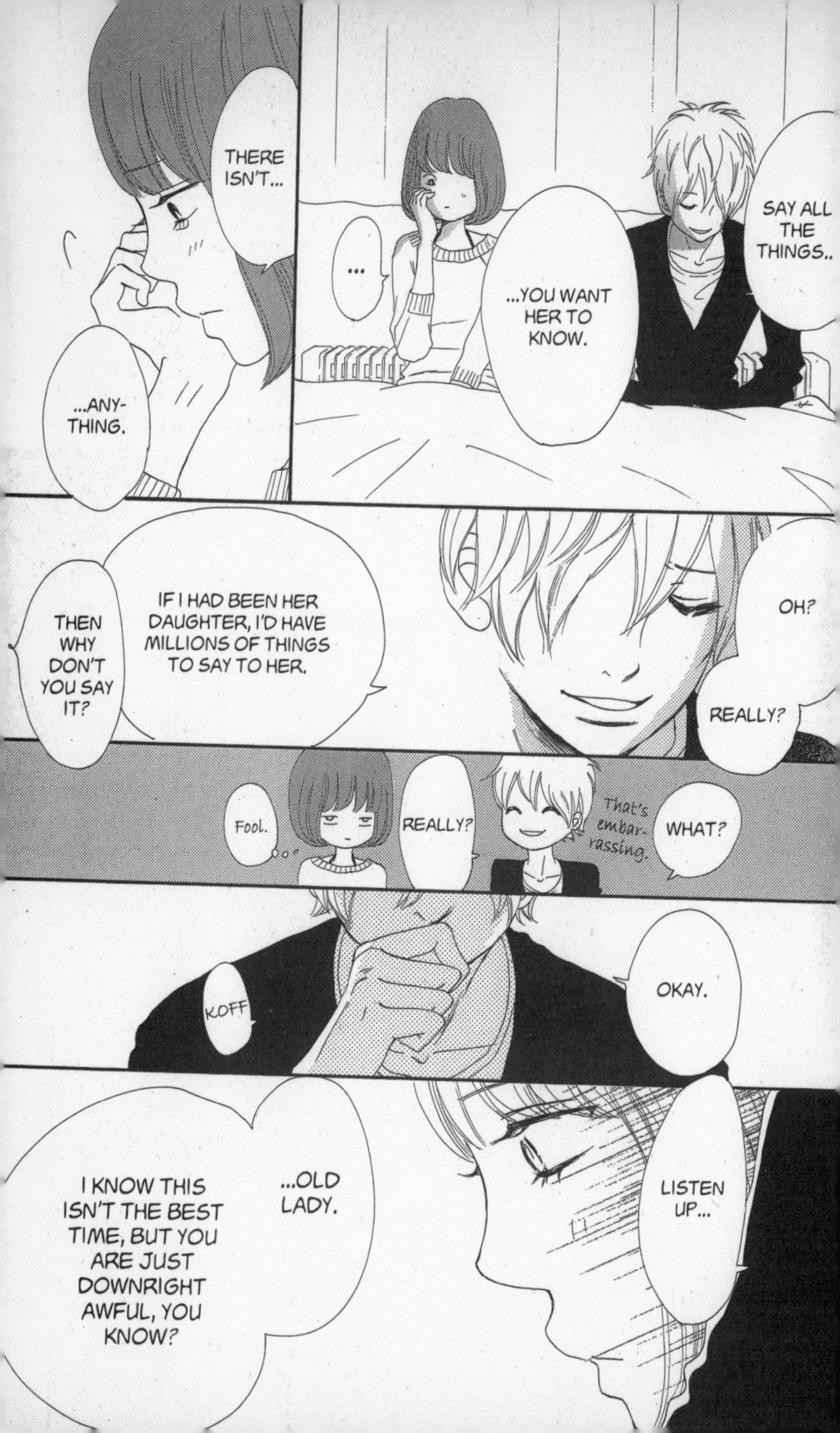
SAY ALL THE THINGS..
...YOU WANT HER TO KNOW.
...
THERE ISN'T...
...ANY-THING.
OH?
REALLY?
IF I HAD BEEN HER DAUGHTER, I'D HAVE MILLIONS OF THINGS TO SAY TO HER.
THEN WHY DON'T YOU SAY IT?
WHAT?
That's embar-rassing.
REALLY?
Fool.
OKAY.
KOFF
LISTEN UP...
...OLD LADY.
I KNOW THIS ISN'T THE BEST TIME, BUT YOU ARE JUST DOWNRIGHT AWFUL, YOU KNOW?

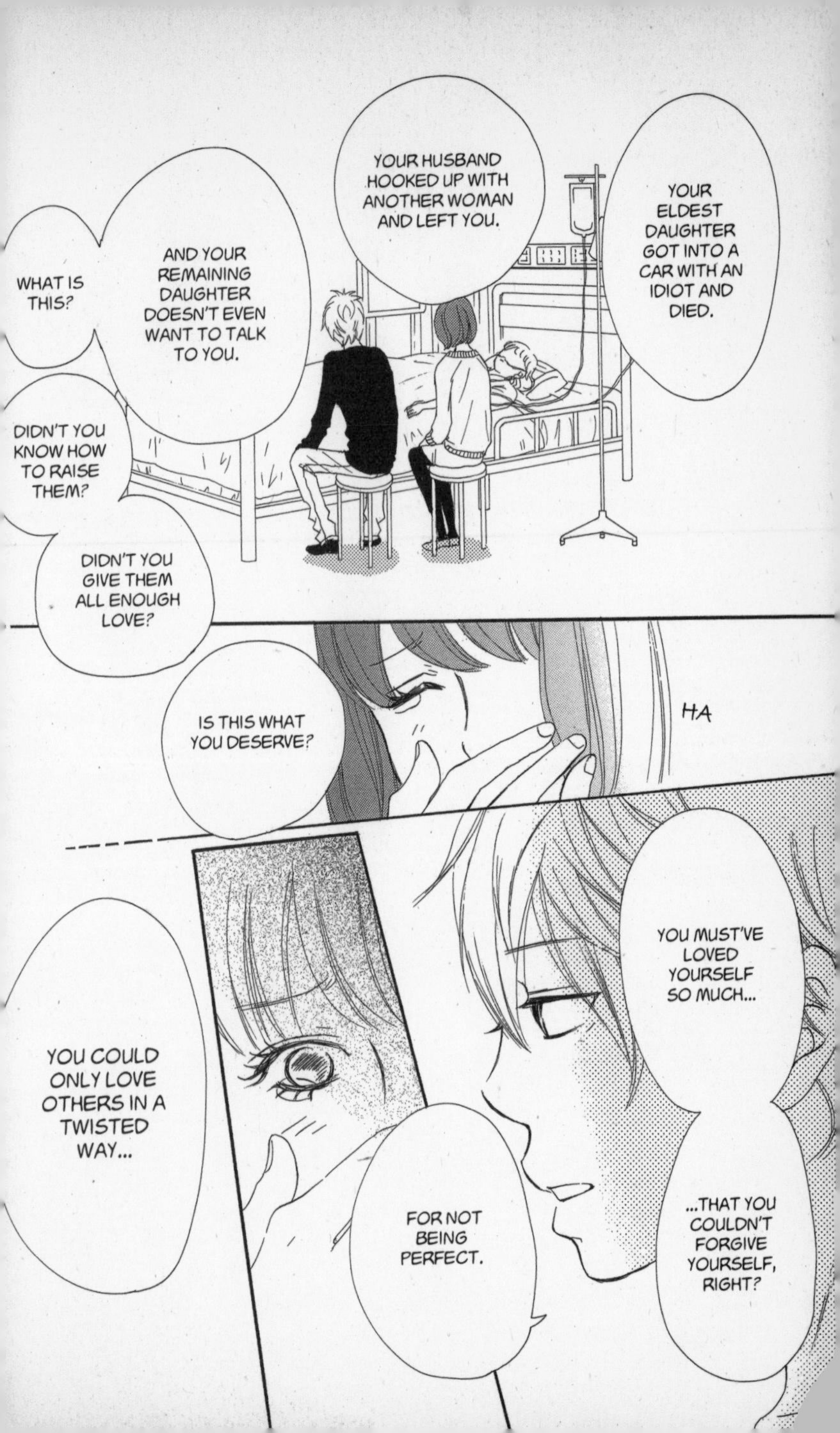
YOUR ELDEST DAUGHTER GOT INTO A CAR WITH AN IDIOT AND DIED.
YOUR HUSBAND HOOKED UP WITH ANOTHER WOMAN AND LEFT YOU.
AND YOUR REMAINING DAUGHTER DOESN'T EVEN WANT TO TALK TO YOU.
WHAT IS THIS?
DIDN'T YOU KNOW HOW TO RAISE THEM?
DIDN'T YOU GIVE THEM ALL ENOUGH LOVE?
HA
IS THIS WHAT YOU DESERVE?
YOU MUST'VE LOVED YOURSELF SO MUCH...
...THAT YOU COULDN'T FORGIVE YOURSELF, RIGHT?
FOR NOT BEING PERFECT.
YOU COULD ONLY LOVE OTHERS IN A TWISTED WAY...

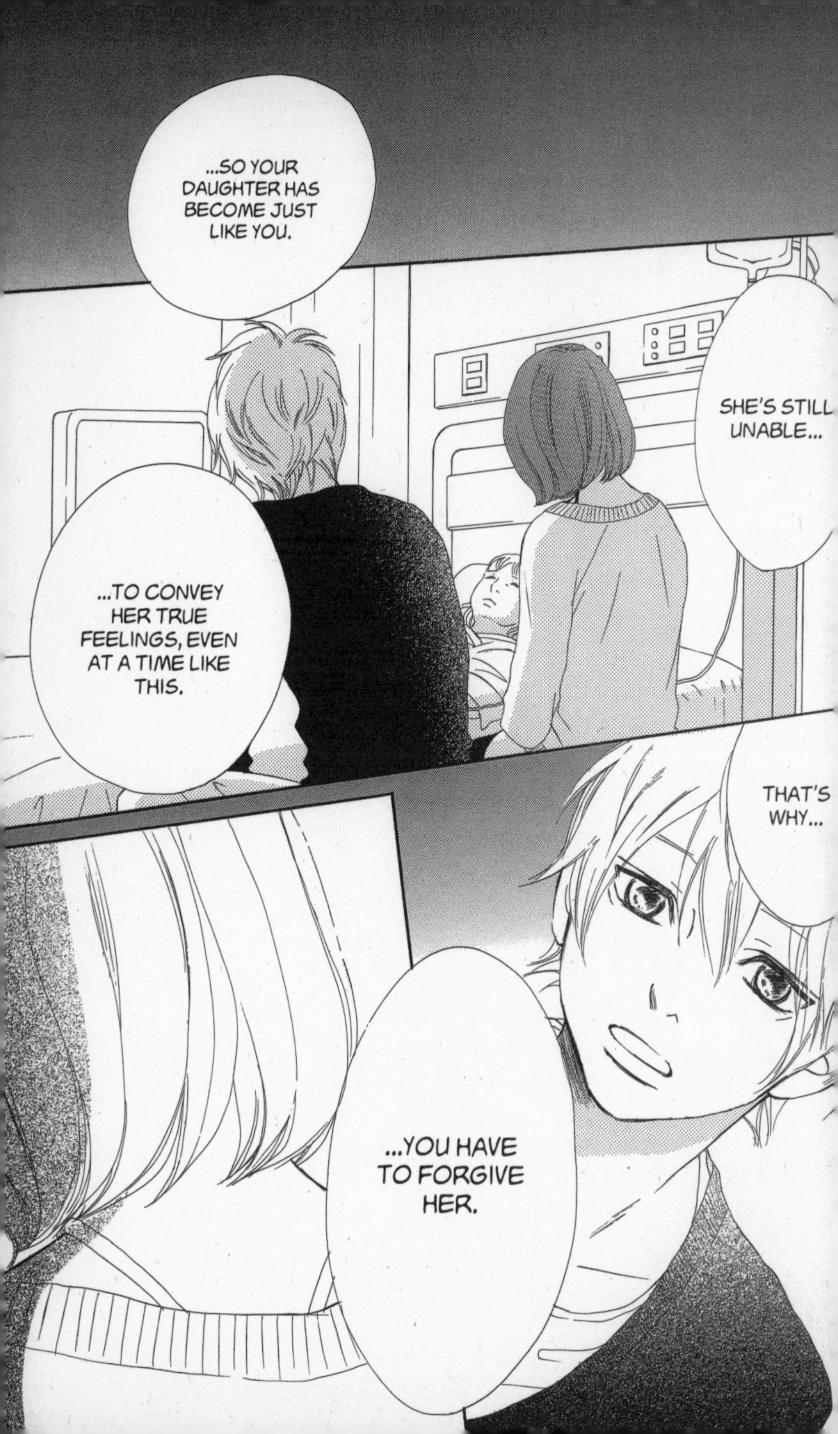
...SO YOUR DAUGHTER HAS BECOME JUST LIKE YOU.
SHE'S STILL UNABLE...
...TO CONVEY HER TRUE FEELINGS, EVEN AT A TIME LIKE THIS.
THAT'S WHY...
...YOU HAVE TO FORGIVE HER.

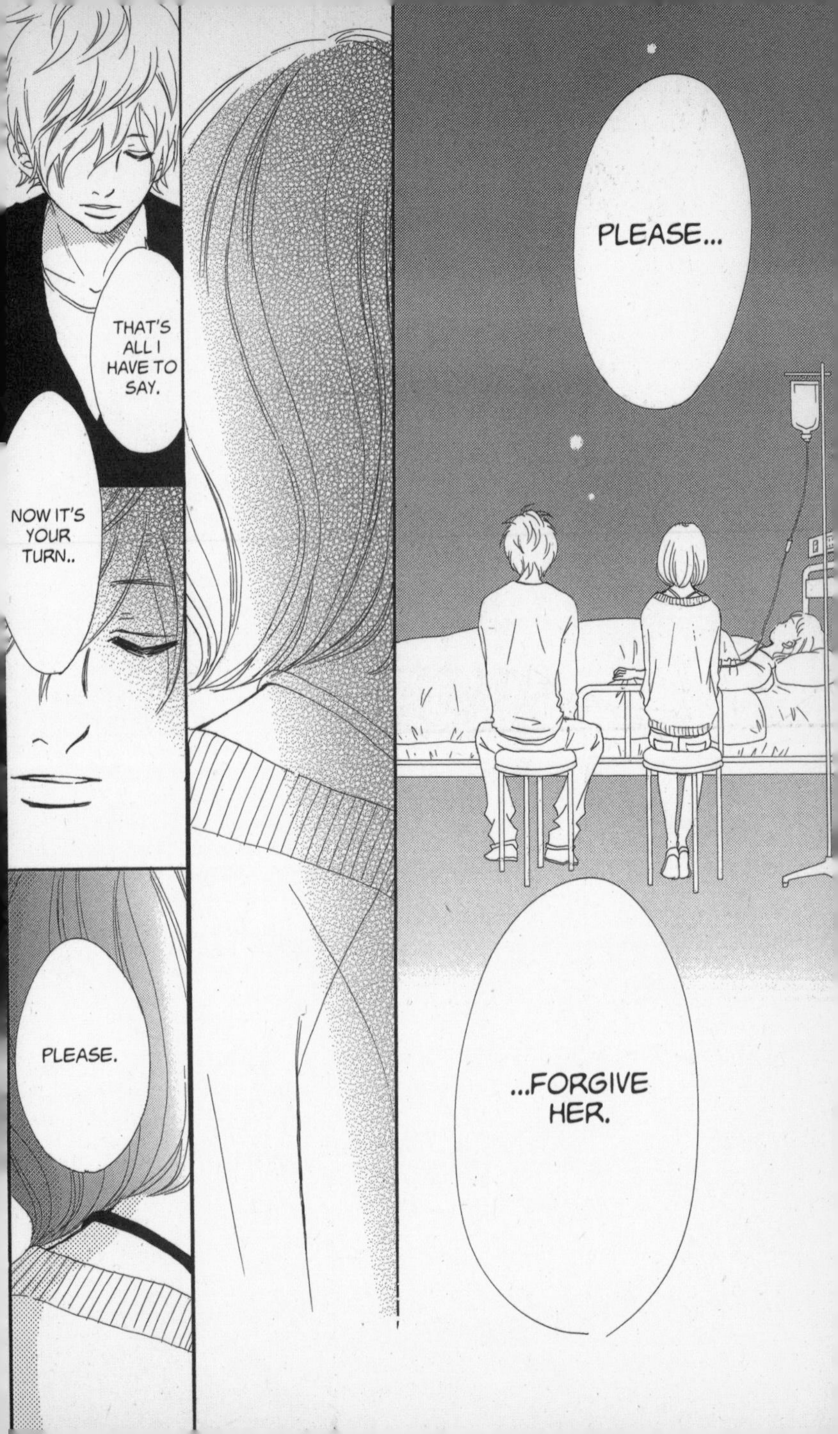
PLEASE...
...FORGIVE HER.
THAT'S ALL I HAVE TO SAY.
NOW IT'S YOUR TURN..
PLEASE.

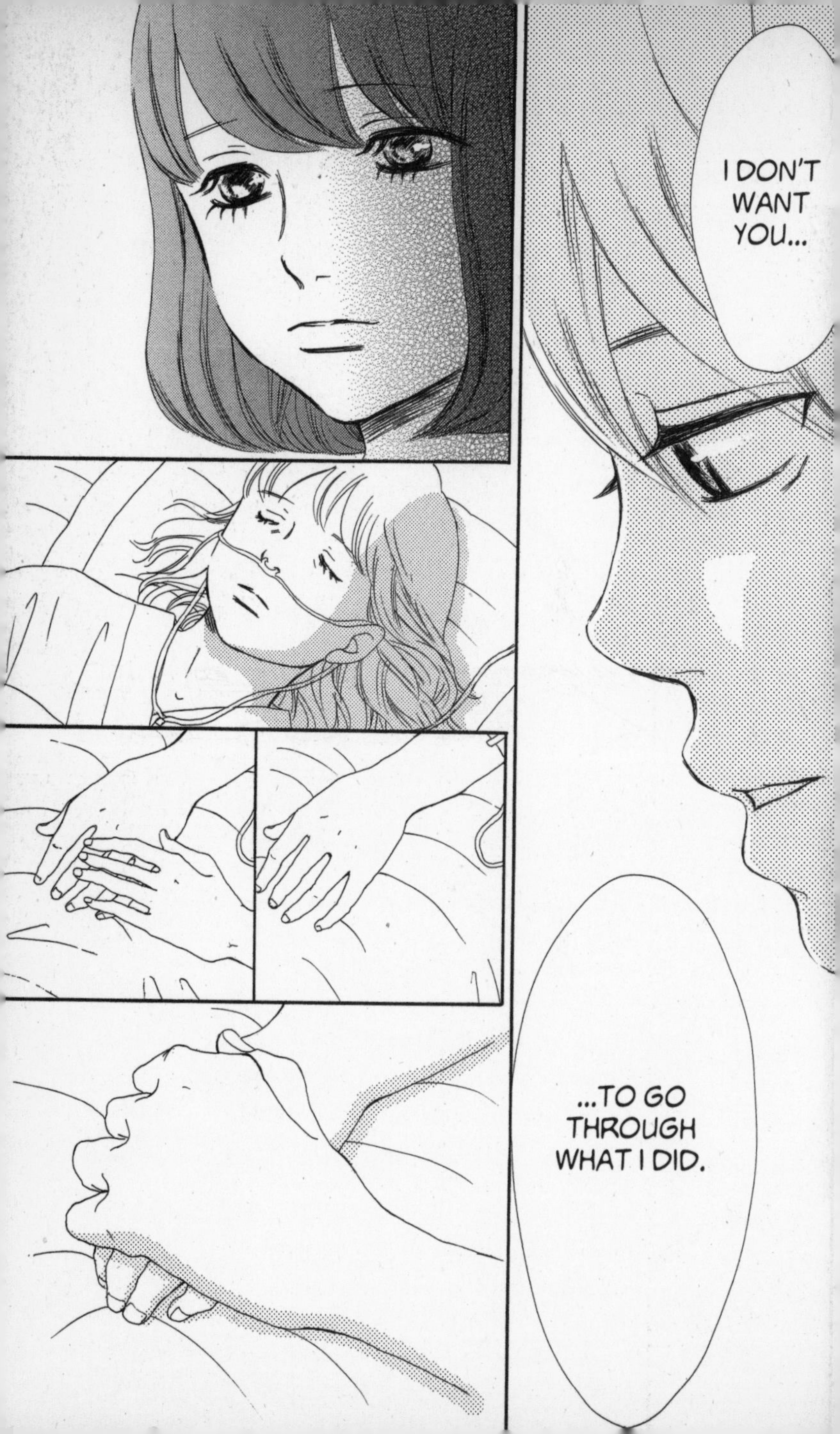
I DON'T WANT YOU...
...TO GO THROUGH WHAT I DID.

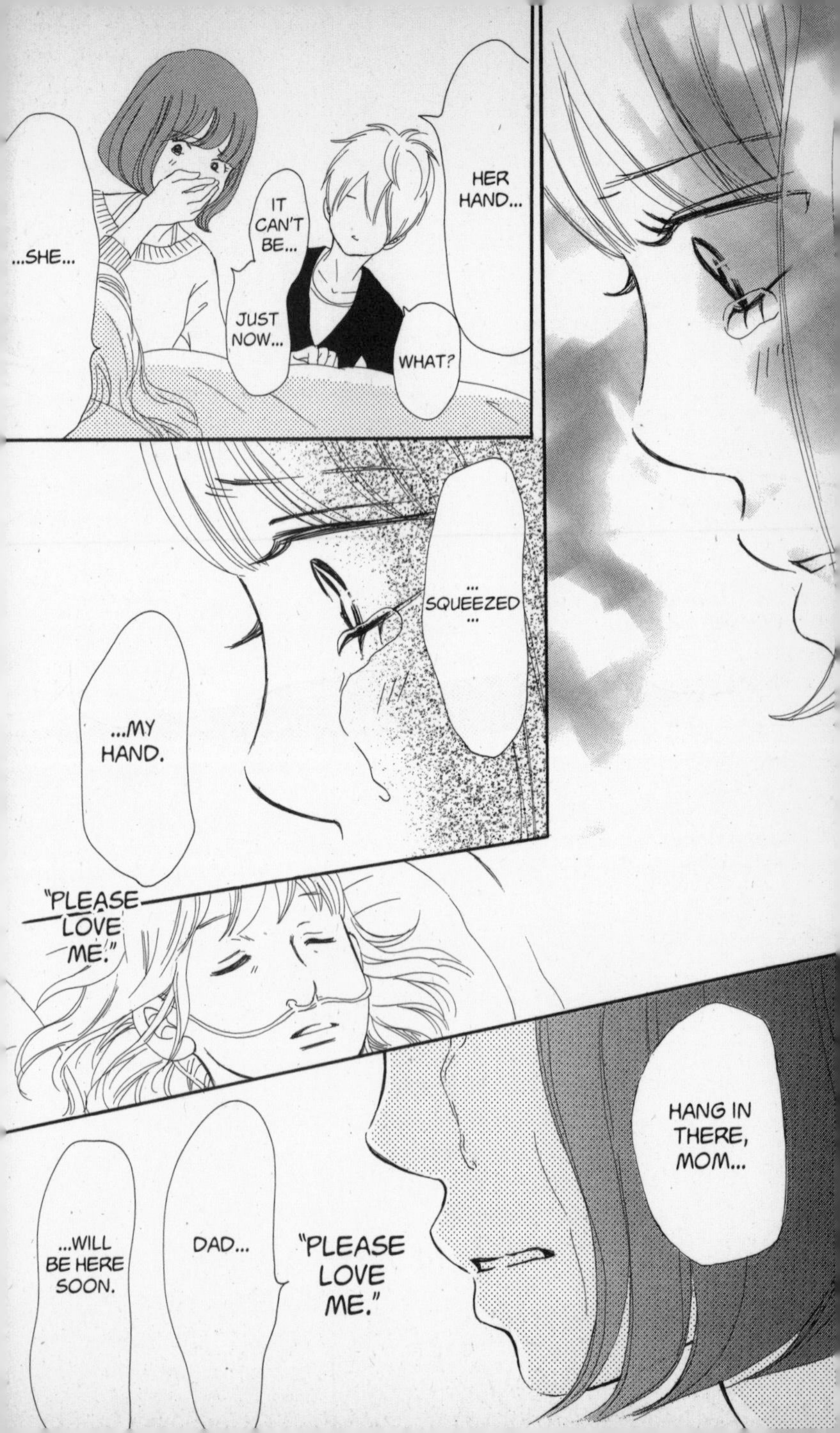

HER HAND...
WHAT?
IT CAN'T BE...
JUST NOW...
...SHE...
...SQUEEZED...
...MY HAND.
"PLEASE LOVE ME."
HANG IN THERE, MOM...
"PLEASE LOVE ME."
DAD...
...WILL BE HERE SOON.

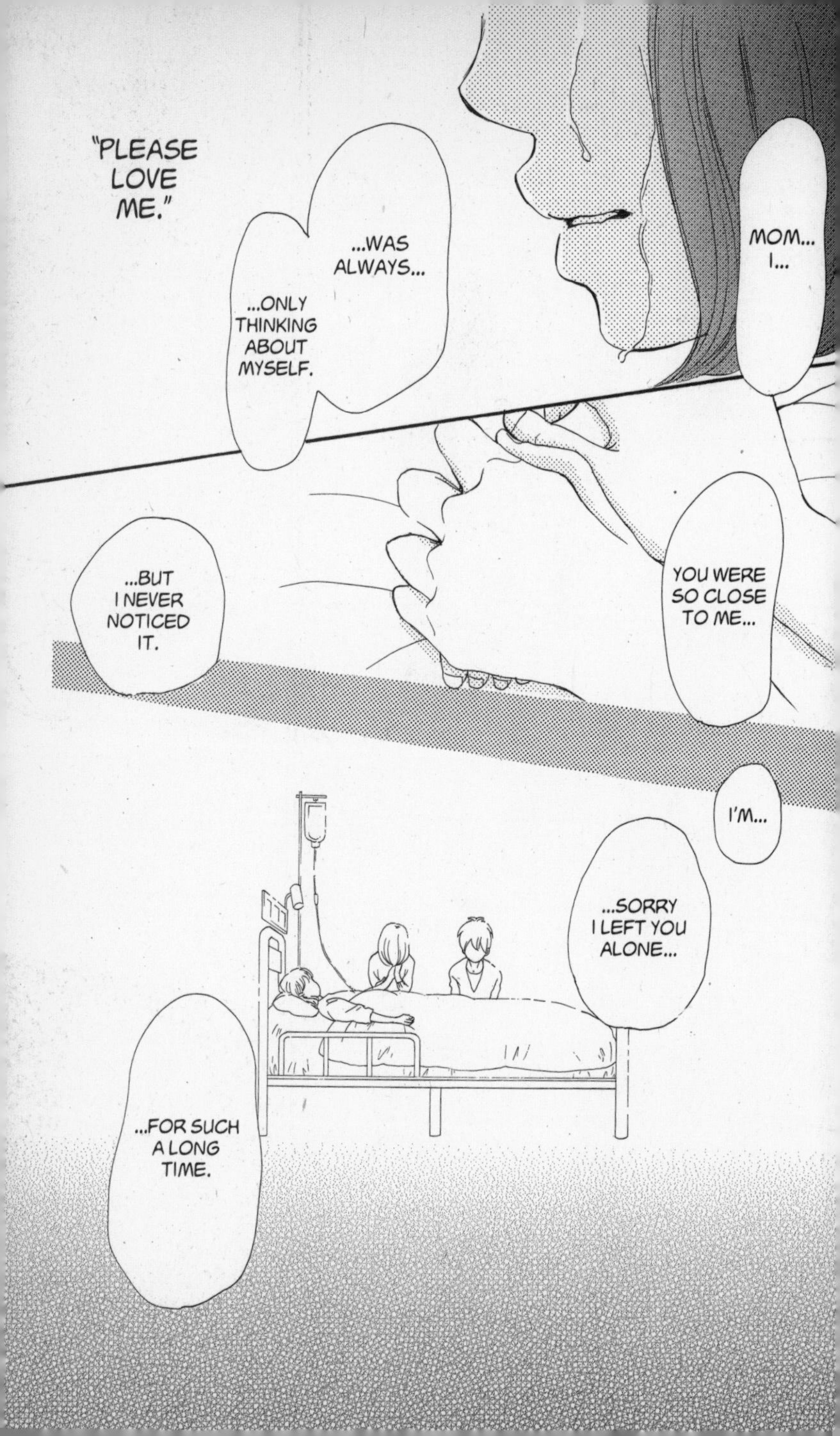
MOM... I...
...WAS ALWAYS...
...ONLY THINKING ABOUT MYSELF.
"PLEASE LOVE ME."
YOU WERE SO CLOSE TO ME...
...BUT I NEVER NOTICED IT.
I'M...
...SORRY I LEFT YOU ALONE...
...FOR SUCH A LONG TIME.

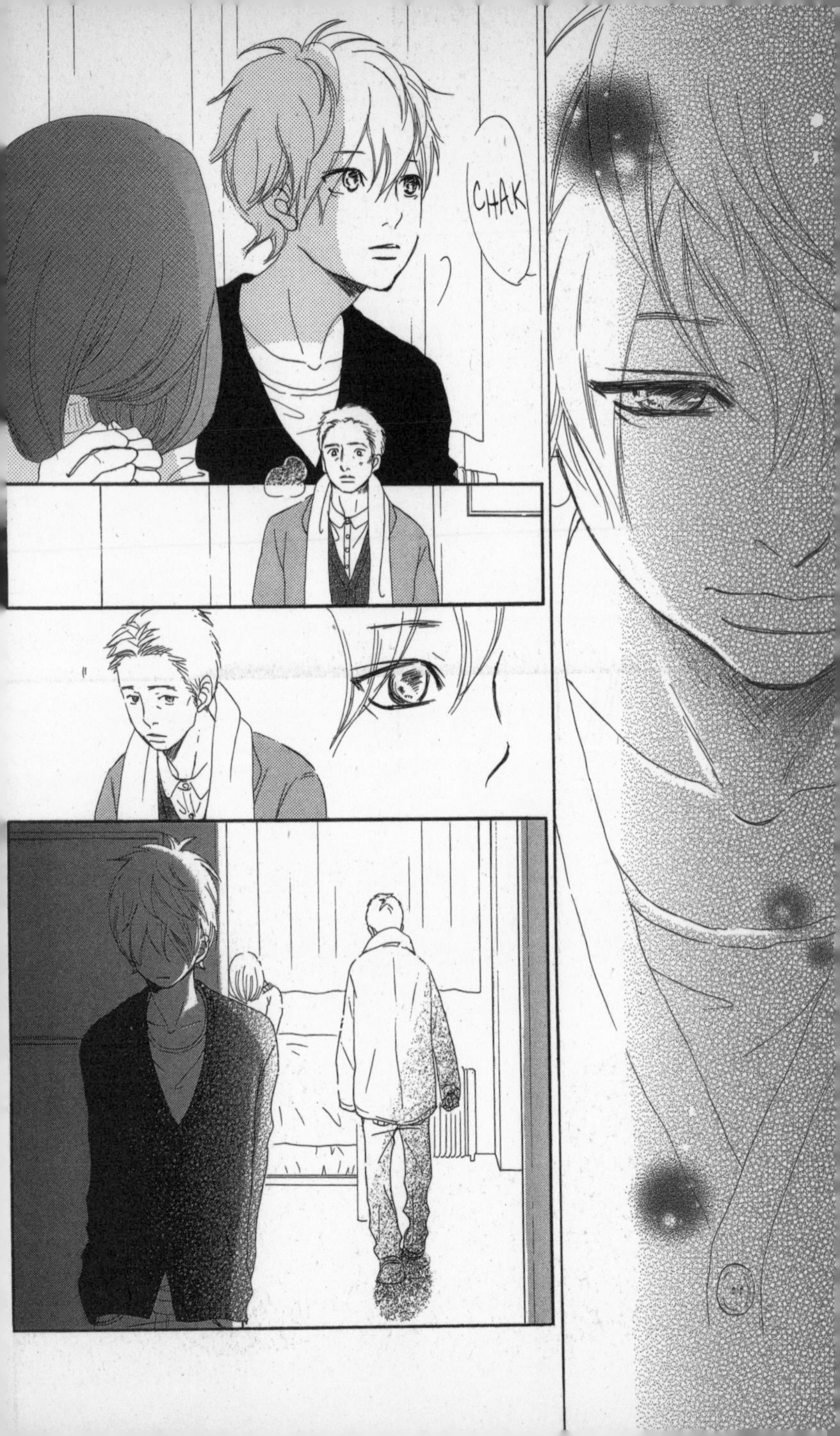
CHAK

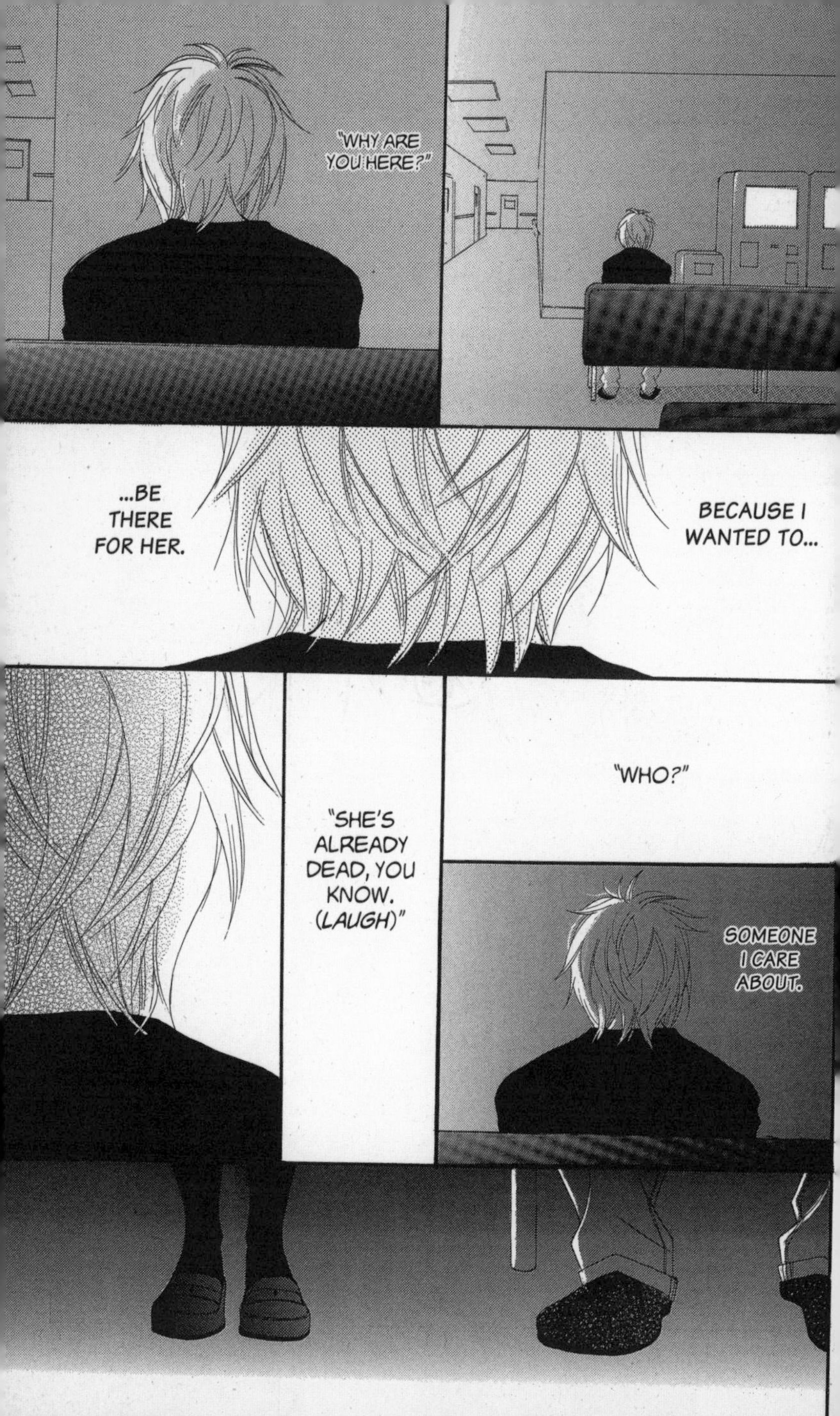
"WHY ARE YOU HERE?"
BECAUSE I WANTED TO...
...BE THERE FOR HER.
"WHO?"
SOMEONE I CARE ABOUT.
"SHE'S ALREADY DEAD, YOU KNOW. (LAUGH)"

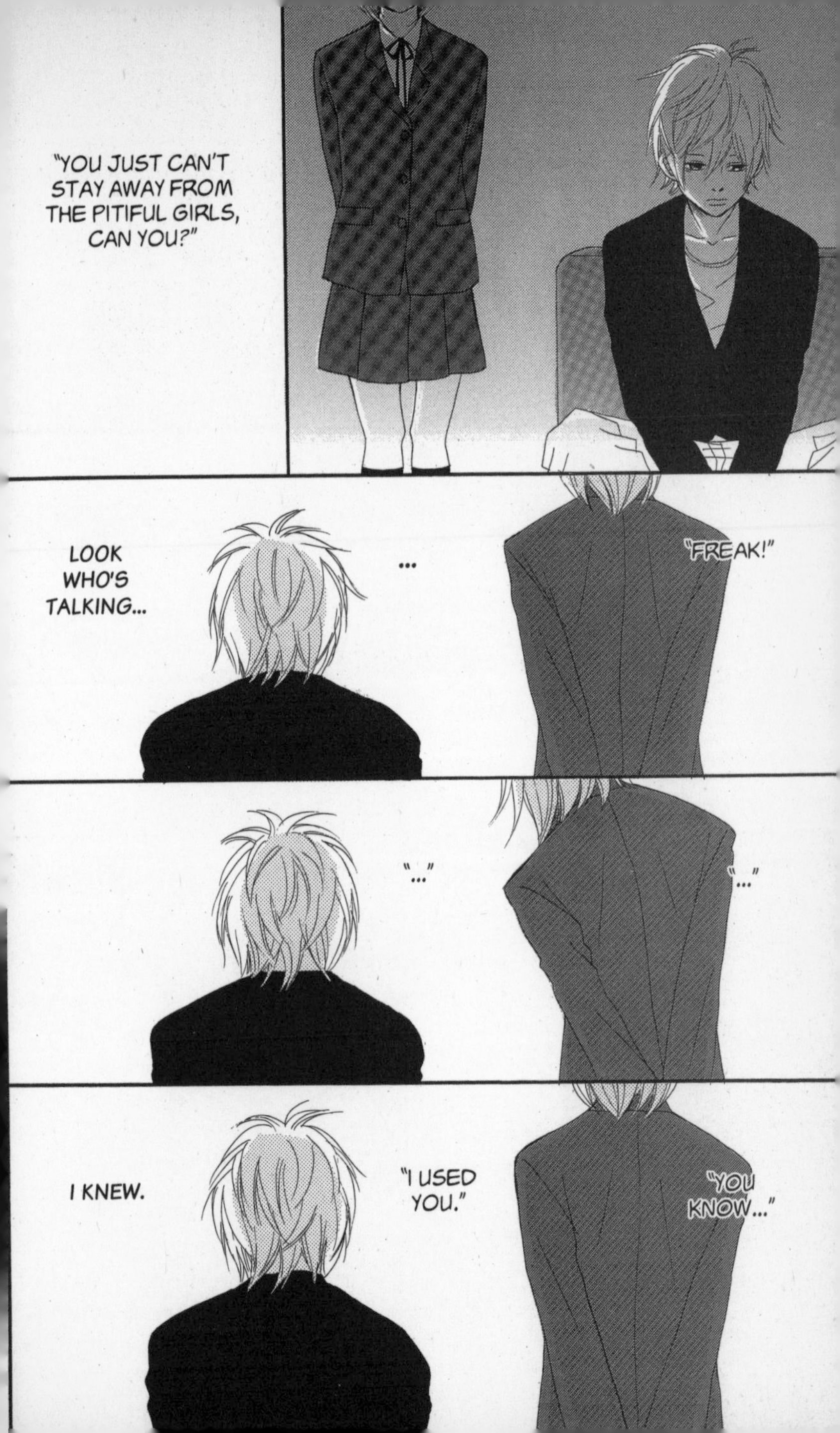
"YOU JUST CAN'T STAY AWAY FROM THE PITIFUL GIRLS, CAN YOU?"
"FREAK!"
...
LOOK WHO'S TALKING...
"..."
"..."
"YOU KNOW..."
"I USED YOU."
I KNEW.

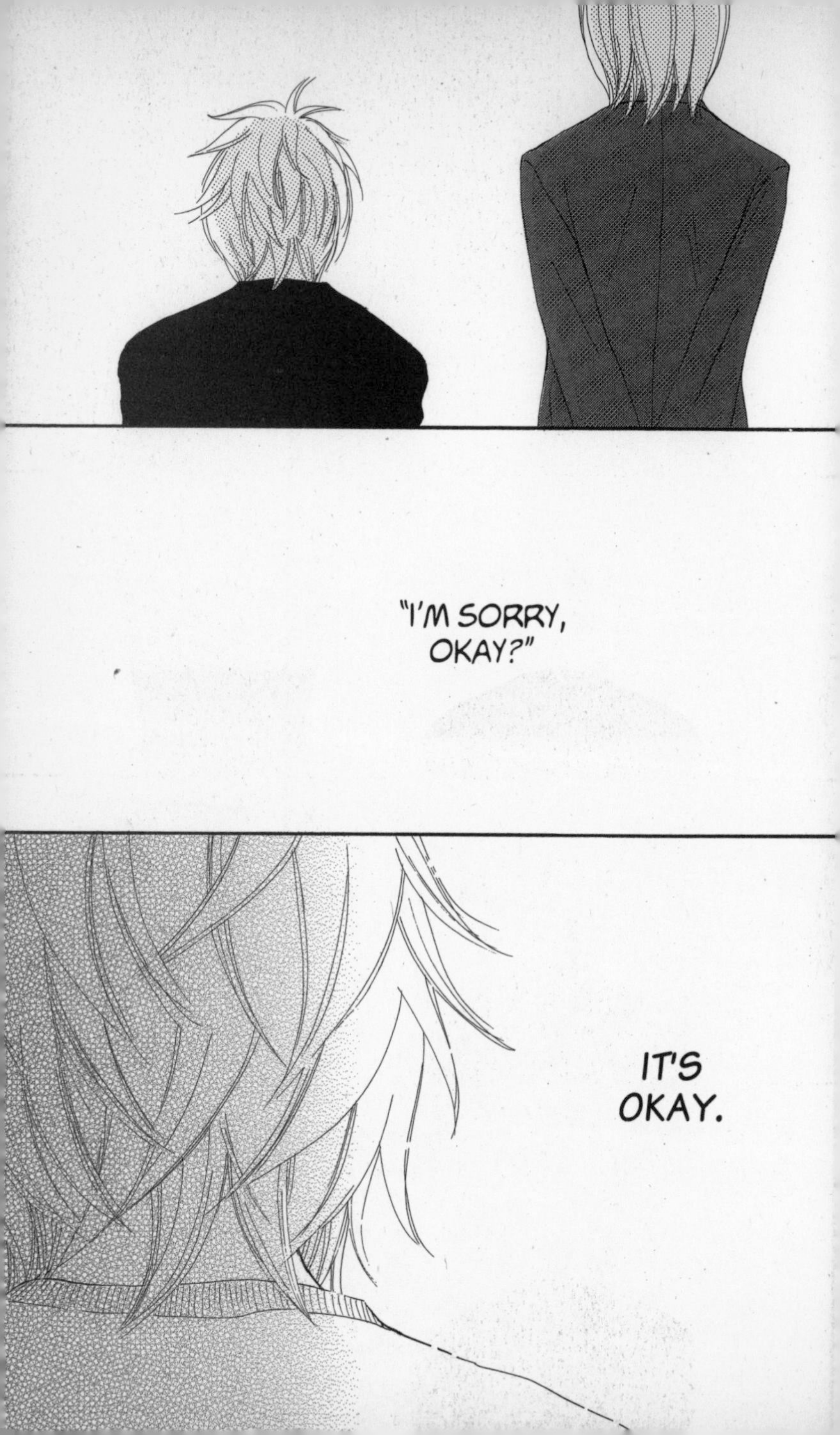
"I'M SORRY, OKAY?"
IT'S OKAY.

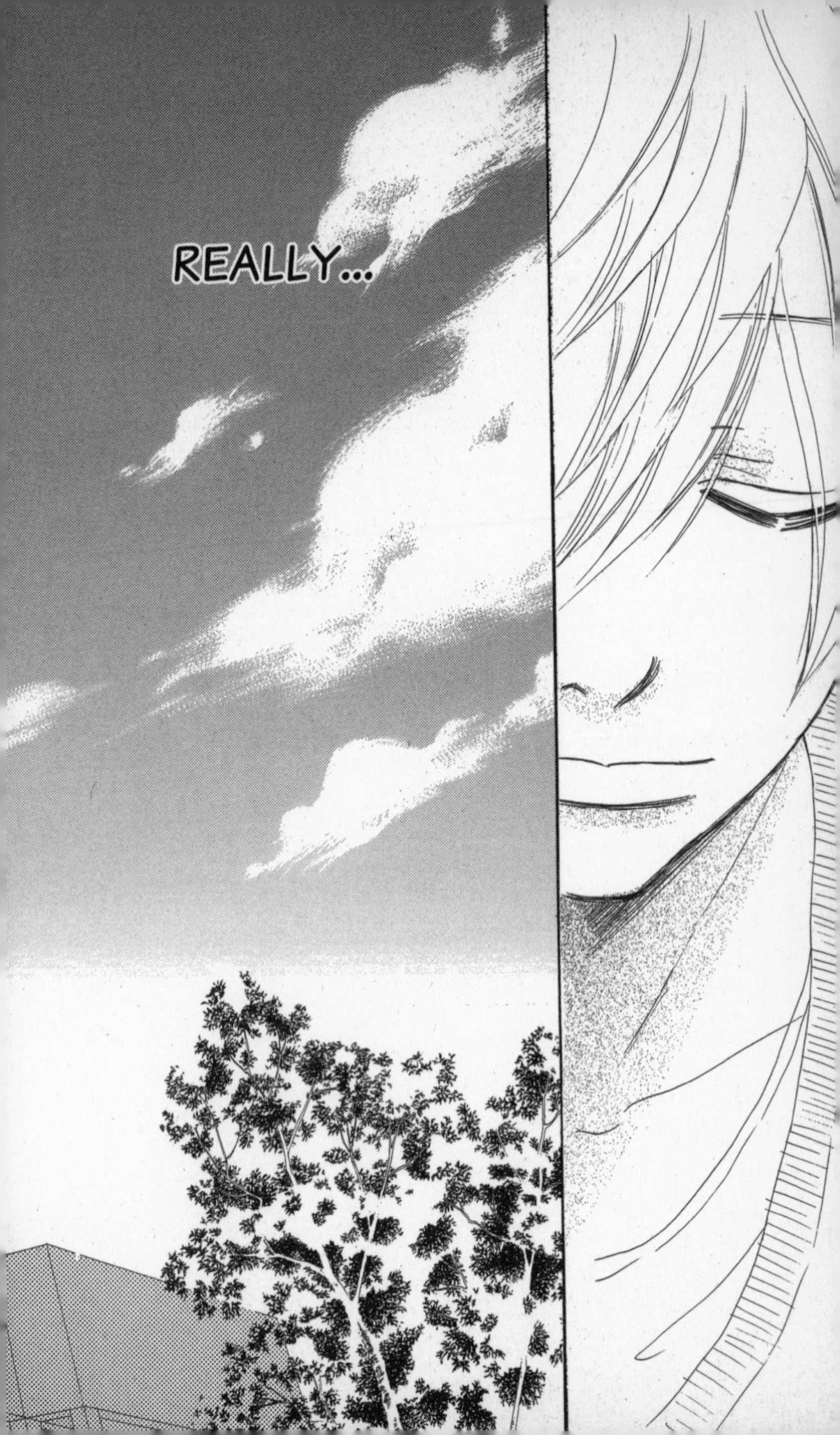
REALLY...

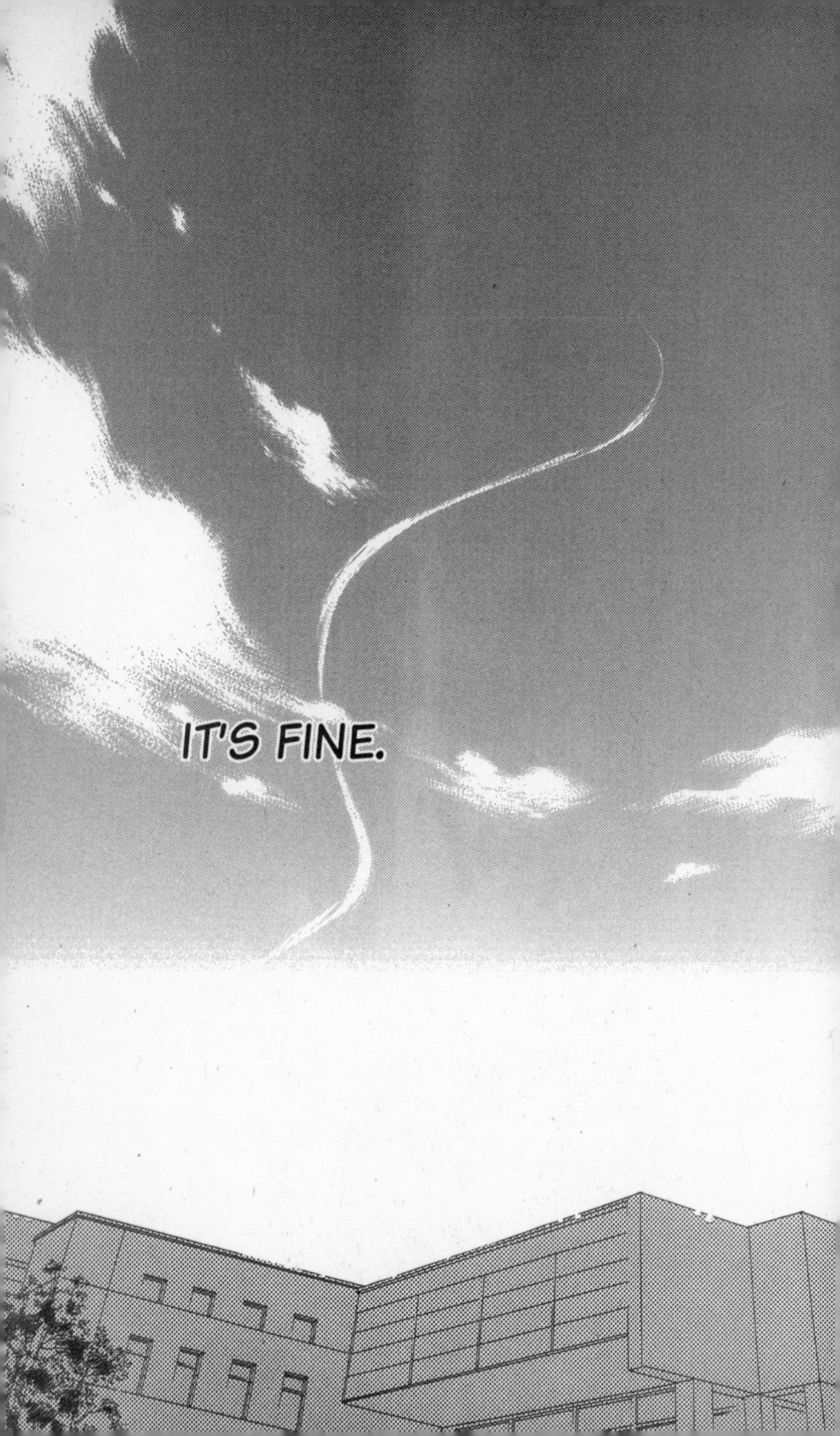
IT'S FINE.

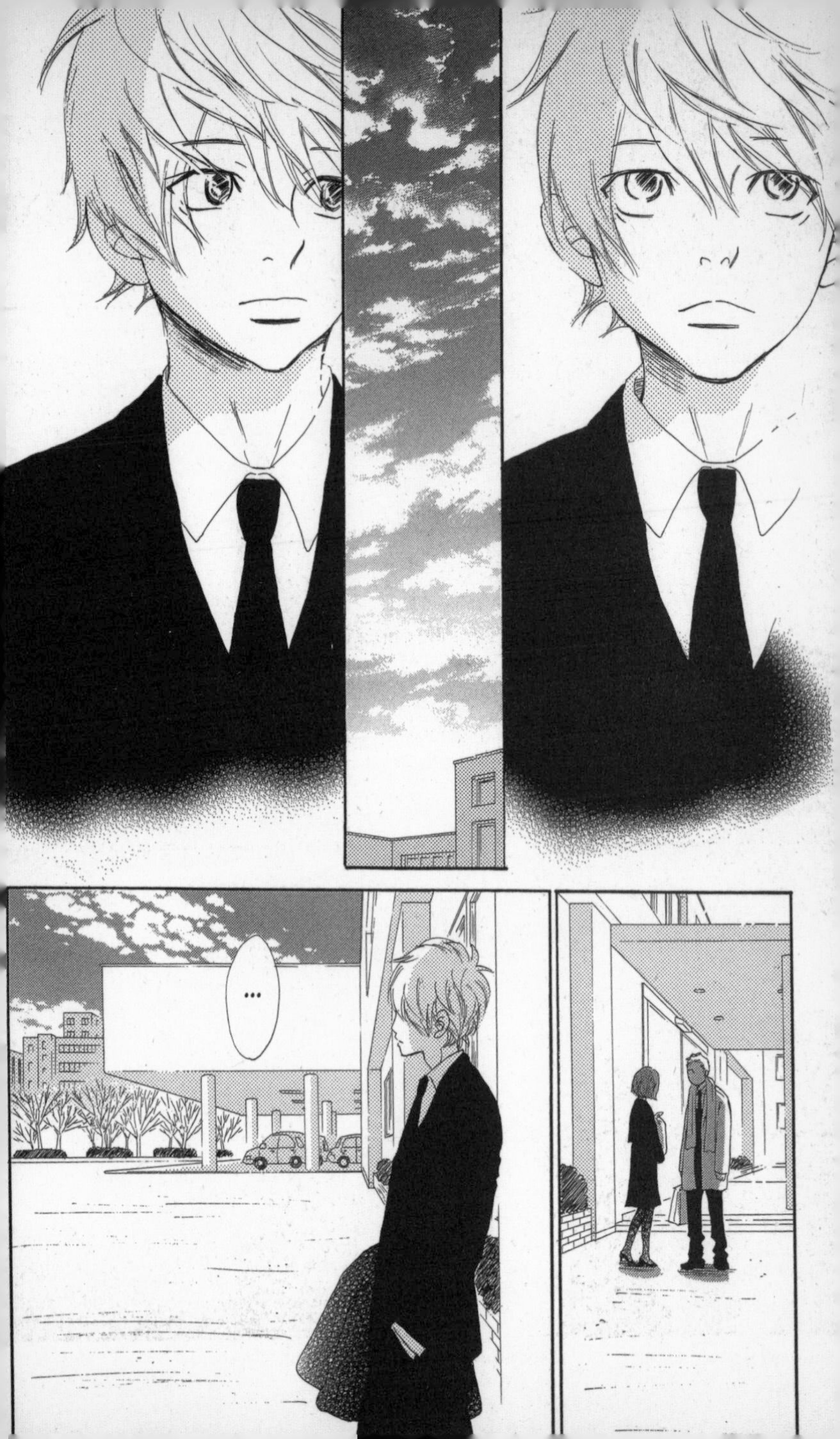
...

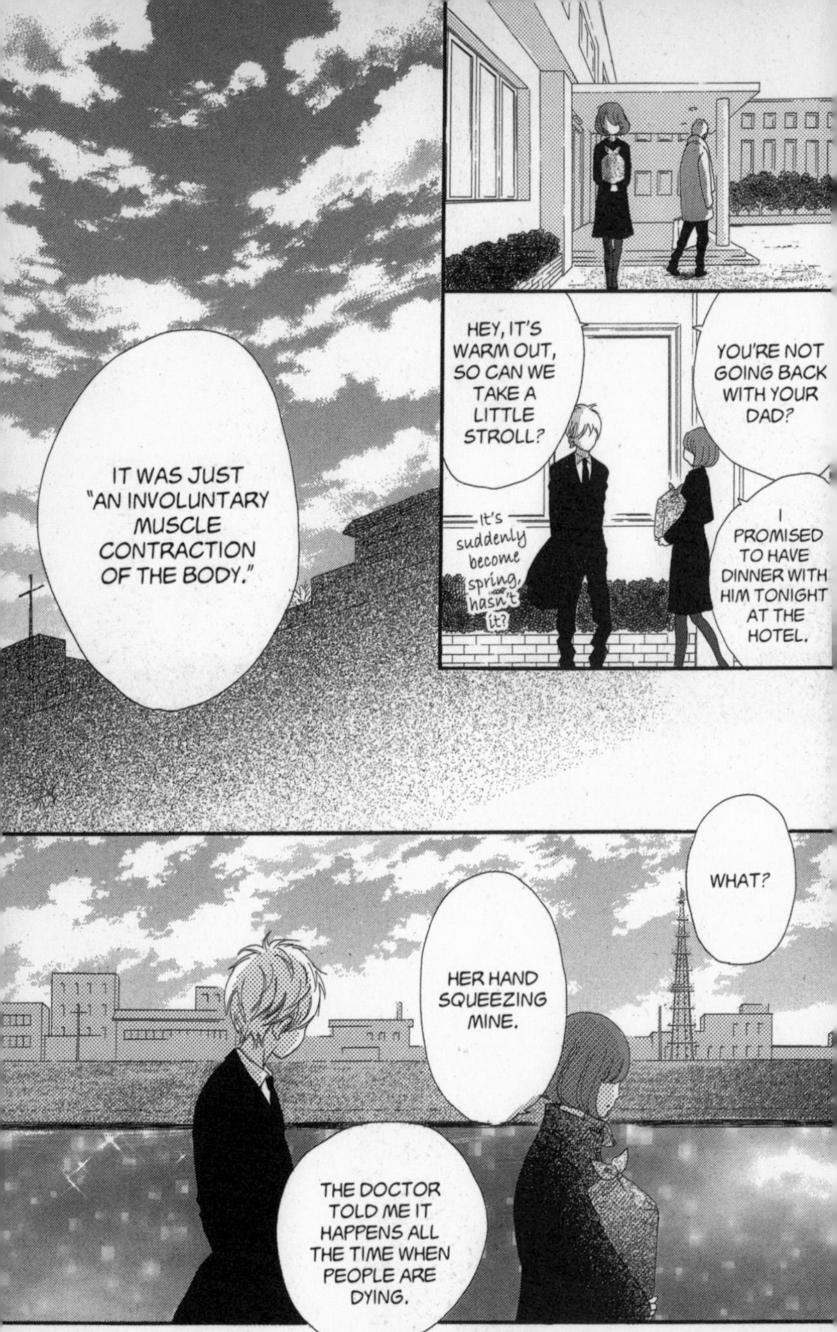
HEY, IT'S WARM OUT, SO CAN WE TAKE A LITTLE STROLL?
YOU'RE NOT GOING BACK WITH YOUR DAD?
I PROMISED TO HAVE DINNER WITH HIM TONIGHT AT THE HOTEL.
It's suddenly become spring, hasn't it?
IT WAS JUST "AN INVOLUNTARY MUSCLE CONTRACTION OF THE BODY."
WHAT?
HER HAND SQUEEZING MINE.
THE DOCTOR TOLD ME IT HAPPENS ALL THE TIME WHEN PEOPLE ARE DYING.

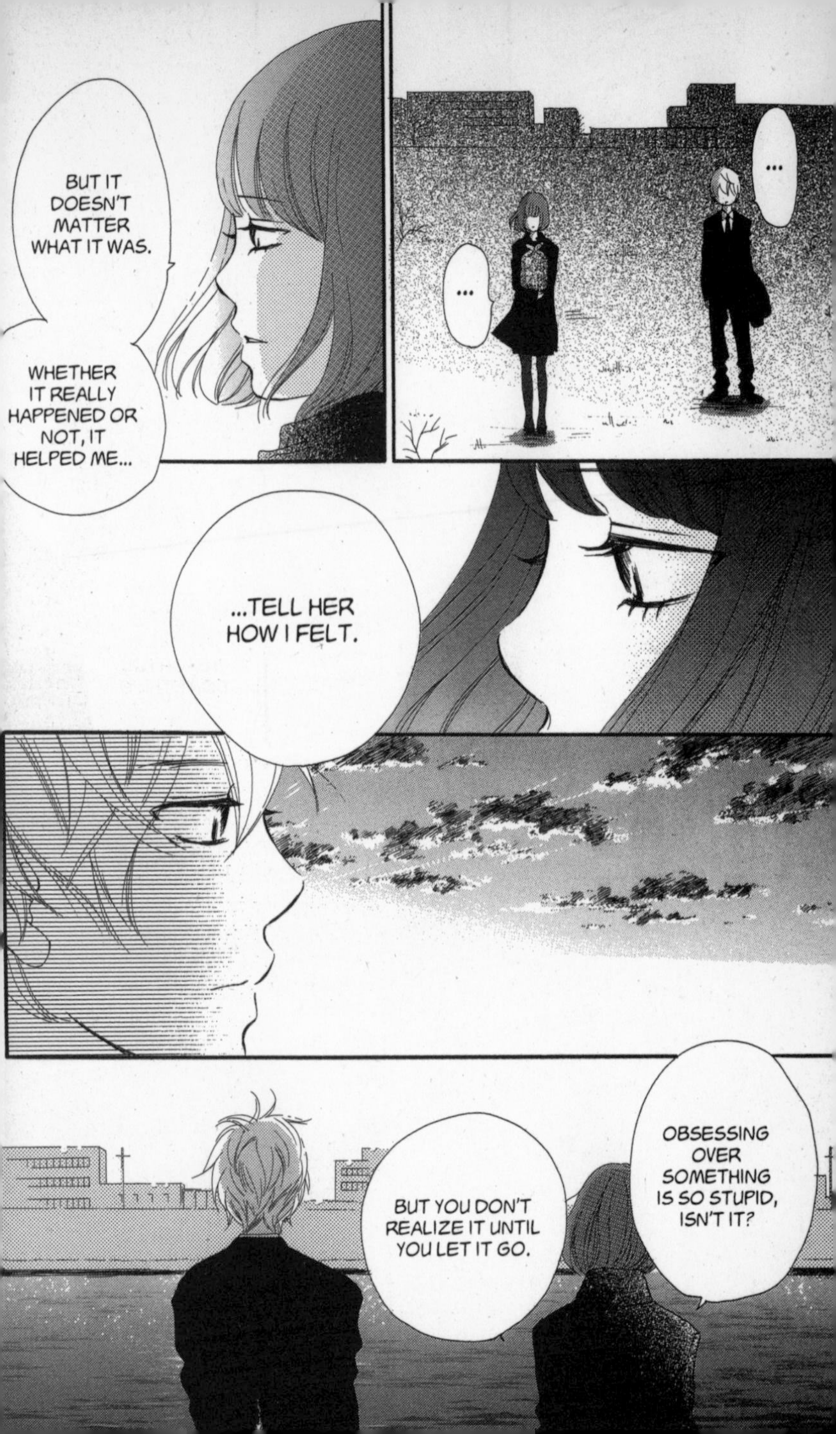
...
...
BUT IT DOESN'T MATTER WHAT IT WAS.
WHETHER IT REALLY HAPPENED OR NOT, IT HELPED ME...
...TELL HER HOW I FELT.
OBSESSING OVER SOMETHING IS SO STUPID, ISN'T IT?
BUT YOU DON'T REALIZE IT UNTIL YOU LET IT GO.

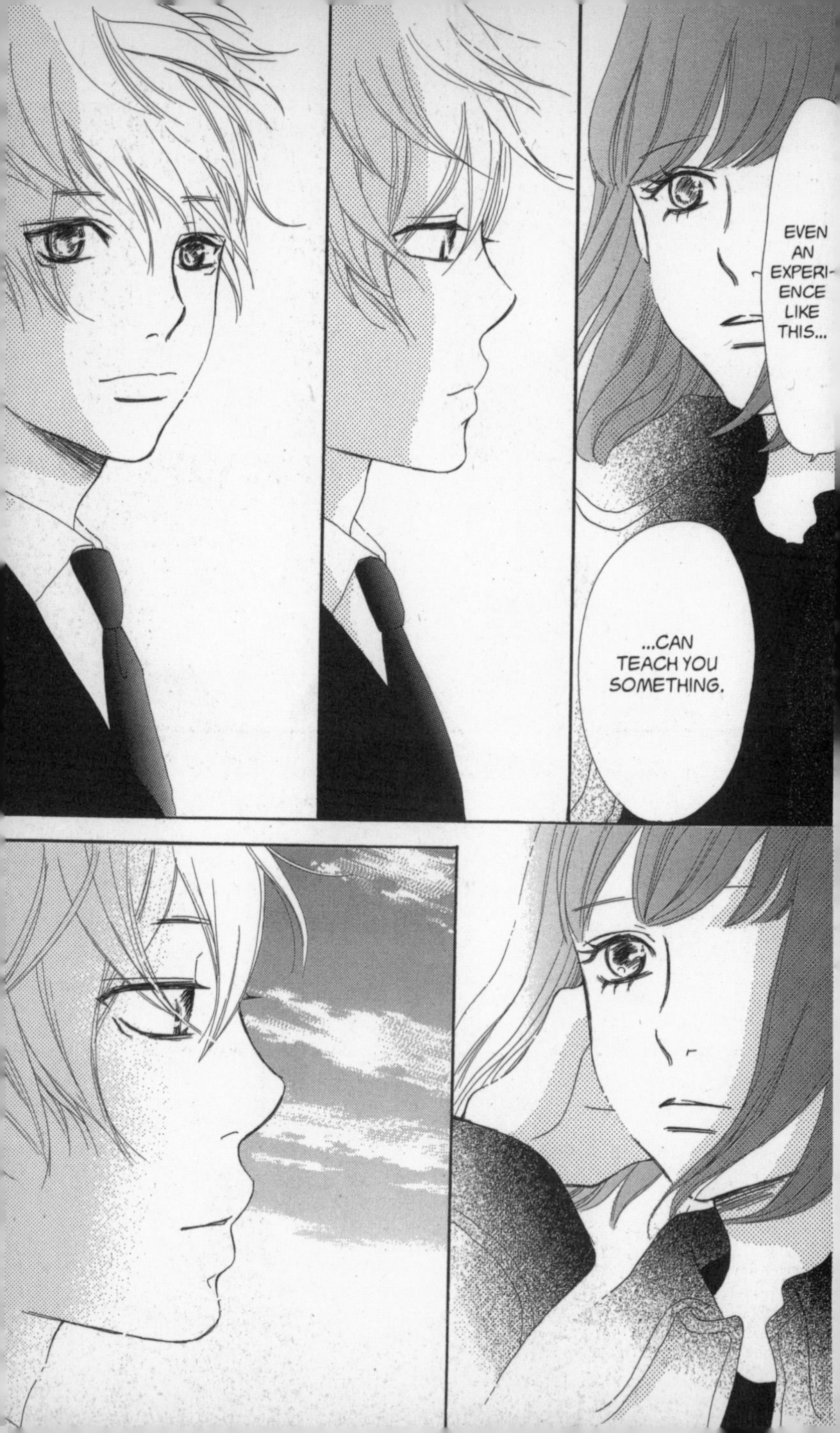
EVEN AN EXPERIENCE LIKE THIS...
...CAN TEACH YOU SOMETHING.

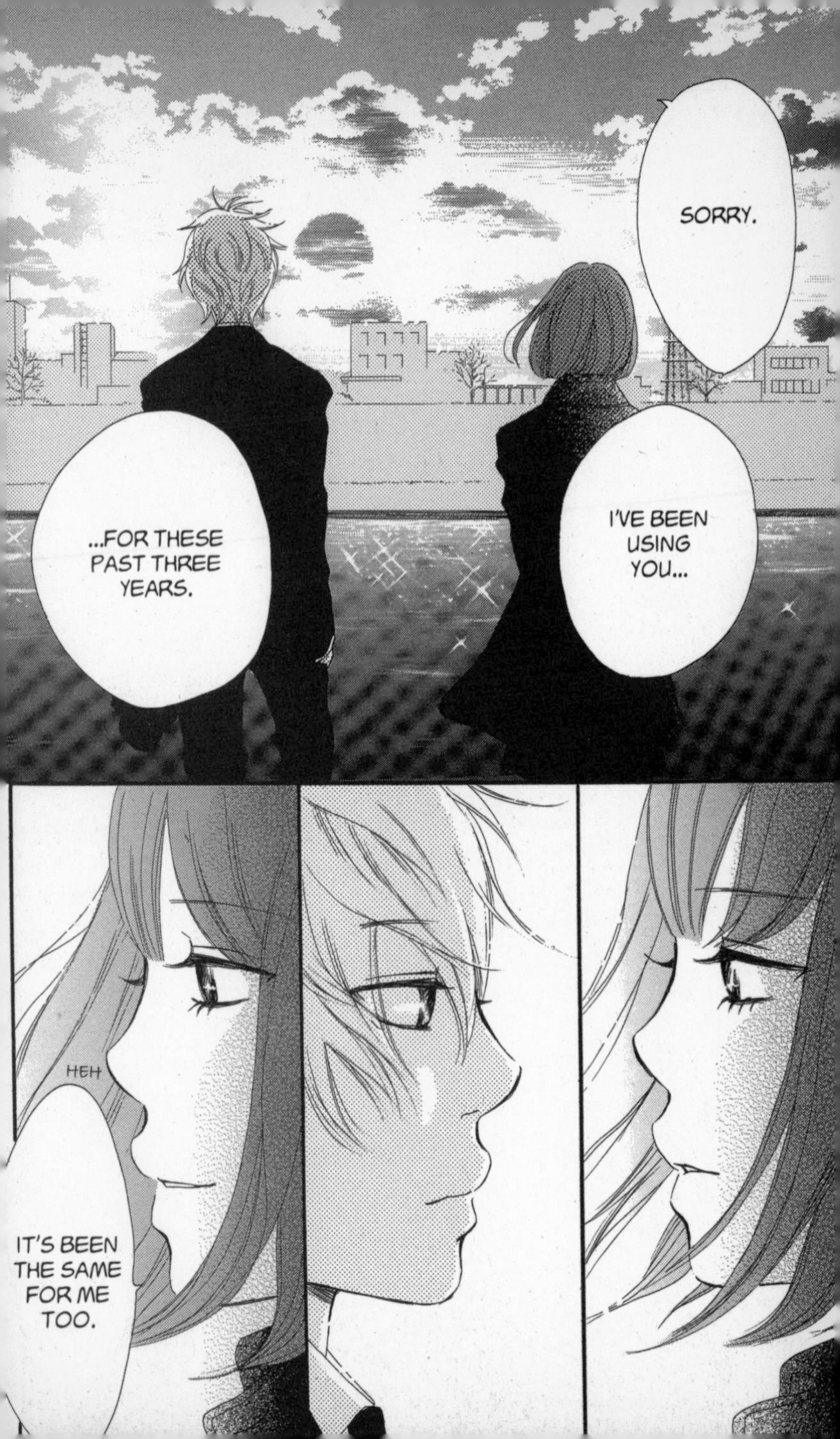
SORRY.
I'VE BEEN USING YOU...
...FOR THESE PAST THREE YEARS.
HEH
IT'S BEEN THE SAME FOR ME TOO.

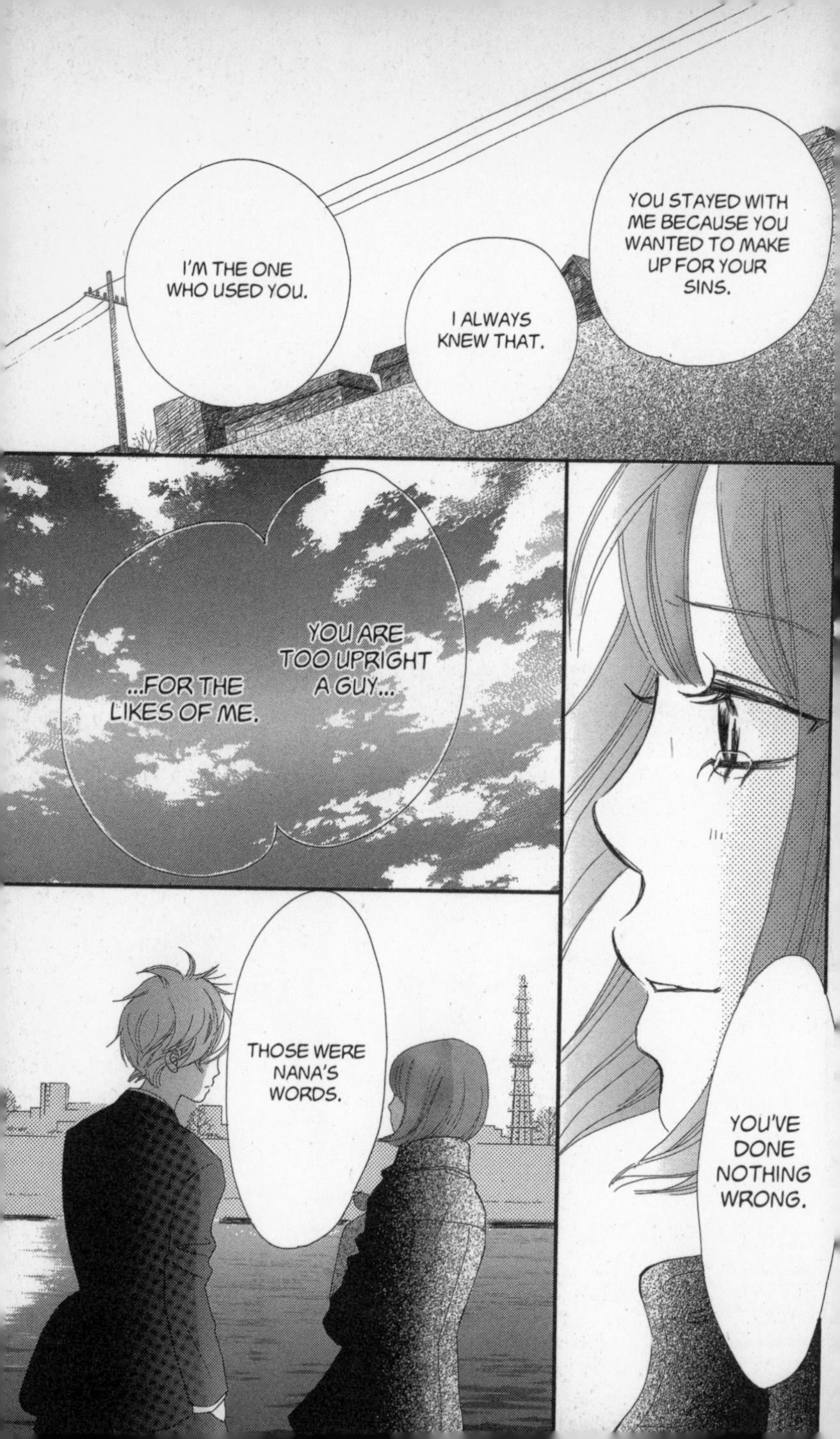
YOU STAYED WITH ME BECAUSE YOU WANTED TO MAKE UP FOR YOUR SINS.
I ALWAYS KNEW THAT.
I'M THE ONE WHO USED YOU.
YOU'VE DONE NOTHING WRONG.
YOU ARE TOO UPRIGHT A GUY...
...FOR THE LIKES OF ME.
THOSE WERE NANA'S WORDS.

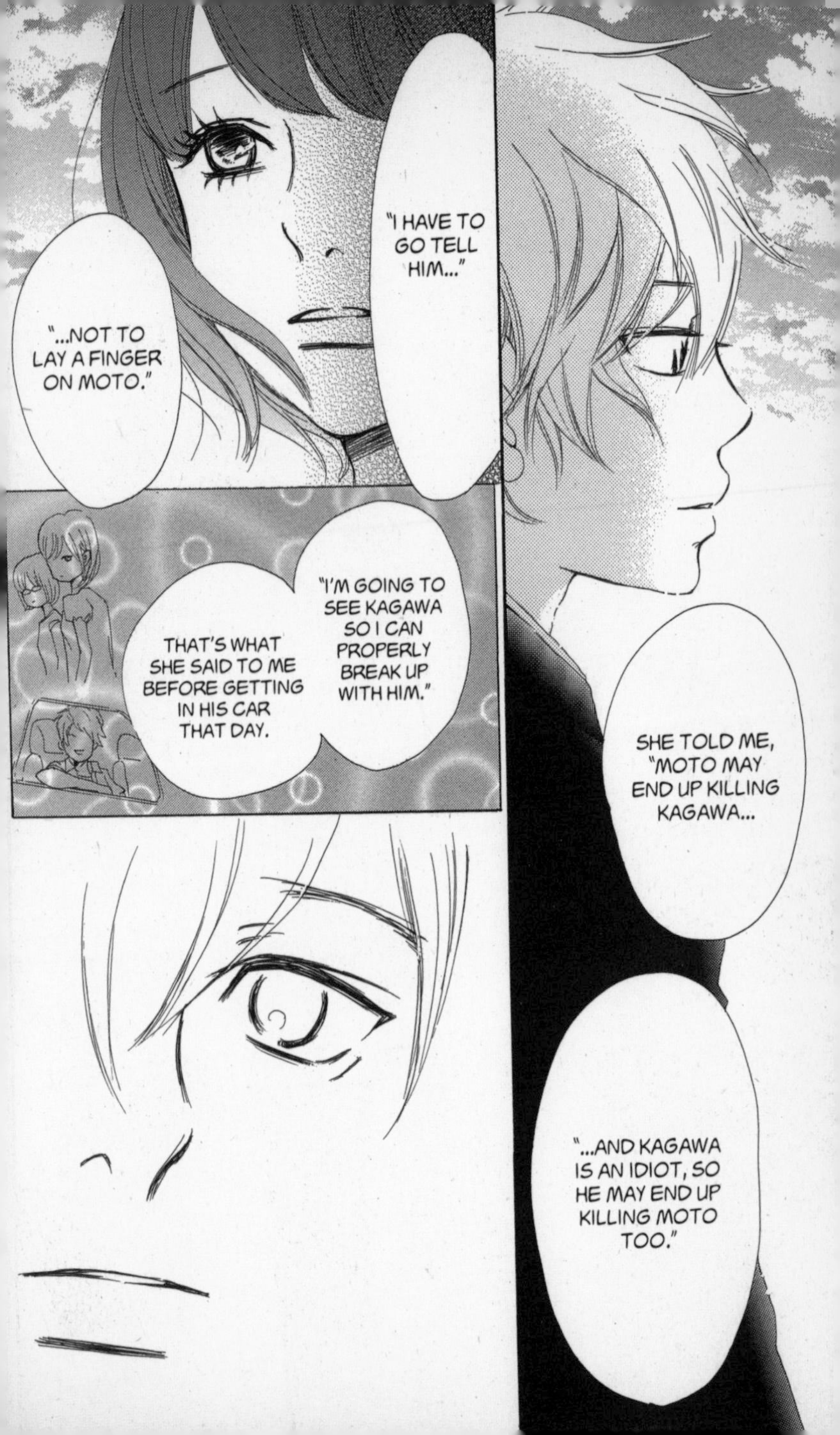
SHE TOLD ME, "MOTO MAY END UP KILLING KAGAWA...
"...AND KAGAWA IS AN IDIOT, SO HE MAY END UP KILLING MOTO TOO."
"I HAVE TO GO TELL HIM..."
"...NOT TO LAY A FINGER ON MOTO."
"I'M GOING TO SEE KAGAWA SO I CAN PROPERLY BREAK UP WITH HIM."
THAT'S WHAT SHE SAID TO ME BEFORE GETTING IN HIS CAR THAT DAY.

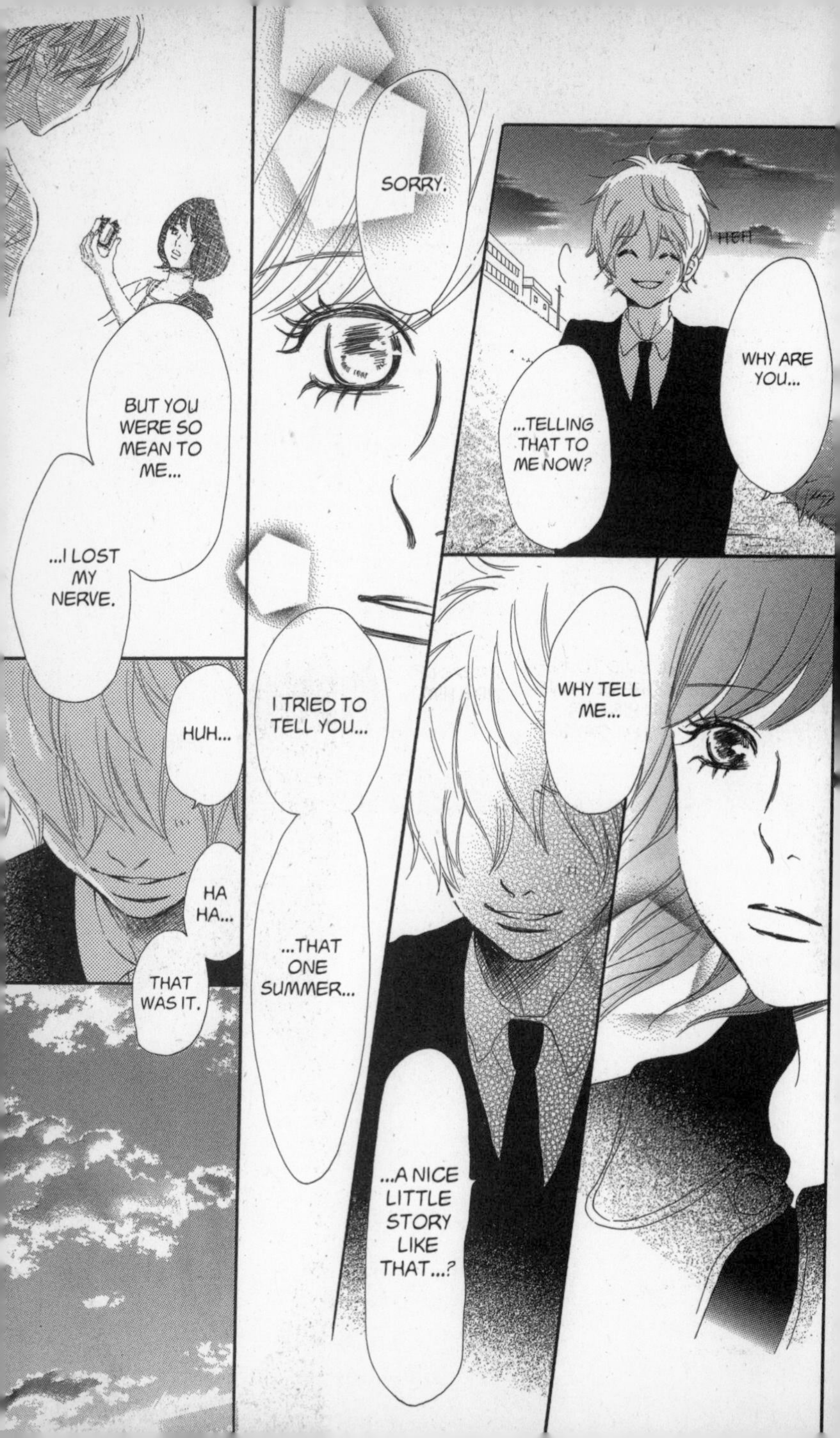
HEH
WHY ARE YOU...
...TELLING THAT TO ME NOW?
WHY TELL ME...
...A NICE LITTLE STORY LIKE THAT...?
SORRY.
I TRIED TO TELL YOU...
...THAT ONE SUMMER...
BUT YOU WERE SO MEAN TO ME...
...I LOST MY NERVE.
HUH...
HA HA...
THAT WAS IT.

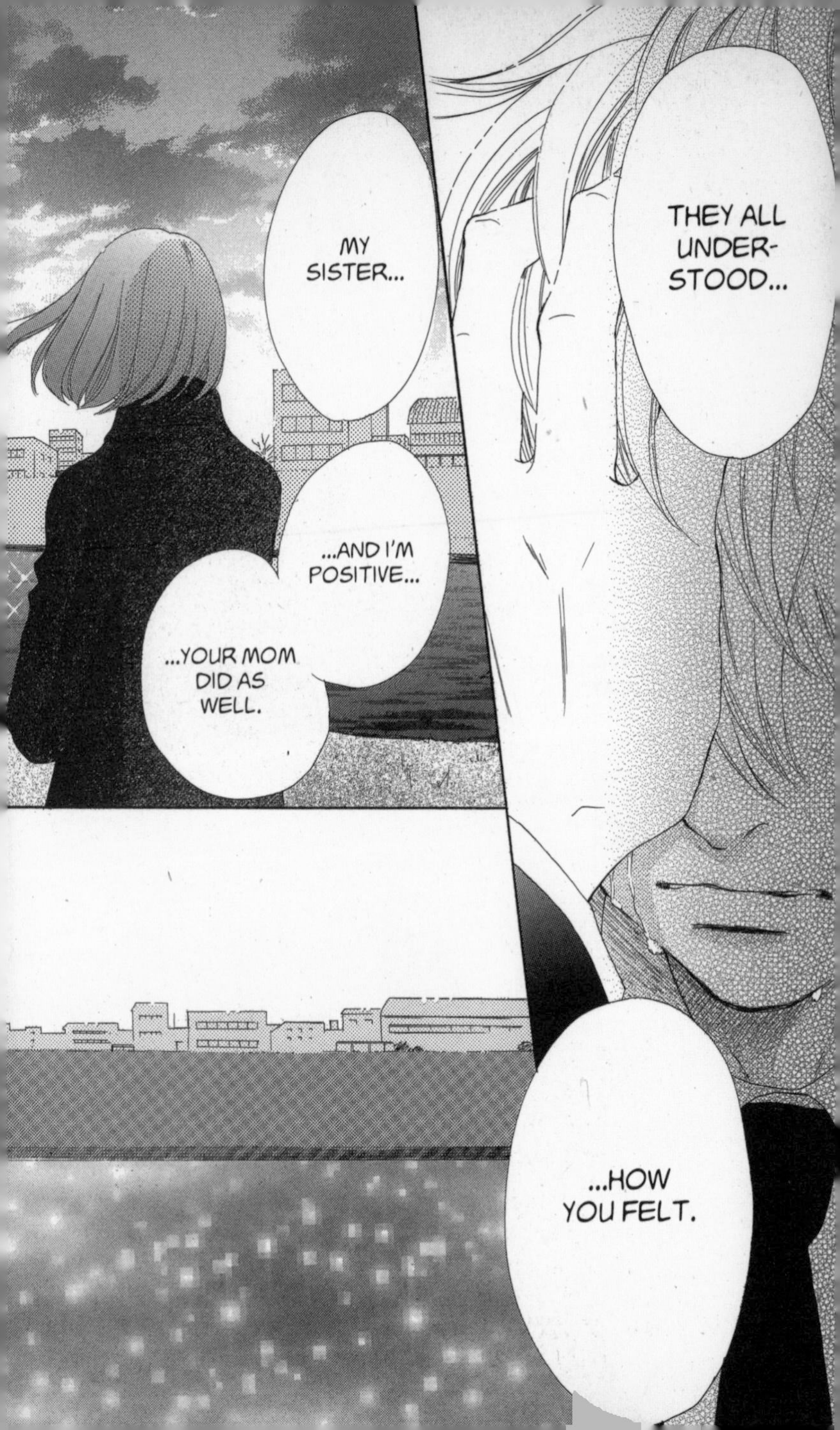
THEY ALL UNDER-STOOD...
...HOW YOU FELT.
MY SISTER...
...AND I'M POSITIVE...
...YOUR MOM DID AS WELL.

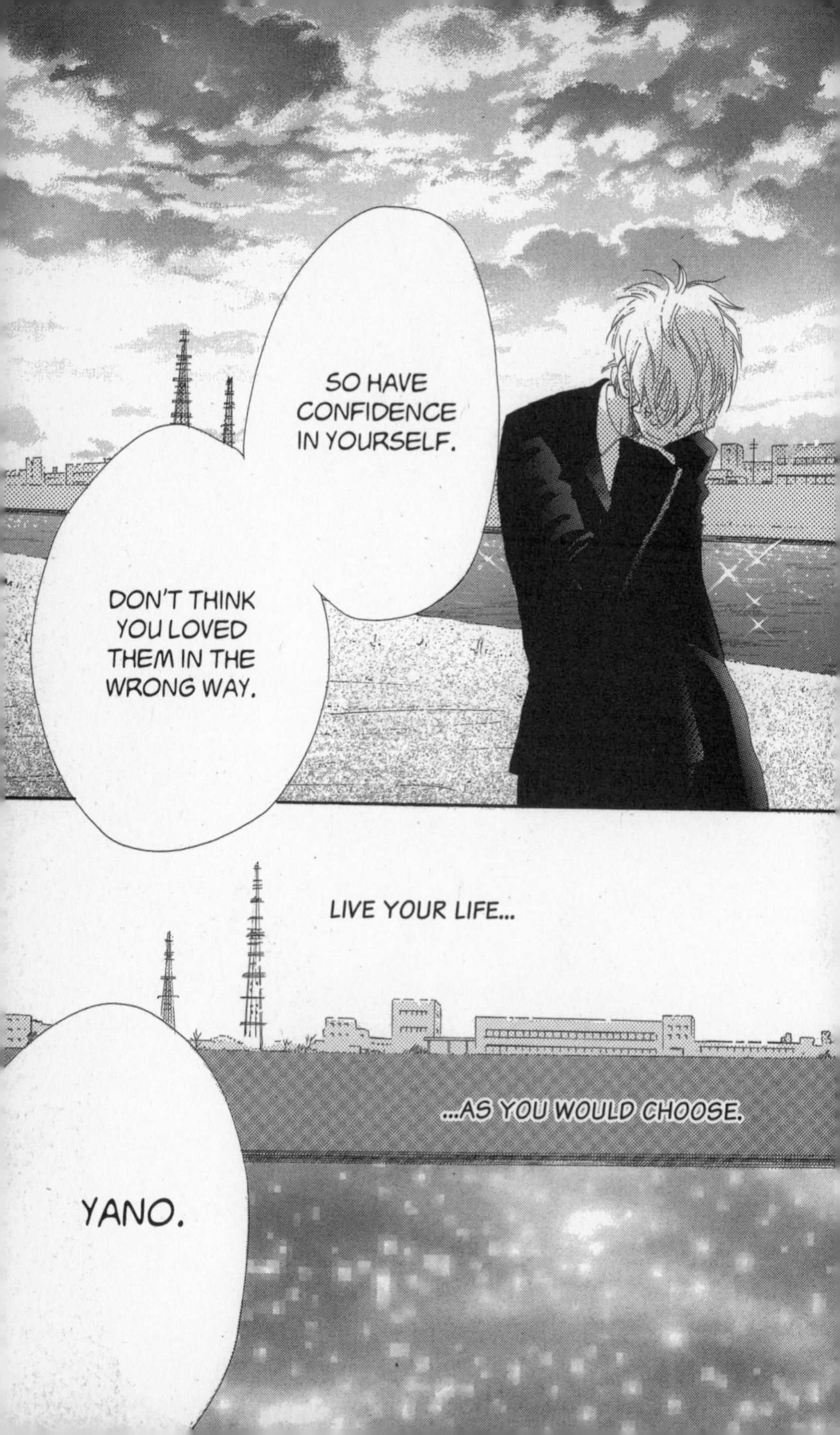
SO HAVE CONFIDENCE IN YOURSELF.
DON'T THINK YOU LOVED THEM IN THE WRONG WAY.
LIVE YOUR LIFE...
...AS YOU WOULD CHOOSE.
YANO.

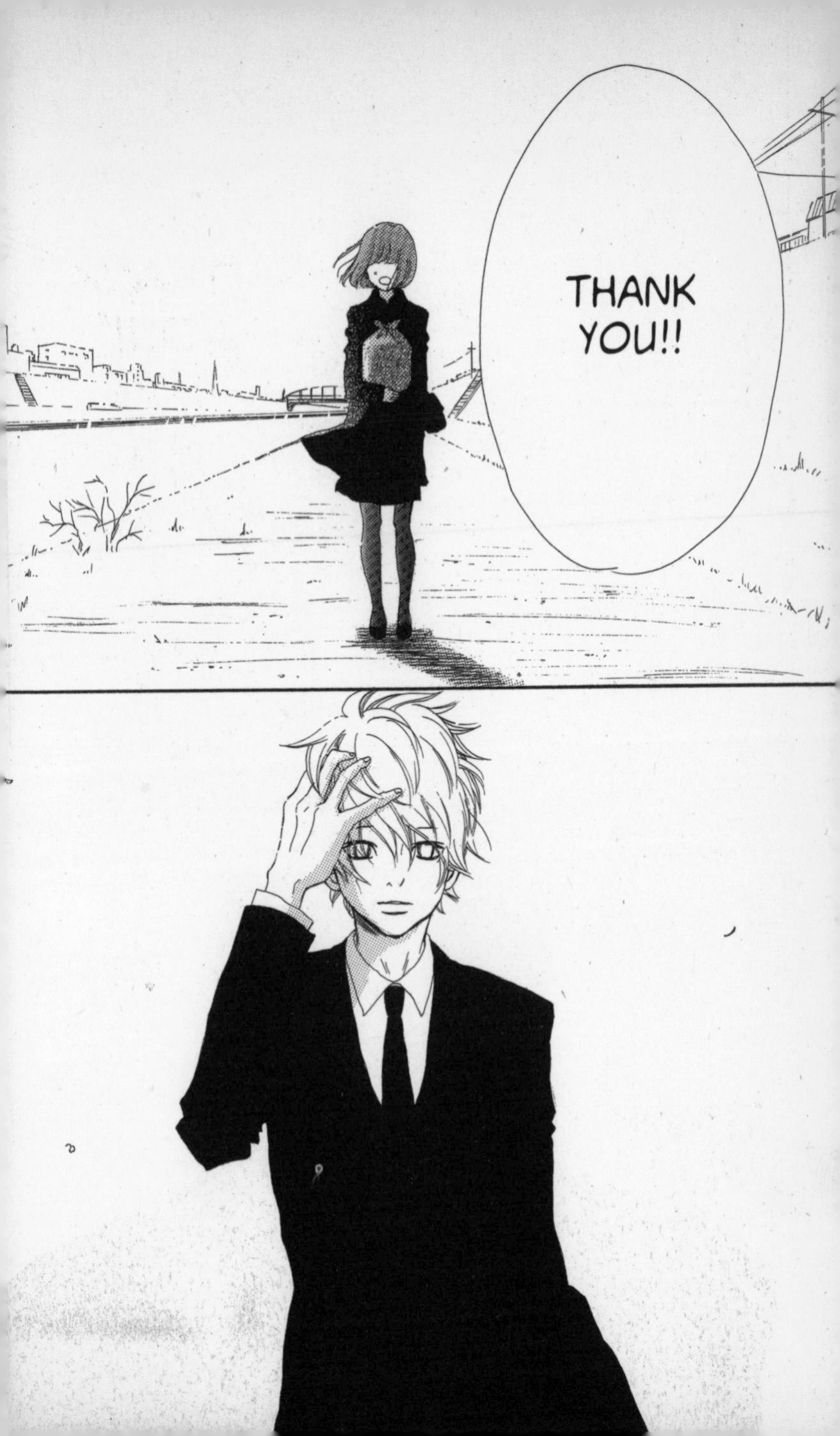
THANK YOU!!

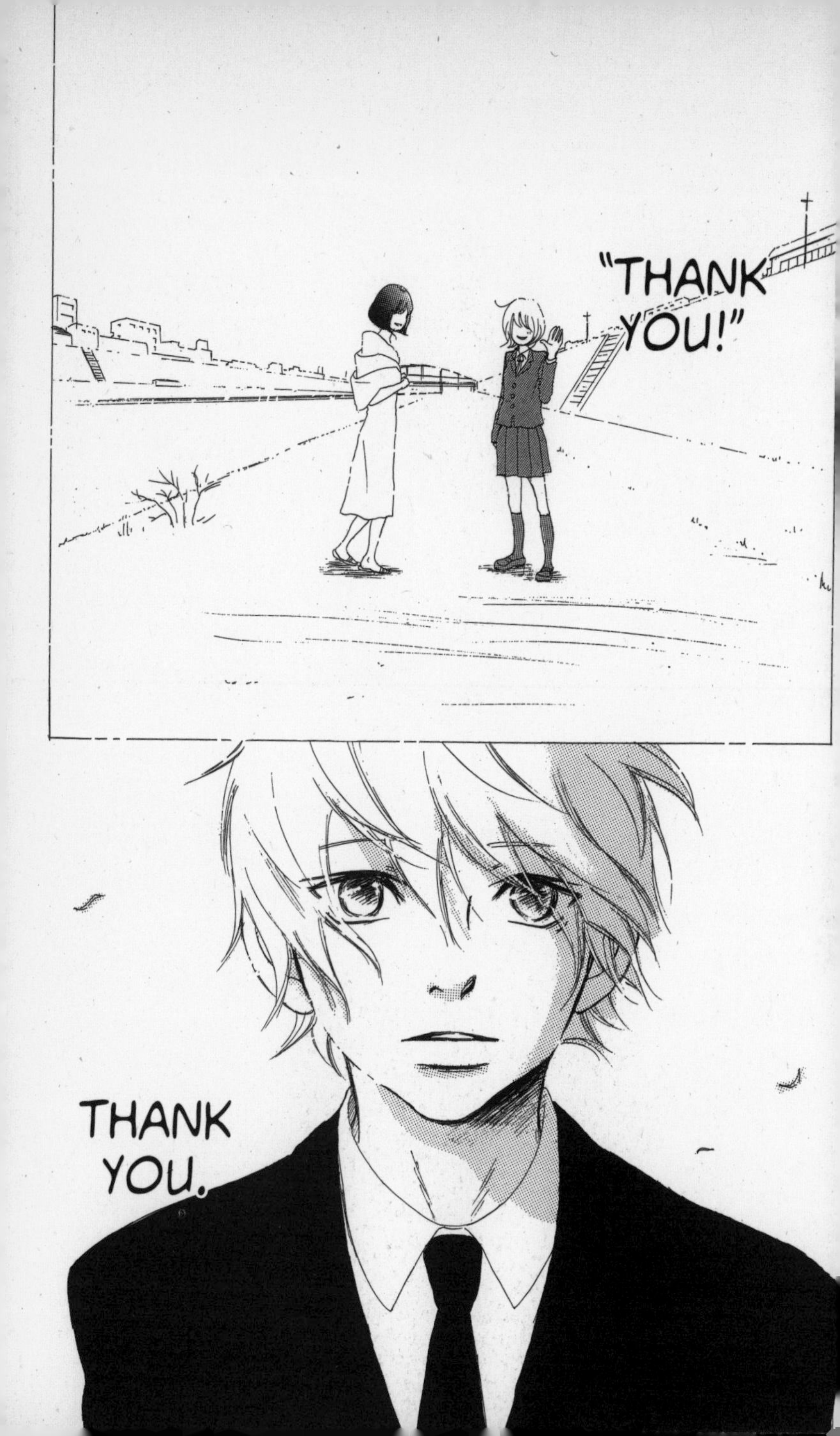
"THANK YOU!"
THANK YOU.

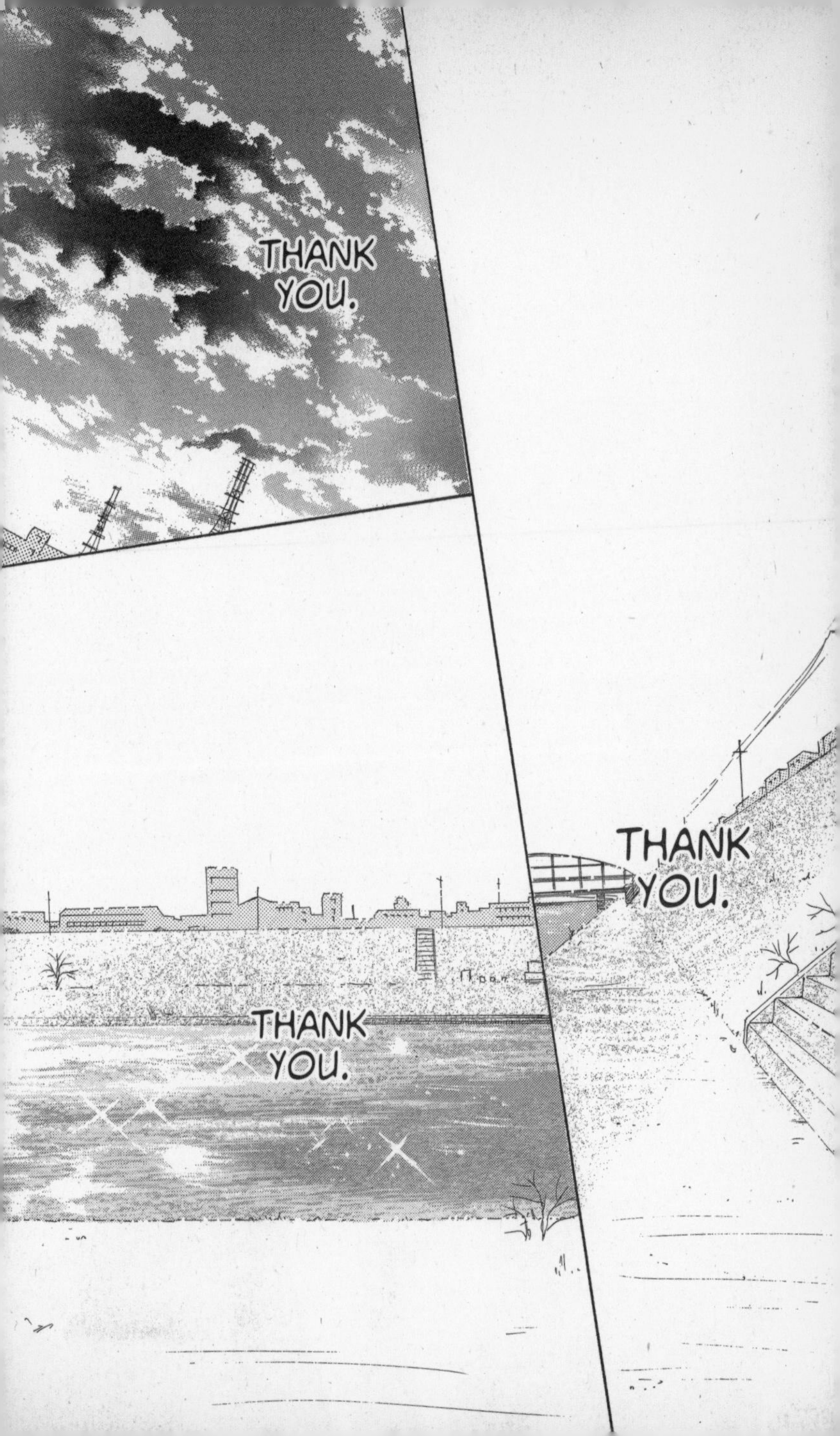
THANK YOU.
THANK YOU.
THANK YOU.

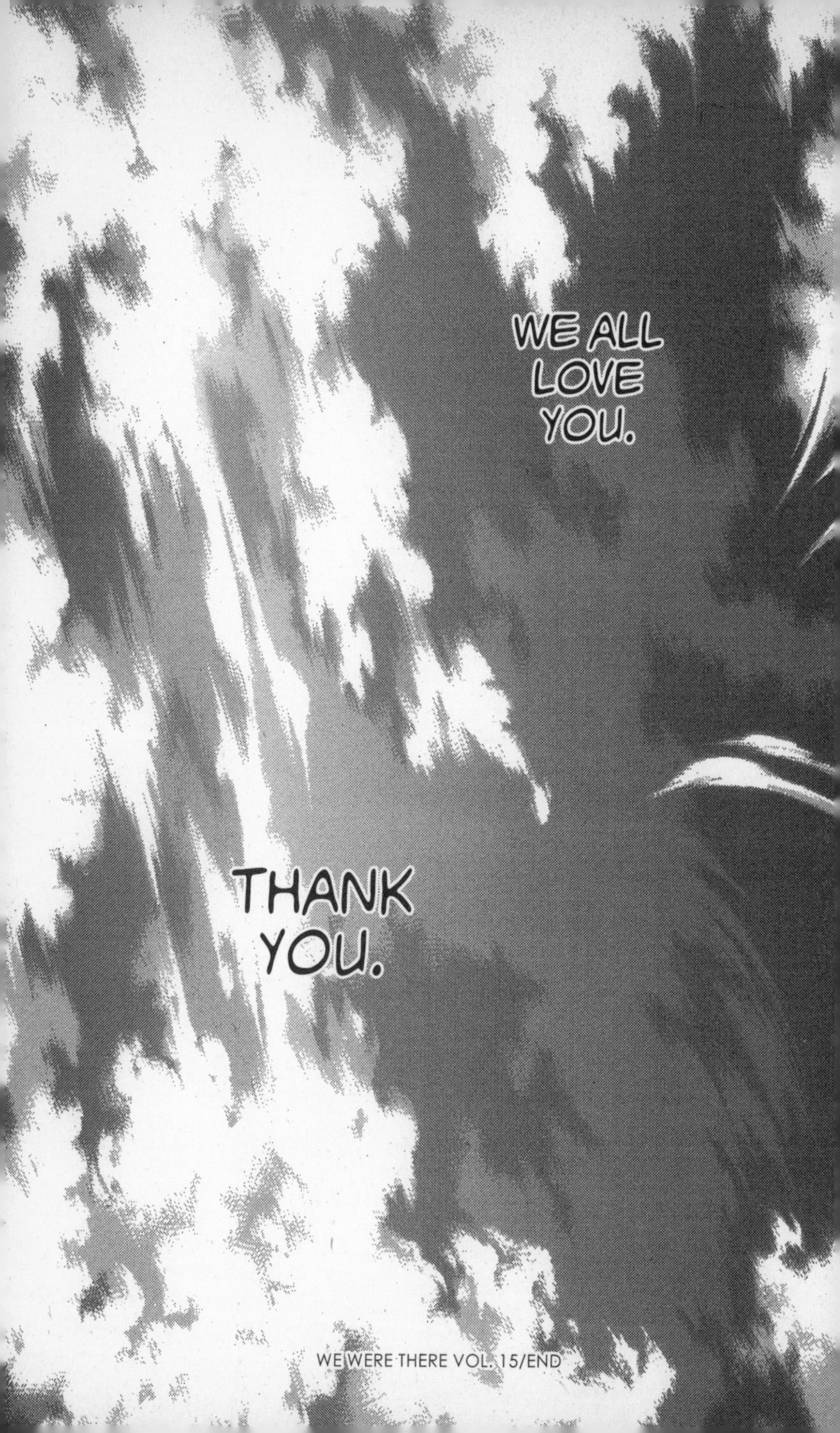
WE ALL LOVE YOU.
THANK YOU.
WE WERE THERE VOL. 15/END

The next volume will be the final one. I'm already starting
to feel a little sad about that... All I'm thinking about
is creating a fitting ending so I have no regrets.
—Yuuki Obata

Yuuki Obata's birthday is January 9. Her debut manga, *Raindrops*, won
the Shogakukan Shinjin Comics Taisho Kasaku Award in 1998. Her
current series, *We Were There* (*Bokura ga Ita*), won the 50th Shogakukan
Manga Award and was adapted into an animated television series. She
likes sweets, coffee, drinking with friends, and scary stories. Her hobby
is browsing in bookshops.

WE WERE THERE
Vol. 15
Shojo Beat Edition

STORY & ART BY
YUUKI OBATA

© 2002 Yuuki OBATA/Shogakukan
All rights reserved.
Original Japanese edition "BOKURA GA ITA"
published by SHOGAKUKAN Inc.

Adaptation/Nancy Thistlethwaite
Translation/Tetsuichiro Miyaki
Touch-up Art & Lettering/Inori Fukuda Trant
Design/Yukiko Whitley, Jodie Yoshioka
Editor/Nancy Thistlethwaite

Printed in Canada

Published by VIZ Media, LLC
P.O. Box 77010
San Francisco, CA 94107

10 9 8 7 6 5 4 3 2 1
First printing, November 2012

www.viz.com   www.shojobeat.com

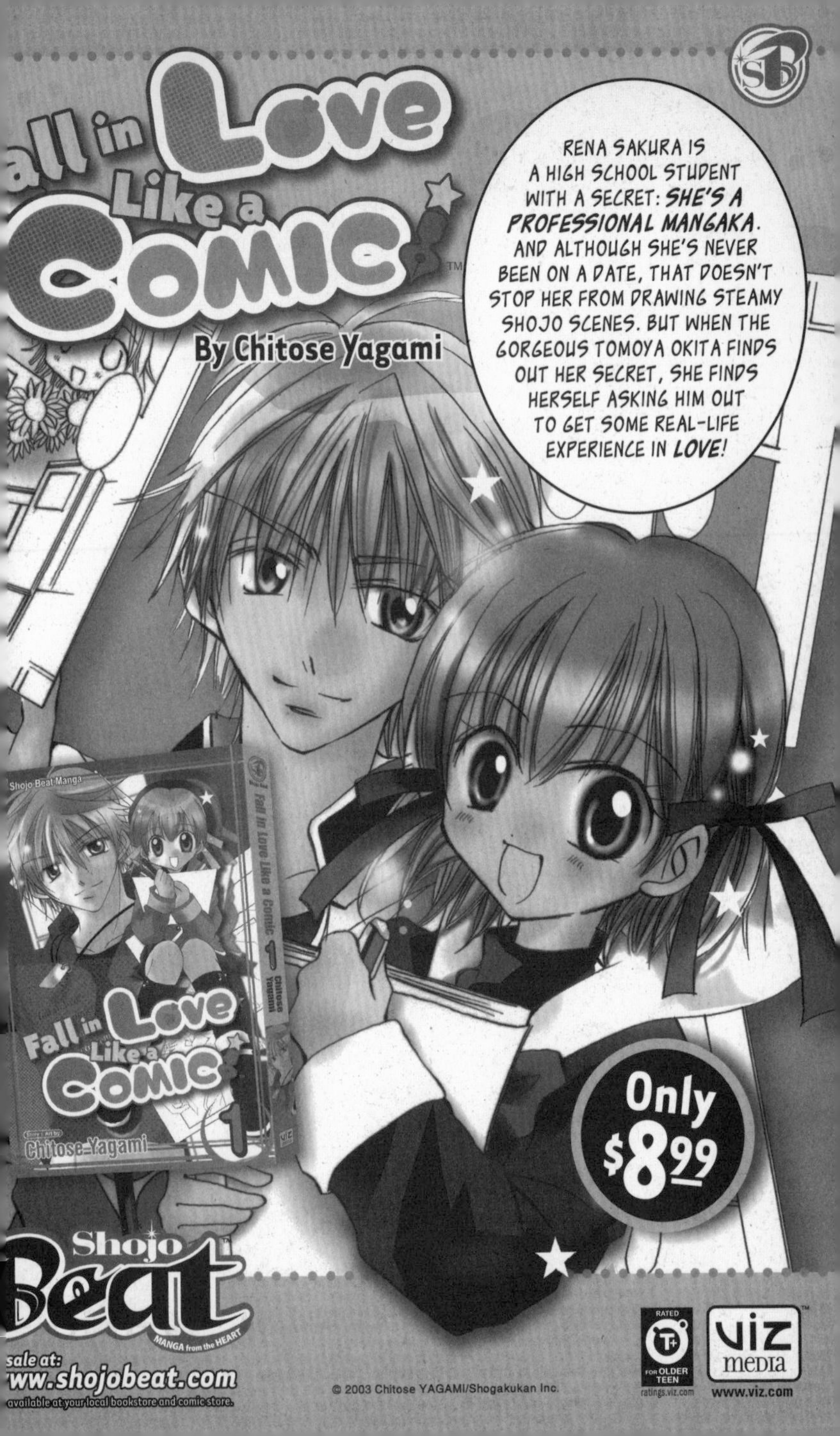
Fall in Love Like a Comic™
By Chitose Yagami
RENA SAKURA IS A HIGH SCHOOL STUDENT WITH A SECRET: ***SHE'S A PROFESSIONAL MANGAKA***. AND ALTHOUGH SHE'S NEVER BEEN ON A DATE, THAT DOESN'T STOP HER FROM DRAWING STEAMY SHOJO SCENES. BUT WHEN THE GORGEOUS TOMOYA OKITA FINDS OUT HER SECRET, SHE FINDS HERSELF ASKING HIM OUT TO GET SOME REAL-LIFE EXPERIENCE IN ***LOVE***!
Shojo Beat Manga
Fall in Love Like a Comic 1
Chitose Yagami
Only $8.99
Shojo Beat™
MANGA from the HEART
sale at:
www.shojobeat.com
available at your local bookstore and comic store.
© 2003 Chitose YAGAMI/Shogakukan Inc.
RATED T+ FOR OLDER TEEN
ratings.viz.com
VIZ media
www.viz.com

FUSHIGI YÛGI
GENBU KAIDEN™
BY YUU WATA

THIS EXCITIN
PREQUEL TO VIZ MED
BEST-SELLING FANTA
SERIES, *FUSHIGI YÛG*
TELLS THE STORY OF T
VERY FIRST PRIESTESS
THE FOUR GOD
THE PRIESTESS OF GENE

Only $8.99

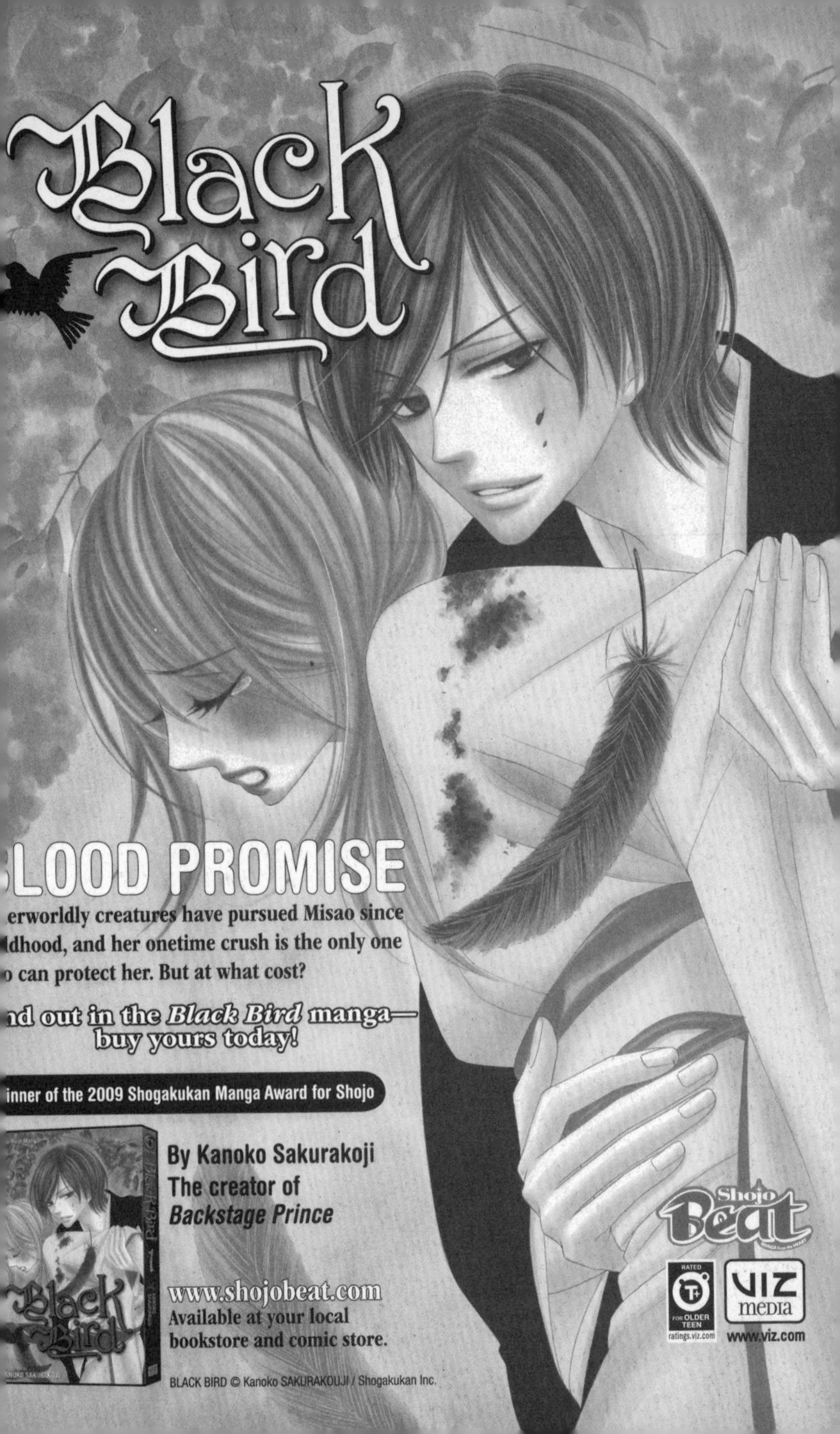
Black Bird
LOOD PROMISE
erworldly creatures have pursued Misao since
dhood, and her onetime crush is the only one
can protect her. But at what cost?
nd out in the Black Bird manga—
buy yours today!
inner of the 2009 Shogakukan Manga Award for Shojo
By Kanoko Sakurakoji
The creator of
Backstage Prince
www.shojobeat.com
Available at your local
bookstore and comic store.
BLACK BIRD © Kanoko SAKURAKOUJI / Shogakukan Inc.
Shojo Beat
RATED T+ FOR OLDER TEEN
ratings.viz.com
VIZ media
www.viz.com

SURPRISE!

You may be reading the wrong way!

It's true: In keeping with the original Japanese comic format, this book reads from right to left—so action, sound effects, and word balloons are completely reversed. This preserves the orientation of the original artwork—plus, it's fun! Check out the diagram shown here to get the hang of things, and then turn to the other side of the book to get started!